THE MIND TOOL

NEILL
GRAHAM

SECOND EDITION THE MIND TOOL

COMPUTERS
AND
THEIR
IMPACT
ON SOCIETY

WEST PUBLISHING COMPANY
ST. PAUL ■ NEW YORK ■ LOS ANGELES ■ SAN FRANCISCO

1st Reprint—1980

LIBRARY OF CONGRESS CATALOGING IN PUBLICATION DATA

Graham, Neill, 1941-
  The mind tool.

  Bibliography: p.
  Includes index.
  1. Computers. 2. Computers and civilization.
3. Basic (computer program language) I. Title.
QA76.G672 1980   001.6'4   79-23703
ISBN 0-8299-0272-4

COVER PHOTO

Photo © Phillip Harrington

The photo shows a very small section of printed circuitry on a computer chip. The computer chip itself is about 1/8″ square. The photograph was taken at approximately 506 times magnification.

PHOTO CREDITS

2 Courtesy Radio Shack. **5** Courtesy Hewlett-Packard. **10** Courtesy Radio Shack. **11** *(top)* Courtesy IBM; *(bottom)* Courtesy Hewlett-Packard. **12** Courtesy Hewlett-Packard. **20, 21, 22, 23, 24, 25, 26, 27** Courtesy IBM. **32** Courtesy Heath Company. **33** Courtesy Radio Shack. **34** *(top)* Courtesy IBM; *(bottom)* Courtesy Intel Corporation. **35** Courtesy Intel Corporation. **37, 38** Courtesy IBM. **40** *(top)* Courtesy Talos Systems; *(bottom)* Courtesy IBM. **41** Courtesy IBM. **42** *(top)* Courtesy Radio Shack; *(bottom)* Courtesy California Computer Products, Inc. (CalComp). **43** Courtesy California Computer Products, Inc. (CalComp). **44** Courtesy Radio Shack. **67** Courtesy Hewlett-Packard. **72** Courtesy Radio Shack. **103** Courtesy Amana Refrigeration, Inc. **104** Courtesy Heath Company. **105** Courtesy Canon, U.S.A. **106** Courtesy Heath Company. **107** Courtesy Radio Shack. **109** Courtesy Heath Company. **112, 114** Courtesy Radio Shack. **122** Courtesy Hewlett-Packard. **135** Courtesy Tektronix. **138, 147** Courtesy Radio Shack. **151** Courtesy Tektronix. **159** *(top)* Courtesy Houston Instrument; *(bottom)* Courtesy California Computer Products, Inc. (CalComp). **160** Courtesy California Computer Products, Inc. (CalComp). **161** *(top)* Courtesy California Computer Products, Inc. (CalComp); *(bottom)* Courtesy Hewlett-Packard. **162** Courtesy California Computer Products, Inc. (CalComp). **163, 165, 183, 186** Courtesy Tektronix. **205, 206, 215** Courtesy Data General. **231** Courtesy Tektronix. **242** Courtesy Radio Shack. **243, 246** Courtesy Tektronix. **249, 250** Courtesy Radio Shack. **253, 254** Courtesy Georgia Railroad Bank and Trust Company. **261** Courtesy Radio Shack. **264** Courtesy Data General. **290** *(top)* Courtesy Hewlett-Packard; *(bottom)* Courtesy Radio Shack.

To My Mother

CONTENTS

vii

PREFACE

While the first edition of *The Mind Tool* was in the final stages of preparation, vast changes began to take place in the way people used computers. Newly developed electronic components called microprocessors began to make computers available at a fraction of their former cost. Hobbyists started buying computers by the tens of thousands; stores selling computers began to spring up in shopping centers and malls; computers started to appear in consumer products such as microwave ovens and cameras.

This "microprocessor revolution" continues to change not only the ways we use computers but the ways we think and feel about them as well. Before microprocessors, computers were mainly the tools of large institutions—government bureaus, corporations, and universities. Beginning in the 1960s, the public became increasingly disenchanted with these institutions, and the computers the institutions used inherited much of the disenchantment. More and more, people came to perceive computers as something that "they" were using against "us".

But now, when computers are used almost everywhere and by almost everybody, it is getting as hard to be "against" computers as it would to be against television sets or automobiles. This does not mean that conflicts do not still arise over how computers should be used—they do, just as they arise over television (are some kinds of programs harmful to children?) and automobiles (what safety features should the manufacturer provide?). But with almost everybody using computers it is easier to view these conflicts not as cases of "us against them" but as disagreements over how to best use a resource that is available to everyone.

The first chapter of this book introduces not only the computer but the theme for the rest of the book: Computers, like most other technological innovations, have the potential for both benefit and harm. It is important for the people to be informed about the capabilities and limitations of computers if they are to insist that beneficial uses and not the harmful ones be realized.

The rest of the book is divided into three parts: *Computers . . ., . . . and Society,* and *BASIC.* The first two parts were also in the first edition; they have both been expanded and completely rewritten for this edition. The third part, which was only an appendix in the first edition, has been expanded into a complete introductory course in BASIC. The book can now be used not only for computer literacy courses but for introduction-to-programming courses that also emphasize computer literacy.

Part 1, *Computers . . .,* concentrates on the computer itself: its history, its hardware, its operation, its software, and its programming. The idea of computer languages is introduced and the basic ideas of programming are illustrated.

Part 2, *. . . and Society,* has been reorganized to reflect the current interest in personal computing. The use of computers by individuals is taken up first. Next come the uses by professionals that serve individuals directly—teachers, artists and entertainers, and doctors. After that come the applications of computers in politics, transportation, law enforcement, and business and finance. A chapter on computers and people discusses some of the guidelines that have been set forth for the humane uses of computers and some of the problems that still remain. The final chapter of this part explores the possibility of artificial intelligence and people's attitudes toward thinking computers.

Part 3, *BASIC,* is a seven-chapter introduction to programming in the BASIC language. More space than usual is devoted to the parts of programming that beginning students find to be particularly difficult, such as the use of variables, expressions having more than one operator, and expressions involving parentheses. Separate chapters are devoted to three important techniques for constructing programs: repetition, selection, and the use of functions and subroutines. The final two chapters focus on the two important data structures available in BASIC: arrays and strings.

The standard minimal BASIC is followed except that some string-processing features are introduced that are available on many computers but are not part of the standard. These features are comparison of strings for alphabetical order, string arrays, and string-manipulating operators and functions. Only in the final

chapter is extensive use made of nonstandard features, and there students are warned that the implementation of the features discussed may vary from one system to another.

Each chapter in this part is provided with problems, which range from easy to intermediate level in difficulty. For the most part the problems are nonmathematical.

I would like to thank the following people, who read the manuscript for this edition, for their helpful criticisms and suggestions: Thomas Dock, Ralph Schiferl, Ted Sjoerdsma, and Kenneth Trester. I also wish to thank the companies who contributed photographs and other materials: Amana Refrigeration Inc.; California Computer Products, Inc.; Canon, U.S.A., Inc.; Data General Corporation; Georgia Railroad Bank & Trust Company; Heath Company; Hewlett-Packard; Houston Instrument; IBM Corporation; Intel Corporation; Radio Shack; Talos Systems, Inc.; and Tektronix, Inc.

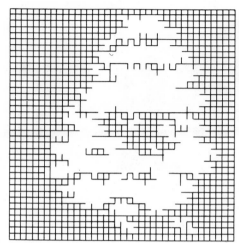

CHAPTER 1

INTRODUCING THE COMPUTER

It used to be that you had to visit a large corporation, a major university, or a government bureau in order to see a computer. But times have changed. These days, computers turn up almost everywhere—in microwave ovens, automobiles, pinball machines, CB sets, stereo turntables, typewriters, electronic games, cameras, and telephones.

Thousands of computer hobbyists operate their own personal computer systems. Some of these systems cost less than $500. Many of them were purchased in the computer stores that are springing up in malls and shopping centers everywhere.

This revolution in the use of computers has been brought about by advances in *microelectronics*, the art of building complex electronic circuits on tiny chips of silicon. What once filled a large cabinet in the computer room (and costs hundreds of thousands of dollars) now can be built on a silicon chip that will fit on the end of your finger (and costs ten dollars or less).

The most important chip used to construct a computer is called a *microprocessor*. The microprocessor contains the circuits that control the operation of the computer as well as those that do all the calculations. Because the development of microprocessors in the

Once computers were so expensive that they could only be used by large corporations and institutions. Now more and more people are putting computers to use in their homes.

early 1970s made small, inexpensive computers possible, the current revolution in computer usage is often called the *microprocessor revolution*.

Because of the microprocessor revolution, computers are no longer hidden away in closely guarded computer rooms. Now they are small enough and inexpensive enough to be used wherever they are needed—in consumer products, in scientific instruments, in hobbyist and educational computer systems.

How does the microprocessor revolution affect you and me? If computers are used intelligently and creatively, they can open up new realms of human comfort, convenience, pleasure, freedom, and intellectual stimulation. But used thoughtlessly, they can threaten our humanity, our privacy, and our freedom. Only if we are aware of the possibilities for both benefit and harm will we be in a position to insist that computers be used *for* people instead of *against* them.

But before getting into ways to use computers, let's look at just what computers are and what they can do.

THE INFORMATION MACHINE

Computers come in many shapes and sizes. To understand computers, then, we should focus our attention on what they can do, not on what they look like or how big they are or how much they cost.

The Computer   Two outstanding characteristics distinguish computers from other machines. These characteristic features let us identify a computer even when it happens to be a part of some other machine.

2 machine.

1. A computer is an information-processing machine. The information to be processed goes into the computer, and the processed information comes out, much as grain goes into one end of a mill and flour comes out the other.

2. The information processing that the computer carries out is controlled by a detailed set of instructions called a *program*. Without a program, a computer will do nothing useful. On the other hand, by changing the program, we can completely change the kind of information processing the computer performs.

The two fundamental ideas of computing, then, are *information processing* and *programming*. Let's take a closer look at each of these ideas.

Information The words *information* and *knowledge* refer to the same thing—facts about ourselves and the world around us. When the facts are inside our heads, we refer to them as knowledge. But when we pass them from one person to another or preserve them, as in books, we call them information. Thus, we speak of possessing knowledge but of receiving, providing, requesting, or looking up information.

Symbols To convey information from one person to another or to store it for later use, we have to represent it in concrete, physical form. Any physical object or physical effect used to represent information is called a *symbol*. Familiar symbols include the sounds of human speech and the characters used in writing and printing. The latter includes letters, numerals, punctuation marks, and special signs, such as the plus and minus signs and the dollar sign.

Speech sounds and printed characters are symbols that nearly everyone uses (although people who speak different languages use them in different ways). Other symbols are used by particular groups of people for special purposes. Examples of these are the special symbols used in music, mathematics, chemistry, chess, dance, knitting, architecture, and electronics.

The kind of symbols we choose to represent a particular piece of information depends on what we want to do with the information. For example, if you want to communicate with someone in the same room, the sound of your voice will suffice. If you want to communicate with someone on the other side of town, you could use a telephone to convert your voice into an electrical signal that travels across town through wires. To communicate with an astronaut on the moon, you would need a radio transmitter to convert your voice into radio waves capable of traversing the emptiness of space.

The sounds in the air, the currents in the telephone line, and the radio waves in space are three different kinds of symbols that can be used to represent the information contained in human speech. Which representation you choose depends on the destination to which you wish to send the information.

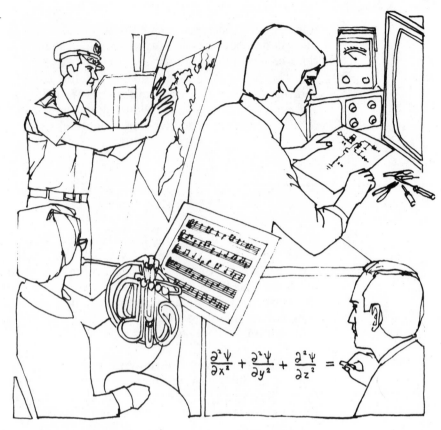

The idea of using different kinds of symbols for different purposes is important in connection with computers. That's because information has to be represented in a special form for computer processing, just as it does for telephone or radio transmission. The information that a computer is to process has to be translated into a code similar in principle (but not in detail) to the Morse code. The codes that computers use are called *binary codes*, which we will look at in more detail later on.

But how do we convert information from the symbols we find convenient (the letters of the alphabet, for instance) to the binary codes the computer can process? This job is done by *input* and *output* devices.

A common example of both an input and an output device is the *computer terminal*, which consists of a typewriter-like keyboard (the input device) and either a printer or a television-like display screen (the output device). When you strike a key on the keyboard, the terminal sends a signal to the computer. The signal carries the binary code corresponding to the key that was struck. When the terminal receives a signal from the computer, it displays the character corresponding to the binary code that was received.

With modern electronics, almost any kind of information can be

4 translated into a form acceptable to a computer. For instance,

A computer terminal. Information to be sent to the computer is typed on the keyboard. Information that the computer sends to the user is displayed on the screen.

pictures and sounds, as well as written material, can be processed. A familiar example of picture processing is the computer portraits that can be purchased on boardwalks and shopping malls.

An increasingly important application of computers is monitoring and controlling other machines. Sensors, such as thermometers and pressure gauges, transmit information about the operation of the machine to the computer. Effectors, such as electric motors, convert information from the computer into motions of parts of the machine.

The symbols used to represent a piece of information are called *data*. If *information* refers to the meaning of the content of a message, then *data* refers to symbols used to represent the message. For example, consider the following sentence:

MY TYPEWRITER IS BLUE.

The information in this sentence is the knowledge you gain about the color of the author's typewriter. The data, on the other hand, is the letter M followed by the letter Y followed by a blank space, and so on.

Information Processing   The following three terms describe what a computer does:

- information processing

- data processing

- symbol manipulation.

Information processing emphasizes the meaning of the symbols that go into and come out of the computer. Since that meaning is what we wish to emphasize in this book, *information processing* is the term we will use most frequently.

5

The terms *data processing* and *symbol manipulation* focus our attention more on the physical symbols that the computer actually works with rather than on their meaning. The term *data processing* is the one used most frequently in the computer industry.

What kinds of information processing can computers do? Much of this book is devoted to answering that question, so we won't try to tell the whole story here. But the following brief examples should give you some idea of the capabilities of computers.

■ *Arithmetic.* Computers originally were invented to do arithmetic. Their ability to carry out numerical calculations rapidly and accurately affects our daily lives in unexpected ways.

For example, one reason you can buy high-quality cameras at reasonable prices is that computers are used to help design the camera lenses. The computer evaluates each trial design by computing the paths of thousands of light rays through the lens. The computer can do this for many thousands of trial designs and select the one that promises the best performance.

Before the advent of computers, optical manufacturers maintained rooms full of people punching desk calculators to do the same job. Because these people worked far more slowly—and expensively —than the computer, many fewer trial designs could be explored. The resulting lens cost more to design and was of poorer quality than if a computer had been used.

Arithmetic provides a familiar example of what we mean by symbol manipulation. When we add, subtract, multiply, and divide numbers, we simply are manipulating combinations of the ten symbols 0, 1, 2, 3, 4, 5, 6, 7, 8, and 9. The manipulations are governed by the rules and tables we learned as schoolchildren.

Since computers were invented to do arithmetic and because they are famous for their ability to do it rapidly and accurately, some people are under the impression that arithmetic is all a computer can do. But this isn't so. Doing arithmetic is not even the most important application of computers.

The following three examples all illustrate the processing of non-numerical information.

■ *Picture Processing.* We already have mentioned computer portraits as an example of picture processing. The picture of the subject is picked up by a TV camera. The signal from the camera is processed by an electronic device called a "digitizer." The digitizer converts the brightnesses of the points in the picture to binary codes, which are sent to the computer. (Remember that binary codes are the symbols used to represent information inside computers.) For each point, the computer selects a printed character that, when seen from a distance, has the same overall brightness as the point. The computer sends the codes representing these characters to a printer to produce a portrait made up of printed characters.

■ *Word Processing.* In word processing, a letter, an article, or a term **6** paper is typed out at a computer terminal and stored in the computer's memory. Once the text is in the computer's memory, you can revise it by typing commands at the terminal to make insertions and deletions or to switch sections of text around. At any time, you can order any part of the text displayed or printed so you can see the results of your revisions. When you are perfectly satisfied with the result, you order the computer to print out a clean copy of the revised text.

The computer also can be connected to a typesetting machine, so that type is set automatically from the text stored in memory. The text can contain special codes to indicate where different typefaces, such as italics and boldface, are to be used. These codes also can specify such things as where space must be left so that a drawing or a photograph can be inserted.

■ *Game Playing.* There are three ways to play games with computers.

First, the computer can provide an electronic gameboard and serve as scorekeeper. The computer is not a participant in the game, but it provides the facilities for human players to compete with one another. Many of the popular video games fall into this category. The users play the game by manipulating hand controllers connected to the computer. The computer translates the motions of the hand controllers into the movements of figures on the TV screen which represent such things as ping-pong paddles and baseball bats. The computer notes when each side scores a point and displays an up-to-date score on the screen.

Second, the computer can simulate some challenging situation in which the player attempts to achieve a particular goal. For instance, the computer can simulate the behavior of a lunar lander, which the player attempts to bring to a soft landing on the moon. The player specifies how the lander's rockets are to be fired, and the computer works out the motion of the lander that results. The computer does not play against the person but simply works out the logical consequences of the person's decisions.

Finally, the computer can be an active participant, playing against a human opponent, usually at some traditional game, such as tic-tac-toe, checkers, backgammon, or chess. For simple games, such as tic-tac-toe, you cannot win against the computer. If you play perfectly, the game is a draw. If you make a mistake, the computer wins. But computers are not necessarily superior to humans at more sophisticated games, such as chess. For many years, the best chess-playing programs played rather poorly. Now the best programs can provide a challenging game for a chess master, but they certainly don't play perfectly.

Programs and Programming Remember, there are two characteristics of computers. First, a computer processes information. Second, the information processing is controlled by a program. Now we'll turn our attention to this second characteristic.

The program determines what kind of information processing the computer carries out. Without a program, the computer will do nothing useful. On the other hand, if we can devise a program that tells it, step-by-step, how to manipulate the symbols that represent the information, it will do any kind of information processing. For this reason, computer pioneer John von Neumann called the computer the "all-purpose machine."

We say that a computer *executes* a program when it carries out the instructions in the program. Usually, the program assumes more importance than the machine that executes it. The way we talk about computers and programs illustrates this. We do not speak of a chess-playing computer but of a chess-playing *program*. In the same way, we speak of a program (not a computer) for word processing or picture processing or designing camera lenses.

We can think of the computer as being like a phonograph. Within the limits set by its construction, a phonograph can reproduce any sound. But the sounds do not originate with the phonograph; they come from the record. Unlike a music box, which always plays the same tune, the phonograph will play any song as long as we put on the right record.

If we think of a computer as being like a phonograph, then the computer's program corresponds to the phonograph record. But what corresponds to the music? What do we get when we "play" a computer program?

A computer program determines how a computer behaves. If we communicate with the computer through a terminal, then the program determines how the computer will respond to what we type at the terminal. If we change the program, the computer's responses will change as well.

We can think of the program as giving the computer a particular personality. We certainly do not mean by this that the computer behaves like a person. But just as we judge a human personality by the way the person responds to us, we can judge a computer's personality by its responses to the input we provide. One computer manufacturer calls the unit containing a program for his machine a "personality module."

We can take the phonograph analogy even further. We do not think of the music as originating with the record anymore than it originates with the phonograph. The music was created by a human artist. The record merely preserved it until the phonograph could reproduce it for our enjoyment.

It is interesting to look at computers and programs in the same light. The way the computer behaves originates, not with the computer, not with the program, but with the human programmer. In writing down a series of instructions for the computer to follow, the programmer creates a particular personality, a particular behavior. The program is merely a means of preserving this creation until the computer can bring it to life for our use.

In the past, programs mainly were written to be useful rather than entertaining. Naturally, they have been all business. But as computers become less expensive, we can afford to put them to uses that do not involve turning a profit. In the future, we may expect to see more and more programs designed to make computers behave in ways that are engaging, amusing, or aesthetically satisfying. The programmer will become an artist as well as a technician.

COMPUTERS LARGE AND SMALL

Now that we have some idea of what computers can do and how they do it, let's look at some of the physical forms these machines can take.

Computers are classified as *general purpose* or *special purpose*.

General Purpose Computers With a general purpose computer, the user easily can change the program that the computer executes and thus completely change the information-processing task the computer is carrying out. The emphasis is on flexibility; by putting in a suitable program, we can instantly adapt the computer to whatever job is at hand.

General purpose computers vary widely in size, cost, speed of operation, memory capacity, and convenience of use. We can classify computers as to cost and capability, much as we classify cars as subcompact, compact, standard, and luxury. The following terms are used to classify computers:

- maxicomputer (also large-scale computer or main frame)

- midicomputer (also medium-scale computer)

- minicomputer ⎫ (also small computer)
- microcomputer ⎭

We will not dwell on the exact criteria for distinguishing, say, a minicomputer from a midicomputer. Instead, we will concentrate on the extreme ends of the scale.

Microcomputers are computers built around microprocessors. These machines first began to appear in 1975. They cost hundreds or thousands of dollars and will fit on the top of a desk or table. A microcomputer system that would be useful for a small business or a professional, such as a doctor or a dentist, is in the same price range as a new car. Most hobbyist computers cost far less.

Maxicomputers are the largest and most costly machines. A maxicomputer is to a microcomputer as a 747 is to a Piper Cub. The cost of a maxicomputer may be a million dollars or more, and the machine may fill a large room. Maxicomputers are used by organizations, such as corporations, universities, and government bureaus, that must do massive amounts of information processing.

When computers are to be shown on television and in the movies, maxicomputers usually are selected since their large size is so impressive. Unfortunately, this has given many people the im-

9

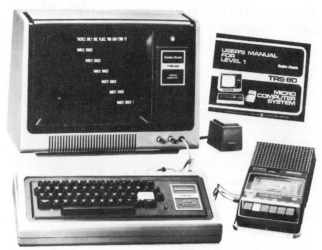

A microcomputer system widely used by hobbyists. The cassette recorder (right) allows programs to be recorded on ordinary audio cassettes and played back into the computer when needed. Prerecorded program cassettes can also be purchased.

pression that all computers are maxicomputers. But this isn't so. In fact, there are more microcomputers in use than all the other kinds put together.

Special Purpose Computers   A general purpose computer is designed to make it as easy as possible to change from one program to another. A special purpose computer is just the opposite; its program is permanently built in and cannot be changed without replacing electronic components inside the machine. Since its program is fixed, a special purpose computer can only do one type of information-processing task.

The computers in microwave ovens, automobiles, cameras, and other consumer products are special purpose computers. Since the computers are built right inside the devices they control, the user may not realize that a computer is used at all if the manufacturer's advertisements do not make a point of the fact.

The pocket calculator is another kind of special purpose computer that is used widely. The heart of a calculator is a microprocessor. This microprocessor can carry out commands only for relatively simple operations, such as adding two single numbers or shifting all the digits of a number one place to the right or left.

Then how are more complicated operations, such as multiplication and division of large numbers, carried out? The calculator contains programs that tell the microprocessor how to realize the more complicated operations by sequences of simpler ones. There is one program for each operation the calculator can carry out.

When you hit a key on the calculator, the microprocessor executes a particular program; there is a different program for each key. When you strike the + key, the microprocessor executes the program for addition, and when you strike the ÷ key, the microprocessor executes the program for division.

The programs are stored on silicon chips called *read only memories* or ROMs. For simple four-function calculators, the pro-

A large-scale computer

A small-scale computer (left) and a medium-scale computer (right). On the corner of the desk top is a so-called "floppy disk," used to store programs and data. In the background is a computer terminal.

grams are stored on the same chip as the microprocessor. The combined microprocessor-ROM chip is a *calculator chip* that needs only to be connected to a keyboard, a display, and a power supply to get a working calculator. More complicated calculators use separate microprocessor and ROM chips.

11

Programmable calculators are calculators that will accept and execute programs written by the user. The user enters a program by switching the calculator to a "store program" mode and then punching the keys for the operations the program is to carry out. After the calculator has been switched back to the "run program" mode, punching a single key causes all the operations specified in the program to be carried out.

Since it is possible for the user to program the calculator, a programmable calculator satisfies all the requirements for a general purpose computer. Despite this, people usually distinguish between calculators and general purpose computers. One basis for the distinction is that programmable calculators only do arithmetic, whereas computers can process many different kinds of information. Another is that calculators have smaller memories than computers and operate at slower speeds. But as more powerful programmable calculators come out each year, it becomes more difficult to maintain the distinction between programmable calculators and general purpose computers.

COMPUTERS AND SOCIETY

Telephones, television, automobiles, airplanes, and other modern technological developments have revolutionized the way we live, work, and play. We can expect the computer to do no less. In fact, the computer ultimately could have a greater impact on our lifestyles than any of the inventions just mentioned.

But one lesson the twentieth century has taught us is that most technological innovations have the potential for both great benefit and great harm. Some people, impressed more by the dangers than

A programmable calculator. User programs can be entered from the keyboard and executed by pressing one of the keys on the top row. Programs and data can be saved on magnetic cards and read back into the calculator when needed. Prerecorded cards containing commonly used programs can be purchased from the calculator manufacturer.

the benefits, shy away from technology all together. But this may be throwing out the proverbial baby with the bath water. Are we not smart enough to reap the benefits of technology while minimizing or eliminating its adverse side effects?

And there *are* benefits to be had from computers. Contrary to what some people think, computers do not necessarily restrict our freedom or threaten to dehumanize us. Instead, their tremendous information processing capacity offers us more control over our lives, greater freedom of choice, and the opportunity for richer interactions with our fellow human beings and the world around us. Many examples of how computers can be used for our benefit will be found in the rest of this book.

Yet we must also approach the widespread use of computers with a healthy caution, for problems are possible. The following is a list of some possible pitfalls.

- If computers are used in such a way that our options are limited to those that already have been programmed into the computer, then our freedom of choice is limited, and our lives become less interesting and more mechanical.

- Computerized data banks can give government agencies greater information about us and, as a result, greater power over us. This is especially true when police agencies operate the data banks.

To be sure, the picture is not entirely grim. The information in data banks can be used to serve us as well as persecute us. But, before such data banks are established, we certainly will want to scrutinize carefully how the information stored in them is to be used.

- If all our financial records are stored in computers, then computer-wise criminals can steal from us merely by changing data in computer memories. Alas, this is already a reality, and more than one person already has gone to jail for computer crime.

- If we come to depend heavily on computer systems, then a failure of one of those systems could affect our lives in unprecedented ways. We are reminded of the failures of electric power systems that have plunged large areas into darkness. It has been suggested that when all our financial records are stored in computers, a widespread failure could cause a "credit blackout" that would plunge large areas into financial chaos.

In the rest of this book, you will see many ways in which computers can help society and many ways in which they can hurt it. You also will learn something about how computers work and how they are programmed. The information you gain should help you form intelligent opinions about how you want computers to be used in your life and the society in which you live.

FOR FURTHER READING

Computers and Computation. San Francisco: W.H. Freeman and Co., 1971.

Fink, Donald G. *Computers and the Human Mind.* Garden City, N.Y.: Doubleday, 1966.

Halacy, D.S. *Computers: The Machines We Think With.* Rev. ed. New York: Dell Publishing Co., 1971.

MacKay, Donald M. *Information, Mechanism, and Meaning.* Cambridge: MIT Press, 1969.

Mader, Chris, and Hagin, Robert. *Information Systems: Technology, Economics, and Applications.* Chicago: Science Research Associates, 1974.

Nelson, Ted. *Computer Lib/Dream Machines.* Chicago: Hugo's Book Service, 1974.

_____ . *The Home Computer Revolution.* South Bend, Ind.: The Distributors, 1977.

REVIEW QUESTIONS

1. Name some familiar consumer products that may contain computers.

2. What is a *microprocessor*? Why are microprocessors important?

3. What two outstanding characteristics distinguish computers from other machines?

4. What is *information*?

5. What are *symbols*? How are they related to information?

6. What is the name for the kind of symbols that computers use to represent the information they process?

7. What are the functions of *input* and *output* devices?

8. What is a *computer terminal*?

9. What is *data*?

10. Give three terms that can be used to describe what a computer does.

11. Give four examples of the kinds of information processing computers can do.

12. What is a computer *program*?

13. Why did von Neumann call the computer the "all-purpose machine"?

14. Compare the relations between the programmer, the program, and the computer with those between the recording artist, the record, and the phonograph. Construct a similar analogy in which the motion picture projector corresponds to the computer.

15. Give four classifications of general purpose computers. Which classifications contain the largest and the smallest computers? Describe briefly the kinds of computers that fit into those two classifications.

16. Distinguish between general purpose computers and special purpose computers.

17. Why do we consider a (nonprogrammable) calculator to be a special purpose computer?

18. Should a programmable calculator be considered a special purpose or a general purpose computer? Why?

19. What are some of the benefits to society that computers can provide?

20. What are some of the pitfalls of widespread computer use?

**DISCUSSION
QUESTIONS**

1. Examine your own attitudes toward computers. Are they based on personal experience or on hearsay? How do you think people's attitudes toward computers might change as the use of computers becomes more widespread?

2. We often hear it said, somewhat contemptuously, that a computer can only do what it is told. Does this imply that computers are limited? Or does it suggest the advantage of the computer over a machine that is designed for a single job and that cannot be reprogrammed for another one? In your discussion, use the analogy of a music box that plays a single tune and a phonograph that will play any music for which we can provide a record.

3. People sometimes criticize computers as "cold" and "unfeeling." Yet it doesn't worry us that a phonograph or a movie projector is "cold and unfeeling." Why should our attitude toward computers be any different?

4. Do present environmental and energy problems caused by the use of technology mean that we should avoid advanced technology in the future? Or would this be throwing out the baby with the bath water? Or is it even possible that more advanced technology is the only thing that will get us out of our present difficulties?

5. Take some familiar technological development, such as the telephone, the automobile, or the airplane, and list as many of its effects on society as you can. Which effects are harmful, and which are beneficial? Most important, which effects might be considered harmful by some people and beneficial by others?

PART ONE

COMPUTERS...

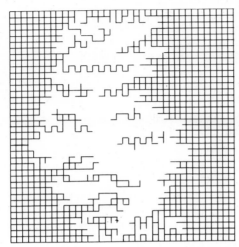

CHAPTER 2

THE DEVELOPMENT OF COMPUTERS

Tools are any objects other than the parts of our own bodies that we use to help us do our work. Technology is nothing more than the use of tools. When you use a screwdriver, a hammer, or an axe, you are using technology just as much as when you use an automobile, a television set, or a computer.

We tend to think of technology as a human invention. But the reverse is closer to the truth. Stone tools found along with fossils show that our ape-like ancestors were already putting technology to use. Anthropologists speculate that using tools may have helped these creatures evolve into human beings; in a tool-using society, manual dexterity and intelligence count for more than brute strength. The clever rather than the strong inherited the earth.

Most of the tools we have invented have aided our bodies rather than our minds. These tools help us lift and move and cut and shape. Only quite recently, for the most part, have we developed tools to aid our minds as well.

The tools of communication, from pencil and paper to television, are designed to serve our minds. These devices transmit information or preserve it, but they do not modify it in any way. (If the information is modified, this is considered a defect rather than a

19

virtue, as when a defective radio distorts the music we're trying to hear.) Important as these tools of communication are, however, they are not our concern here.

Instead, our interest lies with machines that classify and modify information rather than merely transmitting it or preserving it. The machines that do this are the computers and the calculators, the mind tools referred to in the title of the book.

PREHISTORY

The widespread use of machines for information processing is a modern development. But simple examples of information-processing machines can be traced back to ancient times. The following are some of the more important forerunners of the computer.

- *The Abacus.* The abacus is the counting frame that was the most widely used device for doing arithmetic in ancient times and whose use persisted into modern times in the Orient. Early versions of the abacus consisted of a board with grooves in which pebbles could slide. The Latin word for *pebble* is *calculus,* from which we get the words *abacus* and *calculate.*

- *Mechanical Calculators.* In the seventeenth century, calculators more sophisticated than the abacus began to appear. Although a number of people contributed to their development, Blaise Pascal (French mathematician and philosopher) and Wilhelm von Leibniz (German mathematician, philosopher, and diplomat) usually are singled out as pioneers. The calculators Pascal and Leibniz built were unreliable, since the mechanical technology of the time was not capable of manufacturing the parts with sufficient precision. As manufacturing techniques improved, mechanical calculators eventually were perfected; they were used widely until they were replaced by electronic calculators in recent times.

- *The Jacquard Loom.* Until modern times, most information-processing machines were designed to do arithmetic. An outstanding exception, however, was Jacquard's automated loom, a machine designed not for hard figures but beautiful patterns. A Jacquard loom

A Chinese abacus. The Japanese abacus uses one less bead both above and below the divider.

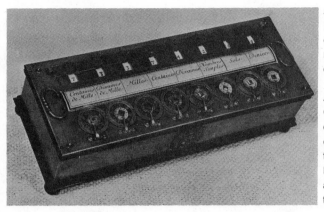

At far left, Blaise Pascal, who built one of the first mechanical calculators.

At left, Pascal's Calculator. The calculator was operated by turning the dials at the bottom, somewhat as one turns a telephone dial.

weaves cloth containing a decorative pattern; the woven pattern is controlled by punched cards. Changing the punched cards changes the pattern the loom weaves. Jacquard looms came into widespread use in the early nineteenth century, and their descendants are still used today. The Jacquard loom is the ancestor not only of modern automated machine tools but of the player piano as well.

THE ANALYTICAL ENGINE

When was the automatic computer invented? In the 1930s or the 1940s? If you think that, you are only off by a hundred years. A computer that was completely modern in conception was designed in the 1830s. But, as with the calculators of Pascal and Leibniz, the mechanical technology of the time was not prepared to realize the conception.

Charles Babbage The inventor of that nineteenth-century computer was a figure far more common in fiction than in real life—an eccentric mathematician. Most mathematicians live personal lives not too much different from anyone else's. They just happen to do mathematics instead of driving trucks or running stores or filling teeth. But Charles Babbage was the exception.

For instance, all his life, Babbage waged a vigorous campaign against London organ grinders. He blamed the noise they made for the loss of a quarter of his working power. Nor was Babbage satisfied with writing anti-organ-grinder letters to newspapers and members of Parliament. He personally hauled individual offenders before magistrates (and became furious when the magistrates declined to throw the offenders in jail).

Or consider this. Babbage took issue with Tennyson's poem "Vision of Sin," which contains this couplet:

Every minute dies a man,
Every minute one is born.

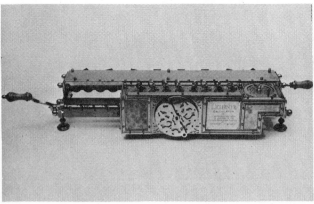

At far left, Gottfried Wilhelm von Leibniz, who built the first mechanical calculator that could multiply and divide as well as add and subtract. He also studied *binary notation*, now used for coding numbers inside computers.

At left, Leipniz's calculator.

Babbage pointed out (correctly) that if this were true, the population of the earth would remain constant. In a letter to the poet, Babbage suggested a revision:

Every moment dies a man,
And one and a sixteenth is born.

Babbage emphasized that one and a sixteenth was not exact, but he thought that it would be "good enough for poetry."

Yet, despite his eccentricities, Babbage was a genius. He was a prolific inventor, whose inventions include the ophthalmoscope for examining the retina of the eye, the skeleton key, the locomotive "cow catcher," and the speedometer. He also pioneered operations research, the science of how to carry out business and industrial operations as efficiently as possible.

Babbage was a fellow of the Royal Society and held the chair of Lucasian Professor of Mathematics at Cambridge University (the same chair once held by Isaac Newton, the most famous British scientist).

The Difference Engine The mathematical tables of the nineteenth century were full of mistakes. Even when the tables had been calculated correctly, printers' errors introduced many mistakes. And since people who published new tables often copied from existing ones, the same errors cropped up in table after table.

According to one story, Babbage was lamenting about the errors in some tables to his friend Herschel, a noted astronomer. "I wish to God these calculations had been executed by steam," Babbage said. "It is quite possible," Herschel responded.

(At that time, steam was a new and largely unexplored source of energy. Just as we might wonder today whether or not something could be done by electricity, in the early nineteenth century it was natural to wonder whether or not it could be done by steam.)

Babbage set out to build a machine that not only would calculate

22 the entries in the tables but would print them automatically as well.

Part of Babbage's Difference Engine.
Babbage never completed the machine.

He called this machine the *Difference Engine*, since it worked by solving what mathematicians call "difference equations." Nevertheless, the name is misleading, since the machine constructed tables by means of repeated additions, not subtractions.

(The word *engine*, by the way, comes from the same root as *ingenious*. Originally it referred to a clever invention. Only later did it come to mean a source of power.)

In 1823, Babbage obtained a government grant to build the Difference Engine. He ran into difficulties, however, and eventually abandoned the project. In 1854, a Swedish printer built a working Difference Engine based on Babbage's ideas.

The Analytical Engine One of Babbage's reasons for abandoning the Difference Engine was that he had been struck by a much better idea. Inspired by Jacquard's punched-card-controlled loom, Babbage wanted to build a punched-card-controlled calculator. Babbage called his proposed automatic calculator the *Analytical Engine.*

The Difference Engine could only compute tables (and only those tables that could be computed by successive additions). But the Analytical Engine could carry out any calculation, just as Jacquard's loom could weave any pattern. All one had to do was to punch the cards with the instructions for the desired calculation. If the Analytical Engine had been completed, it would have been a nineteenth-century computer.

But, alas, the Analytical Engine was not completed. The government had already sunk thousands of pounds into the Difference Engine and received nothing in return. It had no intention of repeating its mistake. Nor did Babbage's eccentricities and abrasive personality help his cause any.

The government may have been right. Even if it had financed the new invention, it might well have gotten nothing in return. For, as usual, the idea was far ahead of what the existing mechanical technology could build.

23

Part of Babbage's Analytical Engine, a nineteenth-century computer. Like the Difference Engine, the Analytical Engine was never completed.

This was particularly true since Babbage's design was grandiose. For instance, he planned for his machine to do calculations with fifty-digit accuracy. This is far greater than the accuracy found in most modern computers and far more than is needed for most calculations.

Also, Babbage kept changing his plans in the middle of his projects so that all the work had to be started anew. Although Babbage had founded operations research, he had trouble planning the development of his own inventions.

Babbage's contemporaries would have considered him more successful had he stuck to his original plan and constructed the Difference Engine. But then he would only have earned a footnote in history. It is for the Analytical Engine he never completed that we honor him as "father of the computer."

Lady Lovelace   Even though the Analytical Engine was never completed, a demonstration program for it was written. The author of that program has the honor of being the world's first computer programmer. *Her* name was Augusta Ada Byron, later Countess of Lovelace, the only legitimate daughter of the poet, Lord Byron.

Ada was a liberated women at a time when this was hardly fashionable. Not only did she have the usual accomplishments in language and music, she was also an excellent mathematician. The latter was most unusual for a young lady in the nineteenth century. (She was also fond of horse racing, which was even more unusual.)

Ada's mathematical abilities became apparent when she was only fifteen. She studied mathematics with one of the most well-known mathematicians of her time, Augustus de Morgan. At about the time she was studying under de Morgan, she became interested in Babbage's Analytical Engine.

In 1842, Lady Lovelace discovered a paper on the Analytical Engine that had been written in French by an Italian engineer. She resolved to translate the paper into English. At Babbage's suggestion, she added her own notes, which turned out to be twice as long as the paper itself. Much of what we know today about the Analytical Engine comes from Lady Lovelace's notes.

To demonstrate how the Analytical Engine would work, Lady Lovelace included in her notes a program for calculating a certain series of numbers that is of interest to mathematicians. This was the world's first computer program.

"We may say more aptly," Lady Lovelace wrote, "that the Analytical Engine *weaves algebraical patterns* just as the Jacquard-loom weaves flowers and leaves." Most aptly said indeed.

BABBAGE'S DREAM COME TRUE

The Harvard Mark I   A hundred years passed before a machine like the one Babbage conceived was actually built. This occurred in 1944, when Howard Aiken of Harvard University completed the Harvard Mark I Automatic Sequence Controlled Calculator.

Aiken was not familiar with the Analytical Engine when he designed the Mark I. Later, after people had pointed out Babbage's work to him, he was amazed to learn how many of his ideas Babbage had anticipated.

The Mark I is the closest thing to the Analytical Engine that has ever been built or ever will be. It was controlled by a punched paper tape, which played the same role as Babbage's punched cards. Like the Analytical Engine, it was basically mechanical. However, it was driven by electricity instead of steam. Electricity also served to transmit information from one part of the machine to another, replacing the complex mechanical linkages that Babbage had proposed. Using electricity (which had only been a laboratory curiosity in Babbage's time) made the difference between success and failure.

But, along with several other electromechanical computers built at about the same time, the Mark I was scarcely finished before it was obsolete. The electromechanical machines simply were not fast enough. Their speed was seriously limited by the time required for mechanical parts to move from one position to another. For instance, the Mark I took six seconds for a multiplication and twelve for a

Herman Hollerith, who pioneered the use of punched cards for data processing in the late nineteenth century. His Tabulating Machine Company was one of the organizations that would be brought together to form IBM.

The Harvard Mark I, "Babbage's dream come true."

division; this was only five or six times faster than what a human with an old desk calculator could do.

ENIAC What was needed was a machine whose computing, control, and memory elements were completely electrical. Then the speed of operation would be limited not by the speed of mechanical moving parts but by the much greater speed of moving electrons.

In the late 1930s, John V. Atanasoff of Iowa State College demonstrated the elements of an electronic computer. Though his work did not become widely known, it did influence the thinking of John W. Mauchly, one of the designers of ENIAC.

ENIAC—Electronic Numerical Integrator and Computer—was the machine that rendered the electromechanical computers obsolete. ENIAC used vacuum tubes for computing and memory. For control, it used an electrical plugboard, like a telephone switchboard. The connections on the plugboard specified the sequence of operations ENIAC would carry out.

ENIAC was 500 times as fast as the best electromechanical computer. A problem that took one minute to solve on ENIAC would require eight to ten *hours* on an electromechanical machine. After ENIAC, all computers would be electronic.

ENIAC was the first of many computers with acronyms for names. The same tradition gave us EDVAC, UNIVAC, JOHNIAC, ILLIAC, and even MANIAC.

EDVAC The Electronic Discrete Variable Computer—EDVAC—was constructed at about the same time as ENIAC. But EDVAC, influenced by the ideas of the brilliant Hungarian-American mathematician John von Neumann, was by far the more advanced of the two machines. Two innovations that first appeared in EDVAC have been incorporated in almost every computer since.

First, EDVAC used *binary notation* to represent numbers inside the machine. Binary notation is a system for writing numbers that **26** uses only two digits (0 and 1), instead of the ten digits (0-9) used in the conventional decimal notation. Binary notation is now recognized as the simplest way of representing numbers in an electronic machine.

Second, EDVAC's program was stored in the machine's memory, just like the data. Previous computers had stored the program externally on punched tape or plugboards. Since the programs were stored the same way the data was, one program could manipulate another program as if it were data. In chapter 5, we will see that such program-manipulating programs play a crucial role in modern computer systems.

A stored-program computer—one whose program is stored in memory in the same form as its data—is usually called a *von Neumann machine* in honor of the originator of the stored-program concept.

THE COMPUTER GENERATIONS

From the 1940s to the present, the technology used to build computers has gone through several revolutions. People sometimes speak of different *generations* of computers, with each generation using a different technology.

The First Generation First-generation computers prevailed in the 1940s and for much of the 1950s. They used vacuum tubes for calculation, control, and sometimes for memory as well. First-generation machines used several other ingenious devices for memory. In one, for instance, information was stored as sound waves circulating in a column of mercury. Since all these first-generation memories are now obsolete, no further mention will be made of them.

The Selective Sequence Electronic Calculator was built by IBM in 1948. This machine was installed at IBM's World Headquarters in New York City. It was perhaps the first giant digital calculator available for commercial use.

Vacuum tubes are bulky, unreliable, energy consuming, and generate large amounts of heat. As long as computers were tied down to vacuum tube technology, they could only be bulky, cumbersome, and expensive.

The Second Generation In the late 1950s, the transistor became available to replace the vacuum tube. A transistor, which is only slightly larger than a kernel of corn, generates little heat and enjoys long life.

At about the same time, the magnetic-core memory was introduced. This consisted of a latticework of wires on which were strung tiny, doughnut-shaped beads called *cores*. Electric currents flowing in the wires stored information by magnetizing the cores. Information could be stored in core memory or retrieved from it in about a millionth of a second.

Core memory dominated the high-speed memory scene for much of the second and third generations. To programmers during this period, *core* and *high-speed memory* were synonymous.

The Third Generation The early 1960s saw the introduction of *integrated circuits*, which incorporated hundreds of transistors on a single silicon chip. The chip itself was small enough to fit on the end of your finger; after being mounted in a protective package, it still would fit in the palm of your hand. With integrated circuits, computers could be made even smaller, less expensive, and more reliable.

Integrated circuits made possible *minicomputers*, tabletop computers small enough and inexpensive enough to find a place in the classroom and the scientific laboratory.

In the late 1960s, integrated circuits began to be used for high-speed memory, providing some competition for magnetic-core memory. The trend toward integrated-circuit memory has continued until today, when it has largely replaced magnetic-core memory.

The most recent jump in computer technology came with the introduction of *large-scale integrated circuits*, often referred to simply as *chips*. Whereas the older integrated circuits contained hundreds of transistors, the new ones contain thousands or tens of thousands.

It is the large-scale integrated circuits that make possible the *microprocessors* and *microcomputers* we have discussed. They also make possible compact, inexpensive, high-speed, high-capacity integrated-circuit memory.

No one has yet proclaimed a fourth generation of computers. But the recent developments just mentioned have resulted in a *microprocessor revolution*, which began in the middle 1970s and for which there is no end in sight.

FOR FURTHER READING

Gleiser, Molly. "Lady Lovelace and the Difference Engine." *Computer Decisions*, May 1975, pp. 38-41.

Goldstein, Herman H. *The Computer from Pascal to von Neumann.* Princeton: Princeton University Press, 1972.

Heath, F. G. "Origins of the Binary Code." *Scientific American*, Aug. 1972, pp. 76-83.

Libes, Sol. "The First Ten Years of Amateur Computing." *Byte*, July 1978, pp. 64-71.

Morrison, Phillip, and Morrison, Emily. *Charles Babbage and His Calculating Engines.* New York: Dover Publications, 1961.

Reid-Green, Keith S. "A Short History of Computing." *Byte*, July 1978, pp. 84-94.

REVIEW QUESTIONS

1. How might technology have contributed to the evolution of mankind?

2. What was the most widely used method of calculation in ancient times?

3. From where do we get the words *abacus* and *calculate*?

4. Name two mathematicians and philosophers who constructed pioneering mechanical calculators.

5. Why were the early mechanical calculators unreliable?

6. What distinguishes the Jacquard loom from the abacus and the mechanical calculators?

7. What determines the pattern woven by a Jacquard loom?

8. In what century was the automatic computer invented?

9. What facets of Charles Babbage's character might have made it more difficult for him to get his inventions taken seriously?

10. What inspired Charles Babbage to start work on the Difference Engine?

11. Contrast the Difference Engine and the Analytical Engine.

12. Where did Babbage get the idea for using punched cards to control the Analytical Engine?

13. Who wrote a program for the Analytical Engine and so became the world's first computer programmer?

14. What was the main shortcoming of the Mark I and the other electromechanical computers?

15. What was the distinguishing feature of ENIAC?

16. What were the two distinguishing features of EDVAC?

17. What is a *von Neumann machine*?

18. Describe the technological features characteristic of each computer generation.

19. What type of computer memory was once so widely used that its name became almost synonymous with "high-speed memory"?

20. What technological developments made (a) minicomputers and (b) microcomputers possible?

DISCUSSION QUESTIONS

1. If Charles Babbage had been able to build a mechanical computer around the middle of the nineteenth century, how would our present uses of computers and our attitudes toward them have been affected?

2. When Babbage conceived the much more important idea of the Analytical Engine, he abandoned the Difference Engine, in which the government had invested a substantial amount of money. Discuss the ethics of this decision.

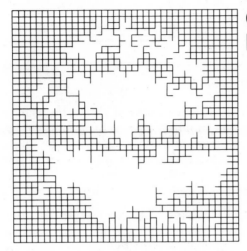

CHAPTER 3

COMPUTER HARDWARE

A *computer system* is composed of *hardware* and *software*. The hardware is the physical components that make up the computer system—the transistors, integrated circuits, microprocessors, tape decks, disk drives, card readers, printers, computer terminals, and the like. The software consists of the programs that the computer executes. We will look at the hardware in this chapter and the next and the software in chapter 5.

Of course, you don't have to understand how the hardware works to use a computer anymore than you have to understand how a television set works to watch the late movie. But you will be able to form a better mental picture of what we are talking about in the rest of the book if you do know a few things about computer hardware.

THE PARTS OF A COMPUTER

Figure 3-1 shows the parts of a computer. These parts are connected to each other by a group of wires called a *bus*. (The number of wires

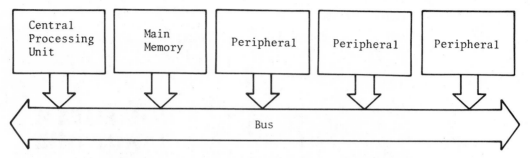

| Central Processing Unit | Main Memory | Peripheral | Peripheral | Peripheral |

Bus

Figure 3-1. The parts of a computer. The parts are connected together by a group of around 50-100 wires called a *bus*.

making up the bus varies from one computer to another but is usually from fifty to one hundred.) All information going from one unit to another flows along the bus. Usually, the bus has sockets installed along it. The various components are built on circuit boards that plug into the sockets.

The individual components are as follows:

- *The Central Processing Unit* (often abbreviated CPU). The central processing unit executes the user's program. It fetches program instructions from memory, one by one. It carries out the arithmetical or other operations requested by each instruction. It also sends commands to any other components whose services are required to execute an instruction.

- *Main Memory.* This is the computer's scratch pad. It holds the data and the program the computer currently is working on. The term *storage* is sometimes used instead of *memory*.

- *Peripheral Devices.* These include input devices, output devices, and auxiliary memory.

We already have seen that input and output devices convert data between forms useful to humans (text, pictures, sounds) and the binary codes the computer requires.

Not all the information to which a computer must have access will fit into main memory. The rest is stored in auxiliary memory. If

This cabinet houses the central processing unit, the main memory, and the device controllers for a small computer.

A small computer and some of its peripherals. On the left are two floppy-disk drives, used for auxiliary memory. On the right is a printer for printed output. The keyboard and the display screen are also considered to be peripherals. The central processor and main memory are inside the case that holds the keyboard.

main memory is the computer's scratch pad, auxiliary memory is its library and filing cabinets.

Each peripheral has a *device controller* that plugs into the bus and is connected to the device by wires (not part of the bus). The device controller converts between the binary codes on the bus and the sensing and control signals needed to monitor and control a particular device.

THE CENTRAL PROCESSING UNIT

The central processing unit (or central processor, for short) is *the* essential component of a computer. Other components, such as auxiliary memory or input and output devices or even main memory, sometimes can be omitted. But, without the central processor, there is no computer.

Not surprisingly, the central processor is the most complex part of a computer. This is why microprocessors represented such an advance. A microprocessor is simply a central processor constructed on a single silicon chip. Microprocessors make it possible to buy the complex central processor as a single, inexpensive component, instead of having to build it out of many individual transistors and integrated circuits.

The central processor itself is made up of two components—the arithmetic/logic unit, which does the calculations, and the control unit, which coordinates the activities of the entire computer.

The Arithmetic/Logic Unit   This is the computer's calculator, and it **33** performs the same jobs for a computer that a pocket calculator

The operator's console and central processor for a large-scale computer.

performs for a human being. The following are some of the jobs the arithmetic/logic unit does.

■ *Arithmetic Operations.* The arithmetic/logic unit adds, subtracts, multiplies, and divides. On some computers, the arithmetic/logic unit will not multiply or divide; for these machines, it is necessary to program multiplication and division in terms of repeated addition and subtraction.

■ *Logical Operations.* Logical operations require some explanation. Suppose we have a compound sentence made up of simple sentences joined with the words *and* and *or*. For example:

It is raining *and* I am home, *or* the sun is shining *and* I am playing baseball.

The Intel 8080 microprocessor, a central processing unit built on a single silicon chip.

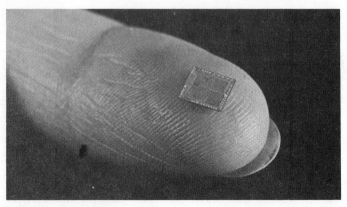

Given whether each of the simple sentences is true or false, the arithmetic/logic unit can determine (under the control of a program) whether the entire compound sentence is true or false.

■ *Comparisons.* The arithmetic/logic unit can determine such things as whether two alphabetic characters are the same or whether one number is less than, equal to, or greater than another. This information is passed to the control unit, which uses it to determine which instruction will be executed next. This feature of the central processor allows the computer to be programmed to make decisions and thus sets the computer apart from other machines.

The Control Unit   When an instruction is fetched from memory, it goes to the control unit. Like all other information in the computer, the instruction is stored in binary-coded form. The control unit decodes the instruction and generates the control signals that cause the other parts of the computer to carry out the instruction.

In particular, the control unit determines what arithmetic or logical operation the arithmetic/logic unit carries out. If we think of the arithmetic/logic unit as the computer's calculator, then we can think of the control unit as "punching the keys" on this calculator.

The control unit oversees the movement of data back and forth between the arithmetic/logic unit and main memory. It also oversees the movement of data between the arithmetic/logic unit and some peripheral devices. (Other peripheral devices transfer data directly to and from main memory, without going through the arithmetic/logic unit.)

The control unit also fetches from main memory the instructions to be executed. Normally, it takes its instructions from successive memory locations, just as a person might start at the top of a list of instructions and work through the list, instruction by instruction.

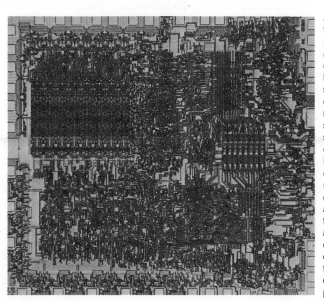

A magnified view of the Intel 8080 microprocessor. The arithmetic/logic unit occupies most of the lower half of the silicon chip. The central processor registers, which serve as a scratchpad during calculations, are at left just above the center. The control unit occupies most of the remaining area. Wires attached to the square pads around the rim of the chip connect it to the computer's memory, the peripheral devices, and a power supply.

But sometimes an instruction will direct the control unit not to fetch the next instruction in sequence but to jump to another part of memory and begin executing instructions there. Usually, the jump is to take place only if a certain condition is true. The control unit has the arithmetic/logic unit check whether or not the specified condition is true. If it is, then the control unit jumps to the designated part of memory for its next instruction. Otherwise, it just fetches the next instruction in sequence.

This feature provides the computer with a decision-making capability by allowing it to execute different parts of a program under different conditions.

COMPUTER MEMORY

Memory is the part of the computer that stores information for later use. It is also sometimes referred to as *the store* or *storage*.

Most computers have both *main memory* and *auxiliary memory*. (Main memory is sometimes referred to as *primary storage*. Auxiliary memory is sometimes referred to as *secondary storage* or *mass storage*.)

Main memory is very fast: the computer can store and recall the contents of a main memory location in a time measured in billionths of a second. Unfortunately, one has to pay for this performance; main memory is more expensive than auxiliary memory with the same capacity. Also, some forms of main memory are *volatile*; that is, the information stored in them is lost when the computer is turned off.

Therefore, most computers also make use of auxiliary memory, which is about a thousand times slower than main memory but costs correspondingly less and is not volatile. The volatility of many forms of main memory makes auxiliary memory essential for permanent files.

Main Memory Currently, computers employ two kinds of main memory—magnetic-core memory and integrated-circuit memory (also called *semiconductor memory*.) The trend is definitely away from the former and toward the latter.

A computer's main memory is divided into a number of individual *memory locations*, each of which can hold a certain amount of data. Each location has an *address*, which the computer can use to refer to it. We can think of a computer's memory as being like an array of post office boxes, each having an address and containing a piece of data.

Main memory is *random-access memory*. That is, the computer can access any memory location chosen at random. (We "access" a location when we store information in it or retrieve information from it.) The computer is not required to access the locations in any particular order. We will see that this is not always true for auxiliary

memory.

When the control unit needs to access a particular memory location—say, to transfer the data in it to the arithmetic/logic unit—it sends the address of that location over the bus to the memory unit. The memory unit decodes the address and sends the contents of the addressed location back over the bus to the arithmetic/logic unit. (The contents of the memory location remain unchanged. The contents of a memory location are changed only when the control unit stores new data in the location.)

Auxiliary Memory Auxiliary memory is used for large, permanent files, such as the accounts of all those who do business with a particular corporation. Libraries of programs also can be stored in auxiliary memory. The computer will execute any program from the library at the user's request. And if the computer's "scratch pad" becomes too large, part of it can be stored in auxiliary memory.

We will look at three kinds of auxiliary memory—magnetic disks, magnetic tape, and magnetic-bubble devices.

Magnetic Disks A disk looks like a grooveless phonograph record. The disk can be rigid, like a phonograph record, or flexible. The latter, called *flexible* or *floppy disks*, are widely used on personal computer systems.

A number of rigid disks (eleven is typical) can be combined to form a *disk pack.*

In use, a disk is mounted on a spindle. The spindle turns the disk at high speed; 1500 RPM or more are typical. A fork-shaped access arm carries two read-write heads, one for the top surface of the disk and one for the bottom. The access arm moves across the disk to store information in, or recall it from, various locations.

The computer can access a given location on the disk in a few ten thousandths of a second. This is an average time. If the read/write head happens to be close to the location to be accessed, the time could be much shorter; if the read/write head is farther away, the time could be much longer.

Magnetic Tape Main memory and magnetic disks are random-access memories: the computer can access the memory locations in

Four disk drives.

At left, three magnetic tape units. Below, a magnetic tape unit is opened revealing the reels of tape inside.

any order. On the other hand, magnetic tape is a *sequential-access* memory. To get to a certain location on the tape, we must pass over all the locations between it and the beginning of the reel.

The difference between random and sequential access is familiar from our everyday experience with phonograph records and tape recorders. If we want to play a particular selection on a phonograph record, we just pick up the tone arm and set the needle down on the part of the record we want to play. But if we want to play a particular selection on a tape recording, we have to wait while the tape winds from the beginning of the reel to the selection we want to play. This is time-consuming, even with the "fast-forward" features of some tape players.

Thus, magnetic tape is at its best when the reel is to be processed straight through, from beginning to end, so that all locations are accessed in the same order in which they were recorded. Otherwise, the time wasted in winding and rewinding becomes intolerable.

Magnetic Bubble Devices Information can be stored in the form of *magnetic bubbles*, magnetized regions in thin films of certain materials, such as garnet. The magnetic bubbles are so called because they have many of the properties of bubbles in a liquid: they can be created and destroyed, and they retain their identities as they are moved about on the film by externally applied magnetic fields.

Magnetic bubble devices, which first became commerically available in the late 1970s, promise to replace disks in many applications. Access to stored data is faster for magnetic bubble devices than for disks. The magnetic bubble devices are more compact than disk drives. And, since they contain no mechanical moving parts (the bubbles are moved about electrically), they are more reliable than disk drives. As with disks, magnetic bubble devices are nonvolatile, so they can be used to store permanent files.

INPUT AND OUTPUT EQUIPMENT

The input and output devices, frequently referred to as *I/O devices*, serve to get information into and out of the computer. They also convert between the symbols that are convenient for humans (such as the letters of the alphabet) and those the computer needs (binary codes).

Card Readers Card readers transfer to the computer information that has been recorded in the form of holes punched in cards. The cards themselves are variously known as *punched cards, computer cards, IBM cards,* and *Hollerith cards.* The last name honors Herman Hollerith, who first used punched cards for data processing.

The most common type of punched card is divided into eighty columns. One character can be punched into each column, so a card holds a maximum of eighty characters. The cards are punched by a machine called a *card punch.* Some card punches, called *key-punches,* are designed to be operated by humans using a typewriter-like keyboard. Other card punches serve as output devices for computers and punch on cards information transmitted to them by the computer.

In addition to the 80-column punched card, there is a 96-column card developed by IBM for use with its System/3 computer system. The 96-column card uses a more efficient method of coding characters as combinations of punched holes than does the 80-column card. Thus the 96-column card is substantially smaller than the 80-column card, even though it carries more information.

This *digitizer* allows a computer to input graphical information. Sketches, graphs, maps, and so on that are drawn on the digitizer pad using a special electrical pen are transmitted to the computer.

A manually operated card punch, commonly known as a keypunch.

Key-to-Tape and Key-to-Disk Equipment　These devices accept information from a keyboard and store it on tape or a flexible disk. The tape or disk takes up much less space than the equivalent number of punched cards, and the tape or disk can be reused, whereas the cards cannot. What's more, the computer can read the information from the tape or disk much faster than it could read it from punched cards.

40

Optical Character Readers Optical character readers read hand-written, typed, or printed characters directly from source documents, such as filled-out forms.

Reading from the source document is the ideal situation, since many errors blamed on computers actually take place during the keypunching or other keyboarding process.

From personal experience, I can cite one example of how many errors occur. Typists and keypunch operators frequently spell my first name *Neil* (the usual spelling) instead of *Neill* (the correct spelling). Perhaps unconsciously, they ignore what is on the source document and type what they "know" to be the correct spelling.

Unfortunately, present optical character readers cannot cope with human handwriting or even ordinary typing or printing. The characters must be carefully hand printed according to certain rules, or they must be typed or printed, using special typefaces designed for optical character recognition. Since much work is being done on optical character recognition, however, improvements may well be forthcoming.

Printers At present, most output from computers is printed. Various high-speed printers currently available can print hundreds or thousands of lines per minute. Printer technology runs the gamut from typewriter-like impact printers to those using exotic techniques, such as laser beams or ink jets, to form the characters.

Computer Output Microfilm Computer output can be recorded on either microfilm or microfiche. Both are more compact and less expensive than the equivalent amount of paper. On the other hand, a special reader is necessary in order to view the microfilm or microfiche. Some people find that extensive use of the special readers produces eyestrain. And those who are used to marking up their computer printout no longer can do so.

Typewriter Terminals A typewriter terminal consists of a keyboard and a typewriter-like printer, a combination that resembles an

A line printer.

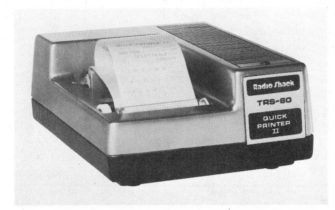

An inexpensive printer intended for use with small computers.

electric typewriter. Information typed on the keyboard is sent to the computer. Information received from the computer is typed out by the printer.

CRT Terminals   CRT terminals are similar to typewriter terminals except that the printer is replaced by a television-like display. (CRT stands for *cathode ray tube,* which is the engineer's name for a television picture tube.) Some CRT terminals can only display text; others can display drawings (including graphs and charts) as well.

In some CRT terminals, the display and the keyboard are built into the same cabinet. Others use a separate display. This can be an ordinary video monitor, such as is used in a closed-circuit TV system. In some cases, an ordinary TV set can be used, but a TV set usually is not as satisfactory as video monitor.

Plotters   Plotters allow the computer to make drawings. They are often used to plot graphs or draw maps. Another common use is to draw the patterns from which integrated circuits are manufactured.

A flatbed plotter.

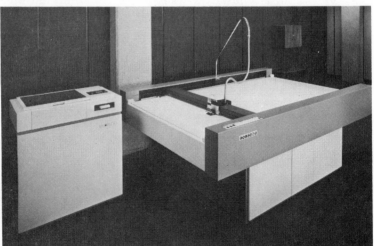

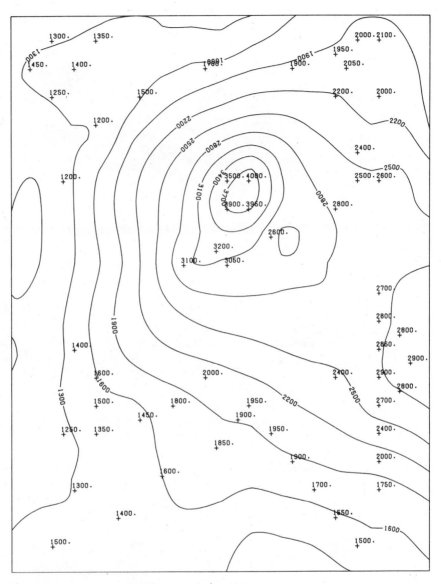

A contour map drawn by a computer using a plotter.

Speech Synthesizers   Computers can talk as well as print. Already on the market are two products that use speech synthesis—a calculator for the blind and an educational toy that pronounces and spells words.

How does speech synthesis work? The program looks up the words to be spoken in a dictionary in auxiliary memory. The dictionary shows how each word is to be pronounced and stressed. Using this information, the computer sends codes representing each sound to the speech synthesizer, an electronic device that actually produces the sounds.

43

A speech synthesizer intended for use with small computers.

With current hardware and software, the result is not perfect. The computer seems to speak with a foreign accent. But people who really need a talking computer, such as blind persons, have little trouble learning to follow the machine's accent.

The computer's accent can be eliminated if the machine utters only a few stock phrases. A human being chooses the codes to be sent to the synthesizer for each phrase, experimenting with the codes until each phrase sounds just right. Then the codes for each phrase are stored in the computer's memory and recalled when needed.

With a speech synthesizer, a Touch-Tone phone can be used as a computer terminal, at least in a limited way. Using the synthesizer, the computer can ask questions over the phone. The listener responds by pushing buttons on the phone. The buttons send tones over the phone line that the computer can easily decode.

Equipment to let the computer recognize spoken sounds is under development, and some actually is being used. At present, however, speech recognition is not as highly developed as speech synthesis.

FOR FURTHER READING

Computers and Computation. San Francisco: W. H. Freeman and Co., 1971. See the following articles:

Evans, David C. "Computer Logic and Memory."

Rajchman, Jan A. "Integrated Computer Memories."

Slotnick, D. L. "The Fastest Computer."

Sutherland, Ivan E. "Computer Inputs and Outputs."
————. "Computer Displays."

Winograd, Shmuel. "How Fast Can Computers Add?"

Flores, Ivan. *Computer Organization.* Englewood Cliffs, N. J.: Prentice-Hall, 1969.

Scientific American (special issue on microelectronics), September 1977.

Vacroux, André G. "Microcomputers." *Scientific American,* May 1975, pp. 32-40.

1. What are the two components of a *computer system*?

2. What is *computer hardware*?

3. What is *computer software*?

4. What are the three main hardware components of a computer system?

5. What is the function of the *central processing unit*?

6. What is the function of *main memory*?

7. Give two functions performed by *peripherals*.

8. What is the *bus*, and what is its function?

9. What is a *device controller*?

10. What are the two parts of the central processing unit?

11. Describe three functions of the *arithmetic/logic* unit.

12. Describe the operation of the *control unit*.

13. Describe the operation of the instruction that gives the computer a decision-making facility.

14. Give the advantages and disadvantages of main and auxiliary memory.

15. What does *volatile* mean in reference to computer memory?

16. What two types of main memory are used in modern computers?

17. Describe three forms of auxiliary memory.

18. Distinguish between random access and sequential access.

19. Why are magnetic bubble devices likely to be more reliable than either tape or disk drives?

20. Identify briefly each of the following methods of input and output:

    (a) punched cards
    (b) key-to-disk and key-to-tape equipment
    (c) optical character readers
    (d) printers
    (e) computer output microfilm
    (f) typewriter terminals
    (g) CRT terminals
    (h) plotters
    (i) speech synthesizers

**DISCUSSION
QUESTION**

This chapter discussed only the most widely used input and output devices. Many more are used for special purposes. Have you encountered any of these in your everyday experience? If so, describe the devices and how they were used.

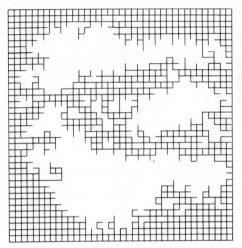

CHAPTER 4

HOW DOES A COMPUTER WORK?

In chapter 3, we looked at the parts that make up the hardware of a computer system. Two things we touched upon there but did not discuss in detail were (1) how data and programs are represented inside a computer and (2) how the various parts we mentioned work together to execute a program. Now it's time to explore these matters in greater detail.

BINARY CODES

A *binary code* represents information using combinations of the two symbols 0 and 1. The symbols 0 and 1 are called *binary digits* or, for short, *bits*.

Binary codes are extremely well suited for electronic computers, since it is easy to represent the 0s and 1s electrically. For instance, we might represent a 1 by an electric circuit with a current flowing in it and a 0 by a circuit in which no current is flowing. Or we might represent a 1 by a point at which an electrical voltage is present and a 0 by a point at which no voltage is present.

There are also convenient nonelectrical ways of representing 0s and 1s. The most common of these uses holes punched in cards. The presence of a hole signifies a 1 and the absence of a hole signifies a 0.

In our everyday writing, we employ an alphabet that consists of the twenty-six lowercase letters a-z, the twenty-six uppercase letters A-Z, the digits 0-9, and a number of punctuation marks and special signs (twenty-six of them on my typewriter). Printed books use far more symbols, since text can be set in italics or boldface, and different type sizes can be used.

But actually this profusion of symbols is unnecessary. Only two symbols will suffice to represent any information that could be represented using the eighty-eight symbols on the typewriter or the much larger number used in printing. The two symbols 0 and 1 are the "letters" of the computer's alphabet. The computer uses them just as we use the ordinary letters, digits, punctuation marks, and special signs.

Representing Alternatives Representing information boils down to representing alternatives. For instance, suppose you wish to represent the state in which a person lives. Since there are fifty states, you must be able to represent fifty alternatives. Put another way, the question what state do you live in? has fifty answers, and we must provide a distinct code for each answer.

The post office uses two-letter codes for the names of the states—FL for Florida, GA for Georgia, WV for West Virginia, and so on. Since there are 26 letters in the alphabet, there are 26 × 26 or 676 possible combinations of two letters. Thus there are far more two-letter codes than are needed to represent the fifty states. We may assume that if any reasonable number of new states joins the union in the future, the post office is unlikely to run out of two-letter codes.

Now let's look at the number of alternatives we can represent using a binary code with a given number of bits. We start with a single bit, which can be either 0 or 1, and thus can represent two alternatives. Put another way, we can use a single bit to record the response to any question that has only two possible answers.

The simplest question of this kind is one whose answer is either "yes" or "no." For instance, suppose you are asked, "Are you going home this weekend?" Unless you change the subject to avoid answering, you have exactly two possible responses—"yes" and "no." Let's agree to have 0 represent "no" and 1 represent "yes." Then we can represent your answer inside the computer by a single bit. If the bit is 0, your answer was "no." If the bit is 1, your answer was "yes."

Physically, the computer could use a single electric circuit to store your answer. If no current is flowing in the circuit, representing 0, then your answer was "no." If the current is flowing in the circuit, representing 1, then your answer was "yes." Figure 4-1 illustrates this way of representing the two possible answers.

But what about questions with more than two answers? For instance, suppose a waiter asks you what flavor of ice cream you

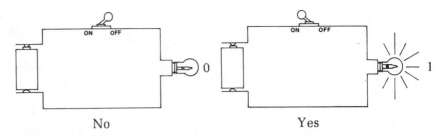

No   Yes

Figure 4-1. A single electric circuit can store the answer to a yes-or-no question. If a current is flowing, the answer to the question is "yes." If no current is flowing, the answer to the question is "no."

want to order. The four flavors on the menu are vanilla, chocolate, strawberry, and peach. How many bits are needed to record your choice?

Two bits will do the job. With two bits, we have four possible codes—00, 01, 10, and 11. For example, we could agree to represent the four flavors of ice cream as follows:

Flavor	Code
Vanilla	00
Chocolate	01
Strawberry	10
Peach	11

(Any other correspondence between flavors and codes would work just as well. The only requirement is that we be consistent; once we decide on a correspondence, then we must use the same one all the time.)

If you ordered strawberry ice cream, then this fact would be represented inside the computer by the code 10. Physically, two circuits could be used to record your preference. Current would be flowing in the first circuit (representing 1) and not flowing in the second circuit (representing 0). Figure 4-2 shows how we can represent each of the four flavors as combinations of currents that are flowing or not flowing in two electric circuits.

Using one bit, we can represent 2 alternatives. With two bits, we can represent 2 × 2 or 4 alternatives. So we will not be too surprised to find that with three bits we can represent 2 × 2 × 2 or 8 alternatives. In fact, the 8 possible three-bit codes are as follows:

000	100
001	101
010	110
011	111

(Can you think of a good reason why the number of alternatives must double every time we add another bit to the code?)

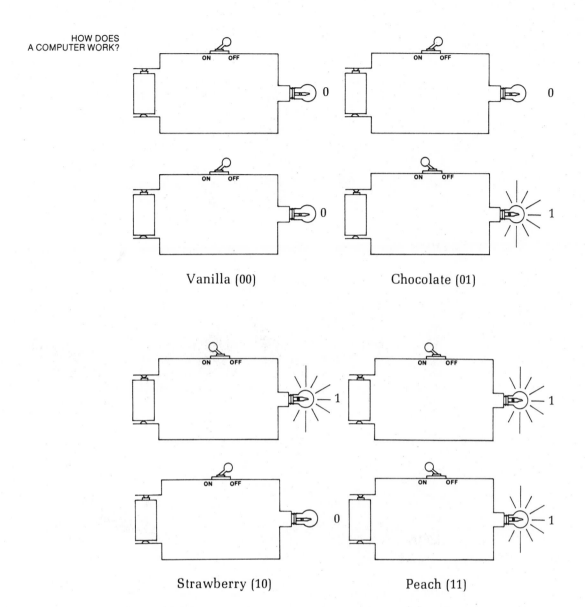

Vanilla (00)   Chocolate (01)

Strawberry (10)   Peach (11)

Figure 4-2. By using two two electric circuits we can represent four alternatives, such as four flavors of ice cream.

We can see a pattern forming for the number of alternatives that can be represented with a given number of bits. We saw that there were 2 one-bit codes, 2 × 2 two-bit codes, and 2 × 2 × 2 three-bit codes. We expect (and are correct in expecting) that there will be 2 × 2 × 2 × 2 four bit codes, 2 × 2 × 2 × 2 × 2 five-bit codes, and so on.

Mathematicians have a shorthand notation for repeated products, such as 2 × 2 and 2 × 2 × 2. They write 2 × 2 as 2^2, 2 × 2 × 2 as 2^3, and so on. For completeness, 2 can be written as 2^1. Using this

49

shorthand, we can say that there are 2^1 possible one-bit codes, 2^2 two-bit codes, 2^3 three-bit codes, and so on. The numbers 2^1, 2^2, 2^3 and so on are called the *powers of two*. We find the values of the powers of two by multiplying the specified number of 2s together in each case. This is easy to do with a calculator, but, to save you the trouble, here is a table of the first seven powers of two:

Power of Two	Value
2^1	2
2^2	4
2^3	8
2^4	16
2^5	32
2^6	64
2^7	128

We can use this table to determine how many bits are needed to represent a particular number of alternatives. For instance, if we want to represent the decimal digits 0-9, then we must be able to represent ten alternatives and, therefore, need four bits. (Three bits, with only eight alternatives, would not be enough.) Since four bits provide sixteen alternatives and we only need ten, six combinations of bits will be unused. In fact, the decimal digits often are represented as follows:

Digit	Binary Code	Digit	Binary Code
0	0000	5	0101
1	0001	6	0110
2	0010	7	0111
3	0011	8	1000
4	0100	9	1001

The six codes 1010, 1011, 1100, 1101, 1110, and 1111 are not used.

In the same way, to represent the twenty-six letters of the alphabet we need five bits. Since five bits give us thirty-two codes and we need only twenty-six of them, six codes will be wasted.

The ASCII Code When we strike a key on a computer terminal, a binary code representing the key struck is sent to the computer. And when the computer needs to display a character, it sends the corresponding binary code to the terminal.

Therefore, we need a code for the characters found on the keyboard of a computer terminal (which are, with a few exceptions, the same ones found on a typewriter keyboard). Ideally, all terminals should use the same code so that any terminal could be used with any computer system. But, in reality, there is more than one character **50** code in widespread use.

A standard code has been defined, however, and is widely used. This is the American Standard Code for Information Interchange, which usually is abbreviated ASCII (pronounced ass'key).

The ASCII code uses seven bits to represent each character. Therefore, there are 2^7 or 128 possible ASCII characters.

With 128 codes at our disposal, we can represent the uppercase and lowercase letters, the digits, the most commonly used punctuation marks, a handful of mathematical signs, and a number of *control characters*. The latter are used to control special functions of terminals. Examples are *carriage return* (return the typing element to the left margin), *line feed* (go to the next line), and *bell* (ring the bell on the terminal).

Figure 4-3 shows the ASCII code. The groups of three bits along the top of the table give the leftmost three bits of each code. The groups of four bits along the left side of the table give the rightmost four bits of each code. Thus, the ASCII code for A is 1000001, the ASCII code for B is 1000010, and so on.

The two- and three-letter abbreviations in the table represent control characters. For instance, CR stands for *carriage return*, LF for *line feed*, and BEL for *bell*. Some of the control characters come in handy when one computer is communicating with another. For instance, STX (start of text) and ETX (end of text) can be used to "frame" a computer-to-computer message.

Notice that a blank space has its own code, 0100000. People sometimes erroneously believe that the computer ignores spaces. Actually, it treats spaces just like any other character.

Figure 4-4 shows a message coded in ASCII.

Binary Notation   Numerical values are an important type of data that a computer must be able to deal with. One way to represent numerical values would be to retain the familiar decimal system of notation, which uses the digits 0-9, but to represent each digit by a four-bit code, as we did earlier in this chapter. This technique for representing numbers is called the *binary-coded-decimal representation*. In the binary-coded-decimal representation, the number 3249 would be written

0011 0010 0100 1001

The binary-coded-decimal representation almost invariably is used in pocket calculators. But it suffers from some drawbacks, the most serious of which we have already seen. For each digit, there are six bit combinations that are not used. Because of these wasted bit combinations, a number in binary-coded-decimal form will require more bits than if a representation had been used that did not waste any bit combinations.

The solution to this problem is to abandon the decimal system entirely. Instead of trying to represent each decimal digit by a binary code, we express our values in a number system that only uses the two digits 0 and 1 in place of the 0-9 of the decimal system. This

51

Leftmost Three Bits

		000	001	010	011	100	101	110	111
	0000	NUL	DLE	space	0	@	P	`	p
	0001	SOH	DC1	!	1	A	Q	a	q
	0010	STX	DC2	''	2	B	R	b	r
	0011	ETX	DC3	#	3	C	S	c	s
	0100	EOT	DC4	$	4	D	T	d	t
	0101	ENQ	NAK	%	5	E	U	e	u
Rightmost	0110	ACK	SYN	&	6	F	V	f	v
Four	0111	BEL	ETB	'	7	G	W	g	w
Bits	1000	BS	CAN	(	8	H	X	h	x
	1001	HT	EM	)	9	I	Y	i	y
	1010	LF	SUB	*	:	J	Z	j	z
	1011	VT	ESC	+	;	K	[	k	{
	1100	FF	FS	,	<	L	\	l	|
	1101	CR	GS	-	=	M	]	m	}
	1110	SO	RS	.	>	N	^	n	~
	1111	SI	US	/	?	O	_	o	DEL

Figure 4-3. The ASCII code. The leftmost three bits of the code for a character are found at the head of the column in which the character lies. The rightmost four bits of the code are found to the left of the row in which the character lies.

C	o	m	p	u
1000011	1101111	1101101	1110000	1110101
t	e	r	s	
1110100	1100101	1110010	1110011	0100000
a	r	e		f
1100001	1110010	1100101	0100000	1100110
u	n	.		
1110101	1101110	0101110		

Figure 4-4. A message coded in ASCII. Notice that the spaces between the words are coded in the same way as the letters that make up the words and the period at the end of the sentence.

system is called the *binary number system*, and numbers written using it are said to be in *binary notation*.

To see how binary notation works, think of an odometer (the mileage indicator on a car). But suppose that, instead of the usual digits (0-9) on each dial of the odometer, there are only two digits, 0 and 1.

Now suppose the odometer has four dials. When the car rolls off the assembly line, the odometer reads 0000. After the car has driven one mile, the odometer reads 0001. (We are ignoring the dial on the right that is used to count fractions of a mile on real odometers.)

What will the odometer read after the car has gone two miles? When the car goes another mile, the rightmost dial will advance one position. Since the dial only has the two digits 0 and 1 on it, advancing one position will take it from 1 back to 0.

Now, remember that on an ordinary odometer when a dial goes from 9 to 0, the next dial to the left advances one position. In binary notation, 1 plays the same role that 9 does in decimal notation. So when a dial goes from 1 to 0 on the binary odometer, the next dial to the left advances one position. After the car has gone two miles, then, the binary odometer reads 0010.

Figure 4-5 illustrates the operation of the binary odometer.

The following table gives the reading of the binary odometer after the car has traveled zero miles, one mile, two miles, and so on:

Miles Traveled	Odometer Reading	Miles Traveled	Odometer Reading
0	0000	8	1000
1	0001	9	1001
2	0010	10	1010
3	0011	11	1011
4	0100	12	1100
5	0101	13	1101
6	0110	14	1110
7	0111	15	1111

53

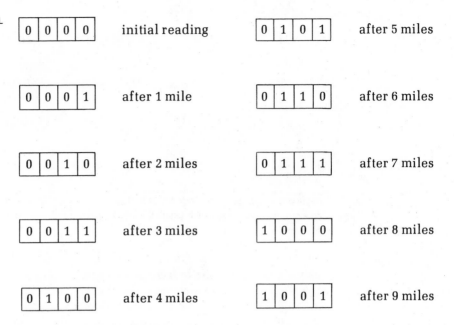

0	0	0	0	initial reading
0	0	0	1	after 1 mile
0	0	1	0	after 2 miles
0	0	1	1	after 3 miles
0	1	0	0	after 4 miles
0	1	0	1	after 5 miles
0	1	1	0	after 6 miles
0	1	1	1	after 7 miles
1	0	0	0	after 8 miles
1	0	0	1	after 9 miles

Figure 4-5. The binary odometer. Each dial on the odometer contains just two digits, 0 and 1.

Notice that the next reading after 0111 is 1000. This corresponds to the situation where a decimal odometer reads 0999 and changes to 1000 after one more mile has been traveled.

The entries in the Odometer Reading column are the binary numbers corresponding to the decimal numbers in the Miles Traveled column. As in decimal notation, we can drop unneeded zeros on the left, so 0001 can be written as just 1, 0010 can be written as 10, and so on. By dropping the unnecessary zeros, we get the following table for the binary numbers from zero through fifteen:

Decimal Number	Binary Number	Decimal Number	Binary Number
0	0	8	1000
1	1	9	1001
2	10	10	1010
3	11	11	1011
4	100	12	1100
5	101	13	1101
6	110	14	1110
7	111	15	1111

What would you expect the binary number corresponding to sixteen to be?

There is another way to look at binary numbers. As we all learned in school, the positions in a decimal number represent

54

(reading from right to left) units, tens, hundreds, thousands, and so on. Thus, the decimal number 3429 can be analyzed as follows:

Thousands	Hundreds	Tens	Units
3	4	2	9

Therefore, 3429 represents three thousands, four hundreds, two tens, and nine units.

We can use the same method for binary numbers, except that instead of units, tens, hundreds, and thousands, we have units, twos, fours, and eights. Thus, we can analyze the binary number 1101 as follows:

Eights	Fours	Twos	Units
1	1	0	1

Therefore, 1101 represents 1 eight, 1 four, and 1 unit for a total of 13 (8 +4+1 = 13).

Notice that the value each position represents is twice as great as the value for the position immediately to the right. Thus, the position to the left of the eights position represents sixteens, the position to the left of that represents thirty-twos, and so on.

BINARY ARITHMETIC

Arithmetic can be done in the binary system just as easily as in the decimal system. We don't intend to examine binary arithmetic in depth here, but we will look briefly at addition and multiplication as examples of manipulations that a computer can carry out on binary-coded data.

Addition The following is the addition table for binary numbers. (Remember that 10 represents 2 in binary notation.)

$$0 + 0 = 0 \qquad 1 + 0 = 1$$
$$0 + 1 = 1 \qquad 1 + 1 = 10 \text{ (that is, 0 and 1 to carry)}$$

Notice how simple this is compared to the huge decimal addition table we all had to learn as children. Here's another argument for binary notation: the addition (and, as we will see in a moment, the multiplication) tables are so simple that they are easily built into the computer's circuits.

With the help of this table, we can easily work out a binary addition:

```
  1010
+ 1011
------
 10101
```

Notice the carries that took place when we added the second and fourth columns from the right.

Multiplication   The binary multiplication table is even simpler than the binary addition table, since no carries are involved:

$0 \times 0 = 0$ $1 \times 0 = 0$
$0 \times 1 = 0$ $1 \times 1 = 1$

Using this table, we can easily work out a binary multiplication:

```
      1010
    × 1101
    _____
      1010
      0000
     1010
    1010
    _____
 10000010
```

Notice that actually doing the multiplications is no job at all. Each of the partial products (the numbers between the two horizontal lines) is either equal to the multiplicand (1010) or is zero (0000). The only work involved is in positioning the partial products correctly and then adding them up.

A MODEL COMPUTER

Now we want to see how the computer components described in chapter 3 work together to carry out the computations specified in a program.

However, we certainly don't want to get into the technical details of central processors, memory units, disk drives, and the various electrical signals they send to one another along the bus. Therefore, we will focus our attention on a model computer instead of a real one. In the model, computer components will be represented by familiar objects, such as post office boxes, calculators, and telephones.

The following list shows how each computer component is represented in the model. The pictures on these pages illustrate the parts of the model.

COMPUTER COMPONENT	REPRESENTATION IN MODEL
Main Memory	A set of post office boxes. Each box has a numerical address that can be used to refer to it. In each box is a card bearing

either a data item or a program instruction. A card can be read and then put back in the box, or it can be removed and replaced with another card.

Arithmetic/Logic Unit	A desk calculator
Control Unit	A clerk who repeatedly fetches instruction cards from memory and carries out the instruction on each card.
Program Counter	The control unit uses the program counter to keep its place in the program being executed. The program counter always contains the memory address (box number) of the next instruction to be executed. The program counter is represented by an ordinary hand counter (exaggerated in the illustrations for clarity).
Data Channels	These carry information to and from the peripheral devices, such as input/output equipment and auxiliary memory. We represent them by telephones.

Now let's watch our model computer in action.

The Fetch-Execute Cycle A computer operates by fetching program instructions from memory and executing them. The computer repeats the same fetch-an-instruction-and-execute-it cycle over and over again. No matter what the program may be doing, whether it is making up a payroll or playing a game of chess, the hardware is merely fetching and executing one instruction after another.

When the execution of a program begins, the program counter contains the address of the first instruction of the program. After the computer fetches each instruction, it updates the contents of the program counter so that the program counter contains the address of the next instruction to be fetched.

The fetch-execute cycle works like this. The clerk (who represents the control unit) notes the number in the program counter, goes to the box with that number, and reads the instruction card inside. The clerk then operates the counting mechanism on the program counter so that the number in it is increased by one.

For the execute part of the cycle, the clerk carries out the instruction that was just fetched from memory. Here are some of the things the instruction might call for.

- Obtain data from a certain address and enter it into the calculator.

57 - Store the result displayed on the calculator at a certain address.

THE MODEL COMPUTER

FETCH I

- Obtain the data from a given address and enter it into the calculator as before. But after punching in the data, hit one of the operation keys $+$, $-$, $\times$, or $\div$.

- Change the contents of the program counter to a specified value, thus causing the computer to jump to another part of its program.

- Contact a peripheral device on one of the telephones to obtain data from it, send data to it, determine its status, or send it a command.

When the execution of the instruction is complete, a new fetch phase begins. The contents of the program counter may have been changed by the execution of the previous instruction. But if they were not—the usual case—the next instruction will come from the box whose address is one greater than the address of the box that contained the previous instruction.

A Program for the Model Computer Now let's look at a simple program for the model computer. Here's the problem we want our program to solve. A salesperson earns a 10 per cent commission if that person's sales for the week were less than $1000. If the sales were $1000 or over, however, the salesperson earns a 15 per cent

commission. Given the weekly sales, the program is to compute the salesperson's commission.

The first thing we have to do is reserve space in memory for our data. We will need memory locations to hold Weekly Sales and Commission. We also need to store three constants—1000, 0.1 (10 per cent in decimal form), and 0.15 (15 per cent in decimal form). The following "memory map" shows which memory locations hold which data items:

Memory Locations

Address	Contents
1000	Weekly Sales
1001	Commission
1002	1000
1003	0.1
1004	0.15

Now for the program, which follows immediately after the data, **60** starting at memory location 1005.

Program

Address	Instruction
1005	Read a value for Weekly Sales from the terminal and store it in location 1000.
1006	Enter the contents of location 1000 into the calculator.
1007	Subtract the contents of location 1002 from the value entered in the calculator.
1008	If the value displayed on the calculator is negative, jump to location 1013.
1009	Enter the contents of location 1000 into the calculator.
1010	Multiply the number entered in the calculator by the contents of location 1004.
1011	Store the number displayed on the calculator in location 1001.
1012	Jump to location 1016.
1013	Enter the contents of location 1000 into the calculator.
1014	Multiply the number entered in the calculator by the contents of location 1003.
1015	Store the number displayed on the calculator in location 1001.
1016	Display the contents of location 1001 on the terminal. This is the commission earned.
1017	Stop.

The instruction in location 1005 reads the value of the Weekly Sales from the terminal and stores this value in loction 1000.

The program must distinguish between two cases: (1) Weekly Sales is less than $1000, and (2) Weekly Sales is greater than or equal to $1000. A different calculation is required for each case.

In order for the correct calculation to be done for each case, the instructions in locations 1006 and 1007 subtract 1000 from weekly sales. If the result is negative, the instruction in location 1008 causes the computer to jump to location in 1013. Otherwise, the computer continues execution with the instruction in location 1009. Therefore, the instructions to handle case (1) begin at location 1013. The instructions to handle case (2) begin at location 1009.

The instructions in locations 1009-1011 multiply Weekly Sales by 0.15 (15 per cent) and store the result in location 1001. The instruction in location 1012 causes the computer to jump to location 1016.

The instructions in locations 1013-1015 multiply Weekly Sales by **61** 0.1 (10 per cent) and store the result in location 1001.

Notice carefully that *regardless of which case occurred*, the computer arrives at location 1016. What's more, the result of the calculation has been stored in location 1001.

When the computer gets to location 1016, then, the value of Commission has been calculated and stored in location 1001. The instruction in location 1016 displays the contents of location 1001 on the terminal. The value displayed is the calculted commission.

The instruction in location 1017 terminates the execution of the program.

FOR FURTHER READING

Chu, Yaohan. *Introduction to Computer Organization*. Englewood Cliffs, N. J.: Prentice-Hall, 1970.

Crowley, Thomas H. *Understanding Computers*. New York: McGraw-Hill Book Co., 1967.

Fink, Donald G. *Computers and the Human Mind*. Garden City, N. Y.: Doubleday, 1966.

Flores, Ivan. *Computer Design*. Englewood Cliffs, N. J.: Prentice-Hall, 1967.

Tanenbaum, Andrew S. *Structured Computer Organization*. Englewood Cliffs, N. J.: Prentice-Hall, 1976.

REVIEW QUESTIONS

1. What is a *binary code?*

2. What are *bits?*

3. Why are binary codes particularly well suited for use with electronic computers?

4. How many different symbols will suffice to represent any information that could be represented using the eighty-eight characters on a typewriter keyboard?

5. What symbols can we think of as the "letters" of the computer's alphabet?

6. What is the advantage of having far more two-letter codes available than are necessary to represent the fifty states? *Hint:* Suppose we were so short of two-letter codes that we had to represent Florida by ZQ instead of FL?

7. Give some examples of your own showing that representing information is a matter of representing alternatives.

8. Describe how to determine the number of bits necessary to represent a given number of alternatives.

9. What is the *ASCII code?*

10. Give two functions that can be served by *control characters.*

11. Using figure 4-3, give the ASCII codes for A, Z, p, q, ?, $, and a blank space.

12. In figure 4-3, what do CR, LF, and BEL stand for?

13. Show how a simple message (other than the one illustrated in the book) can be coded in ASCII.

14. Describe the *binary-coded-decimal* representation for numerical values.

15. Describe the *binary number system*. What is another name for the binary number system?

16. Give the addition and multiplication tables for binary numbers.

17. Since the addition and multiplication tables for binary numbers are so simple compared to those we had to learn in school, some people have suggested that humans as well as computers should adopt the binary system. What's wrong with this suggestion? *Hint:* One thousand in binary is 1111101000, and one million is 11110100001001000000.

18. Describe how each of the following is represented in the model computer discussed in this chapter:
    (a) main memory
    (b) arithmetic/logic unit
    (c) control unit
    (d) program counter
    (e) data channels

19. Describe the fetch-execute cycle in terms of the model computer.

20. What is the effect of a jump instruction on the program counter?

EXERCISES

1. How many bits are required to represent:
    (a) the Seven Wonders of the World?
    (b) the nine planets in the solar system?
    (c) the fifty states of the union?
    (d) the eighty-eight characters on the typewriter keyboard?
    (e) the students in your class?

2. According to legend, the inventor of chess was told by the king to name his own reward. The inventor replied, "Give me one grain of wheat for the first square of my chessboard, two grains for the second square, four grains for the fourth, and so on for all sixty-four squares of the chessboard." The king thought this was a reasonable request. But, on consulting his advisors, he found the inventor had asked for more wheat than there was in the kingdom or even in the world. Express the number of grains of wheat the inventor requested in binary notation.

3. Show that the binary number 110010110001 represents the same value as the decimal number 3249. Compare the binary representation with the binary-coded-decimal representation given in the text. What advantage does the binary representation have over the binary-coded-decimal representation?

4. In our sample program, the instructions were given as English language descriptions. Inside the computer, they would be represented in coded form. Suppose the instructions are coded as follows.

Code	Instruction
01	Read a value from the terminal and store it in memory.
02	Obtain a value from memory and display it on the terminal.
03	Obtain a value from memory and enter it into the calculator.
04	Store the value displayed on the calculator in memory.
05	Add the value obtained from memory to the value displayed on the calculator.
06	Subtract the value obtained from memory from the value displayed on the calculator.
07	Multiply the value obtained from memory by the value displayed on the calculator.
08	Divide the value obtained from memory into the value displayed on the calculator.
09	Jump to the specified memory location.
10	Jump to the specified memory location *if* the value displayed on the calculator is negative.
11	Stop.

Every instruction except Stop refers to a memory location. The address of the location referred to is placed immediately after the instruction code. Thus, 011000 means "read a number from the terminal and store it in location 1000", 031000 means "obtain the value from memory location 1000 and enter it into the calculator"; 061002 means "subtract the value in location 1002 from the value displayed on the calculator."

These instructions are known as *machine code* or *machine language*. In a real computer, the instructions are represented as binary codes. In our model computer, we have represented them as decimal numbers for convenience.

Give the machine-language version of the sample program. To get you started, the first few instructions are as follows:

Address	Machine Code
1005	011000
1006	031000
1007	061002

5. Play the role of the computer and work through the instructions in the sample program. Use boxes drawn on the blackboard to represent memory locations. Your instructor will give you the value that is read from the terminal.

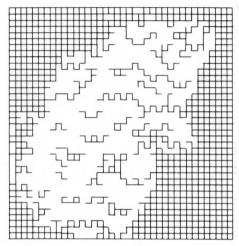

CHAPTER 5

COMPUTER SOFTWARE

The software for a computer is made up of the programs that the computer executes. These programs bear the same relation to the computer that records do to record players and movie films do to movie projectors.

There are two kinds of software—*application software* and *system software*.

Application software consists of the programs that do the jobs we bought the computer to do in the first place. Programs that play games, design camera lenses, make up payrolls, and guide spacecraft are all examples of application software.

System software consists of programs designed to help people write and execute other programs. Programs that translate other programs from one computer language to another are examples of system software, as are programs that supervise the execution of other programs on the computer.

Application software is as varied as the applications of the computer itself. We will be looking at many of these applications in the rest of this book. When we look at a particular computer application, we also are looking at the software that makes it possible for the computer to carry out that application. We will examine

Software for small- and medium-scale computers is often stored on floppy disks, such as the one shown being inserted into a business computer.

application software in depth in the part of this book devoted to BASIC, where we will learn how to write programs for simple applications.

Because most of the rest of this book is devoted to application software, we will say nothing more about that subject here. The rest of this chapter discusses system software.

General purpose computer systems are designed so that the software can be changed as quickly as possible when we want the computer to do different jobs. In fact, some system software is concerned with making such changes as rapidly as possible. But sometimes, particularly for special purpose computers, we want to install the programs permanently so the user won't have to bother putting the programs in memory, and the programs cannot be erased accidentally.

Such permanently installed programs are called *firmware*. The only difference between software and firmware is that software is easy to change and firmware is not. Therefore, we usually won't have to distinguish between the two.

PROGRAMMING LANGUAGES

Machine Language The instructions a computer executes are stored in memory in coded form, and it is only these codes that the computer hardware is designed to understand.

In problem 4 of chapter 4, we looked at a machine-language program for the model computer described in that chapter. The first few instructions of that machine-language program are as follows:

011000
031000
061002

Each machine-language instruction consists of two parts—an *operation code*, which specifies the operation the computer will carry out, and a *memory address*, which specifies the memory location that will be referenced. In the instructions for the model computer, the first two digits of each instruction are the operation code, and the remaining four digits are the memory address. In the example just given, the operation codes are 01, 03, and 06; the memory addresses are 1000 and 1002.

A machine-language programmer, then, has to know the operation code for each operation the computer can carry out. Many computers have hundreds of operation codes, and the machine-language programmer has to carry around a reference card that gives the proper code for each operation.

The machine-language programmer also has to keep track of all the addresses that are referred to in the program instructions. These may number in the hundreds or thousands. With only the addresses to go by, it is difficult to remember the significance of the data stored in each location. It is easy to make a slip and write an instruction that causes the machine to refer to the wrong memory location.

Still another problem is that, if we modify a program, we probably will have to change the addresses of some of the memory locations the program uses. When we change the address of an instruction or data item, we have to change the address part of every instruction in the program that refers to the changed item. Changing the address of one instruction or data item may require us to change the address parts of a large number of machine codes.

A final problem is that thousands of machine-language instructions are required to make the computer carry out any reasonably demanding application.

For these reasons, then, machine-language programming is extremely tedious. A programmer might write a few machine-language instructions for some special purpose, such as to make a correction to an existing program, but very few programmers would write a program of any size in machine language.

Assembly Language   Assembly language allows us to use convenient abbreviations, called *mnemonics*, for operations and memory locations. For instance, the part of the machine-language program just given might look like this in assembly language:

```
RD    SALES
LD    SALES
SB    CUTOFF
```

RD, LD, and SB are abbreviations for operation codes. RD stands for the code that *reads* a value from the terminal and places it in memory; LD stands for the code that *loads* a value from memory into the computer's calculator; SB stands for the code that *subtracts* a value in memory from a value previously entered into the calculator.

SALES and CUTOFF stand for the memory addresses 1000 and 1002. The names are chosen by the programmer to suggest the significance of the contents of the locations named. SALES reminds us that the named location holds the salesperson's weekly sales. CUTOFF reminds us that the named location holds the lowest sales amount for which a 15 percent commission will be paid.

The computer hardware cannot understand assembly language, of course; it only understands machine code. We can, however, program the computer to translate programs from assembly language to machine code. The machine code can then be executed by the computer. The program that causes the computer to do the translation is called an *assembler*. The assembler program is an example of a *language processor*. Language processors make it possible for the computer to accept programs written in languages other than machine language.

Assembly language, then, makes it possible for the programmer to use convenient mnemonics instead of obscure codes for operations and memory locations. Also, since memory locations are referred to by name rather than by address, the programmer can modify the program without worrying that the modifications will change some addresses and thus require still further modifications. Addresses are assigned by the assembler, which does the job anew each time a modified version of the assembly-language program is translated.

On the other hand, the assembly-language programmer still has to write a line of assembly language for each machine instruction, so substantial assembly-language programs are thousands of lines long. Also, the assembly-language programmer must worry about technical details of the computer, such as how much data will fit into a memory location and what operations are available for manipulating the data.

Thus, although assembly language is vastly superior to machine language and used far more widely, assembly-language programming is still tedious and requires specialized technical knowledge.

Higher-Level Languages What is needed is a language that hides the internal details of computer operation. The programmer then could write the program in the same terms that would be used to describe to a colleague the procedure to be carried out.

Programming languages that do this are called *higher-level* languages. As you might expect, different users and uses call for different languages. As a result, higher-level languages have proliferated: currently, about 170 of them are in use. The number in *widespread* use, however, is much less—around ten.

Among the most popular higher-level languages are COBOL
(COmmon Business Oriented Language) for business data process-

ing, FORTRAN (FORmula TRANslator) for scientific and engineering problems, and BASIC for education and personal computing.

For example, here is how a command to add two numbers could be given in each of the three languages just mentioned:

```
ADD PRICE, TAX GIVING TOTAL.    (COBOL)
TOTAL = PRICE+TAX               (FORTRAN)
LET T1 = P+T2                   (BASIC)
```

The names PRICE, TAX, and so on name memory locations, just as in assembly language.

None of the statements refers to any machine components or operations. The business programmer who prefers English-like sentences to algebra-like formulas can have them with COBOL. The scientific programmer who prefers the formulas gets them with FORTRAN. The computer hobbyist who is willing to trade drastic abbreviations for the ability to use the language on a small computer will be happy with BASIC.

Higher-level language programs are much shorter than machine-language programs. A single statement in a higher-level language may correspond to five, ten, or even more machine-language instructions.

The software program that translates a higher-level language program into machine language is known as a *translator* or *compiler*. Computer manufacturers often provide translators for the most popular languages, such as COBOL, FORTRAN, and BASIC. Translators also can be purchased from companies that specialize in computer software. Translators for the more obscure languages usually are written at universities or other research centers. Computer users can write their own translators. But writing a translator may take several years of effort, so it's not a task to be undertaken lightly.

Another approach to executing programs in higher-level languages is to use an *interpreter*. The interpreter program analyzes the higher-level language statements and carries out the operations they specify. No translation into machine language takes place.

It may take much longer to execute an interpreted program than a translated one, since the interpreter may have to analyze many times a statement that a translator would analyze and translate into machine code only once. Nevertheless, interpreters are often the most convenient way to implement a higher-level language, particularly when a large number of machine instructions are required to carry out the commands in a single higher-level language statement.

Interpreters, particularly for BASIC, are popular on small computers. Often the interpreter is included in firmware; as far as the user is concerned, the computer understands BASIC. The user never has to worry about machine language.

Translators and interpreters are both examples of language **70** processors.

This desktop computer contains a firmware interpreter for the BASIC programming language. Software written in BASIC is stored on magnetic-tape cartridges. One of these can be seen on the table at lower left; another can be seen inserted into the computer, just to the right of the display screen.

THE OPERATING SYSTEM

The *operating system* is a program that supervises the execution of other programs. It is also known as the *supervisor, monitor,* or *master control program.* By means of *system commands,* the user requests the operating system to execute particular programs and to give them access to particular data. The operating system handles all the details necessary to comply with the user's requests.

Here are some of the functions a modern operating system can perform.

Program Loading Many computer systems maintain a program library in auxiliary memory. Upon request from the user, the operating system will load a program from the library into main memory and see that the computer executes it. Also, the user who has written a program in a higher-level language can request that the program be translated into machine code and that the machine code be executed. The operating system handles all the details of loading the translator, executing it, then loading the machine code the translator produced (the translation of the user's program), and executing that.

Control of Peripherals Peripheral devices often require complex, tedious, and hard-to-write programs to transfer data between the devices and the computer. To write such a "device handler" program requires detailed technical knowledge about the operation of the device.

For this reason, the device handlers usually are written once and for all and included in the operating system. A user-written program transfers information to or from a peripheral device by requesting the operating system to do the job. The form of the request to the operating system is the same for all devices, even though the coded commands that actually must be sent to the device vary widely from one device to another.

As we will see shortly, one advantage of modern operating systems is their ability to allow many programs to execute on the computer at the same time. Under these circumstances, the operating system must supervise the use of the peripherals. If more than one program tried to use the same peripheral at the same time, chaos would result.

(Once upon a time, there was an operating system that, due to an error, allowed more than one program to use the printer at the same time. The printer would print a line of one program's output, then a line of another program's output, then a line of still another program's output, and so on. Needless to say, the various users were not enthusiastic about their joint printout.)

Data Management   Not only do computer systems maintain program libraries in auxiliary memory, they store data files there as well. Examples of such files would be the accounts of the customers of a company or the data collected in a scientific experiment.

When a program needs data from one of these files, it requests it from the operating system. The operating system first must find the desired file in auxiliary memory (a tape or a disk may contain many files). Then it must find the particular data requested and pass that on to the program. Data that a program wishes to store in a file is handled much the same way.

Many operating systems handle files and I/O devices in exactly the same way. A programmer can write a program to take information from certain files, process it, and store the results in other files. Only when it's time to execute the program does the user have to specify which "files" are actually files in auxiliary memory and which are I/O devices. This specification might be different each time the program is executed; what was a disk file on one execution could be a card reader on the next.

Virtual Memory   Often a computer program and the data it is manipulating are too large to fit into main memory at one time. Therefore, only the parts of the program and data that are being used at the moment are kept in main memory. The remainder reside in auxiliary memory until needed. During execution, parts of the program and data must be swapped back and forth between main

73 memory and auxiliary memory.

It is tedious for the programmer to have to divide the program and data up into parts and worry about making sure that the needed parts are always in main memory. We would like to free the programmer to concentrate on the problem being solved instead of on such computer-oriented technicalities as main and auxiliary memory.

With virtual memory, the operating system takes over the task of dividing the program and data into parts and juggling the parts between main and auxiliary memory. The programmer writes the program as if the computer had a very large main memory. The operating system takes care of the rest.

We speak of *virtual* memory since the computer appears to have a very large main memory, which does not really exist. Any part of a computer system that appears to be present as a result of programming but does not physically exist is said to be *virtual*. For instance, language processors are sometimes thought of as implementing virtual computers, imaginary computers that accept higher-level languages as their machine languages.

Accounting Computing resources, such as computation time and memory space, are expensive, particularly on large-scale machines. In many organizations, it is necessary to keep track of the resources each job uses, so that each department in the organization can be charged for the computer resources it uses. This accounting task is given to the operating system.

Security From what has been said so far, you may think that the operating system will honor any user request it can. In fact, on a large system with many users, there are usually requests that should be denied.

For instance, some data files may contain confidiential information. Others might contain records that someone could benefit from changing, such as bank accounts, student grades, or payroll information. In defense industries, some files and programs might even be military secrets. Even in an academic environment, programs and files must be protected against malicious mischief. It is up to the operating system to identify users and make sure that their jobs use only the programs and files that the users are authorized to have access to.

Security is a weak point with many current operating systems. The security provisions of more than one operating system have been defeated by a clever twelve-year-old with a computer terminal.

MULTIPROGRAMMING, MULTIPROCESSING, AND TIME SHARING

Fast Computers and Slow Peripherals The central processor, being electronic, is very fast. The peripheral devices, being mechanical, are comparitively slow.

For example, many computer terminals send and receive characters at the rate of thirty characters a second. (For sending, this rate is purely theoretical, since no one really can type that fast.) On the other hand, a fast computer can execute millions of instructions each second. While the computer is waiting for the terminal to send or accept one character, it could have executed 30,000 instructions or more. Obviously, if the computer is made to wait on the terminal, it will waste a great deal of its time.

There are two solutions to this problem. One is simply to use an inexpensive computer, so that the wasted time will not really matter. The other (more interesting) solution is to arrange for the computer to work on another program while one program is waiting on a peripheral device. Execution of the first program is not resumed until the request to the peripheral device has been fulfilled.

Multiprogramming   The situation where a single central processor works simultaneously on a number of programs at the same time is known as *multiprogramming*.

Normally, each program is executed for a short time, called a *time slice* or a *time quantum*. Before the operating system gives a particular program control of the computer, it sets an electronic timer that will interrupt the computer after the time quantum has expired. When the timer interrupts, control is returned automatically to the operating system. The operating system then moves on to the next program awaiting execution, sets the timer again, and gives that program temporary control of the computer.

In this way, the operating system goes from program to program in round-robin fashion. Each program is executed briefly, after which the operating system goes on to the next program. Since the central processor executes programs, we can think of the programs in memory as getting brief turns at the central processor, one after another. A particular program continues taking its turn at the central processor until its execution is complete.

When a program has to wait on a peripheral device, it simply loses its turn at the central processor until its request to the peripheral device has been satisfied. But while that program is waiting, the central processor is busy working on other programs.

This is another reason why requests to peripheral devices should be handled through the operating system. The operating system must be able to keep track of which programs are waiting for peripheral devices and which are ready to take their turns at the central processor.

Time Sharing   Time sharing is a form of multiprogramming in which users can communicate with their programs while those programs are executing.

Many users are connected to the computer by means of terminals. Each user can send commands to his program and obtain results **75** from it as the program executes. The user is not aware that the computer is working on other programs or switching from one program to another. Each user seems to have the computer all to himself. But while one user is thinking or typing, the computer is working on other users' programs.

What distinguishes time sharing from other forms of multi-programming is its responsiveness. When a user makes a request of a program, the program should respond promptly; a second or two is usually the longest delay tolerable. This means that every program has to get a turn at the central processor frequently enough to respond promptly to its user. If the number of programs being executed is large, the time quantum for each program must be short.

Another characteristic of time sharing is that there may be a large number of users—around a hundred, say—and therefore, a large number of programs being executed at the same time. Usually the number of programs is too large for all of them to fit into main memory at one time. As a result, the operating system continually must swap programs and data between main and auxiliary memory so that each program will be in main memory when its turn to execute comes up.

Multiprocessing   So far, we have confined our discussion to computer systems having a single central processor, which is switched from one program to another. However, some computer systems have more than one central processor. On these systems, different programs can be executed at the same time by different processors. This is known as *multiprocessing*.

In the past, multiprocessing has been limited because of the expense of multiple central processors. But microprocessors have made central processors much less expensive, and multiprocessing is becoming more common. Not nearly so much is known about multiprocessing as about multiprogramming. Discovering ways to use multiple processors effectively is a subject of continuing research.

FOR FURTHER READING

Denning, Peter J. "Third Generation Computer Systems." *Computing Surveys*, Dec. 1971, pp. 175-216.

Donovan, John H. *Systems Programming*. New York: McGraw-Hill Book Co., 1972.

Fano, R. M., and Corbató, F.J. "Time-Sharing on Computers." *Computers and Computation*. San Francisco: W. H. Freeman, 1971, pp. 79-87.

Katzen, Harry. *Computer Systems and Organization*. Chicago: Science Research Associates, 1976.

Sammet, Jean E. *Programming Languages: History and Fundamentals*. Englewood Cliffs, N. J.: Prentice-Hall, 1969.

Tannenbaum, Andrew S. *Structured Computer Organization*. Englewood Cliffs, N. J.: Prentice-Hall, 1976.

1. Distinguish between *application software* and *system software*.

2. What is *firmware*? How is it related to software?

3. What is *machine language*?

4. What are some of the disadvantages of machine language?

5. What is *assembly language*?

6. How is assembly language related to machine language?

7. What is an *assembler*?

8. Why is assembly language still not convenient for many applications in spite of its advantages over machine language?

9. Give two advantages of higher-level languages over assembly language.

10. Name three widely used higher-level languages, and give the application areas in which each is most likely to be used.

11. What is a *language processor*?

12. Give three examples of language processors.

13. Distinguish between *translators* and *interpreters*.

14. What is an *operating system*?

15. Give three alternate names for operating systems.

16. Give six functions the operating system performs.

17. Describe *multiprocessing, multiprogramming,* and *time sharing*.

18. How are the relative speeds of the central processor and the peripherals related to the need for multiprogramming?

19. What is a *time slice*?

20. Explain how multiprogramming works.

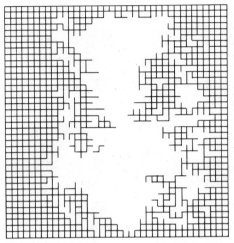

CHAPTER 6

THE ART AND CRAFT OF COMPUTER PROGRAMMING

What is it like to program a computer? Why do some people find programming so fascinating that they take it up as a hobby, while others have to struggle to write even the simplest programs? In this chapter, we will try to see just what programming is and how it is done.

Compared to many arts and crafts that have endured for centuries, programming is in its infancy. Only since the early 1950s have substantial numbers of people programmed computers. What we can expect to find in this chapter, then, are not the time-tested principles of a long-established discipline but a glimpse at work in progress. This glimpse will reveal some of the insights that programmers have arrived at so far as they struggle with the complexities of their machines and the world those machines serve.

WHAT IS PROGRAMMING?

The "High-Speed Moron" As we have seen in previous chapters, a

computer can carry out only a small number of simple operations. A computer can do a job only if the job can be broken down into a sequence of these simple operations. For the computer to do something that seems straightforward to humans may require a program containing thousands of instructions.

Given these facts, people are moved to speak of the computer as a "high-speed moron," capable of doing only the most trivial things but able to do them very fast.

Reporters and magazine writers seem particularly fond of talking about the "high-speed moron." They like to compare programming a computer to giving instructions to an idiot. The reader gets the impression that programming is nothing but the endless tedium of grinding out one instruction after another in hopes of getting the electronic idiot to do what could be explained to any intelligent person in a few words.

We cannot challenge the reporters' facts. Computers often do need programs containing thousands of instructions to do things people find simple. (And many things people find simple cannot, as yet, be programmed for computers at all.)

Giving instructions to an idiot certainly does not sound inspiring. How are we to account for all those programmers who find their craft "interesting," "challenging," or "exciting"? Or for all the thousands of people who took up programming as a hobby when home computers became available?

Let's try to come up with a better analogy. Consider a book. A book certainly is made up of a large number of individual characters. This book, for instance, has nearly a million. The author must strike the typewriter keys nearly a million times to produce the book. Surely this is nothing but endless tedium, striking one key after another, over and over again.

Well, writing a book is indeed work, but no author would think of it as a tedious process of typing one letter after another. For one thing, the individual characters are not paramount in the author's mind. The author is more concerned with the ideas the book is to express and with its larger units—chapters, sections, paragraphs, sentences, and words. Only occasionally does the author lack the right word or have to look up a spelling in the dictionary. Otherwise, the author concentrates on what he is trying to say, and the words and characters largely take care of themselves.

Matters are much the same with the programmer, who also thinks in terms of much larger ideas than individual machine instructions. This is the level where the programmer creates. Here is where fascinating challenges are met and interesting problems solved.

Eventually, of course, the ideas must be realized as machine instructions. But here the programmer has an advantage over other artists and craftspeople. For the programmer has at hand a vast array of software designed to translate, automatically, high-level (but precisely formulated) ideas into low-level programs. It is as if the author had a machine into which ideas could be fed and which could type out the actual sentences and paragraphs. Or if a painter could feed a conception of a scene into a machine and have the machine supply the actual brush strokes.

What the Programmer Creates   What is the fascination of programming? The impulse is the same one that motivates most creative endeavors—the desire to create something useful, or interesting, or significant, or just pretty.

But what the programmer creates is not a novel or a painting or a piece of furniture but a pattern of behavior for the computer. If the behavior in question is interesting or useful, then the programmer will feel the same satisfaction as someone who has created something clever or interesting or useful from words or paint or wood. When the programmer says, "Look at what my program does," the hope is that we will admire the computer's clever behavior as we would a well-painted picture or a neatly constructed birdhouse.

Ultimately, a program is a message from the programmer to the user, with the computer as the medium. But the program will not say the same things to all users, nor will everyone get the whole message at once. Both the programmer's instructions and the user's inputs combine to determine what the program will do. The program is not static, like a book, nor is its behavior always the same, like a motion picture. A program can respond to and interact with the user. It is more like a fascinating toy that one can play with for hours and hours without ever getting tired of it.

FOUR PROGRAMMING TECHNIQUES

Now let's look at some of the tools programmers use to build sophisticated programs out of simple instructions.

Sequencing   Sequencing is the simplest and most obvious method of arranging actions to accomplish some purpose. It means nothing more than just carrying out a sequence of actions in their proper order, one after another.

We often find sequencing in so-called automatic machines, such as automatic washers. For example, here is a program that could be used to direct an automatic washer. We will write it in what is sometimes called a "pseudolanguage." A pseudolanguage is similar to a higher-level programming language except that the commands for the computer are written as informal English statements rather than specially defined words and symbols. We enclose these informal statements in parentheses:

ALGORITHM WASHING-MACHINE
   (Fill tub with wash water and soap)
   (Agitate)
   (Drain wash water)

(Fill tub with first rinse water)
(Agitate)
(Drain first rinse water)
(Fill tub with second rinse water)
(Agitate)
(Drain second rinse water)
(Spin dry)
END WASHING-MACHINE

One of the first things likely to strike your eye is the word ALGORITHM. An algorithm is simply a set of instructions for achieving a particular result. When the instructions are stated in general terms, we speak of an algorithm. When the instructions are written up in a programming language and are ready to execute on a computer, we speak of a program. To convert an algorithm into a program, we have to realize each of the actions called for in the algorithm by means of operations that can be expressed in a particular programming language.

It is customary to give algorithms descriptive names; we call ours WASHING-MACHINE. The lines ALGORITHM WASHING-MA-CHINE and END WASHING-MACHINE serve to frame the actual text of the algorithm.

But the important things are the parenthetical commands. The essence of sequencing is that the commands will be obeyed one after another in the order in which they are written. Thus, the washing machine first will fill the tub with wash water and soap; then it will agitate; after that, it will drain the wash water; after that . . . but you get the idea.

Notice two things: First, the order of the actions is crucial to the success of the algorithm. Rinsing the clothes before washing them would be as futile as trying to take off your socks before your shoes. Second, the sequence gives no alternatives or choices of actions. The algorithm will do exactly the same things in the same order every time it is executed, regardless of what conditions may hold each time.

Programmers sometimes use diagrams called *flowcharts* to show the order in which actions are to be taken. On a flowchart, the starting and stopping points are shown as ovals, and the commands are enclosed in boxes. Figure 6-1 is a flowchart of the washing-machine algorithm.

Selection   The behavior of a program will be very rigid unless the computer can choose between alternate courses of action depending on the conditions that prevail at execution time. The technique for providing such choices is called *selection*. Selection is none other than the decision-making capability of computers that we already mentioned in connection with jump instructions. At the machine-language level, selection is implemented by means of jump instructions. In higher-level languages, however, other selection constructions are more convenient.

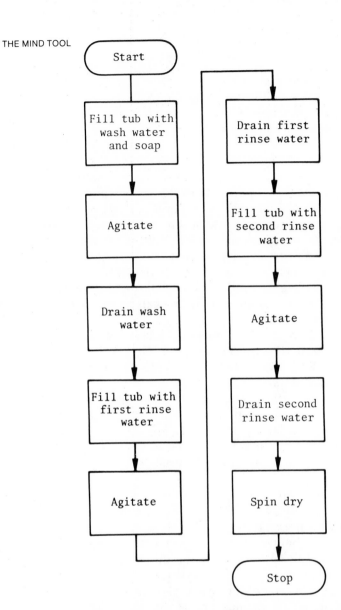

Figure 6-1. The flowchart of the washing-machine algorithm illustrates sequencing.

A good exercise to illustrate such programming ideas as selection is to write algorithms that a person could follow in carrying out everyday activites. Consider, for instance, the decision a driver must make in approaching a stoplight:

```
ALGORITHM STOPLIGHT
    IF (the light is red) THEN
        (Stop the car)
    ELSE
        (Proceed through the intersection)
    END IF
END STOPLIGHT
```

The words IF and ELSE and the phrase END IF set off a particular grammatical construction in our pseudolanguage, the selection construction. It works like this. Immediately following the word IF is a *condition*—"(the light is red)." The condition is a statement that can be either true or false. If the light *is* red, then the statement is true. If the light is green or yellow, the statement is false.

Now, if the condition is true, then any commands between THEN and ELSE are to be carried out. If the condition is false, then the commands between ELSE and END IF will be executed. Thus, if (the light is red) is not true, then (Proceed through the intersection) is executed.

Figure 6-2 illustrates the flowchart for selection. The diamond-shaped symbol indicates a decision point. If the condition inside the diamond is true, the branch labeled TRUE is followed. If the condition is false, the branch labeled FALSE is followed. The two branches eventually rejoin at the small circle, called a *collector circle*.

We can improve the stoplight algorithm and, at the same time, look at another form of selection. The previous version of the algorithm treats a yellow light the same as a green light, which certainly is not correct. The following version takes into account that the light can have three possible colors.

Figure 6-2. The flowchart of the simple stop-light algorithm illustrates selection.

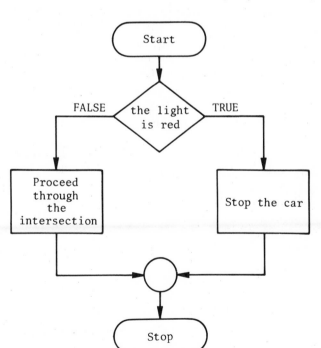

ALGORITHM STOPLIGHT
    IF (the light is red) THEN
      (Stop the car)
    ELSE IF (the light is yellow) THEN
        IF (the car has entered the intersection) THEN
          (Proceed with caution)
        ELSE
          (Stop the car)
        END IF
    ELSE
      (Proceed through the intersection)
    END IF
END STOPLIGHT

What we have here is one selection construction nested inside another. The outermost selection construction has the following form:

IF (the light is red) THEN
   (command for case of red light)
ELSE IF (the light is yellow) THEN
   (command for case of yellow light)
ELSE
   (command for case of green light)
END IF

If the light is red, then the command for the red light is executed, and the commands for the yellow light and the green light are skipped. If the light is not red, then we check to see if it is yellow. If the light is yellow, then the command for the yellow light is executed, and the one for the green light is skipped. If the light is neither red nor yellow, then it must be green. Therefore, the command for the green light is executed if neither (the light is red) nor (the light is yellow) is true. Figure 6-3 shows a flowchart of this selection construction.

The commands for the red light and the green light are straightforward. But the command for the yellow light is itself a selection construction.

IF (the car has entered the intersection) THEN
   (Proceed with caution)
ELSE
   (Stop the car)
END IF

Thus, after we know that the light is yellow, we must determine whether or not the car has entered the intersection before we can specify the correct action.

Notice the way the lines are indented. Without the indentation, it

would be hard to figure out which ELSE or ELSE IF or END IF went

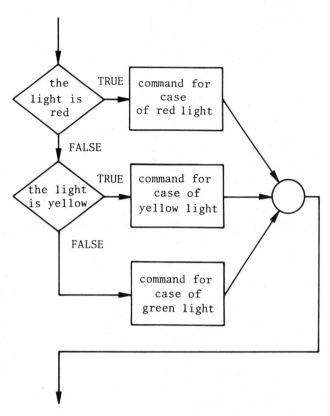

Figure 6-3. The flowchart of the three-way selection construction in the improved stop-light algorithm.

with which IF. Many programming languages use indentation to display the structure of the statements.

Figure 6-4 shows a flowchart of the improved stoplight algorithm. Notice that there is one decision diamond and one collector circle for each selection construction.

Repetition   Repeating instructions is a fundamental programming technique. If each step in a program were to be executed only once, then it probably would be easier to do the calculation by hand than to write a program and let the computer execute it. So just about any job worth programming a computer to do involves repetition. Of course, this could mean that the whole job had to be done many times so that the entire program is used repeatedly. But, more commonly, some of the commands in the program will be executed repeatedly each time the program is executed.

Let's illustrate repetition with an algorithm for sharpening a pencil. Here's our problem: When we write the algorithm, we have no idea how many times the crank of the pencil sharpener will have to be turned in order to sharpen a particular pencil. We must find some way of instructing the person or machine executing the algorithm when to stop turning the crank.

85

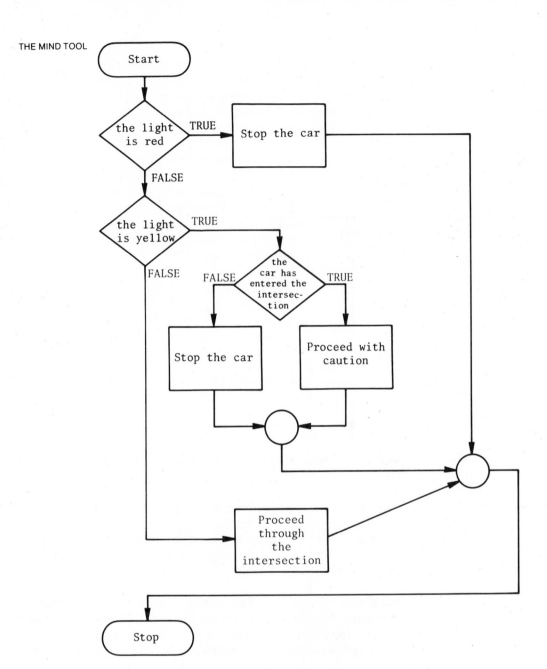

Figure 6-4. The flowchart of the improved stop-light algorithm.

We can write a pencil-sharpening algorithm like this:

ALGORITHM SHARPEN-PENCIL
   (Insert the pencil into the sharpener)
   REPEAT
     (Turn the crank)
   UNTIL (the crank turns easily)
   (Remove the pencil)
86   END SHARPEN-PENCIL

The repetition is brought about by the REPEAT-UNTIL construction. After turning the crank, we know whether or not it turned easily. If it did, no further repetitions are necessary, and we can go on to the next command. But if the crank did not turn easily, then we go back and repeat (Turn the crank) again. The repetitions continue until (the crank turns easily) is true.

Figure 6-5 illustrates the REPEAT-UNTIL construction. Notice that the decision diamond checks the condition after the action-to-be-repeated has been carried out. The TRUE branch goes on to the next command; the FALSE branch goes back for another repetition.

The important point is that when we write the algorithm, we do not know how many times the crank will be turned. We want to specify that the person or machine executing the algorithm should

Figure 6-5. The flowchart of the simple pencil-sharpening algorithm illustrates the REPEAT-UNTIL construction.

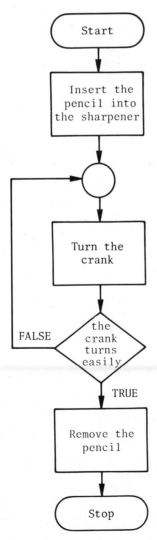

turn the crank *enough* times. The REPEAT-UNTIL construction allows us to do this, provided we can specify precisely how to recognize when the crank has been turned enough.

Of course, the fact that the crank turns easily is not a guarantee that the pencil is sharp. It could be sharp on one side only. An improved algorithm that takes this into account also introduces another repetition construction:

```
ALGORITHM SHARPEN-PENCIL
    WHILE (the pencil is not sharp)
      (Insert the pencil into the sharpener)
      REPEAT
        (Turn the crank)
      UNTIL (the crank turns easily)
      (Remove the pencil)
    END WHILE
END SHARPEN-PENCIL
```

The WHILE construction differs from the REPEAT-UNTIL construction in two ways. First, for the WHILE construction, the repetition takes place while a certain condition is true, rather than until a condition becomes true. Second, in the WHILE construction, the condition is checked before each repetition, instead of afterwards as is the case with REPEAT-UNTIL. Figure 6-6 is a flowchart of the WHILE construction. Compare it carefully with the flowchart of REPEAT-UNTIL.

The improved algorithm, then, starts out by checking whether or

Figure 6-6. The flowchart of the WHILE construction.

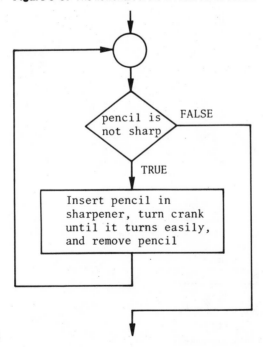

not the pencil is sharp. If it is, we jump immediately to END WHILE, and the algorithm terminates. Otherwise, everything between WHILE and END WHILE is repeated as long as the pencil is not sharp. Figure 6-7 shows a flowchart of the improved pencil-sharpening algorithm.

Figure 6-7. The flowchart of the improved pencil-sharpening algorithm.

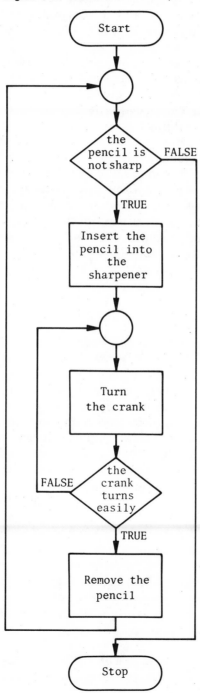

Notice that any flowchart containing a repetition contains a (roughly) circular path. This path is called a *loop*. Any command or series of commands that gives rise to a repetition is also known as a loop.

Subroutines A subroutine is a program that can be called upon by another program to do a particular job. When the subroutine finishes its work, it returns control to the program that called it. The calling program then continues from where it left off when it called the subroutine.

Subroutines are one reason computer programming is not as painful and tedious as outsiders sometimes picture it. Although the computer can carry out only simple operations, we can write subroutines to do much more complicated ones. These subroutines can, in turn, be used as building blocks for more complicated subroutines, which can be used to build still more complicated ones, and so on.

Another way to look at it is that subroutines allow us to build on our previous work, instead of having to start out anew each time we write a program. For example, most computer systems have libraries of previously written subroutines stored in auxiliary memory. When we write a program, we can use any of the available subroutines that will serve our purpose. And any subroutines we write in the process can be stored for us or somebody else to use later.

TO ERR IS HUMAN

A Problem with Bugs You might expect that reasonable care would be sufficient to avoid program errors, known as *bugs*. Alas, this is not so. Even the most careful programmer becomes resigned to the fact that a program is unlikely to work right the first time it is executed. If the program is at all complex, weeks or months may pass before it can be fully *debugged*, or corrected. Some large programs may never be fully debugged. It is a rare computer system that will not *crash* (stop working) every now and then because an erroneous instruction in the operating system has been executed (or an erroneously omitted instruction was not executed).

The problem is that no one knows any sure-fire way to find all the bugs in a program. Some bugs can remain undetected for years until just the right (or wrong) combination of circumstances causes the erroneous part of the program to be executed. Bugs turn up all too often in the software issued by respectable computer manufacturers and written by teams of highly skilled programmers. Nor is it unusual for a program revision designed to cure one bug to cause another one.

The problem of bugs is probably the most serious one facing computer technology today.

Why Programs Are Hard to Debug Why not just test a program thoroughly to find all the bugs before putting it on the market? This turns out to be easier said than done. The problem arises because of selection, which causes branching in the flowchart. As a result of the branching, there are many possible paths through the flowchart. A test input to the computer will cause it to follow one path. To test the program thoroughly, we have to use enough test cases to cause the computer to follow every possible path through the flowchart.

Unfortunately, for large programs the number of paths through the flowchart is enormous.

Suppose the flowchart contains a single decision diamond, as shown in figure 6-8a. Then there are two paths through the flowchart. The computer can follow either path, depending on which exit it takes when it leaves the decision diamond. To test the program thoroughly, we need to test both paths. So we need two sets of test data. One set must cause *condition-1* to be false, so the computer will follow the path labeled FALSE. The other set must cause *condition-1* to be true, so the computer will follow the path labeled TRUE.

Now suppose that, in each of the paths in figure 6-8a, we put another decision diamond, as shown in figure 6-8b. Now we have four paths to test. To test all four, we need four sets of test data. As the following table shows, one set must cause both *condition-1* and *condition-2* to be false, another set must cause *condition-1* to be false and *condition-2* to be true, and so on.

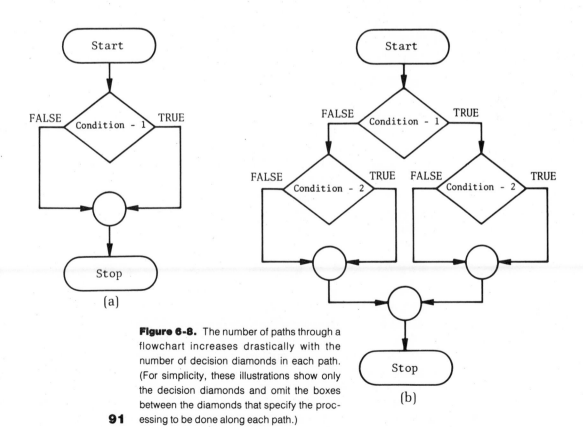

Figure 6-8. The number of paths through a flowchart increases drastically with the number of decision diamonds in each path. (For simplicity, these illustrations show only the decision diamonds and omit the boxes between the diamonds that specify the processing to be done along each path.)

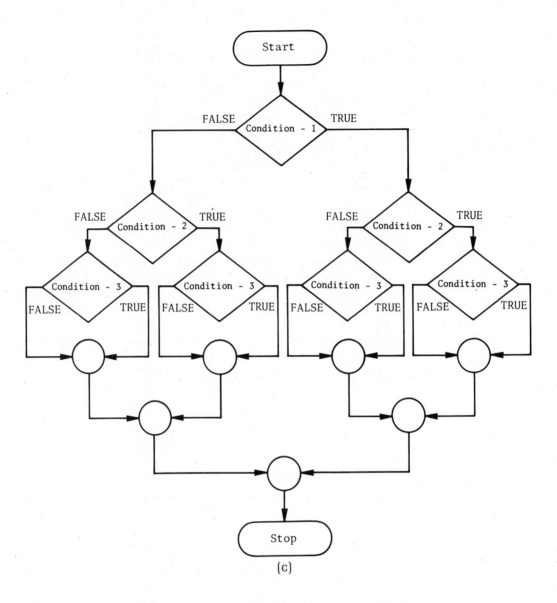

(c)

Path to be Tested	Condition-1	Condition-2
1	false	false
2	false	true
3	true	false
4	true	true

(Designing sets of test data that cause particular combinations of conditions to be true or false may not be easy to do, since the conditions can depend on the test data in very complicated ways. But we ignore that problem here and just concentrate on the number of sets of test data required.)

Let's look at one more example. Suppose we add another
92 decision diamond to each of the paths of figure 6-8b. Figure 6-8c

shows the result. Now we have eight paths to be tested. The following table shows the eight combinations of truth values that the eight sets of test data must produce:

Path to be Tested	Condition-1	Condition-2	Condition-3
1	false	false	false
2	false	false	true
3	false	true	false
4	false	true	true
5	true	false	false
6	true	false	true
7	true	true	false
8	true	true	true

You may have noticed that every time we added another condition, the number of paths doubled. Two, four, and eight paths are no trouble to test. But what about programs that have fifty or a hundred conditions? (Many have far more than this.) The following table illustrates how the number of paths through the flowchart varies with the number of conditions to be tested:

Number of Conditions	Number of Paths
10	1,024
20	1,048,576
50	1,125,899,906,842,624
100	1,267,650,600,228,229,401,496,703,205,376

For 100 conditions, the number of paths through the flowchart is astronomical. And so is the number of sets of test data that would be needed to test the program thoroughly by forcing the computer to follow each path at least once.

Of course, actual flowcharts are more complicated than those shown in figure 6-8. Paths that separate will later rejoin. Loops cause the computer to pass through some decision diamonds many times, perhaps taking a different exit each time around. But, in spite of these details, the general conclusion (if not the exact numbers) still holds: the number of paths through the flowchart of a complex program is astronomical. And so is the number of sets of test data needed to test the program thoroughly.

For those of us who consider programs fascinating objects, these figures are heartening. They assure us that a program can be a "deep" or a "rich" object whose almost endless possibilities cannot be fully explored in even a lifetime of effort. It is precisely things that offer this kind of rich variety which people find worthy of their interest.

Yet the same figures are frightening when we come down to earth and face the task of writing a program to do its job reliably. The very depth and richness we admire threaten to keep us from ever

finding all the bugs.

STRUCTURED PROGRAMMING

If we cannot test a large program adequately, then we'll just have to learn how to write it correctly in the first place. Nobody has any sure-fire scheme for doing this, and we still have a *lot* to learn about the art of writing correct programs. But here are three currently popular approaches that do seem to yield better results than the older, more haphazard approaches to program design.

Modularity   When we think about some complicated machine, such as an automobile, we don't try to grasp the operation of the entire machine at once. Nor do we spend much time thinking about how the machine is constructed from its most basic raw materials—steel, glass, plastic, and so on.

Instead, we visualize the automobile as made up of much larger parts—tires, an engine, a radiator, a battery, and so on. Some of these parts are, in turn, made up of still smaller parts. The engine, for instance, is made up of a block, pistons, connecting rods, a crankshaft, valves, and so on.

On the other hand, some of these parts can be combined into "systems" that are larger than any single part but still smaller than the entire car. For instance, the battery, the horn, the lights, the spark plugs, and the ignition coil are all part of the electrical system.

Each of the parts and systems is called a *module*. We can visualize the car as a hierarchy of modules, with many modules being divided into smaller modules, which are themselves divided into still smaller modules.

At the top of the automobile hierarchy, for instance, is the entire car, which forms a single module. This module can be broken down into other large modules, such as the cooling system, the electrical system, and so on. These can be divided still further into such modules as the battery and the radiator. And, of course, those, too, can be divided still further. The battery, for instance, can be broken down into plates, electrolyte, terminals, and so on.

At the bottom of the hierarchy are the modules that cannot be broken down further, such as shafts, springs, and bolts. Also included are those we could break down further but have no reason to do so. We do not make a light bulb, for instance; we buy it at the auto store. Therefore, we think of it as a single part and have no interest in its internal construction.

It's helpful to think of a computer program as being made up of modules, just as a car is. Like each part of a car, each module of the program performs a distinct function. When we are designing one module, we can focus all our attention on that part of the program and the function it performs. For the moment, we can forget about the rest of the program.

The different modules of a program even can be designed by different people, who may specialize in different kinds of modules. To return to the car analogy, we can be sure that its engine and its tires were designed by different specialists. Surely the engine designer wasted no time worrying about the problems of designing tires, nor did the tire designer worry about the problems of designing engines.

The same ideas extend to repair—or debugging for programs. When a car has a flat tire, we quickly localize the trouble to the tire and concentrate all our efforts there. While changing the tire, we probably won't worry about whether the engine needs tuning or the radiator needs more water. We concentrate on finding and fixing one problem at a time.

Again, all this applies just as well to programs. When a bug turns up, we can pin it down to a single module. We can confine our efforts to correcting the offending module. Even if those efforts cause new problems, the new problems still will be confined to the module we are working on. So we can stick with the one troublesome module until we get it to work right, forgetting about the rest of the program in the meantime.

Everyone who followed the moon landings in the late 1960s and the early 1970s became familiar with such terms as *lunar module*, *command module*, and *service module*. Most people probably dismissed these terms as just more space-age jargon. Undoubtedly, few realized that without a modular approach to design and testing, the space program would never have gotten off the ground.

Top-Down Design and Testing The hierarchical arrangement of modules inspires us to design and test a program by starting with the top-level module and working downward.

To see how this works, consider how an author might apply the technique to writing a book. First, he would decide what the entire book (the top-level module) is to cover. The next step is to break the material down into chapters (the second-level modules). Each chapter is divided into sections (the third-level modules). As each section is written, the author must deal with paragraphs (fourth level), sentences (fifth level), and words (sixth level).

(We could consider the characters in the words to be a seventh level, but we won't. Just as we can buy a light bulb at the auto store, we can find the spellings of words in the dictionary.)

When a program is designed in top-down fashion, we can test it in the same way. That is, as soon as the top-level module is designed and written, we can test it before writing any of the lower-level modules. The same can be done after each lower-level module is written. An advantage of this approach is that each newly written module is tested in the context of a complete program, all of whose higher-level modules are already working. A module can be tested "in place," so to speak, being called on by the same higher-level modules that will call on it in the finished program.

A difficulty with top-down testing, however, is that when we test any particular module, the lower-level modules that it must call on have not yet been written.

The solution is to replace these yet-to-be written modules with *program stubs* during testing. A program stub is a short dummy program that prints out the fact that it has been invoked, reports the data that was passed to it, and passes a dummy result back to the module that invoked it. Thus, we can see that the yet-to-be written module is being invoked when it should be and is being passed the correct data and that the result it returns is being used correctly.

Simple Control Structures   How are we to build a module out of lower-level ones? What programming techniques should we use to combine the calls on lower-level modules into the program for the higher-level module?

The advocates of structured programming recommend using only the control constructions described in this chapter—sequencing, selection, repetition, and calling subroutines. Many other control constructions can be made up on the spur of the moment by drawing flowcharts in arbitrary ways. But these do-it-yourself control constructions are apt to be tricky, with subtle pitfalls for the unwary. By sticking to the well-understood control constructions, we can have much greater confidence that our program is actually going to work as we expect it to.

Modularity, top-down design and testing, simple control constructions—these seem to be the first steps along the path to reliable programs and a discipline of software engineering.

FOR FURTHER READING   *Computing Surveys* (special issue on programming), Dec. 1974.

Dahl, O.J.; Dijkstra, E.W.; and Hoare, C. A. R. *Structured Programming.* New York: Academic Press, 1972.

Knuth, Donald E. "Computer Programming As an Art." *Communications of the ACM,* Dec. 1974, pp. 667-673.

Strachey, Christopher. "Systems Analysis and Programming." *Computers and Computation.* San Francisco: W. H. Freeman, 1971, pp. 70-77.

Yourdon, Edward. *Techniques of Program Structure and Design.* Englewood Cliffs, N. J.: Prentice-Hall, 1975.

REVIEW QUESTIONS   **1.** Why is programming considered to be in its infancy compared with many other arts and crafts?

2. Why is the computer sometimes considered to be a "high-speed moron"? What are some reasons why this term is misleading?

3. Compare the creations of the programmer with those of other craftspeople and artists.

4. What is a *pseudolanguage?*

5. Explain *sequencing.*

6. What is an *algorithm?* How is it different from a program?

7. In the algorithm for the washing machine, what is the purpose of the phrases ALGORITHM WASHING-MACHINE and END WASHING-MACHINE?

8. Give some examples of everyday actions in which incorrect sequencing would lead to absurd results.

9. What is *selection?*

10. What machine-language instructions are used to implement selection?

11. If we wish to provide for selection from more than two alternatives, how is the pseudolanguage selection construction modified?

12. Give an example of how one selection construction can be nested inside another.

13. What is *repetition?*

14. Why do most algorithms and programs make some use of repetition?

15. In this chapter, we looked at two repetition constructions. Distinguish between the two constructions, and illustrate each with a flowchart.

16. What are *subroutines,* and how are they used?

17. Explain why it is not practical to test every possible path through the flowchart of a large program.

18. What is a *module?* Give an example of modular structure, besides those mentioned in the book.

19. Describe the process of top-down design and testing. What is a *program stub?*

20. What control constructions do advocates of structured programming recommend?

**DISCUSSION
QUESTIONS**

1. From your experience with professions, hobbies, and recreations, give an example of some art, craft, or sport that might seem tedious and frustrating to an outsider but that isn't viewed that way by the persons who practice it. Explain why some people find this activity challenging and rewarding in spite of the apparently tedious and frustrating details.

2. Consider some hobby or craft that you enjoy. What do you get out of it? Do you enjoy the work itself, the challenge of producing good results, the results themselves, or the admiration of other people for your skills? Use the results of your analysis to explain why some people enjoy writing computer programs.

1. Using the pseudolanguage described in this chapter, write an algorithm for the sales-commission calculation that we programmed for our model computer. Draw a flowchart of the algorithm.

2. Write an algorithm for some everyday activity, such as changing a tire or making candy. Try to choose an activity that involves selection, repetition, or, preferably, both.

3. An important feature of algorithms is that, if certain conditions hold, the algorithm can be guaranteed to give the desired results if its instructions are faithfully carried out. Consider the pencil-sharpening algorithm in this light. What is the desired result? What conditions must hold if the desired result is to be guaranteed? *(Hint: What if the pencil sharpener was defective?)* Assuming the necessary conditions hold, give arguments proving that:

1) the algorithm terminates—that is, none of the repetitions go on forever; and
2) when the algorithm terminates, the desired result will have been achieved.

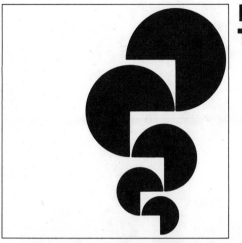

PART
TWO

...AND SOCIETY

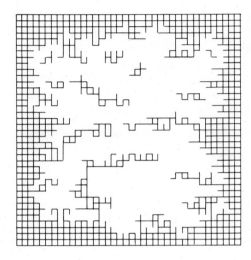

CHAPTER 7

PERSONAL COMPUTING

Personal computing refers to the use of computers by individuals rather than by organizations, such as schools, businesses, and government bureaus.

Before 1970, computers were just too bulky and expensive for personal use. Then, in the early 1970s, large-scale integrated circuits, such as microprocessors and low-cost memory chips, appeared on the market. For the first time, computer use by individuals became practical. Even more, computers no longer were restricted to problems that required massive data processing or sophisticated mathematics. Now they were inexpensive enough to be applied to everyday human problems, such as turning on the oven at the proper time or changing channels on the TV set.

Currently individuals are using computer technology in four areas: (1) calculators, (2) computers in consumer products, (3) computers in games, and (4) hobby computers. Computer hobbyists aside, the people involved usually are quite unaware that they are even using computers.

(The field of personal computing is changing so rapidly that it will not be at all surprising if additional applications for personal **101** computers have become important by the time you read this book.)

CALCULATORS

In preceding chapters, we discussed the workings of pocket calculators, so there is little more to be said here. But since calculators use computer technology, they do deserve mention in the chapter on personal computing. The more advanced programmable calculators satisfy all our criteria for a computer; any distinction between programmable calculators and computers is rather arbitrary. And even the simplest four-function calculator has a microprocessor inside.

In the long run, calculators may have a greater social impact than many other computerized consumer products. The fact that a computer can mind the oven does not drastically change the way we cook our food; the computer just provides added convenience to an already familiar appliance. Yet calculators are drastically changing the way we do arithmetic. Slide rules already are obsolete, and paper-and-pencil calculations seem ready to follow them into oblivion.

THE HIDDEN COMPUTERS

Surely one of the most important developments of the 1970s was the widespread use of microprocessors in consumer products. The computerized products can do things that their manually operated predecessors could not do, and they are easier to operate besides. Functions that once required the close supervision of a human operator now can be carried out automatically. In many cases, an easy-to-use keyboard for giving commands to the computer replaces a variety of dials, switches, and other adjustments.

The built-in computers are not intrusive; the user never has to worry explicitly about "working the computer." Indeed, the user remains unaware that a computer is even involved, unless the manufacturer's advertising makes a point of the fact. (Some manufacturers of computer-controlled appliances use "computer" or "microprocessor" in their advertising. Others, perhaps fearful that "computer" will scare customers, stick to the more familiar "solid state.")

A microcomputer for appliance control usually consists of the following components:

- A microprocessor

- A read-only memory containing the program for the microprocessor (The program is permanently installed when the read-only memory is manufactured and cannot be changed by the user.)

- A random-access memory (This is the computer's scratch pad. Usually only a small amount of random-access memory is needed, since appliance-control computers rarely have to do extremely complex calculations or process large amounts of data.)

■ Circuits for interfacing the computer to the sensors and effectors that actually will monitor and operate the appliance (Designing these sensors and effectors can be the most difficult part of adapting an appliance to computer control.)

In the remainder of this section, we'll look at some representative computerized consumer products. (Since new ones are being announced every day, complete coverage is out of the question.)

It may strike you that some of the applications described are rather trivial—turning the oven on and off, for instance. Yet, in a way, this triviality is one of the most important points to make. Machines that are only good for solving specialized problems will be used only by specialists; they can only have an indirect impact on the general public. Only when a machine can solve the simple (but annoying) problems of everyday life will ordinary people make it a part of their lives.

In a certain sense, all household appliances are trivial. After all, we *could* use a washboard instead of a washing machine, a wood stove instead of an electric range, a broom instead of a vacuum cleaner. But we would rather not, and there's no reason why we should.

Microwave Ovens   The computer allows the user to specify when cooking will begin, how long the food should be defrosted, and how long it should be cooked. Or, instead of specifying cooking time, the user can specify that the food be cooked until it reaches a certain temperature. A probe inserted in the food transmits the temperature of the food to the computer. After the food is cooked, the computer will see that it is kept warm until it is served.

Although computer control first became popular in microwave ovens, it is now beginning to appear in conventional ovens as well. With a computer-controlled oven, you can put your food in the oven before leaving the house. At the proper time, the oven automatically will defrost the food, cook it, and keep it warm until you return.

Computers in Automobiles   We can use computers in automobiles in two ways—(1) to make the car run better and (2) as a convenience to the driver.

A computer can monitor continuously such variables as engine speed, power demand, and power output. Using this information, it

A microprocessor-controlled microwave oven.

continuously adjusts such things as fuel-air mixture, fuel-feed rate, and spark timing for maximum engine performance. In effect, the computer continuously "tunes up" the car as it runs. The driver has the benefit of an "engineer" that devotes its full attention to getting the best performance out of the engine.

Not only does the continuous tuning improve the performance of the engine, it reduces exhaust emissions as well. This should make it possible to eliminate the expensive and troublesome catalytic converter as well some other antipollution measures that reduce engine performance instead of improving it.

For the driver's convenience, a computer can display, at the touch of a button, such things as miles traveled or miles to go on a trip, estimated time of arrival at a destination, and gasoline consumption in miles per gallon and costs per mile. An alarm can sound when particular milage points are reached, thus reminding the driver of freeway exits or points of interest. The computer can help the driver determine the brand of gasoline and the cruising speed that give the most economical performance. For highway driving, the computer can maintain the car at a preset speed.

Television Sets A computer in a TV set can periodically display the time and channel number on the TV screen. You can program an entire evening's entertainment in advance: the computer automatically switches to the correct channel at the correct time. In localities where rooftop antennas are required, the computer will see to it that the antenna is always pointed in the correct direction.

(When we talk about programming a consumer product to do certain things, we don't mean writing a complete computer program. The user merely pushes a few clearly labeled buttons to specify what the appliance will do. Only those who haven't bothered to read the instruction booklet will have any difficulty.)

Computers are becoming even more important for television viewing as a result of the growing popularity of video recording. Each evening you will program not only the shows you wish to watch but those you wish to record for later viewing as well. A computer in the video recorder also can oversee the recording of shows while you are away from home.

With this computerized TV set you can program an entire evening's viewing, then just sit back and watch.

A system has been set up whereby television stations transmit captions for persons with impaired hearing. The captions are transmitted in coded form and do not show up on ordinary TV sets. Persons with hearing problems use an attachment to decode the captions and display them at the bottom of the screen.

Cameras For years, a photographer had to choose between a camera in which focus, shutter speed, and lens opening were fixed and one in which these could be adjusted. The inexperienced photographer usually chose the camera that required no adjustments and accepted the limited conditions under which pictures could be made. The professional usually had to choose the adjustable camera and accept the hassle of making adjustments before each shot.

Today, computer-controlled cameras greatly reduce the number of adjustments that must be made. For instance, the exposure of the film is governed by both lens opening and shutter speed. The photographer specifies one of these, depending on the kind of picture to be taken: for instance, action shots require a fast shutter speed; pictures in which there are objects both close to the camera and distant from it require a small lens opening so that both the near and the distant objects will be in focus. Whichever adjustment the photographer did not specify, the computer adjusts automatically to get the correct exposure for each shot. But if there is no other way to get the correct exposure, the computer may take the liberty of changing the adjustment that the photographer fixed.

A recent innovation is a sonar-like device for setting the focus. The camera bounces a (harmless) pulse of ultrasonic waves off the subject. By noting how long it takes for the pulse to travel from the

This automatic camera uses a microprocessor to control lens opening and shutter speed.

camera to the subject and back, the computer can determine how far the subject is from the camera and set the focus accordingly.

Many automatic cameras have a calculator-like display built into the viewfinder. The display keeps the photographer constantly informed as to what adjustments the camera is making.

Stereo Components So far, computers have found their way into stereo turntables, cassette players, and FM tuners.

A computer-controlled turntable can be programmed to play selections from a long-playing record in any order the user wishes. Using a light-sensitive cell on the tone arm, the computer can locate the spaces between the different bands on the record. By counting the spaces as the tone arm moves across the record, the computer can locate any particular band. By pressing numbered buttons, the user programs the turntable as to which bands are to be played and in what order.

A similar procedure can be used to locate particular selections on a cassette. Under the control of the computer, the tape is scanned at high speed, and the sections of blank tape that separate the selections are counted. The computer counts until it reaches a selection it has been requested to play.

FM turners use computers in much the same ways TV sets do: the user can program the tuner to switch from station to station at preset times. Some tuners show, on a calculator-like display, the call letters of the station being received. And even when using the tuner manually, the user can punch in the frequency of the desired station on a calculator-like keyboard instead of having to adjust a dial.

Telephones A computerized telephone can store frequently called numbers. The phone automatically will dial any stored number at the touch of a button. The same computer that stores and dials the numbers can also serve as a timer and calculator for timing long-distance calls and computing their costs.

Looking toward the future, we can foresee a phone that automatically will call the fire or police department when a fire or burglar alarm is sounded. But in the case of burglar alarms, this may cause a problem: people frequently set off their own burglar alarms

This computerized turntable allows the user to play the different bands on a record in any order desired.

An automatic telephone dialer, clock, and timer.

by accident. Even with businesses, frequent false alarms waste the time of the police. If every homeowner had an alarm that could call the police automatically, the police switchboards might be jammed with false alarms.

It is possible that, in the future, the telephone will evolve into a computer terminal that can handle a large number of tasks automatically by contacting other computers over the telephone lines. But another, perhaps better, alternative is to use the TV cable rather than the phone line for computer-to-computer communication. We discuss this alternative in the next chapter.

Recent changes in Federal Communications Commission regulations have greatly increased the freedom of telephone users to attach to their phone lines equipment not made by the phone company. The result has been increased activity among independent suppliers (and, to meet the competition, among the phone companies as well) in supplying advanced telephones and telephone attachments. Many of these contain microprocessors.

GAMES

Games constitute another area that microprocessors are revolutionizing. Traditionally, game boards have been passive, merely providing the paraphernalia whereby human players could interact with one another. It was no fun to play a traditional game by oneself; another player was needed to make the game entertaining.

With the aid of a built-in computer, however, the game board can take a more active role. For instance, it can have secret information that the players must guess. The computer can provide hints, tell the players how close their guesses are, and so on. And, of course, the computer does all the scoring.

The computers also make games of manual skill possible. Using hand-held controllers, the players attempt to direct the motion of the variously shaped spots of light on a TV screen. The spots of light represent such things as balls, paddles, bats, race cars, missiles, and airplanes.

Currently, there are two kinds of games using computer technology. The *video games* connect to a home TV receiver and use it as the

107

gameboard. The other kind of game uses a more conventional gameboard, augmented with push buttons and perhaps calculator-like displays. These are sometimes called *smart electronic games*, the "smart" referring to the computer's presence.

Both types of games may provide sound effects. The video games use the TV set's sound system; the smart electronic games have built-in loudspeakers.

Smart Electronic Games A distinguishing feature of smart electronic games is that they do not use a TV screen as a display. Instead, some of them use calculator keyboards and displays; in fact, these games look very much like calculators. Other combine the keyboard and display with a more or less conventional gameboard. Playing pieces on the board keep track of the status of the game as usual. But, instead of rolling dice or drawing a card to determine the next move, the player makes an entry on the keyboard.

In still other games, the computer and the playing board are more closely integrated. Instead of a single block of keys, push buttons are placed around the playing surface. Pegs that can be inserted in holes in the board give the computer the locations of the playing pieces. Lights below the playing surface can turn on to indicate moves. However, the calculator-like display is usually still present for scoring purposes.

A number of the electronic games seem to be basically guessing games. Often the players are called upon to guess three-, four-, or five-digit numbers. These games differ mainly in how the players are given clues to the identity of the number to be guessed. To use the clues, the player usually has to engage in mental arithmetic, thus making the game "educational."

Other guessing games are geometrical. The player tries to guess a secret location on a grid or a secret path between two locations. These games can be dressed up in various ways. For instance, the location to be guessed can be presented as a submarine, which the player must locate and destroy with his naval and air forces. Also in the category of geometrical games are those in which the player must find a path through a maze.

Some of these games are frankly educational, designed to develop arithmetic and spelling skills. One spelling game is interesting because it uses a speech synthesizer to pronounce the words to be spelled.

Several computers that play chess with the user are on the market. Chess-playing computers have a colorful history. Interest in a chess-playing machine was first aroused in the eighteenth century, when a fraudulent chess-playing automaton was demonstrated. (The automaton had many interesting features, but its chess-playing skills derived from a human player hidden inside.) When electronic computers first were developed, one of the first questions asked was whether or not the machines could be programmed to play chess.

In the early days of computing, the expense of the machines largely prevented them from being used for such unprofitable activities as playing chess. But as the cost of computers started to come down, more and more chess-playing programs were written for them. There are now yearly national and international chess tournaments in which only computers can participate. Over the years, the chess-playing programs gradually have been improved; those that run on large computers sometimes defeat Class A players, experts, and masters.

The chess-playing computers available to consumers are not so skillful. But, in the United States at least, the average person who plays chess every now and then seldom gets beyond the beginner's stage. These casual players find the electronic chess machines quite challenging.

Some electronic games simulate real-world activities, such as auto racing, football, missile attacks, submarine detection, landing a lunar module, and so on. As we will see in later chapters, computers make quite elaborate and detailed simulations possible. Undoubtedly, these simulation games will become more highly developed in the future.

Video Games In video games, the game board and all the playing pieces are displayed on the TV screen, along with the score. Since the board and the pieces are completely under the control of the computer, it is possible to change completely the game being played by changing the computer program. Most video-game manufacturers now offer a library of different game cartridges that can be plugged into the computer. Each cartridge contains a read-only memory with an appropriate program for the computer.

Many video games provide more challenge for physical skills than for mental ones. Using hand-held controllers, the players move spots of light about on the screen. The spots of light represent balls, paddles, bats, airplanes, missiles, torpedoes, spaceships, racing cars, and the like. Background lines provide a playing field with goals, out-of-bound areas, and so on. Regardless of how these games are dressed up, they all are based on having the players try to hit one spot of light with another.

The types of hand-held controllers vary from one game to another. The simplest are just knobs, like the volume control knob of a radio. Joysticks are frequently used instead of knobs. Moving the stick forward or backward moves the object being controlled up or down on the screen. Moving the stick to the left or right moves the object to the left or right. By combining the forward-backward and

A video game. Note the hand controllers, which are used to move the objects displayed on the TV screen.

left-right motions, the player can move the object in any direction desired.

Some games are equipped with more specialized controllers. For instance, a steering wheel and a "gear shift" let the user control a racing car. A pistol containing a light-sensitive cell makes possible a home shooting gallery.

Some of the more advanced games now offer a cartridge containing a BASIC interpreter. With this cartridge in place, the TV game becomes a general purpose computer, and the user can write and execute programs in the BASIC language. For instance, a player can design his own games by writing programs for them in BASIC (and can learn a lot about programming computers in the process). It could well be that the only contact the majority of the public has with computer programming is through these programmable games.

Both electronic and video games have proved to be extremely popular. This is evident from the number of new ones that appear on the market each year. Soon it may be difficult to sell a nonelectronic game. Youngsters will be so used to game boards that take an active part in the proceedings that they will find the traditional passive games dull.

HOBBY COMPUTERS

Background Ever since the use of computers became widespread, there has been some interest in building and programming them as a hobby. As early as the 1950s, for instance, books and articles appeared telling electronics enthusiasts how to build their own computers using relays—electrically operated switches. But the most these relay machines could do was demonstrate the principles of computer operation; it was not possible to get enough relays in a reasonable amount of space and at a reasonable cost to do useful computations.

Beginning in the mid-1960s, however, a number of ambitious individuals either built their own computers, purchased minicomputers, or subscribed to time-sharing services.

Dedication certainly was imperative in those days, when there were no microprocessors and no computer kits. The complex central processor had to be built up out of individual transistors or out of the then-new integrated circuits, each of which contained only a handful of logic elements. Things that were almost impossible for an amateur to build—core memory and disk drives, for instance—were either bought or scrounged on the surplus market.

Although a few people bitten by the computer bug purchased minicomputers or subscribed to time-sharing services, this solution was reserved for the reasonably well-off. The minicomputers and the time-sharing services were priced for industrial users, not for individuals. And except in the largest cities, time-sharing users could contact their computers only through long-distance telephone calls, the costs of which often far exceeded the charges for computer time.

All this started to change when the first microprocessors began to appear in the early 1970s. The Intel corporation introduced the 8008 microprocessor in 1972. Although the 8008 was primitive by today's standards, it was the first microprocessor capable of supporting a general purpose computer. In 1973, Intel brought out an improved version, the 8080, which is still used in many hobbyist computers. In 1974, the magazine *Radio Electronics* published plans for a computer based on the 8008. Probably around 500 people constructed this machine.

But the breakthrough did not come until 1975. MITS, a company that had manufactured electronic calculator kits and was now having financial problems, designed a computer kit around the Intel 8080. The computer, named the Altair 8800, represented a last-ditch effort to stave off financial disaster. At best, the company hoped for a few hundred orders. Articles about the kit appeared in the December 1974 and January 1975 issues of *Popular Electronics*.

This was the one that caught on. MITS found itself deluged with phone calls inquiring about the $375 kit. At one time, they were receiving up to a thousand phone calls a day. By the end of 1976, MITS reported that it sold over 10,000 Altair 8800s. About 80 percent of these were sold to hobbyists. (The rest were sold to educational institutions and industrial firms, which also were quick to realize the advantages of inexpensive computers.)

Since 1975, a substantial industry has grown up around personal computing. Magazines for computer hobbyists flourish. The seven listed at the end of this chapter are widely read, and a number of others cater to special interests. In any major city (and lots of smaller ones as well), it's possible to walk into a shopping center or mall and buy a computer or at least order one. One phenomenon of personal computing is the computer store, which is devoted to computers, their peripherals, and their software. How different this is from the days when acquiring a computer meant lengthy contract negotiations with a distant company.

But What Do You Do with a Home Computer?   This is one of the first questions that anyone who admits to being a computer hobbyist is likely to be asked. And it's not always easy to come up with a satisfactory answer. As a matter of fact, hobbyists currently are in the process of *discovering* ways to use computers in the home. The final results are by no means in, but the following are some of the uses that have emerged to date.

Game Playing   Like the people who purchase electronic and video games, computer hobbyists also play games with their computers. Since the computer hobbyists write their own programs, they can design their own games instead of being limited to the few available from a game manufacturer. If a hobbyist gets tired of a game, it's **111** easy to give it new life by modifying the program to introduce new

Game playing using
a home computer.

features or change existing ones. Besides, writing the program is often more fun than playing the game.

At least at present, the games computer hobbyists play are often much more sophisticated than those available as electronic or video games. Simulation games, for instance, may put a player in charge of a space battle, a war, or an island economy. Undoubtedly the most popular of the computer-hobbyist games ultimately will appear on the mass consumer market. Some of the number-guessing games available today were pioneered by hobbyists and educators.

Word Processing   In chapter 1, we looked at word processing, which allows the text of a letter, article, report, or other document to be stored in the computer and revised until the writer is satisfied with it. The computer then prints a clean copy of the revised text.

Almost anyone involved in any intellectual field does a lot of writing. This includes students, teachers, executives, and professional persons. The writing invariably requires many revisions and corrections, particularly if the person is not an experienced writer (and may not type very well either). These people can put word processing to good use.

Use with Other Hobbies   A number of other hobbies invite computerization. A model railroad enthusiast, for instance, can use a computer to switch the train from track to track as it moves through the layout and operate the signal and crossing gates along the way. A single computer can control a number of trains at the same time. From the computer keyboard, the railroad enthusiast has complete control of the movement of all the trains.

Music and art offer additional opportunities for the computer hobbyist. Almost any computer will, with an appropriate program, play tunes through a nearby radio. With special music-generating peripherals and music-control languages, the computer can play a wide variety of music. The computer also can serve visual artists as an electronic sketch pad. These capabilities are discussed in more detail in the chapter on the computer in the arts.

Sports   All the sports activities that humans participate in require some kind of scorekeeping. Sometimes this is trivial. But in games such as golf and bowling, it can become complex enough to be annoying to the participants. Even in professional games, players are sometimes penalized for having completed their score cards incorrectly.

A computer easily can keep track of the scores in any sport. All that needs to be fed into the computer are the points won or lost by the various participants. The computer can print almost any kind of summary desired, showing the standings of all the players.

Tournaments require that many matches be set up, often according to elaborate rules and depending on the previous records of the players. A computer easily can be programmed to set up the matches according to the specified rules.

Control of Home Appliances   We have seen that many home appliances can be controlled by built-in microprocessors. Some computer hobbyists are experimenting with using a single central computer to turn appliances on and off throughout the house. Signals for controlling the appliances are sent from the computer to the appliances over the power lines; no additional wiring is necessary.

The computer can turn on the coffee pot in the morning, the lights at dusk, and the TV set in time for the evening news. It can turn down the thermostat at night and turn it back up again in the morning in time for the house to be warm when the family gets up. To confuse prospective burglars, it can turn the lights on and off in a realistic fashion when the family is away. The computer can detect rain and close the windows; of course, electric motors to do the actual closing must be installed. Interfaced with the telephone, the computer automatically can call the appropriate department when fire and burglar alarms are tripped. And the homeowner, when away, can call the computer and request that a certain appliance be turned off. (The request would be transmitted by the buttons on a Touch-Tone phone).

All these monitoring and control tasks make very little demand on the computer. Therefore, the computer can be used for other purposes at the same time, such as word processing or game playing.

If this kind of control becomes popular, we may expect that the appliances of the future will provide means for interfacing the built-in microprocessor with a central household computer.

Home Record Keeping   Computers are old hands at accounting; businesses have used them for this purpose for years. A computer can store all important family records, such as checking accounts, savings accounts, expenses, and income. Using these records, the computer can help the family plan a budget. It also can generate

Using a home computer to plan a family budget.

income tax returns and any other financial reports that government agencies may require.

The computer also can store inventories, such as the kinds and amounts of groceries in the house. It also can help with meal planning. Taking into account the kinds of food currently in the house, nutritional requirements, family preferences, and the family budget, the computer can plan a week's meals and print out the week's shopping list at the same time. Such planning could be particularly helpful when some family members must follow special diets, such as those required by diabetics and persons who must lose weight.

THE FUTURE OF PERSONAL COMPUTING

Calculators and computers built into household appliances and other consumer products are now well established conveniences, just as electronic and video games are popular forms of entertainment. But what about the more advanced forms of personal computing that computer hobbyists are exploring? You may not have been very impressed with the examples offered. You may feel that you can keep household records or turn appliances on and off or keep scores in sports quite well without any help from a computer. Computer hobbyists often encounter this kind of reaction when they try to answer the question, "What do you do with a home computer?"

For the moment, the doubters may even be right. Much personal computing is going through a phase that is common to many new inventions. At the start, the new invention is not the most practical way of doing a particular job, and the average person has little use for it. But enthusiasts use it, not because it is the best way to do the job but because they happen to be interested in the technology. And in experimenting with the technology, the enthusiasts improve it to the point where it is practical for other people as well.

The automobile provides a good example. Early automobile drivers were urged to "get a horse" when their machines broke down. And the scoffers certainly had a point. With poor roads, poor tires, and frequent mechanical breakdowns, the horse was indeed more practical for many trips. But the enthusiasts persisted; the mechanical problems were overcome; the roads were built; and, eventually, the automobile did replace the horse.

Many aspects of personal computing are now at the "get a horse" stage. But this does not mean that they always will be there. The same computer hobbyists who may be laughed at by their friends today are pioneering the home computer applications that will be commonplace tomorrow.

The situation with automobiles and roads is a typical one. Many inventions require extensive support systems to make them useful. Automobiles need highways, telephones need phone lines and central offices, railroad trains need rail systems, and so on.

Personal computers, too, will be much more useful when means are established by which one computer automatically can communicate with others. Then computers can replace mail and telegrams as well as eliminate a lot of the traveling that humans now have to do. For instance, the food-planning system mentioned earlier will make a lot more sense when the home computer can arrange for food to be delivered by contacting the grocery store's computer and arrange for the food to be paid for by contacting the bank's computer. These matters are explored in the next chapter.

FOR FURTHER READING

The best way to find out more about personal computing is to read the magazines published for computer hobbyists. The following seven are recommended:

Creative Computing
On Computing
Personal Computing
Recreational Computing
Byte
Interface Age
Kilobaud Microcomputing

The first four of these will be the easiest for beginners to read. The last three have a higher percentage of technical articles for dedicated hobbyists. *Creative Computing* has a particularly broad coverage, which includes electronic and video games as well as hobbyist computers.

REVIEW QUESTIONS

1. What is *personal computing*? What distinguishes it from other forms of computing?

2. Give four areas in which individuals are benefiting from computer technology.

3. Why do we mention calculators in a chapter on personal computing?

4. Why may calculators ultimately have a greater social impact than many other forms of personal computing?

5. Give two advantages that computer-controlled consumer products have over conventional ones.

6. What are the four components found in most computers used to control consumer products?

7. Give six applications of the built-in computers that are described in this chapter.

8. Are you familiar with any computer-controlled consumer products that are *not* described in this chapter? If so, briefly describe a few of them.

9. Distinguish between the two types of games that use microprocessors.

10. Describe some of the different kinds of smart electronic games.

11. What originally led to the strong interest in chess-playing machines?

12. Describe briefly some of the electronic games you have played.

13. Give two ways in which video games differ from smart electronic games.

14. Describe briefly some video games you have played.

15. What technical developments make hobby computers possible?

16. When did hobby computers suddenly "catch on" with a large number of people? What event brought about this change?

17. What is a computer store? Is there a store in your area at which computers can be purchased?

18. Give five uses for home computers. Question some computer hobbyists you know to find out what they do with their machines.

19. Why are new technological developments often taken up by enthusiasts but ignored by the general public?

20. Give some examples of inventions that became useful only after a supporting system had been established.

1. Describe a day in the life of a housewife or househusband of the twenty-first century. Assume that, by this time, computerized products have become so popular that computers are incorporated in everything for which they conceivably can be justified and perhaps a few for which they cannot. If, for example, the twentieth century can have electric toothbrushes, the twenty-first century can have computerized ones. Assume that the computers are sufficiently advanced to accept verbal instructions and give verbal responses.

2. Discuss possible future developments in electronic and video games. To get you started, imagine a television drama that is also a game. The players make decisions for the various characters, and the future course of the drama depends on the decisions made.

3. Discuss the science-fiction story "The Feeling of Power," by Isaac Asimov (in *Opus 100*, pp. 106-118, Boston: Houghton Mifflin, 1969).

4. Read some of the computer hobbyist magazines and note some of the things that computer hobbyists are doing (or talking about doing) with their computers. Discuss some of these things in relation to two questions. First, do you think a computer is necessary to do the job in question or is even the best way to do it? Second, why do you think that computer hobbyists are interested in using computers this way, even if it doesn't seem that using a computer is the best way to do the job?

5. Discuss an invention, other than the automobile, that (1) was adopted by enthusiasts long before it became practical for the general public to use and (2) required a supporting system before it could be practical for widespread use.

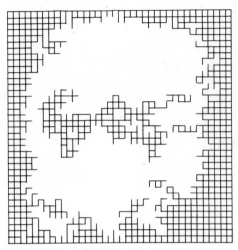

CHAPTER 8

COMPUTER NETWORKS AND INFORMATION UTILITIES

A computer network is any arrangement for computers to communicate with one another. The actual means of communication can range from telephone lines to satellites.

Computers are connected into networks so that they can share information and resources. For example, one computer may have certain large data files. Another may have a very large main memory or a very fast central processor. Still another may have special hardware for carrying out arithmetic on large arrays of numbers. Also, certain types of software, such as a translator for a particular language, may be available on one computer and not on others.

A program submitted for execution to one computer in the network can be sent to another that has the necessary hardware, software, or data files. The routing of programs can be handled by the computer's operating systems; users need not worry about it. Or, the program may be executed on the computer to which it was submitted; but, during execution, it may request data from other computers in the network.

Computer networks have been used successfully by military agencies, businesses, schools, law enforcement agencies, and other organizations. In this chapter, we will concentrate on networks of

personal computers rather than on the use of computer networks by
organizations. Some of the latter will be discussed in later chapters.

As we mentioned in the last chapter, home computers currently
are limited because different people's computers are isolated from
one another. As long as they are isolated, their usefulness to the
general public will be limited. They will be confined largely to
hobbyists who like to experiment with computers. But these hobbyists already have started experimenting with networks to allow
their computers to communicate with one another. When the hobbyist networks are sufficiently widespread and interesting uses for
them have been demonstrated, we may expect that commercial
interests will take up the idea of computer networks for the general
public.

When we speak of personal computers in this chapter we refer to
the general purpose machines used by computer hobbyists rather
than the special purpose computers found in consumer products.

COMPUTER
NETWORKS

Computers can exchange information using any of the usual communication techniques—telephone, coaxial cable (the kind used for
cable TV), radio, and laser beam. Radio includes microwave links
(such as used by telephone companies and many private corporations), as well as radio signals relayed by satellites.

Current plans for hobbyist computer networks use the telephone
system. This is reasonable since the telephone system already exists,
and no group of hobbyists could afford to build up an alternate
system. On the other hand, long-distance telephone calls are expensive. And data transmission over telephone lines is slow, since
the lines originally were designed for voice signals, not data signals.

Computer hobbists who are also amateur radio operators are
experimenting with computers linked by ham radio. But government
regulations present some obstacles here. Amateur radio operators
are required to have technical knowledge and the ability to send and
receive Morse code. Also, there are limitations to the kinds of
messages that can be sent by ham radio: entertainment is forbidden,
for instance, as are messages relating to commercial activities. Thus
amateur radio computer networks are limited to experimental activities.

What is perhaps the most attractive approach to eventual commercial computer networks uses coaxial cables, such as those used
for cable TV. In fact, the cables now used in community television
systems can be adapted to computer networks. Experimental
networks using cable TV facilities already have been demonstrated.

A coaxial cable is particularly attractive because, unlike a
telephone line, it can support many services at the same time. Not
only can a cable carry the television and FM radio programs that it
119   does now, it can handle data communications at the same time.

Computer networks might become just an additional service offered by cable TV companies.

Another feature of data communication simplifies matters. For each private line, a telephone system requires a pair of wires connecting the subscriber's phone to the central office. On the other hand, a large number of subscribers can use the same coaxial cable at the same time. This is unlike a party line because one subscriber does not tie up the cable until his call is finished.

Here's how this works. The computer breaks the message it wishes to send into small blocks called *packets*. Each packet contains all the routing information necessary to get it to its destination. The network handles each packet separately. Only the recipient's computer needs to worry about which packets should be combined to form a complete message.

The various computers connected to a cable take turns using it, much as people take turns using a CB channel. When one computer is ready to transmit a packet, it "listens" until the cable seems to be momentarily free. Then the computer sends its packet. It then waits a certain period of time before using the cable again, in order to give other users a chance.

Each computer monitors all the packets that are transmitted. A computer examines the address portion of each packet. If a particular packet is addressed to it, it stores the contents and sends an acknowledgement (another packet) back to the computer that originated the packet that was received. The computer ignores all packets not addressed to it.

(Since a "nosey" computer could intercept packets not addressed to it, users probably will employ ciphers for private messages. This isn't difficult since the contents of a message are of interest only to the sender and the recipient. The network uses only the addressing information. The contents could be enciphered in any way agreed upon by the two parties. The enciphering and deciphering would be done by the computers at each end, of course, at no inconvenience to the users.)

Should two or more computers try to send their packets at the same time, all the packets would be garbled. For this reason, when a computer sends a packet, it expects an acknowledgement from the receiving computer. If the acknowledgement does not arrive within a certain period of time, then the packet is retransmitted. The computer attempting to send a packet transmits it over and over until the computer to which it is addressed acknowledges receipt.

A single cable TV system would provide a community information exchange through which the computers in a single community could communicate. "Long distance" communications between different community information exchanges also would be available. The communications between the different exchanges could take place over whatever medium was most economical—leased telephone lines, microwave relays, satellites, and so on.

Undoubtedly, these services first would be offered by cable
television companies. As computer networks become more and more

popular and profitable, however, other institutions, such as the telephone companies and the post office, probably woud try to get into the act. Great legal battles ultimately may be fought over who should offer computer network services and what government agencies should regulate them.

So far, we have talked about two-way communication between computers. Another interesting possibiliy is digital broadcasting—one-way transmissions from a broadcasting station to a large number of computers. One thing that makes digital broadcasting interesting is that it presents few technical difficulties. Ordinary FM and television stations also can transmit data without interfering with their normal operations. These data transmissions would be received only by people who had special attachments to their FM or TV sets.

Digital broadcasting could allow broadcasters to provide some of the services now provided by newspapers but not practical with ordinary radio or television. For instance, lengthy tables, such as sports scores or stock market quotations, could be transmitted; people interested in these things would program their computers to store them, and then they could study them at their convenience. People not interested in particular kinds of data would program their computers to ignore them.

Digital broadcasting is easy to accomplish from a technical point of view. The main obstacles are legal, since radio and television stations are regulated by the federal government and cannot change the nature of the signals they transmit without government approval.

INFORMATION UTILITIES

Let's try to imagine how the ideas of the last section might develop in the foreseeable future. We imagine an *information utility* that offers data communication combined with other media, such as radio, television, and facsimile. Users subscribe to the services the utility offers just as they now do for electricity, gas, telephone, and cable television. The computer networking capabilities of the information utility would be used in conjunction with more conventional media, such as radio and television.

A move in the direction of information utilities already has been made. A prototype system called QUBE, to be described in more detail in chapter 13, has been set up on a trial basis in Colombus, Ohio.

In the remainder of this section, we will look at some of the possible applications for the advanced communications and data processsing facilities that information utilities might be able to offer. The required technology would be different for different applications. Most of the applications mentioned could be offered with present-day technology. But, in order to be practical, some, such as person-to-person television communication, would require new developments.

This is one kind of arrangement that people might use to send and receive information over an information utility. Information to be sent would be typed on the keyboard. Information received would be displayed on the screen; if a permanent copy was desired, it would be produced with the printer/plotter.

Communication   The information utility would supply a large number of television and radio programs. These would include sponsor-supported commercial programs, state-supported educational programs, and user-supported "pay TV" programs.

Even more important, broadcast channels could be reserved for individuals or small groups and leased at reasonable cost. For instance, an amateur theatrical company could originate a television program at modest cost.

In addition to broadcasting, the system could be used for person-to-person communication. The parties could exchange pictures, data, sound, or any combination of these, depending upon the need. (The rates the utility charged probably would vary depending on whether data, sound, or pictures were being exchanged, with data being the least expensive and pictures the most expensive.)

This could influence the way we do our work, particularly at the executive level. With advanced communications, there is no reason why executives should waste a good part of their time traveling to and from work. They could do all their work at home. Using an information utility data channel, they could exchange the necessary memoranda and reports with their colleagues. With two-way television, they could participate in meetings and conferences, could even join their colleagues for lunch—they in their homes and their colleagues in theirs.

In a world beset by energy shortages, there is much to be said for substituting communications for travel. At present, the cost of communications is high, but advancing technology promises to reduce this. And as long as the world is short of energy, we can be sure that the cost of travel will continue to increase.

Education   With an information utility, much formal education could take place in the home. The student would spend a certain amount of time at the computer terminal each day, probably far less than would have to be spent in a conventional classroom. A good part of the remainder of his time probably would be spent in front of the TV, where he would continue to be educated as well as entertained.

Laboratory courses could not be taught over the information utility, of course. But much of the information usually imparted by such courses probably could be taught—by television programs demonstrating experiments and the use of equipment, for instance.

With the exception of laboratory experiences, however, the information utility could supply a complete education from pre-school through the university level. When students, working at their own pace, completed a certain segment of their education (the equivalent of high school, for example), they could take a series of examinations, which would certify their progress and qualify them for the appropriate degrees or diploma.

But the greatest beneficiaries of education in the home could be adults instead of children. Currently we ask that youngsters devote most of their time to school at an age when other interests are most compelling. Not surprisingly, many young people drop out as soon as they legally can. Many of them later regret it.

But with education in the home via an information utility, there are no age limits. Education becomes a lifelong affair, with the world of knowledge waiting to be explored when a person feels the need to do so or when the circumstances of life (such as the need to get a particular job) require it. Education can be directed to more specific uses, avoiding the scattergun approach that disenchants some students today.

Publication   Authors could publish directly on the system by putting their latest works in files that readers could access for a fee. The storage for the files would be provided by the information utility, for a fee charged to the author.

A file also could be provided for reader comments on a work. The author might wish to revise the work in response to the comments received. Thus, a work would become a dynamic thing, with both the author and the readers-listeners-viewers participating in the final version.

Would this do away with publishing as we know it? Certainly, publishers no longer would be needed to print a work and distribute copies to readers. The information utility would take care of that.

But we still would need editors and critics, although perhaps the two functions could be combined. Publishing houses receive thousands of manuscripts a year; only a fraction of these are ever published. Authors often charge that some of the rejected books were worthwhile but were turned down because they were unlikely to make large profits. In some cases, this may be true. But the sad fact is that the majority of the manuscripts submitted are just incompetently written by people with nothing to say.

Perhaps you've heard of so-called vanity publishers, who will publish any book as long as the author pays for it. With rare exceptions, vanity press books are worthless. As a result, reputable book stores don't usually stock them, and reputable reviewers don't waste their time reviewing them.

When one and all are invited to publish on an information utility, the majority of works are apt to be in the vanity press category. The poor reader needs someone to help separate the good works from the bad. This function is performed by the editors of magazines and at reputable publishing houses.

So editors still would have plenty to do. The editor would read a large number of works and prepare a "magazine" containing not the works themselves but a list of recommended works with editorial comments for each entry. A user first would access the magazine in order to decide what is worth reading. After making that decision, the user would access the files containing the works themselves. Since the "magazine" does not actually contain the works it recommends, it could be much more flexible than a conventional magazine: it could refer the reader to a large book just as easily as to a short article.

Persons who accessed items such as magazines and books would be charged a fee automatically. The fees would go to pay the authors and editors for their labors.

Because of the ease with which items in electronic form can be copied, not all the problems of how to protect intellectual property and compensate authors for their work have been solved. These problems are tricky today, and electronic media would make them even more complicated. Evidence for this can be found in the lengthy statements on the copyright pages of some books, reserving rights to use the work in information-retrieval and other electronic systems.

Information Retrieval   Conventional library services would also be available through the information utility. From your terminal, you would specify key words characterizing the subjects in which you were interested. The library's computer would scan the "card catalog" and present you with a list of titles that might be appropriate. You could read the recommended books through the terminal or pick up the actual books at the library.

A newspaper might place its entire "morgue" (the file of all the stories it has ever published) on the system. Even now, the *New York Times* maintains a computerized file of its back issues that can be accessed by the public.

The newspaper reporters would update the file daily. Anyone wishing information on a particular subject could access the file and get not only the latest news but, if desired, a complete background briefing on the subject. People probably would watch television news summaries as they do today and then consult the "newspaper" file for in-depth coverage of items of particular interest.

One file could serve as a community bulletin board. It would do the same job as the want-ad section of a newspaper or the conventional bulletin boards sometimes found in public places.

Some libraries and newspapers may be designed specifically for use by computers rather than people. You would ask your computer a question, and it would "look up" the information and give you the answer. Libraries intended for use by computers would have all their information stored in forms convenient for computers rather than people.

Electronic Voting   With an information utility, electronic voting becomes possible. The issues are presented over a television channel. The people return their votes over the information utility. The prototype QUBE system, mentioned earlier, has this capability. More details on electronic voting can be found in chapter 13.

Electronic Funds Transfer   It would be possible to do all your banking business at home over the information utility. In fact, you might turn much of this business over to your personal computer, leaving to you only the approval of unusual or irregular transactions.

It might be possible to do much of your shopping by means of the information utility. Each merchant would maintain a catalog file that could be accessed by prospective customers. Merchants also might offer special television showings of clothing, appliances, furniture, books, records, and many other items.

To make a purchase either from the catalog or a television showing, the customer would merely send an order to the merchant's computer over the network. The order would be delivered at home later in the day or week. (Or, if not delivered, it would be ready for the customer to pick during a visit to the store.)

Programs for Home Use   Publication on the information utility would not be limited to conventional books and magazines. Computer programs would be published as well. These could be executed either on the home computer or on one operated by the information utility.

(Once a program had been transmitted to the home computer, there would be no way to keep the user from making a copy of it. Therefore, certain valuable programs might be available only for execution on the utility's computer. Subscribers could use these programs but could never get copies of them. Therefore, they would have to pay each time they used the program and would not be able to give copies of it to their friends.)

Programs on menu preparation, budgeting, tax preparation, family record keeping, and scheduling of activities would be available. Many of these programs would be able to function only because of information and computer resources available through the information utility.

Game-playing programs, as you might expect, would be very popular. Indeed, we can be sure that game playing will be one of the major applications of the information utility. Large games with players throughout the community or even the country might run more or less continuously.

Many of the programs will be designed to help people with their jobs. A manager, for instance, may call on a computer model to simulate the effects of an important decision. An engineer might call on many programs to do design calculations, to simulate the performance of the resulting structure, and to help produce engineering drawings.

People would use programs in their hobbies as well. An electronics enthusiast could use a program to help design circuits. A weekend pilot could get computer-generated flight plans similar to those the airlines now use. (Detailed weather data would be one of the kinds of information that would be available through the utility.) A woodworking hobbyist could have the computer display a finished piece of furniture from rough sketches and descriptions. When the picture resembled what he wanted, he could have the computer produce a set of detailed plans.

Ordinary people will find uses for computer power that scientists and futurists can hardly imagine. For instance, many people predicted the widespread use of the radio and the telephone. But they did not predict dial-a-prayer or time-and-temperature services. We may be putting too much emphasis on serious applications of computers and information utilities. To a large extent, people will use computers for *entertainment* and for small *conveniences*.

Electronic Mail   The telephone provides instantaneous communication between people in different parts of the world. But the person you are trying to reach may not be in when you call. Or if he is in, he may not want to be disturbed just then. With the information utility, we could have instantaneous transmission without having to interrupt people if the message was not urgent.

Each subscriber to the information utility would have a "mailbox file." Any message addressed to that subscriber would go in his mailbox file. A subscriber would review his mailbox file at his convenience. His personal computer could be programmed to alert him as soon as certain messages arrived—messages from certain people, for instance, or those marked urgent. The computer also could be programmed to eliminate junk mail.

Computer Conferencing   An interesting extension of electronic mail is known as *computer conferencing*. People who wish to discuss a certain subject send all their messages to a common file. Computer conferencing software makes sure that all the messages are properly classified and stored and that they are accessible to all the participants.

Each participant in the conference can address comments to other participants or to the group as a whole. Questions can be asked and answered. Everything said is available to everyone. But not everyone has to be present at his terminal at the same time; anyone can go to his terminal whenever it is convenient, catch up on what has been said, answer other people's questions, and then ask questions or make comments. A person can think as long as necessary before answering a question and perhaps even take time to consult references.

This kind of conference is "cooler" and more detached than a face-to-face meeting. For some purposes, no doubt, the detachment would be a disadvantage. But, for others, particularly where controversial topics are being discussed, anything that would make the comments more reasoned and less emotional could only be for the good.

Computer conferencing is in its infancy. To date, only a small number of experiments with it have been conducted. How useful it will prove to be remains to be seen. But it does provide one example of an entirely new mode of human interaction that information utilities would make possible.

Please don't assume that electronic mail or computer conferencing is intended to take the place of other forms of human contact or that either one would ever do so. The idea is to add new ways in which humans can interact with each other, not to replace the existing ones.

OLIVER   The acronym OLIVER stands for On Line Interactive Vicarious Expediter and Responder; the name was chosen to honor Oliver Selfridge, the computer scientist who first thought of the idea.

An OLIVER would be nothing less than a computerized alter ego. It would perform most of the functions of a good secretary. Although OLIVER originally was visualized as a separate device, it could be just another program in a personal computer.

Your OLIVER could handle your social engagements. It would know whom you wanted to see and whom you wanted to put off with excuses. Should you want to give a party, you would direct your OLIVER to invite your usual friends. It would know who they were and would contact their OLIVERs to make arrangements. Instead of just announcing a date and time, it could consult their OLIVERs in advance and then set the date and time so that as many of your friends as possible could attend.

Your OLIVER would know to which charities you wanted to contribute and how much you wanted to give each one. It would cull their solicitations from your mailbox file and make the donations automatically (by contacting your bank's computer). Since your OLIVER would know your political preferences and your tastes in current fashions, it could vote and buy clothes in your name.

You would hold a dialog with you OLIVER as often as necessary. It would ask you about any matters it could not handle on its own. You, in turn, would give it instructions and perhaps ask it questions. It could answer some questions (What appointments do I have scheduled today?) from information stored in its own memory. For others (Who won the World Series in 1955?), it would have to find the answers with the help of the information utility. (Remember those libraries for computers that we mentioned?)

Since your OLIVER would do most of your ordering for you, it would know which bills were legitimate and authorize your bank to pay them. It also could help manage the family budget, advising you on what you could or could not afford when you asked it to make a purchase.

Many routine meetings that take place between people today could just as easily take place between their OLIVERs. Each OLIVER would represent its master's interests. In fact, much computer conferencing ultimately may be conducted by the computers and not just with the aid of them.

It may sound to you as though the OLIVER would be regulating its user's life, that it would be more like a jailer than a secretary. But, of course, your OLIVER would only take over those functions that you wanted it to. Using it would be voluntary, not compulsory. The whole idea of computers is to take over those intellectual tasks that *humans do not want to do themselves.* Only time will show what things people want to do personally and which ones they would just as soon turn over to computers.

COMMUNITY MEMORY

By now, you may have decided that you can get along just fine without an information utility. This is a common reaction to any new technology. We are so accustomed to the traditional ways of doing things that we find it difficult to imagine alternative ways or to see how they would be useful.

For instance, when housewives and students were questioned about information utilities, they were unimpressed with the idea and even hostile to it. Yet when some of the same services were made

128 available, the same people who were unimpressed by the description found ways to use the real thing in their personal lives.

The Community Memory project in the San Francisco Bay area was designed to get the reactions of ordinary people to a computer-based public-information network. Computer terminals providing access to the network were located in such public places as a nonprofit community record store in Berkeley and a library in San Francisco's Mission District.

The system worked like this. To post something in the community memory, you would type ADD, the item to be posted, and a series of keywords under which the item was to be filed. To retrieve an item, you would type FIND and one or more relevant keywords. A user who typed FIND CAR, for instance, would be told how many items were stored under the keyword CAR. If the number were small, he could type PRINT and have them all displayed. Otherwise, he could enter other keywords to make his request more specific—to distinguish people who have cars for sale, say, from those who want to form car pools.

The system was advertised as an "electronic bulletin board" so people would know what to expect. Public acceptance was strong and immediate. People used it, encouraged their friends to use it, and told one another how to use it.

Here are a few of the uses that developed for community memory:

▪ Searching for student housing (the system was installed during the August housing crunch in Berkeley);

▪ Getting together musicians to form practice groups;

▪ Buying and selling musical instruments;

▪ Assembling car pools;

▪ Organizing study groups;

▪ Finding chess partners;

▪ Passing on tips about good restaurants; and

▪ Publishing poems, graphics, and comments similar to "letters to the editor."

The lesson here is that the reaction to the actual community memory was highly favorable, even though the students and house-wives were not impressed with the idea *when it was described to them.* Except for habitual readers of science fiction, most people find it almost impossible to visualize how a new technology will affect their everyday lives. Even the inventors of the technology themselves often fail at this. The uses of a new technology develop gradually as people get a chance to experiment with it and pass on to one another the ideas for using it that seem to work well.

POSSIBLE PROBLEMS

Security   Any time a number of people use the same computer system, problems with security arise. So an information utility needs ways to identify users positively and make sure that each user can only access the data to which he is entitled. Also, a record of the resources that each person uses must be kept so that the person can be billed for them. If users find they can "take over" the system the way "phone freaks" take control of long-distance switching equip-ment, only chaos can result. Under those conditions, no one would entrust valuable information to the utility.

Privacy   It is important that the security restrictions apply to official government agencies as well as to private individuals. Otherwise, these agencies could build dossiers on individuals by examining their files and monitoring their communications over the system. Anti-wiretapping legislation needs to be extended to prevent government snooping on information utilities.

Education   With an information utility, a child might be almost completely educated by a computer. Would this be desirable? Or would a mixture of human tutoring and computer-assisted instruction be better?

Discipline and supervision also would be problems. The burden of keeping children at their lessons would fall on parents, who might not want it at all. We should never forget that one of the social functions of schools is to serve as baby sitters.

Information Overload   Could we ever suffer from too much information? Could we become so jaded that we never trouble to think deeply about any of the facts that are constantly bombarding us? Or could we become so deeply involved with information that we ignore our bodies' needs entirely?

Future Shock   In his book *Future Shock*, Alvin Toffler defined future shock to be the disorientation and alienation brought about by rapid change. The widespread use of information utilities would produce drastic changes in the way we live our lives. If these changes took place rapidly, future shock might well result.

Vested Interests   The information utility described in this chapter would largely replace the post office, the telephone companies, and television broadcasters. It is inconceivable that these powerful vested interests would give up their markets without a fight. By sponsoring restrictive legislation, they could strangle information utilities in the cradle. Several schemes for pay TV have suffered this fate at the hands of broadcasting and theater interests.

FOR FURTHER READING

Brunner, John. *The Shockwave Rider*. New York: Harper and Row, 1975.

Colstad, Ken, and Lipkin, Efrem. "Community Memory: A Public Information Network." *People's Computer Company*, July 1975, pp. 16-17.

Dickson, Gordon. "Thank you, Beep . . . !" *The Hewlett-Packard Personal Calculator Digest*, Vol. 5, 1979, pp. 2-3, 28-29.

Gardner, Richard. "The Shadow, Buck Rogers, and the Home Computer." *Byte*, Oct. 1975, pp. 58-60.

Kimbleton, Stephen R., and Schneider, Michael G. "Computer Communications Networks: Approaches, Objectives, and Performance Considerations." *Computing Surveys*, Sept. 1975, pp. 129-173.

McCarthy, John. "On the CIU" (letter). *Communications of the ACM*, May 1975, pp. 300-301.

Press, Laurence I. "Arguments for a Moratorium on the Construction of a Community Information Utility." *Communications of the ACM*, Dec. 1974, pp. 674-678.

Steinwedel, Jeff. "Personal Computers in Distributed Communications Networks." *Byte*, Feb. 1978, pp. 80-82, 94-101.

Toffler, Alvin. *Future Shock*. New York: Random House, 1970.

Turoff, Murray. "Computerized Conferencing: Present and Future."

Creative Computing, Sept.-Oct. 1977, pp. 54-57. See other articles in the same issue on computer conferencing.

Wilber, Mike. "CIE Net: A Design for Community Information Exchanges." *Byte,* Feb. 1978, March 1978, April 1978.

REVIEW QUESTIONS

1. What do we mean by a *computer network?*

2. What are some of the reasons for connecting computers together into networks?

3. Name some kinds of organizations that have used computer networks successfully.

4. Give some applications of personal computing that require the computers to communicate with one another.

5. Give some of the means of communication that computers can use.

6. What means of communication are the first hobbyist networks using?

7. What are some of the problems of using amateur radio for computer networks?

8. What makes coaxial cables so much more attractive for computer networks than telephone lines?

9. What is a *packet?*

10. Explain how transmission of information in packets allows a number of computers to share the same coaxial cable.

11. What do we mean by an *information utility?*

12. List a number of possible uses of information utilities. Can you think of some that were not mentioned in the book?

13. Give some ways in which an information utility might influence education.

14. Describe how authors might publish their works through an information utility. What are some of the problems this kind of publication raises?

15. Describe some of the kinds of computer programs that might be published through an information utility.

16. How would *electronic mail* work?

17. What is *computer conferencing?*

18. List some of the functions that would be carried out by an OLIVER.

19. Describe the Community Memory Project. Compare its acceptance with the way people respond to questionnaires about information utilities.

20. Describe briefly some of the problems that information utilities might cause.

**DISCUSSION
QUESTIONS**

1. Advanced communications facilities tend to replace *travel* with *communication*. Discuss the advantages and disadvantages of this. Illustrate your discussion with examples of how radio, television, and other modern communications devices contributed to this change.

2. Read Gordon Dickson's science-fiction story "Thank you, Beep . . . !" (see readings for this chapter). Discuss the effects on people's lives if Dickson's "Beeps" were used as widely as pocket calculators are today.

3. Describe some ways you could put a Community Memory to good use if one were available in your area?

4. *Technological assessment* is the idea of having a panel of judges evaluate a proposed new technology before encouraging (or allowing) its development. Considering the difficulties of predicting how people will use a new technology, discuss the advantages and disadvantages of technological assessment.

5. Discuss the arguments for and against information utilities given by Press and McCarthy (see readings for this chapter). Has the growth of personal computing and the fact that computer hobbyists are actively experimenting with information networks changed the force of any of the arguments?

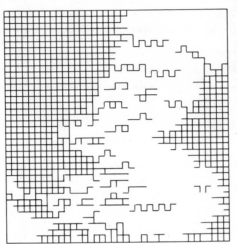

CHAPTER 9

THE
MODEL
BUILDERS

Making decisions is an essential part of life. Sometimes the decisions are small ones that affect only a single person. Sometimes they are large ones, made by corporations or governments, that can affect a city, a state, or the entire world.

To make decisions rationally, we must understand the political, social, and economic systems that will be affected by the decisions. The most successful approach to understanding is experiment. We "poke" the system we are investigating to see how it reacts. By poking in enough places and recording the reactions of the system, we collect the data needed to understand how the system operates.

But experimenting with the systems that are vital to the well-being of a country, such as its economic system, will never do. Such experimentation may be impractical, costly, dangerous, unethical, or, frequently, all four at the same time.

Fortunately, we have an alternative. We can program a computer to *simulate* the behavior of the system we want to study. The computer program is then a *model* of the system. We conduct our experiments and make our trials and errors on the model rather than on the real system with real people in it.

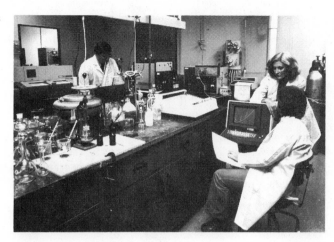

With computer models of chemical molecules, the properties of compounds can be predicted before the compounds are actually synthesized in the laboratory.

THE SYSTEMS APPROACH

What are Systems?   When we talk about a *system*, we mean nothing more than a collection of parts acting together to accomplish some purpose.

A human being is a system, as is a cat, a tree, an automobile, or a television set. One system can include other systems as parts. For instance, a human being is a system that has, among other things, a nervous system, a respiratory system, a circulatory system, and a digestive system.

If it occurred to you that these systems sound a lot like the modules we talked about in chapter 5, you are absolutely right. *Modules* and *systems* are different terms that different groups of people use for the same basic idea.

Here we are interested in large systems that include many people as well as various kinds of equipment. Some examples that can be found in almost every city are an educational system (schools, libraries, educational television stations, and so on), a water system (the people as well as the pipes and pumps), and a criminal justice system (police, courts, prisons).

Management and Planning   Traditional approaches to management and planning often concentrate on a small part of the system and ignore the rest. Management and planning techniques that try to take the entire system into account sometimes are referred to as *the systems approach.*

There are two aspects to the systems approach—systems design (or planning) and management science. The system designer tries to plan a new system in such a way that it will fulfill its purpose as well as possible. The management scientist studies the day-to-day operating decisions that have to be made to keep the system serving its purpose.

Both the planner and the manager have to take into account the five major characteristics of a system.

135

- *The goals or objectives of the system.* How do we judge the performance of the system? Exactly what do we mean when we say the system is working well or poorly?

- *The environment of the system.* These are the outside constraints under which the system must operate—existing laws and regulations, for example.

- *The component parts of the system.* These parts seldom correspond with traditional departments and bureaus. For instance, the part of the criminal justice system that apprehends wanted criminals involves a number of local, state, and federal police agencies.

- *The resources of the system.* These are the personnel and equipment that the system uses to accomplish its purposes.

- *The management of the system.* Management is a part of the system, both influencing and being influenced by the system it manages.

A Scientific Approach   The systems designer and the management scientist try to study systems scientifically. They hope to apply the results of their studies in order to better manage existing systems or to design new ones.

Today, "scientific" is very much a catchword. Every television commercial seems to have "scientific" proof that the product it touts is the best ever. What does a "scientific approach" really mean?

Observation and *reasoning* are the keys to the scientific method. A scientist starts by observing the behavior of a system. He then applies reasoning to the observations to devise a theory that explains the observed behavior.

But, most important of all, a scientist compares the predictions of the theory with the actual behavior of the system. If the two do not agree, then the theory must be changed. Testing and correction are the steps most often missing from nonscientific approaches.

COMPUTER MODELS

What Is a Model?   A model is something that, in one way or another, represents a real system. Usually the model does not represent every detail of the real system, but only those that are of interest to the model builder.

Take a model airpane, for example. Some model airplanes are scaled-down reproductions of actual airplanes. They look exactly like fighter planes or passenger jets, but they cannot fly. On the other hand, we have model airplanes that can fly but do not look very much like actual airplanes, at least not like fighters or passenger jets.

Neither of the two kinds of models completely represents the airplane. One kind respresents the appearance of the plane. The other kind represents the ability of the plane to fly. And there are

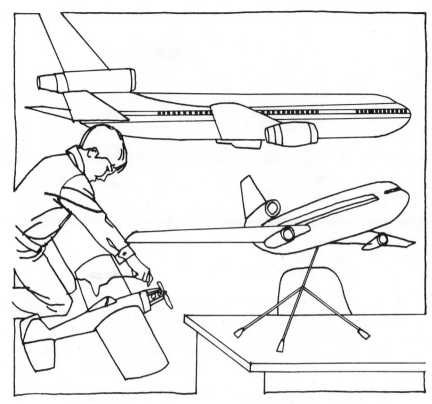

features of real planes that neither model represents, such as the ability to carry passengers or cargo.

Neither model is suitable for every purpose. The kind that looks like a real plane could serve to decorate an airline office. The kind that flies would be of more interest to a person interested in radio-controlled models. As a rule, there are no all-purpose models.

Kinds of Models   People often build models of physical systems (such as airplanes) out of wood, metal, or plastic. But these materials are of little help when we want to model economic and social systems. For those, we must rely on logical models.

A *logical model* is a set of statements that describes the system. From these statements we can, using logical reasoning, deduce facts about the system. When the statements are in the form of mathematical equations, we speak of a *mathematical model*.

A *theory* is just another word for a logical model. If the theory is particularly clear and simple, we think of it as not only describing the system but of explaining it as well.

When the model is mathematical, then the logical reasoning involves solving equations and doing other kinds of mathematical reasoning. If the model is complex, the number of equations will be **137** large, and the use of the computer will be indispensible. For instance, economic models often involve tens of thousands of equations, which would require years to solve by hand. And, by the time they were solved, the structure of the economy would have changed, so the solutions finally reached no longer would be of interest.

A computer program also can model a system directly, instead of just solving the equations of a mathematical model. For instance, the program might accept the present state of the system as data and print out a prediction of the state of the system at some future time. Or the program might accept as data the *inputs* to the system—operating funds, for example. The printout would predict certain *outputs*—number of students graduated, say, or number of criminals apprehended.

We refer to a computer program used to model a system as a *computer model.*

AN EXAMPLE

In this section, we'll look at an example of a computer model. The example comes from the traditional theory of *queues,* or waiting lines. Since it's common for one component of a system to have to wait until the activities of another component are completed, queues play an important role in many models.

A Model Queue We don't have to look far to see a waiting line. We see them everywhere we turn. To pick a familiar one, we will take the line at a supermarket check-out counter as our example.

Suppose, for instance, that the supermarket manager is planning to install a new kind of cash register, or he expects an increase in trade because of a new housing development nearby. The manager needs to know how long a line to expect at each check-out counter if the anticipated changes take place. And how many minutes, on the

With computer modeling the properties of an electronic circuit can be studied without actually constructing the circuit.

average, will a customer have to wait in line before getting checked out?

Using a computer model, the manager can determine these facts in advance and plan remedies (such as hiring more checkers) if the waiting times turn out to be too long. Thus, the manager can avoid the customer dissatisfaction that would result when people found themselves faced with lengthy waits.

This example is fairly trivial, of course. But the same principles can be applied to much larger and more significant problems.

The state of the check-out-counter system is a description of the line at the counter. If the length of the line is all we're interested in, then all we have to keep track of is the number of people in line. But if we also want to find the average time needed for a person to get checked out, then the computer must keep a list showing the time at which each person got in line.

Two events can change the state of the system: a new person can get into line, and the person at the head of the line can finish getting checked out.

Now, no one can say precisely at what times people will get in line on a particular day, nor can we say exactly how long it will take to check out each person. But if we consider all the people who will use the store over a period of time, we can predict with confidence that a certain percentage of them can be checked out in one minute, another percentage can be checked out in two minutes, and so on. We also can predict the percentage of cases in which people arrive at the end of the line one minute apart, two minutes apart, and so on.

These statistics may well vary with the time of day, the day of the week, the month of the year, the condition of the economy, and other variables as well. So we must be certain that the conditions under which we use our model are the same as those ones under which the statistics were collected. Once we take that precaution, we find that we can predict what percentage of a large group of people will do a certain thing, even though we are completely powerless to predict the actions of a single individual.

Suppose we make our observations and get the following results: 20 percent of the customers are checked out in one minute after reaching the check-out counter; 40 percent in two minutes; 30 percent in three minutes; and 10 percent in four minutes. How can we incorporate this data into our model?

Imagine a large drum, the kind used for raffles. Each raffle ticket in the drum has "one minute," "two minutes," "three minutes," or "four minutes" written on it. Of all the tickets in the drum, 20 percent have "one minute" written on them, 40 percent have "two minutes" written on them, 30 percent have "three minutes," and 10 percent have "four minutes."

As in a real raffle, we will have a pretty blindfolded girl draw tickets from the drum. Whenever a customer arrives at the simulated check-out counter, the girl draws a ticket. If the ticket reads "one minute," then it takes that person one minute to check out. If the ticket reads "two minutes," then it takes two minutes to check out that person. Thus our simulation begins to resemble one of those games where each player draws a card or rolls dice to see what happens on that move.

With another raffle drum, we can use a similar procedure to determine when customers arrive at the end of the line.

What we are doing, you see, is using random chance to determine the things we cannot predict—the exact times people will arrive at the end of the line and how long it takes each person to check out. But we prepare the cards in the raffle drum in such a way that the percentages of people who arrive at a certain time or take a certain amount of time to check out agree with the percentages that have been observed.

To make the model we have imagined into a computer model, we replace the raffle drum with a table in the computer's memory and the pretty girl with a program called a *pseudorandom number generator*. The pseudorandom number generator produces seemingly random numbers that can be used to select entries from the raffle-drum table.

Using the outlined procedure, the computer follows people through the check-out line. Of course, both the people and the line exist only in the computer's memory.

We aren't interested in the minute-by-minute behavior of the simulated line. After all, the arrival and check-out times have been chosen at random, so it's extremely unlikely that the minute-by-minute behavior of the actual line will duplicate that of the simulated line on any particular day. But suppose the computer runs the model for some time and calculates *averages*, such as the average length of the simulated line or the average time a customer is kept waiting. Then we can expect these averages to agree with those observed for the actual line. We use averages (and statistics in general) to make up for our lack of knowledge of the detailed behavior of the customers.

APPLICATIONS

Economic Modeling *Econometrics* is the discipline that uses mathematical equations to express the relationships between different sectors of the economy. Frequently hundreds, thousands, or tens of thousands of equations have to be used. By solving these equations (with the help of a computer, naturally), we can better understand how the economy behaves under different circumstances. We can even predict the future course of the economy, provided unforeseen events do not upset our assumptions.

Models based on econometrics are called *econometric models*. The first of these was set up in the 1940s at the Wharton School of Business at the University of Pennsylvania.

An econometric model bases its predictions on patterns of production, inventories, capital investments, return on investments, consumer buying, interest rates, bank deposits, and countless other **140** details.

Some models include a huge input-output table. For each industry, the table shows what inputs (raw materials, products of other industries, labor) that industry needs to product its outputs (products). With an input-output table (and a good computer), we can determine how a shortage or a surplus of one commodity will affect the activities of many industries.

Econometric models are vulnerable to surprises. An Arab oil embargo, a sudden turnabout of a key political leader—these are the kinds of things that will make the best thought-out predictions look foolish.

These kinds of surprises often arise from the actions of individuals, actions no model can ever predict. Sometimes these individuals are legislators, heads of state, or their advisors. But they can be ordinary people—writers, journalists, advocates for some cause— whose ideas happen to catch the public fancy and become the basis of a new cause or movement. An example from recent history is the tax-cutting propositions that caught many politicians by surprise.

For these reasons, it is unrealistic to expect an econometric model to predict *the* future. Claims that these models are crystal balls have stimulated much controversy about them. It is more realistic to try to predict a small number of futures, each based on the assumption that certain key events will take place. (Often the possibilities are at least known; complete surprises are rare.) One then can try for policies that will produce some gain in each of the possible futures and no disasters in any of them.

In short, econometric modeling promises to reduce the uncertainty about the future, but it is doubtful that the uncertainty can ever be completely eliminated. In the future, we may be told that there is a "20 percent chance of a recession in the coming year" much as we may be told today that there is a "20 percent chance of rain tomorrow."

The Whole-Earth Model In 1972, the Club of Rome, an international group of scientists, educators, economists, and industrialists, published a report called *The Limits of Growth*. The report disclosed results that were obtained using a computer model of the entire world. The model predicted that, if present trends continue, civilization will collapse before the year 2100.

The world model takes into account the interaction of about eighty factors, the most important of which are population, food production, natural resources, industrial output, and pollution.

A key feature of the model is the presence of *positive feedback loops*. A positive feedback loop is a vicious circle in which an increase in one quantity leads to further increases in the same quantity. Birth rate is an example. The more people are born, the more people there are to have more children. In the absence of other factors, the population will increase explosively.

This is just the opposite of a *negative feedback loop*, where the effect of an increase in a quantity is to produce a decrease in the same quantity. A thermostat is an example of negative feedback.

141

When the house gets too hot, the thermostat turns off the furnace, causing the temperature to decrease.

A negative feedback loop stabilizes a quantity. A positive feedback loop makes it grow explosively. The world model's dire predictions result from an explosive growth of population, pollution, and other quantities caused by positive feedback loops.

These unpleasant predictions certainly have not been accepted uncritically. In fact, *The Limits of Growth* has been widely attacked on the grounds that the model did not take certain important factors into account. For instance, the report predicts a steadily explosive growth of population. But recent data indicate a leveling off of population growth in developed countries. Also, the model does not take into account the effects of new technology. Yet some people argue that new technology, such as thermonuclear fusion or manufacturing in outer space, is precisely what will save us.

This last point is particularly serious. People who believe the predictions of the model urge that we limit our industrial growth to conserve our resources. Yet, to develop the new technology that might save us, we will have to do just the opposite.

But despite the criticisms and regardless of whether the detailed predictions turn out to be right or wrong, the model has served its purpose. It shows what will happen under the certain assumptions. Now the arguments can focus on whether those assumptions represent the real world accurately. And, of course, people who think that other sets of assumptions describe the real world better are free to build their own models and offer the results obtained as alternatives.

Business Games It is often easy to build a model that exhibits the same kind of behavior as some system in the real world. It is much harder, sometimes impossible, to take enough factors into account so that the model can be used for accurate predictions. This suggests that the models might prove more useful as training tools than as crystal balls.

The aerospace industry uses models this way. Before a pilot ever touches the controls of a real aircraft or spacecraft, he spends hours in a simulator, a mock-up of the real craft controlled by a computer. The computer takes as input the positions of the pilot's controls and produces as output all the sensations and instrument readings that the pilot would experience on an actual flight.

The simulator is a combination of a physical model and a computer model. The flight deck of the aircraft or the spacecraft is modeled in metal and plastic. But the training flights take place only in the computer's imagination.

These simulators are important for two reasons. First, the expense of operating an actual aircraft for training purposes is avoided; the simulator is far cheaper to operate than a large airplane. Second, no one gets hurt in a simulator; training flights risk not only expensive airplanes but the lives of student and instructor as well.

Why can't the same thing be done in the social and economic

sciences? Why can't managers make their mistakes on simulations before they are turned loose on real systems?

Business seems to be the only area in which this idea has caught on. In many business schools, the students play (for credit) computer-based business games. The computer models a situation in which several firms are in direct competition. The students are divided into teams, and each runs one of the simulated firms.

The corporations are as realistic as possible. Each management team decides how many people to hire, how large the plants will be, how much of each product to produce, and how much to charge for each product. The students must worry about financing, advertising, and research and development. The managers are bound by union contracts that place limits on how much the work force can vary and how much overtime can be required from each worker. And the union insists that the workers be paid time-and-a-half for overtime, of course.

The instructor can throw in surprises, such as oil embargoes or stock market crashes. Or the instructor may play the role of an irate stockholder, demanding explanations for unsound business practices.

Of course, models don't have to be this elaborate for students to learn from them. A simple model limited to one narrow facet of the world, such as population growth, energy resources, or political elections, can as be enlightening, too. And the simple models don't demand as much of the students' time as do the more elaborate ones.

Finally, students who can program can write their own models. It is impossible to construct a realistic model of anything without learning far more about it than one is likely to learn from reading a textbook or listening to a lecture.

CAUTIOUS OPTIMISM

Computer simulation is still in its infancy. Much remains to be learned about the general techniques and the specific details of simulating real-world systems.

An invalid model could do much social harm, particularly in the hands of a person who treats all computer output as gospel and whose answer to every question is "But the computer says . . ."

Another danger is that the structure of the model and, therefore, the predictions that come out of it may reflect the social and economic views of the builder. Some of the people affected by the predictions of the model may strongly disagree with those views. This danger is particularly obvious in economics, where we have "liberal" and "conservative" economists.

But, in spite of these cautions, there seems room for optimism that computer models, carefully used with an awareness of their limitations, can provide an important tool for dealing with the complexities of the real world.

143 And here's one more thing to think about. Everyone who reads the newspapers knows that our world is beset with many difficult problems—over-population, pollution, crime, the arms race, and so on and on. People have not had much success in dealing with these problems. Perhaps the problems are just too difficult to be solved by people alone. Perhaps we will *have* to use computers to attack our pressing problems if we are going to survive at all.

FOR FURTHER READING

Ahl, David. "How to Write a Computer Simulation." *Creative Computing*, Jan.-Feb. 1978, pp. 88-93.

Chadbourne, Robert D. "Real World Games." *Creative Computing*, Sept.-Oct. 1978, pp. 78-80.

Churchman, C. West. *The Systems Approach*. New York: Dell Publishing Co., 1968.

French, Nancy; Holmes, Edith; and Ward, Patrick. "Econometrics: Can It Be Trusted?" *Computerworld*, Jan. 29, 1975.

_____. "Government Econometrics: Science or Politics?" *Computerworld*, Feb. 5, 1975.

_____. "Surprises Can Throw Models out of Line." *Computerworld*, Feb. 12, 1975.

Gotlieb, C. C., and Borodin, A. *Social Issues in Computing*. New York: Academic Press, 1973, pp. 110-139.

Meadows, Dennis L. *et al. The Limits of Growth*. New York: New American Library, 1972 (Second edition, 1974).

REVIEW QUESTIONS

1. Why is it imperative that we understand the political, social, and economic systems that affect our lives?

2. What is the most successful approach to understanding a system?

3. Why is it usually not possible to experiment with real social and economic systems?

4. What is the alternative to experimenting with real-world systems?

5. Define a system and give several examples. Your examples should include both physical and social systems.

6. What are the goals of (a) the systems designer and (b) the management scientist?

7. Describe the five major characteristics of a system.

8. What do we mean by a *scientific approach* to the study of systems?

9. What is a model? Give a number of examples. Include logical models as well as physical ones. *(Hint:* Scientific theories are logical models.)

10. What is a *mathematical model?*

11. What is a *computer model?*

12. In order to construct the model of the check-out counter, what data had to be collected by observing customer behavior in the store?

13. In the model of the check-out counter, what roles were played by the raffle drum and the girl who drew tickets from it? What would replace these in a computer model?

14. Why are we not interested in the minute-by-minute behavior of the simulated check-out line? What features of the simulated check-out line are we interested in?

15. What is a *pseudorandom number generator?*

16. What are some of the economic indicators used in econometric models?

17. In what way are econometric models (as well as most other social and economic models) particularly vulnerable?

18. What is a *positive feedback loop?* Can you explain inflation in terms of a positive feedback loop?

19. Name an industry that uses models extensively for training purposes.

20. Describe how managers can be trained using business games.

DISCUSSION QUESTIONS

1. Devise and discuss examples illustrating situations in which experimenting with real social and economic systems would be (a) impractical, (b) costly, (c) dangerous (either to society or to the experimenter), and (d) unethical.

2. This question is for those who have read (or who are willing to invest the time to read) *The Foundation Trilogy,* a collection of science-fiction stories by Isaac Asimov (Doubleday, 1951). Compare the kind of social and economic modeling we have been talking about here with the science of "psychohistory" described in the stories. Do you think that computer modeling is ever likely to reach the state of perfection ascribed to psychohistory? Why or why not?

3. Imagine a future in which politicians are required to develop their abilities on computer models before being allowed to assume real legislative and executive responsibilities. What laws and regulations would be needed to implement such a system? What would be the nature of the social and economic models used in the training? What steps should be taken to make sure that the majority of the public agrees with the political philosophy on which the models were based? How could we be sure that the models used were based on an adequate understanding of the political, social, and economic systems?

CHAPTER **10**

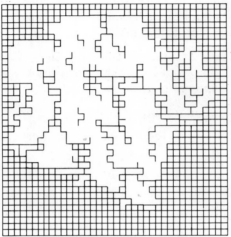

COMPUTERS IN THE CLASSROOM

The early 1960s saw the advent of time-shared computer systems and simplified programming languages, such as BASIC. These developments made computers look attractive for classroom use. But, for many years, costs still kept computing out of many schools; and those schools that did get involved with computers often did so only in a limited way.

But the microprocessor revolution changed all that. Now a computer costs little more than a movie projector, a video recorder, or many other standard classroom tools. These days, it is a rare high school that doesn't own at least one computer. Not many years ago, just the opposite was true.

How should we use computers in the classroom? Can they really lead to any improvements over traditional teaching methods? These are the questions we will explore in this chapter.

EDUCATION AND THE COMPUTER

Since the days of ancient Greece, educators have realized that the **146** ideal learning situation consists of a single student working with a

Inexpensive computers such as the one shown here have as much place in the classroom as the phonograph, the movie projector, and the television set.

well-qualified instructor. This kind of one-on-one instruction has long been the privilege of the children of European aristocrats as well as students at the famous English universities of Oxford and Cambridge. But most American schoolchildren never enjoy the benefits of individualized instruction.

The reason, of course, is that in the United States we are committed to universal education. Everyone is to be educated, not just the privileged few. As a result, there are always far more students than there are teachers.

As justifiably proud of this sytem as we are, we must recognize its drawbacks. Perhaps the worst of these is that all students are forced to work at the same pace. Inevitably, the pace is geared to the average student. The poorer student gets lost; the better student is bored. Neither is learning very much, and both are apt to become disenchanted with education.

Another problem is that with traditional methods of instruction, the flow of information is largely one way. The student reads the text and listens to the teacher but has little opportunity to become personally involved with the subject.

Skilled teachers have developed many ways for trying to get around these problems. Some of these ways work better than others. But with too many students and not enough time, even the best teacher is hard put to overcome the obstacles of traditional education.

The computer is a tool that can be used to avoid some of these obstacles. Used properly, it may be the next best thing to individualized instruction. In some circumstances, it may even be better, since a computer program is infinitely patient, something that even **147** the most saintly of teachers often finds it difficult to be.

The computer makes possible a compromise between responsive, individualized instruction on the one hand and universal education on the other. We don't expect a computer to provide all the responsiveness and individual attention of a private tutor. On the other hand, it can go further in this direction than most traditional methods of mass education. And computer-assisted instruction, unlike private tutors, can be brought to all students.

A computer engages a student in a dialog. Conversation is the most natural way of communicating for most youngsters. The student interacts with the program and has considerable control over what will be presented next. The computer covers material at the student's pace, not that of the teacher or the rest of the class. A computer has all the patience the slowest student might need, yet it can proceed as rapidly as the brightest one could desire.

Nor will a (properly programmed) computer ever imply by word or expression that one student is less capable than others. It will keep its calm no matter how many times a student has failed to grasp the lesson. And when a student has to be told that he is wrong, the news may well be less painful if delivered by an impersonal machine. Computers are sometimes criticized for their impersonality, but, in some situations, this can be an asset.

The human teacher and the computer make a good team. The computer, with its tremendous information-handling capacity, can provide individualized instruction to everyone in the class at the same time. With a good library of instruction programs, it can give advanced instruction to the better students in areas where the teacher may not be qualified. Teachers, freed from the burden of administering routine drills, can spend more time with individual students. They can answer students' questions, explore their interests, invite them to share experiences; in short, teachers can put their human understanding and feelings to good use.

COMPUTER-ASSISTED INSTRUCTION

Programmed Instruction   Programmed instruction is a teaching technique based on the work of the well-known Harvard psychologist, B.F. Skinner. Much of computer-assisted education is based on Skinner's ideas.

Two ideas lie at the heart of programmed instruction:

1. *Active Responding.*   Students must respond actively to each piece of information that is presented to them. Usually, they are asked to respond by answering a question that involves the piece of information they are supposed to have learned.

2. *Immediate Confirmation.*   When students respond, they must be told immediately whether or not their responses are correct.

A lesson designed for programmed instruction is called a *learning program.* This should not be confused with a computer program, although we will see that computer programs can be used to implement learning programs.

A learning program presents a student with a series of *frames*. Each frame either introduces a new piece of information or reinforces an old one. Each frame ends with a question that the student must answer before going on to the next frame.

Proponents of programmed learning disagree about how the frames should be arranged. Skinner and his followers advocate *linear* programs, in which the frames come one after another, just like the pages of a book. Each student who uses the program works through every frame. The frames are constructed so that students will make as few errors as possible in answering the questions. The ideal situation would be if the student could go through the entire program without making any errors; thus, wrong answers wouldn't be learned inadvertently.

Although experiments show linear programs to be effective, students often find them unappealing. Since every student has to work through every frame, linear programs contribute little to individualized instruction. And because no one is supposed to make any mistakes, the program must be geared to the poorest students. The average and better-than-average students have to suffer through many frames that reinforce concepts they have long since learned. Boredom is inevitable.

Fortunately, there is another kind of learning program, the *intrinsic* program. In an intrinsic program, the answer to the question in one frame determines which frame the student goes to next. Different students work through different frames, depending on how they answer the questions.

Thus, a good student who masters a fact quickly can proceed immediately to more advanced material. The student who gives a wrong answer is directed to additional frames that cover the troublesome concept in more detail. These frames also may review concepts that already have been covered, if the answer to the question indicates that they might not have been understood the first time.

In short, the student sees just those frames necessary for understanding the material and no more.

What is the best physical form for learning programs? For linear programs, all we need is a conventional book with its pages divided into frames. Linear programs are also easy to adapt to "teaching machines." These are mainly for those students who cannot be relied on to use the book properly or who might peek ahead at the answers to questions. Simplicity of implementation, then, is the best thing that can be said for linear programs.

The more flexible intrinsic programs are far more difficult to present through conventional media, such as books. To be sure, there are so-called scrambled books: after each frame, the student goes thumbing through the book to find the next one. But this becomes tedious after a while. And a book of average size can cover only a small amount of material, since it has to contain so many alternate sequences treating the same material at different levels of difficulty.

Another drawback to scrambled books is that the question in each frame has to be a multiple-choice question. (The choice the student picks tells him which frame to go to next.) But learning theorists tell us that, for best results, students should construct their own responses instead of merely selecting from among those given.

The computer can get around all these problems. It can store a many-branched learning program in memory and always present the correct frame, depending on the student's response to the current one. This is all done automatically: the student may well be unaware that there are alternate paths through the learning program.

A technique known as pattern matching can be used to examine the student's answer for key words and phrases. This means the student can construct his own responses instead of choosing from among alternatives. Also, by allowing the computer to control audio-visual equipment, the computer can coordinate the learning program with audible and visual materials to provide a true multi-media approach to learning.

For instance, in the system known as Plato, slides can be projected on the same screen that is used for computer display. The computer output can be superimposed over the slides to explain and point out what the student is seeing.

What programming languages should we use for writing computer-assisted-instruction programs? We could use standard languages, such as BASIC. But computer-assisted instruction, like most special problem areas, has its own specially designed programming languages, which are much easier to use than the standard languages. Simplicity is the watchword, since overworked teachers have neither the time nor the inclination to become immersed in complicated programming languages.

One of the most widely used of these languages is *Pilot*, which uses single-letter abbreviations for commands. For instance, T stands for Type, A for Ask, and M for Match. Here is a short sample of a Pilot program:

```
T:  Who was the first president of the United States?
A:
M:  Washington
T Y:  You are correct. George Washington was the
T Y:  first president of the United States.
T N:  No, the first president of the United States
T N:  was George Washington.
```

The first line of the program causes the question

Who was the first president of the United States?

to be displayed on the student's terminal. The second line causes the computer to accept the student's response. The third line causes the computer to check whether or not the student's response contains the word *Washington*.

In the last four statements the Y and N stand for *Yes* and *No* and refer to whether or not the student's response was found to contain the word *Washington*. If it did, the T Y commands are executed, and the computer prints

You are correct. George Washington was the
first president of the United States.

If the student's response did not contain the word *Washington*, then the T N commands are executed, and the computer prints

No, the first president of the United States
was George Washington.

Other Pilot commands would make it possible to direct the computer to jump to different parts of the Pilot program, depending on whether or not the student's response contained the word *Washington*.

BEYOND PROGRAMMED INSTRUCTION

When most teachers and school officials refer to computer-assisted instruction, they are referring to the kind of programmed instruction just described.

As with all other teaching materials, the quality of computer-assisted-instruction programs varies. A program written by a skilled, creative teacher draws the student into an interesting, informative

A computer terminal can display a variety of graphs and diagrams that are extremely difficult for a teacher to draw accurately.

conversation. But when the writer is less imaginative, the result may be more like chunks of text interspersed with examination questions. This can be as boring and tedious as any text ever was, particularly after the novelty of using the computer has worn off.

Not surprisingly, then, this form of computer-assisted instruction has its critics. One of the strongest is the author, lecturer, and researcher, Ted Nelson. Some of his criticisms are presented in this section, along with the alternatives he suggests.

According to Nelson, traditional computer-assisted instruction perpetuates many of the faults of the classroom. The central problem is that the student has little real choice of what to study. The material has been divided into subjects and lessons by teachers and administrators. The student does not have the option of digressing from the lesson to explore the connections between the current subject and another one. The computer program controls the lesson. Which material the student covers is determined not by an informed choice but by whether or not the exam questions are answered correctly.

The solution is to put the student in complete control of the lesson. Nelson calls the means for doing this *hypertext*.

Hypertext is a form of writing that branches. At certain choice points, the reader is given the choice of what he wants to see next. This is something like those novelty movies where the film is stopped every now and then so the audience can vote on how the movie should continue. Should the hero get the girl, for instance, or should he be rebuffed?

At each branch point, the student is given a list of alternatives, like a menu (and often referred to as such). One alternative might be to go back over the previous topic in more detail. Another might be to go back and review a previously covered topic. Still another alternative might be to skip further introductory material and get on with something new.

Hypertext also would have something equivalent to the asterisks for footnotes that appear in ordinary text. But instead of leading to footnotes, the asterisks would lead to entirely different pieces of text. Thus, the reader constantly would be invited to explore related subjects. Hypertext emphasizes not only the separate subjects but the relationships between subjects as well.

Here are two methods that Nelson has suggested (and his organization is developing) for displaying information. In each case, the idea is to put the reader in control of the material as much as possible.

Stretchtext The reader has a control that determines in what detail the text covers the topic. When the control is turned in one direction, new words, phrases, and sentences appear in the text, making it more detailed. When the control is turned in the other direction, material is deleted, making the text less detailed. When something strikes the reader's interest, he has only to turn the control in the proper direction to have more details provided. When bored, he can turn the control the other way, to drop details and get a quick summary.

Hypergrams These are animated drawings that perform at the viewer's request. By pointing out various parts of the drawings with a special pointer called a light pen, the user can do the following things.

■ The viewer can make the drawing move. That is, a drawing of a machine might go through a cycle of operation as the viewer moves one part with the light pen, much as you might move a part of a model machine with your finger.

■ A selected part of a drawing can be magnified and shown in more detail.

■ The viewer can request an explanation of the function of any selected part.

■ The viewer can request that a drawing be dissected. When he indicates a part to be removed, the computer would remove that part from the drawing, revealing what was underneath it.

Of course, a lot of work will be needed to make these ideas technically and educationally feasible. But the main idea can be applied even to programs written in languages like Pilot. The object is to give the student as much free choice over the material as possible, instead of having all the choices automatically depend on whether or not questions are answered correctly.

OTHER USES FOR CLASSROOM COMPUTERS

There are many ways to use computers in teaching besides computer-assisted instruction. Some of these are particularly appropriate for certain subjects, such as science and mathematics.

Drills It is easy to program a computer to generate drills, particularly mathematical ones. For instance, the computer can display an addition problem. The student enters his answer, and the computer tells whether it was right or wrong. If it was wrong, the student is given the correct answer. The drill then continues with another problem.

These drills easily can be turned into games to keep the interest of young children. Several of the smart electronic games on the market are just slightly disguised drills in arithmetic or spelling. Some of these are calculator-like devices decorated to appeal to children. One of these is marketed under the trade name of "The Little Professor."

Simulation As was pointed out in the chapter on computer models, there are few better ways to understand a system than to write a program to simulate it. Simulation is an attractive alternative for the systems studied in science courses. Traditionally, students mastered these systems by laboriously working large numbers of problems. But they might well learn more by writing programs to simulate the systems and letting the computer do the labor.

Teaching Programming   From all the applications of computers described in this book, it should be clear that computer programming is an important skill to have, whether for personal or professional use.

But this is not the only reason to teach students to program. Many students find it more interesting (and less work) to program a computer to solve a problem than to solve the problem by hand. And they probably learn as much or more doing it that way. No one can write a program to solve a problem without thoroughly understanding the method of solution. Only the mind-numbing, hand-cramping drudgery of manual arithmetic is missing.

Computer-Managed Instruction   The computer does not have to teach students directly. It can oversee their instruction but direct them elsewhere for the actual learning experiences.

For instance, the computer can ask students to read certain books, listen to certain tapes, see certain films, and so on. When the students complete the assignments, they return to the computer terminal for testing and further assignments.

Since each student is managed individually, each can proceed at his own pace. Yet the students are not limited to materials that can be presented on a computer terminal. They can see movies, television, works of art, and so on. Also, the computer can summarize test results in a form that makes it easy for the teacher to judge each student's progress.

THE OUTLOOK
FOR COMPUTER-ASSISTED
INSTRUCTION

Cost   For a long time, cost was the main obstacle to computer-assisted instruction. As long as computers were expensive, computer-assisted instruction cost five to ten times as much as conventional instruction. Most school districts simply could not afford it. But now that microprocessors have lowered the cost of computers so drastically, computer-assisted instruction is within the budget of almost every school.

Will the Computer "Depersonalize" the Students?   There is no reason to think that a computer will be any more depersonalizing than a movie projector, a record player, or a TV set. The computer is simply a machine that allows the programmer to communicate with the student in a much more flexible manner than is possible with conventional media.

154   The best learning programs reflect the fact that they are written by human beings. They are replete with congratulations, admonitions, asides, and jokes. In short, any kind of communication can be personal or impersonal. The same is true for computer-assisted instruction.

Of course, it would be as undesirable for children to spend all their time with a computer as it would be if they spent it with a record player, a movie projector, or a TV set. But no one suggests doing away with human teachers and classmates. The students should not lack for human contacts just because a computer has assumed part of the task of teaching them.

Quality of Learning Programs   This may turn out to be the biggest problem of all. Writing good learning programs *is not easy*. It calls for the combined skills of a creative writer, a skilled teacher, and an expert in the subject matter. Such people are not easy to find and neither are well-written learning programs.

The Promise of Computer-Assisted Instruction   This approach to education is in its infancy, and much still has to be learned about it. But some of its possibilities are quite exciting. For instance, programmed learning has been used to train even pigeons to exhibit highly complex behavior. If pigeons can be trained, then surely even very poor students, those who get very little out of traditional education, can nevertheless be trained for almost any skill they will need to lead a normal, useful life. And superior students can be helped to overcome the limited backgrounds of their teachers and classmates.

**FOR
FURTHER
READING**

Brown, Dean. "On Computers and Learning." *Computer Decisions,* May 1974, pp. 41-12.

_____ and Cole, Phyllis M. "The Classroom Microcomputer." *Computer Decisions,* Feb. 1975, pp. 34-35.

Nelson, Ted. "No More Teacher's Dirty Looks." *Computer Lib/Dream Machines.* Chicago: Hugo's Book Service, 1974, pp. DM16-DM19.

Nold, Ellen. "Writing CAI." *People's Computers,* July-Aug. 1977, pp. 36-37.

_____ and Cannom, Sallie. "Pilot." *People's Computers,* July-Aug. 1977, pp. 11-15.

Rubin, Sylvan. "A Simple Instructional Language." *Computer Decisions,* Oct. 1973, pp. 17-18.

Skinner, B. F. "Teaching Machines." *Scientific American,* Nov. 1961.

Suppes, Patrick. "The Uses of Computers in Education." *Computers and Computation.* San Francisco: W. H. Freeman, 1971, pp. 249-259.

1. What developments led to the first uses of computers in the classroom?

2. What are some of the problems with traditional teaching methods?

3. In what kinds of situations could the impersonality of the computer be an asset?

4. What are the two fundamental ideas of programmed instruction?

5. What is a *frame?*

6. What is a *linear program?*

7. What is an *intrinsic program?*

8. Give the advantages and disadvantages of linear and intrinsic programs.

9. Give three methods of implementing learning programs.

10. What advantages does a computer have over other methods of implementing learning programs?

11. What are some of the criticisms that have been leveled against the programmed-learning form of computer-assisted instruction?

12. What is *hypertext?*

13. What is *Stretchtext?*

14. Give four things that a *Hypergram* will do at the request of the viewer.

15. Name two subjects for which drills are available in the form of smart electronic games.

16. What are the advantages of students writing simulation programs?

17. Explain *computer-managed instruction.*

18. What problem with computer-assisted instruction has been all but eliminated by the microprocessor revolution?

19. Explain how the fear that computers might somehow "depersonalize" students is irrational.

20. Why are good learning programs so difficult to find?

1. Drawing on your own experience as a student, discuss the strengths and weaknesses of traditional methods of education. Can you think of any situations in which you personally could have benefitted from computer-assisted instruction? Can you think of situations in which you were perfectly satisfied with the traditional approach, and the use of a computer would have been superfluous or detrimental?

2. With computer-assisted instruction, home computers, and information utilities, it is possible that a large part of a child's education could take place in the home. Discuss the advantages and disadvantages of this. For instance, in cases where parents have sought legal permission to educate their children at home, school officials have argued that school is an important social experience, which the child should not be denied.

3. What steps might be taken to encourage the production of high-quality learning programs?

4. Discuss the impact on society if computer-assisted instruction were developed to the point that almost anyone could acquire technical knowledge quickly in any area and could be trained for almost any routine job.

5. Read and discuss the science-fiction story "The Fun They Had," by Isaac Asimov (in *Earth Is Room Enough*. Garden City, N. Y.: Doubleday, 1957).

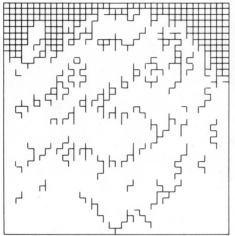

CHAPTER 11

COMPUTER ART AND MUSIC

A visual artist works with patterns of light, dark, and color. A musician works with sounds. A writer works with printed characters. With suitable input and output devices, a computer can manipulate all these things.

The computer offers the artist new ways to control these media. The visual artist gets an "electronic canvas" of great flexibility and versatility. The musician can command an electronic orchestra to play pieces no real orchestra would dream of attempting. And even though computer processing of natural language is still experimental, the writer and the poet can benefit from the computer's versatility.

Computers can be applied in both the useful arts and the fine arts. On the useful side, computers can generate pictures of proposed buildings or automobiles from engineer's descriptions. And computers are making possible new animation techniques that can be seen in everything from television commercials to science-fiction films.

The fine-arts side of computer art is less developed. But pictures produced by computers have been displayed in art museums and published in art collections. A number of recordings of computer-performed music have been issued. So, clearly, this dimension of computer art is being developed, too.

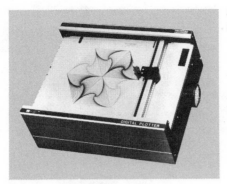

A not-too-expensive plotter intended for use with small computers.

Computer art may turn out to be one of the most important applications of personal computers. Many of us are frustrated artists; we appreciate a particular art form and would like to experiment with it, but we have been unable to devote the years of work required to learn to draw or paint or play a musical instrument. With a computer, we can overcome our deficiencies by letting the computer help translate the ideas in our heads into pictures and sounds. We supply the ideas; the computer supplies the manual skills.

COMPUTERS IN THE VISUAL ARTS

Computer Graphics Computer graphics refers to the use of computers to form images. There are several ways to do this.

A *plotter* produces a pen-and-ink drawing. The computer sends instructions to the plotter for every point or line segment that is to appear in the drawing. Following these instructions, the plotter laboriously executes the drawing, point by point and line by line.

A drum plotter.

159

A close up of the drum plotter showing the three-pen assembly. By moving the pens, the paper, or both, the computer can position a pen over any point on the paper.

Plotters are most useful for large, complex drawings with many fine details. Examples are maps, engineering drawings, architectural plans, and the complex patterns used to manufacture integrated circuits.

Plotters are slow. When the requirements for fine detail are less stringent and when the user would like to interact with the computer producing the drawing, a CRT display is better than a plotter.

CRT, as we mentioned before, stands for *cathode ray tube*, the engineer's term for a television picture tube. The fine details of a CRT vary, depending on whether it is to be used in a TV set, a radar set, a laboratory instrument, or a computer display. But, in each case, its principles of operation are the same.

The computer produces a spot of light on the fluorescent screen of the CRT by aiming a beam of electrons at the point in question. The screen glows where the electrons hit. The brightness of the glow depends on the amount of current flowing in the electron beam.

In a color CRT, such as those used in color TV sets, there are three phosphors corresponding to the three "additive" primary colors—red, green, and blue. (A phosphor is a substance that produces light when struck by electrons. Different kinds of phosphors produce light of different colors.)

The three phosphors are arranged in a pattern of either lines or dots, depending on the design of the CRT. A complex electronic system sees to it that the beam carrying blue information strikes the blue phosphor, the beam carrying red information strikes the red phosphor, and so on. Colors other than red, green, or blue are represented by some combination of the primary colors.

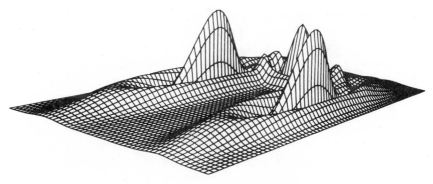

A computer-generated perspective drawing of a surface in three dimensions.

(You can see the pattern of red, green, and blue phosphors on a color TV by examining the screen with a magnifying glass.)

The electron beam can only strike one point on the screen at a time. As soon as the beam has left a point, that point starts to fade. The beam must return to that point before the eye notices the fading.

The usual procedure is for the electron beam to scan the screen methodically from left to right and top to bottom. (If you look closely at a TV screen, you can see the lines along which the electron beam scans the screen.) As the beam reaches each point, the computer adjusts the current in the beam to produce the desired brightness at that point. For a color display, the computer must adjust the currents in three beams to produce the desired combination of red, green, and blue.

The scanning must take place so fast that it is not noticeable to the eye. A home TV, a video monitor, and many CRT terminals scan the complete screen thirty times each second.

An ordinary TV set can be used for computer graphics and is so used by many computer games and personal computers. But, in almost every case, a video monitor will give better results. This is

Using a CRT to
display a bar graph.

161

particularly true of color TVs. Color was added to black-and-white TV as an afterthought, and the method of transmitting and receiving color TV leaves much to be desired in the way of resolution.

Computer graphics can be recorded directly on video tape. Signals from the computer are fed directly to the video tape recorder instead of the CRT display. This technique is often used when computer graphics are used to make TV commercials.

To make computer movies, a movie camera is focused on a CRT display. The camera is equipped with an "animation motor"; instead of running continuously, it photographs one frame each time it is triggered by the computer.

A movie camera has one advantage over video tape. With the latter, the image must be produced in "real time." That is, thirty separate frames have to be computed each second. For complex animations, only the fastest computers can keep up with the video recorder. With the movie camera, however, the computer can work as slowly as it needs to, taking perhaps several minutes per frame. This is because the movie camera does not photograph a frame until triggered by the computer.

Inputting Pictures How do the pictures that are going to be processed get into the computer in the first place? Aside from mathematical patterns, which the computer generates from formulas, the artist needs some way to provide the computer with the pictorial raw materials from which it will work.

A TV camera is a common source of input. The output of the TV camera is an electrical signal, but the signal is not in the binary-coded form required by the computer. A device known as a *digitizer* converts the electrical signal from the TV camera into a series of binary codes that the computer can process. Each code represents the

Another computer-generated perspective drawing.

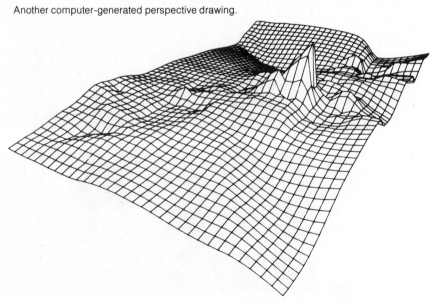

brightness of one point. If the picture is in color, then the brightness of each of the three primary colors must be given for each point.

The TV camera can be focused on a live subject. This is done to make computer portraits. The subject sits in front of the camera, and the camera sends the computer (via the digitizer) the information necessary to print the portrait.

We also can focus the camera on a drawing, a photograph, or a painting. Thus, the artist can start with a conventional drawing or painting and feed it into the computer for modification. The starting point also could be a film, which would be scanned by a projector-camera combination like those used to broadcast films on television.

The most interesting way to put a drawing into a computer is to draw it with a *light pen*, the electronic pointer mentioned in the chapter on computer-assisted instruction. This also is the easiest way to input a drawing, since the computer can be instructed to help out with the drawing process.

The light pen consists of a pen-like case with a light-sensitive cell at its tip. The cell is connected to the computer by a cable. The user holds the light pen over a particular point on the screen. When that point is scanned, the cell in the pen sees a burst of light and sends an electrical impulse to the computer. Since each point on the screen is scanned at a different time, the computer can tell *where* the tip of the light pen is from *when* the electrical impulse arrives. Since the screen is scanned so frequently, the computer easily can keep track of the position of the light pen as the user moves it across the screen.

The simplest way to use the light pen is to point it at a certain part of the display. A schoolchild can use the light pen to point out the

Using a digitizer pad to input a drawing into a computer. The digitizer pad is an alternative to the light pen that is discussed in the text.

correct answer to a multiple-choice question. A medical patient can point out "where it hurts" on a diagram of the body. A refinery operator can point out on a diagram of the refinery the particular valve that should be opened or closed. Once a particular point has been located, a conventional keyboard can be used to tell the computer what it is to do with that particular point.

But the most fascinating way to use the light pen is to draw with it. The computer tracks the pen as it moves across the screen and fills in a line behind it.

Drawing with Light   With the help of graphics software, a computer can offer a number of services to anyone who draws. These include not only creative artists but people who draw for practical reasons, such as engineers and architects. It also includes the "frustrated artists" who like to draw but have never had time to master artistic skills.

For instance, the computer can improve on the lines drawn with the light pen. It can convert a crudely drawn line into a perfectly straight one. Or it can convert a lopsided circle into a perfectly round one.

Under your guidance, the computer will build up drawings from basic geometrical shapes. You might start with a cube, for instance. Now, suppose you wanted a circular hole through the cube. With the light pen, you would position a cylinder where you wanted the hole and instruct the computer to "subtract" the cylinder from the cube. To make a slot in the cube, you would position a rectangular solid where the slot was supposed to go and subtract it. You could construct a wide range of figures by repeatedly adding or subtracting cubes, spheres, cylinders, and pyramids.

This technique is particularly useful for drawing man-made objects, which usually are made up of simple geometrical shapes. It is not as helpful for natural objects, such as people and trees, which are not so closely related to simple geometrical forms.

The computer can modify drawings in other ways as well. On command, it will enlarge or reduce a figure by a specified amount. Or it will move the figure to any part of the screen to fit it into an existing drawing. Stock figures (besides simple geometrical forms) can be called forth from memory, modified as necessary, and fitted into the drawing.

The computer can rotate a figure so that we see it not straight on but from an angle. This solves one of the most difficult problems of drawing, that of determining what a complicated figure looks like when viewed from a given distance and a given direction. Without some kind of help, it's hard to determine this even for a simple circle.

One of the best ways to display a three-dimensional object in a two-dimensional drawing is to have the computer continuously rotate the object. As the object rotates and we see it from all sides, its three-dimensional structure stands out, even though this structure was not obvious from a single view. Complex chemical molecules are often

164   displayed this way. On the television series *The Ascent of Man*, this technique was used to display the DNA molecule, the one that carries the genetic code, the key to life.

The computer also can show three-dimensional scenes in perspective—that is, the way they would look from a particular point of view. Figuring out the shape of each object when seen from the given viewpoint is not difficult for the computer. What is difficult is working out which parts of the drawing are to be visible and which are to be hidden behind other parts. It's easy to program a computer to produce a "stick figure," in which all lines are visible and which looks transparent. It's much harder to get the computer to draw a solid-looking figure, in which the only lines showing are those that would be visible to an actual viewer.

When an artist completes a drawing, he can store it in the computer's memory for later use. In effect, he keeps an electronic sketch book stored in the computer's auxiliary memory.

Computer Animation   Animation is not just a technique for making cartoons and TV commercials. It can be used for more serious work as well; for example, J. R. R. Tolkien's famous trilogy, *The Lord of the Rings*, has been produced as an animated film. Animation is particularly useful for science fiction and fantasy, since the unworldly backgrounds of these kinds of stories make them incredibly expensive to film.

When the user is satisfied with a drawing as it appears on the screen of a computer terminal, he can use a plotter to produce a permanent copy.

Unfortunately, conventional animation requires a vast amount of labor. Each frame of the film has to be painted separately on transparent plastic sheets called *cels*. (Hence conventional animation is called *cel animation*.) Each minute of showing time calls for 1,440 separate frames. Anything that moves has to be redrawn for each frame.

As a result, animated features are usually produced by large teams of animators. Animated films by individual artists almost invariably are short, and, even then, heroic labors are required to make them.

What is needed is a way for the animator to draw a series of snapshots showing various stages of the action and have a computer fill in the thousands of frames necessary to get from one snapshot to another. The artist still would be in control of the film. But the computer would do all the tedious work of drawing the same figure over and over again in slightly different positions. Research is being done on this kind of animation, which is still very much in the experimental stage.

People are experimenting with other ways of directing a computer to produce animations. One of these is *animation languages*, which describe the figures and their movements in programming-language form. Still another approach is to have the artist wear a harness carrying sensors connected to the computer. The artist goes through the desired motions, and the computer moves the animated figures in such a way as to duplicate them.

Entertainment is not the only use for animation. Often the results of calculations can be presented effectively in animated form. If we are studying, say, the movement of an airplane wing, we can have the computer produce a motion picture that *shows* how the wing moves in response to changing forces. A movie like this can be worth thousands of pages of numerical printout.

Sometimes it's useful to let the viewer interact with an animated picture as it is generated. In an aircraft simulator, for instance, an animated picture can show what the pilot sees through the windscreen as he lands his plane. As the student pilot manipulates the controls of the simulator, the display changes accordingly.

In short, there are many useful applications for computer graphics and computer animation. But serious visual artists are just beginning to be interested in using the computer. It will be fascinating to see what they do with the new possibilities that have been opened up to them.

COMPUTER MUSIC

Electronic Music The sounds available to a traditional composer are limited to two things—the capabilities of traditional musical instruments and the abilities of the people who play them.

Frequently, young composers don't appreciate these limitations

and write pieces that experienced musicians label "unplayable."
The music they compose simply cannot be performed by human
beings with only ten fingers and a limited amount of wind. Or, if the
music can be played at all, it is only by virtuosos, not the ordinary
competent musicians found in most orchestras. Eventually, the composer learns to write playable pieces but only at the expense of
limiting his creativity.

Some composers have gone so far as to invent new musical
instruments. But then the problem is to find someone to play the new
instrument. Mastering a musical instrument requires practically a
lifetime of study. And that study is based on the accumulated wisdom
of generations of players. Skilled performers and advanced playing
techniques simply are not available for newly invented instruments.

Electronics offers a solution. Electronic devices called *oscillators*
can be used to generate any desired sounds. (Actually, the oscillators
generate electrical sigals that produce the sounds when they are fed
to an amplifier and speaker.) Other components, called *filters*,
modify the signals generated by the oscillators and so affect the
quality of the sounds that are produced. Also, it's possible to combine
the output of a number of different oscillators to obtain sounds with a
particular quality.

The electronic organs found in homes and some churches make
use of these principles. So do the synthesizers found in rock and jazz
bands.

With electronic equipment, we can produce any sound that could
ever be heard over an electronic reproduction system, such as a
stereo set. To be sure, this is not quite the same as every possible
musical sound. The problem is mainly in loudness: live music
contains passages that are both softer and louder than those an
electronic reproduction system can handle. But since far more music
is heard electronically reproduced than live these days, this limita-
tion is not likely to be noticed.

Once we have the oscillators and filters, the problem becomes
one of controlling them to produce the desired sounds. A musical
tone has four attributes, all of which we must control:

- *Pitch*, which is controlled by adjusting the oscillator;

- *Quality* (which distinguishes a note on a violin from the same note
on the trumpet), which is controlled by adjusting the filters or the
mixture of tones from several oscillators;

- *Attack* and *decay* (the way the note builds up and dies out), which
is controlled by the keying circuits that start and stop each note; and

- *Loudness*, which is controlled by adjusting the gain of an amplifier,
just as we control the volume of a radio or TV set.

All these adjustments have to be made separately for each note
of the composition. The trick is to do this fast enough to keep up with
167 the music.

One solution is to use a keyboard like that of a piano or organ to select the notes, with additional controls to adjust quality, loudness, attack, and decay. This is the approach taken by organs and synthesizers. With a synthesizer, for instance, the keyboardist plays the keyboard with one hand and adjusts a multitude of knobs, sliders, and switches with the other. But, except for certain "glide" or "bending" effects, the keyboard is limited to the standard musical scale. And the composer still must depend on the virtuosity of the performer.

Punched paper tape similar to a player-piano roll has been used to control synthesizers. But special equipment is required to punch the tape. And it is difficult to correct a note if the wrong one is punched or to insert a note that inadvertently has been left out. If the composer wants to make changes after hearing the result, the entire tape may have to be repunched.

Some of the techniques used by early workers in electronic music were tedious beyond belief. For instance, they would record each of the thousands of tones in a composition on a separate piece of magnetic tape. Each tape was then cut to the correct length to give the tone the proper duration. Finally, thousands of these little pieces of tape would be spliced together to give the finished composition.

Enter the computer. A computer can produce sound in two different ways. In one way, the computer calculates a series of numbers representing the strength of an electrical signal at different instants of time. A device called a *digital-to-analog converter* changes the numbers into the corresponding electrical signal. When this signal is fed to an amplifier and speaker, it produces the sound.

The other way a computer produces sound is for it to control the oscillators and filters of a conventional synthesizer. The synthesizer works as usual, but the computer, not a human performer, "plays the keyboard and twists the knobs." (Of course, the computer actually uses special control signals instead of physically pressing keys or twisting knobs. A number of synthesizers now on the market are designed to be controlled by computers.)

The first of the two methods is the most flexible. The sound generation is completely under the control of the computer program. You can invent any musical instrument you want just by telling the computer how to calculate the numbers representing the sounds the instrument makes. The sounds can be varied in any imaginable way, such as changing instruments in the middle of a note, for instance. With the second method, on the other hand, the sounds that can be produced are limited by the design of the synthesizer. The computer only can control the sounds in the ways provided for in the design of the synthesizer.

The first method makes the greatest demands on the computer. To produce music in "real time," so that it can be heard as it is being produced, the computer must calculate each second 40,000 of the numbers representing the electrical signal. Each number may be the result of a quite substantial calculation. Only the fastest computers can do this. For slower machines, the numbers for the entire composition would have to be calculated and stored before the composition could be heard. With the second method, it's easy to hear the music as it is generated; controlling the synthesizer places little burden on the computer.

Using one or the other of these methods, composers can specify the sounds they want at a computer terminal. After completing their pieces, or any part of them, they can have the computer play them. If they are not satisfied with the results, they easily can revise and try again.

New computer applications mean new computer languages, and music is no exception. A number of languages have been developed for entering musical scores into a computer. These languages use symbols and terms that are reasonably familiar to musicians. For example, in a language called SCORTOS (Score to Sound System), musical notes are represented by the usual letters—A, B, C, D, E, F, and G. Numbers are used for time values. Thus, B2 represents a half note of pitch B, C4 represents a quarter note of pitch C, and so on.

Languages like SCORTOS are oriented toward pieces that could have been written in traditional musical notation. How to describe sounds that transcend the limits of traditional musical notation is still an unsolved problem.

One problem that young composers experience is actually hearing their works played by an orchestra. It is difficult to write music if you can't hear how it sounds. And the piano, on which most composers work out their compositions, can give only a poor imitation of the sounds of a real orchestra.

Therefore, it might be worthwhile for music schools to set up computer music systems such as those just described. A composer could practice by entering his composition into the computer and letting the computer play it as it would sound if played by an orchestra. Even if the computer did not duplicate exactly the sound of the orchestra, it would come a lot closer than a piano does.

The electronic music produced so far has not been of superior quality. Composers need time to learn to cope with new freedoms. Much experimenting will be necessary before the possibilities of electronic music are understood. But then, perhaps, we can look forward to electronic works that can rival anything composed by the classical masters.

Computer Composition Computers have been programmed not only to play music but to compose it as well. The computer uses a pseudorandom number generator to produce a series of numbers that represent the pitches and durations of the notes. The output of the random-number generator is rejected where it does not conform to certain rules of composition, based on the principles of harmony and melody. The final composition is random except to the extent that the rules constrain it.

Actually, this kind of random composing was practiced long before computers came along. Schemes for composing music by rolling dice date back to the seventeenth century, and one such method was published by Mozart. Such schemes can produce pleasant music and even music in the style of a particular composer. But the composition are bland and lack variety.

Still, the attempts are interesting. From time to time, psychologists and philosophers have advanced theories about what goes on in a composer's mind during composition. How can we test such theories? One way is to program a computer to compose music according to the principles set forth in the theory being tested. Then we compare the music the computer produced with that of the human composer whose methods we are trying to explain. This kind of research is interesting, even if we never succeed in getting the computer to compose great music.

Finally, we should remember that "serious" musical performances have consisted of turning radios on and off at random, dropping junk on the piano strings, or simply having a musician sit at a piano without playing. If this is the future of music composed and performed by humans, then perhaps there's room for computer composition after all.

OTHER APPLICATIONS TO THE ARTS

Computer Poetry Computers have been programmed to write poetry. They string together randomly selected poetic-sounding phrases, sometimes constrained by some kind of poetic rules, sometimes not. The result actually sounds like some modern poetry. But it might be more accurate to say that some modern poetry sounds as though it were written by a computer.

Actually, there are two areas in which computers are able to duplicate the human use of natural language well enough to fool an uninformed observer. One is writing poetry. The other is imitating the conversation of an insane person.

The reasons are similar for the two cases. We do not expect an insane person to be consistent or logical. And we grant a poet the license to be inconsistent or illogical on the surface, in hopes that, out of the apparent nonsense, some deeper meaning will emerge. If there really is no deeper meaning, our imagination may be willing to supply one.

Dance Notation As mentioned in chapter 1, there is a notation used to describe dances, just as musical notation is used to describe musical performances. In fact, there are two dance notations, each with its own adherents.

Unfortunately, the notations are so complex that it may take a year or more to write out a complex dance. However, a computer system has been developed that considerably shortens this time by letting the notation be entered and edited from a computer terminal. After editing, the computer prints out a perfect copy of the score.

The computer can check for certain common errors. For instance, the writer may put in a symbol that places the dancer in a bent-over position but forget to put in a symbol later to straighten him up again. Or a dancer may be given too many clockwise twirls without an equal number of counterclockwise ones. The computer can determine where the score seems unreasonable and point out possible errors to the user.

Literary Research Computers have proved extremely valuable to researchers in languages and literature.

For example, a powerful research tool for studying any written work is a *concordance*, an index to every occurrence of every word in the work. Preparing such a list manually is pure tedium, but a computer can do the job in a fraction of the time at a fraction of the labor. And the result probably will be more accurate than if it had been done by hand.

These kinds of indexes constantly are needed for literary research. Almost always the computer is the proper tool to do the job. The main obstacle to using a computer is converting the text to be studied into a form the machine can read. Often, it laboriously must be punched on cards, typed in at a terminal, or typed with a special typeface that an optical character reader can recognize. But if the work originally was produced using computer typesetting, then it may be possible to get a machine-readable version from the publisher.

It is possible to characterize the style of an author by certain statistics, including the average lengths of the sentences and paragraphs, the percentage of words having a certain number of syllables, and so on. A comparison of the statistics of two different works can determine whether or not they were written by the same person. Several cases of disputed authorship have been settled this way. Needless to say, the best way to collect and analyze these statistics is with a computer.

Writers can use these statistics to judge whether or not their styles are suitable for particular audiences. The statistics would be different for writing in, say, a popular magazine and a scientific journal. For some time, readability researchers such as Rudolf Flesch have urged writers to monitor their styles this way.

Word-processing programs easily could collect the statistics as the manuscript was typed in and update them as it is revised. Of course, if the statistics indicate that the style is poor, it is still up to the writer to figure out what changes must be made. On that point, neither statistics nor computers are of any help.

FOR FURTHER READING

Altmayer, Nancy. "Music Composition: A Different Approach." *Creative Computing*, April 1979, pp. 74-85.

Computers and Computation. San Francisco: W. H. Freeman and Co., 1971, pp. 113-122.

Greenberg, Donald P. "Computer Graphics in Architecture." *Scientific American*, May 1974, pp. 98-106.

Leavitt, Ruth. *Artist and Computer*. New York: Harmony Press, 1976.

Moorer, James Anderson. "Music and Computer Composition." *Communications of the ACM*, Feb. 1972, pp. 104-113.

North, Steve. "Computer Music." *Creative Computing*, March-April 1978, pp. 28-37.

Schneider, Ben Ross, Jr. *Travels in Computerland*. Reading, Mass.: Addison-Wesley, 1974.

Creative Computing, May-June 1978, special section on computer art and animation, pp. 82-107.

Taylor, Hal. "SCORTOS: Implementation of a Music Language." *Byte*, Sept. 1977, pp. 12-21, 206-208.

REVIEW QUESTIONS

1. What does the computer offer the artist?

2. What is *computer graphics*?

3. What is a *plotter*? What are some of its applications? What is its main drawback?

4. Describe the operation of a CRT.

5. Describe how computer movies are made.

6. Describe two ways of inputting drawings into a computer.

7. What is a *light pen*, and how is it used?

8. Give two ways the computer can improve a drawing made with a light pen.

9. Describe how a drawing can be built up from simple geometrical forms.

10. What is the most difficult problem in depicting three-dimensional scenes?

11. Why are animated films so difficult to produce without the aid of a computer?

12. Describe three experimental approaches to computer animation.

13. What are some of the limitations imposed on a composer who writes for traditional musical instruments?

14. What problems does the composer who invents his own musical instruments face?

15. What are the four attributes of a musical tone?

16. What two electronic components can be used to generate musical tones?

17. Describe two control techniques used by early workers in electronic music.

18. What are two ways a computer can generate music?

19. Did the idea of basing musical compositions on random numbers originate with computer music?

20. Describe three additional applications of computers to the arts.

DISCUSSION QUESTIONS

1. Would you be interested in using computers to explore areas of the visual arts and music that you could not explore by conventional means because you lack the necessary skills? Discuss why the idea of doing this does or does not interest you.

2. Look at some art created with the aid of computers. (For instance, see the book by Leavitt in the readings for this chapter.) Play the role of the art critic, and discuss what you do and do not like about computer art.

3. Listen to some computer music. (The music department probably can recommend recordings that are available on campus.) Try to listen both to computer-composed music and music composed by human beings but performed with the aid of computers. As in question 2, play the role of the music critic, and discuss what you did or did not like about what you heard.

4. How might computer music change the way music is performed and listened to?

5. Discuss the output produced by a poetry-writing program. Such a program, written in BASIC, can be found in David Ahl's *101 BASIC Computer Games*. (Maynard, Mass.: Digital Equipment Corp., 1975).

CHAPTER **12**

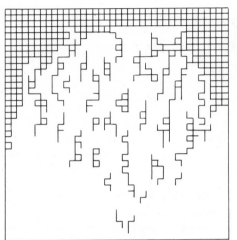

COMPUTERS IN MEDICINE

No one doubts that the best source of a medical diagnosis is a trained physician, up-to-date in the relevant field of medicine, with all the latest research at his (or her) fingertips and all the time necessary to concentrate on the case. Alas, these ideal conditions are seldom met. And when they are not, computers can make an important contribution to medical diagnosis.

Computers also can contribute to routine but time-consuming procedures. These include collecting medical histories, medical record keeping, hospital administration, patient billing, and laboratory analysis.

One of the most important applications of computers to medicine is patient monitoring. The computer receives data from sensors attached to a seriously ill patient. It maintains a constant vigil, ready to alert medical personnel the moment a change for the worse occurs. The data the computer collects during its vigil can be used later for diagnosis.

Finally, the computer has important applications in medical

research.

COMPUTER-ASSISTED DIAGNOSIS

The Information Explosion Twentieth-century medical research has produced a flood of new information about diseases and their treatment. The problem is to get the research results to the practitioners who need them.

Of course, every doctor tries to keep up with the latest results in his specialty. He reads the medical journals, attends seminars, takes refresher courses. But to really keep up, he would have to spend all his time doing these things, and he would have no time left to treat any patients.

A specialist in a narrow field has a better chance of keeping up, of course. But since he might not even know of the existence of results in another specialist's field, he may not know when or to whom he should refer a particular patient.

The Diagnostic Computer Now imagine the following scene. After your doctor has listened to your complaint and has made his examination, he enters the information he has obtained in a computer terminal on his desk. The computer displays a list of possible diseases or disorders whose symptoms match those that were entered. For each disorder, the computer suggests additional tests to determine if that disorder is indeed the problem.

The process of making tests and entering the results might be repeated several times until the cause of the problem was determined. At this point, the computer could supply a list of standard treatments, with statistics on the effectiveness of each one. If still more information were needed, the computer could supply references to the medical literature and perhaps even the relevant papers themselves.

It may sound as though the computer is threatening to replace the doctor, but this isn't so. For one thing, the doctor would call on the computer only for puzzling cases, not for everyday complaints. And the doctor certainly would not accept the computer's suggestions blindly. He would consider them in the light of his own knowledge and experience. Before following them, he almost certainly would look up in medical journals the papers cited by the computer. The purpose of the computer is not to replace the doctor but to suggest things to him that he might otherwise overlook.

Nurses and Paramedics When medical decisions have to be made by persons less well trained than a doctor, then the help of a computer becomes even more important.

A nurse in a school or industrial plant, for instance, has no authority or expertise to treat major illnesses. But she (or he) does have to make recommendations. She must either tell a patient that his problem is minor and not to worry, or she must urge him to consult a physician at once.

Thus, a nurse could benefit greatly from an interactive program that would suggest what questions to ask, what tests to make, and so

175

on. When all the information has been entered, the computer displays a list of possible disorders and the seriousness of each.

This kind of help would be even more vital to paramedics who must give first aid in emergencies. Sometimes they have to treat major illnesses and injuries until the patient can be moved to a hospital. The current practice is for the paramedics to communicate with a doctor by radio. But a portable computer might well be able to give as good advice as a doctor who has not actually seen the patient.

In the future, a portable medical computer probably will be an essential piece of equipment for people such as mariners, mountain climbers, explorers, astronauts, and anyone else who plans to be out of touch with civilization for a while.

MYCIN MYCIN is a computer program designed to diagnose bacterial blood infections and recommend treatment.

To be sure, the agent causing the infection could be identified in the laboratory. But to do this requires growing a culture, which may take a week or so. Treatment cannot be delayed that long. It must be begun immediately. If the bacteria causing the infection cannot be identified, then a broad-spectrum antibiotic (which kills many types of bacteria) must be used. But this approach is considered inferior to using an antibiotic that specifically attacks the bacteria causing the infection.

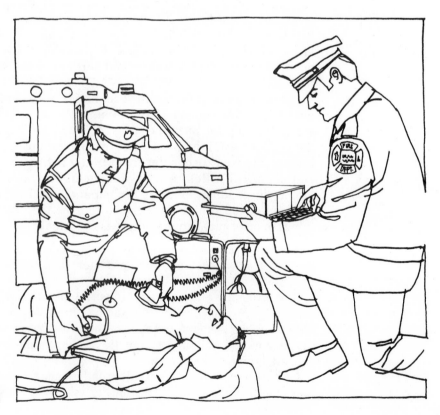

In a dialog with a nurse or doctor, MYCIN attempts to pin down the cause of the infection. It starts by collecting general information —the patient's name (for reference), sex, and age and the time the symptoms appeared. The questions then become more specific asking what tests have been made and what results were observed.

After all the questions have been asked and answered, the program lists the organisms that could be responsible for the symptoms and the results of the tests. It then recommends specific dosages of specific antibiotics, telling which suspected organism each antibiotic is intended to combat.

An important feature of MYCIN is that the physician can question the program about the reasons for its conclusions and recommendations. The program keeps a record of its chain of reasoning—why it made each assumption and how it reached its conclusion. This feature is essential for any diagnostic system. Doctors are unlikely to use any system if they are expected to accept its results blindly.

Characteristics of Diagnostic Systems A medical diagnostic system must have several abilities. The performance of such systems will depend on the progress of research in providing these capabilities.

- *Database Management.* The system must have access to a large collection of medical data. Such a collection of information is called a *database*. Even more important, the computer has to find in the database the information it needs for a particular diagnosis. This means that the information must be indexed in various ways—by disease, by symptons, by drugs used, and so on.

- *Natural Language Processing.* Because busy medical workers don't have time to learn computer languages, the computer must speak to them in their own language. For American doctors, this would be English augmented by a vocabulary of medical terms.

- *Reasoning.* The system must be able to do the same kind of reasoning a doctor does. Logic is seldom so simple in the real world as in the ideal world of the pure mathematician. For instance, some of the necessary data may not be available. Some of the facts may be uncertain; an error may have been made in a test, for instance. Under these circumstances, reasoning becomes a matter of educated guessing, of finding the most likely conclusion consistent with known facts.

The Intelligence Amplifier Computer-assisted diagnosis is a good example of what we mean when we call a computer an *intelligence amplifier*. In the foreseeable future, we are unlikely to turn medical diagnosis entirely over to computers. But when a computer is placed in the hands of a trained doctor, nurse, or paramedic, the two working together can function at a far higher level than either one could alone. The computer amplifies the skills of the human. This kind of man-machine interaction should become increasingly common in the future.

COLLECTING MEDICAL HISTORIES

Improving the Use of Trained Medical Personnel   An up-to-date medical history is crucial for effective diagnosis and treatment. Yet highly trained doctors and nurses can spend an inordinate amount of time collecting the necessary information. Nurses often spend as much as half their time interviewing patients. And doctors are not much better off.

In order to use these trained individuals more effectively, some hospitals and clinics have started to use computers to conduct the preliminary medical interview.

Patient Reactions   Do patients feel this procedure "dehumanizes" them or "turns them into numbers"? Apparently not. Many patients even prefer to be interviewed by a computer instead of by a human nurse or physician.

Why? For one thing, the computer allows the patient some control over the interview. The patient can take as long as necessary to answer a question. The computer never gets impatient. The patient has the privilege of not entering any answer at all to a particular question; this is considerably easier than telling a doctor or a nurse, "It's none of your business."

Patients may positively prefer the computer when it comes to sensitive matters, such as sexual disorders. Talking about these can be especially embarrassing when the patient and a human interviewer are of different sexes.

Equipment and Procedures   Any computer terminal can be used for asking the questions and entering the responses, but those with display screens are by far the best. The need to type answers should be minimized or eliminated. Patients with certain disorders may be unable to operate a typewriter. And the typewriter keyboard is supremely confusing for those who aren't used to it.

An alternative is to ask a question and then display a "menu" of possible responses (including "none of the above"). The patient uses a light pen to point out the correct response. The questions may be accompanied by diagrams of the human body. The patient can use the light pen to point out the locations of pain or other problems on the diagrams. Some systems use slides in addition to the computer display screen.

Medical Information Systems   The medical history interview would not have to be repeated so often—perhaps never have to be conducted at all—if the medical records of each patient were kept in a central data bank. The data bank would be available to the entire medical community. After each examination, the doctor would update the patient's records in the data bank.

Naturally, care would have to be taken to protect the patient's

privacy and the confidentiality of the doctor-patient relationship. No one should have access to the patient's file without his consent, except possibly in cases of medical emergency where the patient is in no condition to give consent.

Other Legal Problems   Privacy is not the only legal question raised by computerized patient interviewing and medical information systems. What if the computer does not ask the right questions to elicit some vital piece of information? Or what if it omits some crucial information from the report it prepares for the doctor? Or gets patients' records mixed up?

Who will bear the legal responsibility in these cases? The hospital? The doctor? The manufacturer of the hardware and software? Or perhaps a service bureau that runs the system for the hospital? As with most legal questions, the answers to these probably will have to await judges' rulings in actual cases involving alleged malperformance of medical information systems.

PATIENT MONITORING

Most hospital patients require little monitoring besides the occasional check by a doctor or nurse. But a few, such as those suffering from heart conditions, have to be monitored constantly so that any adverse change can be countered immediately.

179

A computer is well suited to this task. Not only can it monitor a large number of patients at the same time, it also can monitor a large number of variables for each patient. And the computer will never allow its attention to be distracted from the job at hand.

The following are some of the variables a computer might monitor: blood pressure, heart rate, PVC (premature ventricular contraction) rate, cardiac output, venous pressure, and even urine output.

Most monitoring systems use sensors attached to the patient's body, like those used in the space program to send medical information on the astronauts back to earth. The information the computer is monitoring also can be displayed on a screen or chart at the patient's bedside for use by attending physicians and nurses.

In the simplest kind of monitor, the physician assigns a highest permissible value and a lowest permissible value to each quantity being monitored. When the value of one of these quantities falls outside the preassigned range, the computer sounds an alarm. It displays at a central location the name of the patient, the room number, the offending variable, and its value.

A more elaborate system might look for patterns in the values of the variables that indicate the imminent onset of certain conditions. This kind of system could warn of impending trouble before a life-and-death emergency occurred.

Portable Medical Monitors Microprocessors have made possible miniature medical monitors that easily can be carried by seriously ill patients.

A heart patient, for instance, could wear a portable computer that continuously would monitor his electrocardiogram, the electrical signals the heart generates and the doctors use to analyze its action. When the computer detected an abnormality, it would warn the patient in time for him to get to a hospital before an attack occurred. If the abnormality were less serious, the computer could warn the patient to lie down and rest, to take certain medicine, or to consult a doctor. If an attack occurred, the monitor could sound an alarm audible to bystanders.

Portable monitors also can aid diagnosis by collecting and recording the details of important events that occur only rarely. For instance, people with heart disease suffer from arrhythmias, momentary disturbances in the natural rhythm of the heart. Electrocardiograms of these arrhythmias provide valuable information about the condition of the heart.

The difficulty is that only a few of the hundred thousand heartbeats in a twenty-four-hour period are arrhythmias. Thus, a twelve- to twenty-four-hour electrocardiogram is needed in order to detect any arrhythmias at all. And, even then, finding them is tedious, since each arrhythmia is buried among many normal heartbeats.

The solution to the problem is a recently developed portable

heartbeat monitor. A microprocessor inside the monitor analyzes the

electrocardiogram of each heartbeat. It ignores the electrocardiograms for normal heartbeats but stores in memory those for arrhythmias.

The patient can wear the portable monitor through a normal
day's activities. At the end of the day, the patient connects his
monitor to a *modem*, which is a device for transmitting data over
telephone lines. The data on the arrhythmias for the day is sent over
the telephone to the hospital computer, which stores them for
analysis.

This is an important application of what is called *pattern recognition*. The monitor must be able to distinguish arrhythmias from
normal heartbeats. That is, it must recognize the patterns in the
electrocardiogram that signal an arrhythmia. It must be able to do
this in spite of electrical interference that the monitor might pick up.
Also, the pattern-recognition program must be adaptable, since an
arrhythmia for one patient is a normal heartbeat for another.

The hospital computer that analyzes the arrhythmias also will
apply pattern recognition in trying to extract medically useful information from the electrocardiograms it has received.

HOSPITAL
ADMINISTRATION

A modern hospital is a complex organization. The activities of many
people must be coordinated in order to care for a single patient.

One area in which this complexity shows up is record keeping. The results of each of the many tests and procedures have to be recorded for use by the doctor, and the cost of each must be recorded so the patient can be billed for it. If the bill is to be paid by insurance, as is so often the case now, then more paperwork must be done for the insurance company.

More and more hospitals are using computers to handle the records. When a person becomes a patient, personal background information is entered on a computer terminal. Thereafter, when any test is performed, medication given, or other procedure carried out, the details are entered on a terminal.

The computer uses these entries to maintain up-to-date records for each patient. When a doctor visits his patients, all he needs to do is query the computer to determine the medical status of each one. And when the patient's stay is over, the computer will produce the necessary bills and insurance applications to assure that everything is paid for.

Computers have become so important in hospitals that there is a special computer language oriented toward hospital computing. The language is called the Massachusetts General Hospital Utility Multi-Programming System. The reason it is called that is because the name abbreviates to MUMPS.

COMPUTERS IN MEDICAL TECHNOLOGY

Physicians do not work alone. They require the support of an elaborate medical technology to make tests that range from a simple blood-cell count to elaborate probes of the body with x-rays and ultrasound. Computers are now used extensively in medical technology.

Interpreting the Outputs of Analytical Instruments Several of the most important instruments for chemical analysis work in similar ways. The sample to be analyzed is separated into component parts that differ in some physical property, such as mass. The instrument draws a graph with several peaks, one for each component. From the locations and the sizes of the peaks, a chemist can deduce the composition of the original sample.

Interpreting the graph is a time-consuming and error-prone procedure. But, instead of drawing a graph, the instrument can send the results of its measurements to a computer. The computer compares the output of the instrument with patterns stored in its memory. After making the comparisons and doing any necessary calculations, the computer prints out an analysis of the sample. The operator gets a finished analysis instead of a graph, which would require further interpretation.

The graphs produced by some types of analytical instruments can be displayed on a computer terminal. Programs are under development that will interpret such graphs and display the composition of the sample that was analyzed.

Automating Laboratory Procedures Most laboratory analyses require performing certain operations (mixing reagents, heating, centrifuging, and so on) and noting the results (color changes, formation of precipitates, and so on). A complete analysis calls for many such steps. Which step is to be carried out at a particular point may depend on the results obtained in previous steps.

Progress has been made toward automating these procedures. When this automation has been perfected, a computer will be able to control the entire analysis from start to finish. The computer will direct all the tests, collect the results, and print out the analysis afterwards.

But even when this degree of automation is not practical, technicians still can save time and reduce errors by entering the results of each test on a computer terminal. The computer keeps track of all the tests made on each sample. It can guide a technician through a complicated series of tests. And, when all the tests have been performed, the computer will carry out any necessary calculations and print a summary of all the data collected for the sample as well as the final analysis.

Computed Tomography Some modern medical examination procedures simply would not be practical without computers. These procedures require extensive computation to get the desired results from the data collected. Without the computer, the calculations would take months or years, and, by then, the results probably would be too late to be of any use.

Computed tomography is the best example of such a procedure. *Tomography* comes from a Greek word meaning *slice,* an indication of exactly what tomography does. It presents the physician with a picture of a cross-sectional slice of the human body.

183

Tomography uses x-rays to look inside the body. But it differs from conventional x-ray pictures in several ways. A conventional x-ray picture is simply a collection of shadows, since x-rays cannot be focused with lenses. It is related to a true picture of the inside of your body much as your shadow is related to your photograph.

The internal organs of the body do not stand out well in conventional x-ray pictures, because these organs differ only slightly from the surrounding tissues in their ability to absorb x-rays. (To make them stand out better, patient's may have to endure unpleasant procedures, such as having their organs inflated with air or swallowing obnoxious substances.) Finally, in conventional x-ray pictures, the shadows of several organs may overlap, obscuring the details of each.

In tomography, x-rays are sent through the body in different directions. The degree to which the body absorbs the x-rays in each direction is measured. From this information, the computer can construct a detailed picture of one slice through the human body.

Figure 12-1 illustrates the setup. The patient lies horizontally. A mechanism carrying a source of x-rays and x-ray detectors rotates around the patient in a vertical plane; that is, the x-ray source goes from above the patient to below the patient and back above again.

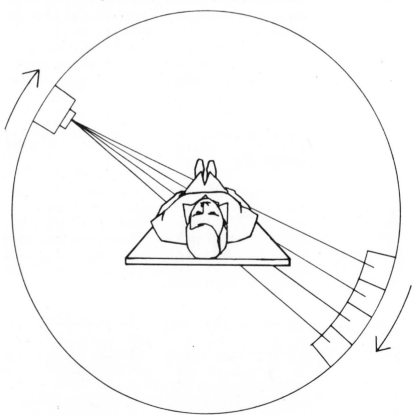

Figure 12-1. The setup for making a tomogram. The patient lies horizontally. The x-ray source and the x-ray detectors rotate around the patient in a vertical plane.

The x-ray detectors move so that they are always on the opposite side of the patient from the x-ray source.

As the mechanism rotates around the patient, the x-ray source sends out bursts of x-rays. These pass through the patient and on to the detectors, where their intensities are recorded. All the x-rays pass through the slice that is being observed. The angle at which each burst passes through the patient, as well as its intensity when it reaches the detectors, is recorded.

From the recorded data, it is easy to determine the degree to which an x-ray beam is absorbed as it passes through the patient in different directions. But without further processing, this information is of little use. That's because each x-ray beam passed through many different organs as it traveled through the patient's body. Part of the x-ray beam was absorbed by each organ it passed through. Therefore, the degree to which the beam was absorbed in passing through the patient's body tells us nothing about any particular organ.

Here's where the computer comes to the rescue. By taking the absorption data for beams sent through a slice of the body from many different directions, the computer can work out the degree to which the beams must have been absorbed at each point inside the slice. The results are presented as a picture in which different colors correspond to different degrees of absorption. The internal organs stand out vividly in this picture.

Since thousands of items of absorption data have to be processed and since the results have to be calculated for thousands of points inside the observed slice, the entire procedure would be impractical without computers.

COMPUTERS IN MEDICAL RESEARCH

The uses of computers in research are many and varied. The following are a few of the most common ones.

■ *Controlling laboratory apparatus and collecting data.* The computer allows experiments to be run for long periods of time without constant human attention.

■ *Statistical analysis of the results of experiments.* Statistical analysis allows useful results to be extracted despite unavoidable errors in the data.

■ *Reducing experimental data to a useful form.* The readings from laboratory apparatus are seldom the final sought-after results. Computations have to be performed to extract useful information from the raw data. Tomography is an example of this.

■ *Simulations of real systems.* The purpose of a simulation can be either to do experiments on the model that would be impractical with the actual system or to test our knowledge of the actual system by

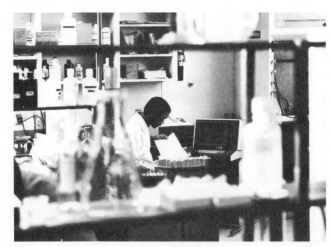

Computers are widely used in medical research to control laboratory apparatus and to analyze and display the data obtained from experiments.

incorporating our ideas into a model and comparing the model's behavior with that of the actual system.

The following are three specific examples of the use of computers in medical research.

Cineangiograms   A key indicator of heart performance is the way the volume of the left ventricle changes as the heart pumps. These volume changes can be observed by taking a *cineangiogram*, an x-ray motion picture of the heart.

Unfortunately, a manual frame-by-frame analysis of the cineangiogram is tedious, fallible, and time-consuming. The results may come too late for a seriously ill heart patient.

But a computer can do the same analysis in five minutes. Researchers are working to develop computer-analyzed cineangiograms into a powerful diagnostic technique.

Contour Maps of the Body   Studies of such things as spinal deformation in children or weight loss in astronauts require highly accurate three-dimensional measurements of the human body. In a technique similar to aerial mapping, overlapping photographs are taken of the body. A plotting device identifies reference points in each photograph. Over 40,000 reference points are used. A computer converts the reference points into a contour map of the human body.

Model of the Inner Ear   Millions of people suffer from hearing disorders that can be traced to the inner ear, or cochlea. Little is known about the inner ear; it is difficult to get at and extremely sensitive to damage.

These facts just about rule out experiments with live subjects. But now, a mathematical model of the inner ear has been constructed, and from it has been developed a computer model. The experiments that cannot be done on the actual inner ear can be simulated on the computer. These experiments could lead to new methods of diagnosis and treatment for inner-ear disorders.

FOR FURTHER READING

Brus, John M. "A New Generation of Biomedical Instruments." *Creative Computing*, July-Aug. 1977, pp. 40-41.

Forbes, Farhad; Garland, Harry; and Takao, Tsuiki. "The Telltale Heart: EKG Processing by Microprocessor." *Creative Computing*, July-Aug. 1978, pp. 48-51.

Hastings, Susan. "Psychiatric Assessment via Computer." *Creative Computing*, July-Aug. 1977, p. 34.

Holmes, Edith. "Mini Report on Medicine." *Computerworld*, April 9, 1975, pp. 7-11.

Spencer, Donald. *Computers in Society.* Rochelle Park, N. J.: Hayden Book Co., 1974, pp. 28-50.

Swindell, William, and Barrett, Harrison H. "Computerized Tomography." *Physics Today*, Dec. 1977, pp. 32-41.

Weintraub, Pamela. "The Miraculous Medical Microprocessor: A Look into the Future." *Creative Computing*, July-Aug. 1977, pp. 41-42.

REVIEW QUESTIONS

1. Why is it difficult for even the most conscientious and energetic doctor to stay up-to-date on the latest medical developments?

2. How can a computer help a doctor make a diagnosis?

3. What medical personnel other than doctors can benefit from computer-assisted diagnosis? Is their need likely to be greater or less than that of doctors?

4. Describe the MYCIN program.

5. Give three necessary characteristics for computer diagnostic systems.

6. What do we mean when we say that a computer serves as an *intelligence amplifier*?

7. What is gained by turning the collection of medical histories over to computers?

8. What are typical reactions of patients whose medical histories are recorded by computers?

9. What are some legal problems raised by computer-collected medical histories and medical information systems?

10. What situations indicate computer monitoring of a patient?

11. What are some of the quantities a computer might monitor?

12. Describe how a portable medical monitor might be used.

13. What is the advantage of using a portable medical monitor to collect data on arrhythmias?

14. What is MUMPS?

15. How can a computer be used to interpret the outputs of analytical instruments?

16. Describe how computers can be used to automate laboratory procedures.

17. What is the advantage of computed tomography over conventional x-ray pictures?

18. Describe briefly how computed tomography works. Why is a computer essential if the technique is to be practical?

19. In what four ways can the computer be used to aid medical research?

20. Give three specific examples of the use of computers in medical research.

DISCUSSION QUESTIONS

1. In what situations do you think society might allow a person less skilled than a doctor to practice medicine with the aid of a computer? Discuss the moral and ethical questions such situations would raise.

2. What legal and ethical problems would arise if a doctor relied on a computer for a diagnosis—and the computer turned out to be wrong?

3. Argue the pros and cons of using computers to collect medical histories. Would you personally prefer to reveal sensitive medical information to a person or to a computer? How is your answer influenced by your past experiences with the medical profession?

4. Discuss the legal and ethical problems raised by medical information systems. For example, under what circumstances should the information in such a system be used without a person's explicit permission? Under what circumstances should it be supplied to insurance companies?

5. Computed tomography has been specifically singled out as a technique that raises the cost of medical care; once the equipment has been purchased, there is a tendency to use it as much as possible. Discuss.

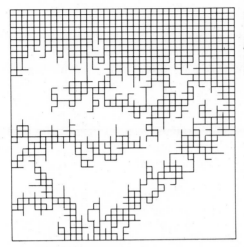

CHAPTER 13

COMPUTERS
AND
POLITICS

One feature of American government of which we are particularly proud is our system of free elections. But this system imposes a heavy burden on the government: tabulating the votes of an entire nation, or even of a state or city, is a tremendous data-processing task.

Nor is the official election the only event that requires data processing. Political campaign managers need to know before the campaign what issues concern the voters, which voters are most likely to be receptive to a particular candidate, and (most important of all) which voters are likely to contribute to the campaign.

Computers are now used extensively for processing election returns and the data collected in political polls. And, for the future, computer technology offers radically different ways of holding elections. We could, for instance, vote from our homes over TV cables or telephone lines. If such techniques could encourage more people to care about good government, our country would benefit enormously.

POLLS
AND
PREDICTIONS

People have always been curious about the future. Once they **189** consulted oracles, astrologers, soothsayers, witches and crystal-ball gazers. Nowadays, they often turn to computers. Sometimes the computers do better than the witches, sometimes worse.

The Poll Takers The concept behind polling is to go around and ask people how they will vote. If you ask enough people and they all tell you the truth and don't change their minds later, then you will know in advance how the election will come out.

Ideally, the poll taker should question every registered voter. But that's out of the question. So pollsters do the next best thing and query a much smaller group called a *sample*.

Choosing the sample is tricky. Bad sample choices caused some early pollsters to make fools of themselves. The most celebrated case of this was the poll the *Literary Digest* conducted in 1936 for the Roosevelt-Landon election. After polling a large number of people, whose names were taken from the telephone directory and automobile registration lists, the *Digest* predicted a landslide for Landon. But, in 1936, automobiles and telephones were not nearly as common as they are now, and many people who had neither favored Roosevelt. Roosevelt won by a landslide, and the *Literary Digest* went out of business shortly thereafter.

There are two ways to choose a sample. One way is to use a *random sample*. As the name implies, the people to be polled are chosen at random. If the sample is large enough—enough people are polled—the randomly chosen sample will be representative of the electorate as a whole.

To get a truly representative random sample may require interviewing a very large number of people. This number can be reduced by using a *stratified sample*. Instead of being completely random, a stratified sample consists of all important groups of voters represented in the proper proportions. Within each group, the individuals to be interviewed are chosen at random.

Thus, a stratified sample would include so many Democrats, so many Republicans, so many whites, so many blacks, so many Catholics, so many Protestants, and so on. The number of, say, Democrats in the sample would be proportional to the number of Democrats in the population as a whole. The same would be true for the other groups.

A stratified sample can be smaller than a random sample because we don't have to depend on chance to see that all important groups of voters are represented in the correct proportions. On the other hand, great care must be taken in deciding what groups to include. To leave out one that should be there may invalidate all predictions.

Planning a poll and interpreting the data after the poll has been taken are major data-processing tasks. Because computers can do the data processing quickly and inexpensively, they make possible more polls during a campaign, with large samples and at reasonable costs to the candidates and the news media.

Election-Night Predictions   All the commercial television networks now predict the outcomes of national elections early on election night. The predictions are based on early returns from key precincts. Here computers are even more important than they are in polling, because the analysis must be done quickly if the predictions are to be useful.

(However, the story is told that once upon an election night the computer broke down at a major network. In desperation, the network staff simplified the prediction procedures on the spot and carried out the processing by hand, with perhaps a little educated guesswork thrown in. No one seemed to notice the difference.)

Politicians have been heard to grumble about election-night predictions. That's because the polls close three hours later on the West Coast than in the East and even later in Hawaii. Therefore, the polls are still open in the West when the networks start issuing predictions based on early returns from East Coast precincts. How will this affect the West Coast voters? Will they stay away from the polls if they think the election already has been decided? Or, worse, will they be influenced to vote for the apparent winner, making the prediction a self-fulfilling one?

Some politicians have gone so far as to propose that the networks be forbidden to broadcast predictions in states where the polls have not closed. But any law to that effect probably would be unconstitutional, since it would conflict with the freedom of the press.

**CAMPAIGN
PLANNING AND
MANAGEMENT**

Networks and newspapers are by no means alone in commissioning polls. The campaign managers themselves use polls before, during, and after the campaign. They also use computers for everything from fund raising and identifying ethnic groups to getting out the vote for their candidates on election day.

Campaign Polling   A campaign may use a variety of different polls for different purposes. The following six types are typical.

(1) Issue Definition Poll.   This poll tries to find out what issues are of concern to different groups of voters.

(2) Bench Mark Poll.   This poll classifies the voters according to age, race, sex, political party, and so on. It tries to determine what the members of each group know about and think of the candidate. This kind of poll can be used to determine whether or not it's worth the candidate's while to run in the first place.

(3) Tracking Poll.   This poll brings the bench mark poll up-to-date. By taking tracking polls throughout the campaign, the campaign manager determines with which groups the candidate is making gains and with which ones more work is needed.

(4) Target Voter Survey.   This poll checks on the effectiveness of the campaign with a particular group of voters, such as the members of a particular religion or the people living in a certain part of the country.

(5) Communications Survey.   This tries to find out how well the campaign's advertising and slogans are getting through to the voters.

(6) Post-Mortem.   A post-mortem poll tries to find out why the candidate lost the election so that the same mistakes won't be repeated next time.

Voter Simulation   For the 1960 election, the Simulmatics corporation introduced a new approach to polling.

Before then, pollsters had to be content with a "statistical snapshot" of the electorate at one moment in time. The snapshot revealed the voters' opinions at that instant but gave no clue as to how those opinions might change in the future. When it was suspected that the opinions might have changed, a new poll had to be taken (such as the "tracking polls" already mentioned). The new polls gave additional snapshots of the voters' opinions.

In fact, the practice often was—and still is—to take a series of polls during the campaign, a kind of "statistical motion picture" of the electorate. This allows opinion changes to be followed but not predicted.

The Simulmatics people were interested not just in observing opinion changes but in predicting them in advance. That way they could tell a candidate beforehand how people *would* react to his raising a certain issue or taking a certain position. Their idea was to construct a computer model of the electorate. They would use the model to simulate the voters' reactions to candidates, issues, and positions.

The Simulmatics model, consisting of a giant table with 480 rows and 52 columns, was stored in the memory of a computer. Each of the 480 rows corresponded to a group of voters as defined by their social, religious, and economic characteristics. One row, for instance, might be for "Southern, urban, Protestant, male, lower-income Democrats," another for "Eastern, rural, Catholic, female, upper-income Republicans," and so on.

The number 480, by the way, achieved minor fame as the title of a political novel by Eugene Burdick. The famous number was largely dictated by the main-memory limitations of 1960 computers. With modern computers, many more groups could be used.

With a few exceptions, each of the fifty-two columns corresponded to a political issue, such as "Attitude toward U.N." or "Concern with rising prices."

Each entry in the table lay at the intersection of a row corresponding to a particular group of voters and a column corresponding to a particular issue. The entry specified how the group of voters in question stood on the corresponding issue. Each entry consisted of four numbers: these gave the number of people polled on the corresponding issue and the number of responses that were for, against, and undecided.

With this information, Simulmatics hoped to be able to predict how each group would react to each issue. Therefore, they could tell a candidate how his stand on a certain position would affect his vote getting.

For example, in the election of 1960, Simulmatics was able to advise John Kennedy that his Catholic religion should be played up rather than down. The simulation showed that Kennedy could not hope for the votes of confirmed anti-Catholics, no matter how he handled the issue. But further airing of the religious issue would put Catholics firmly behind him. Even more, it would gain him further support from Protestants and Jews who were strongly opposed to religious intolerance. Raising the issue could not do him any more harm, and it might well do some good.

Ethnic Identification   Several of the techniques discussed so far have involved classifying voters into groups based on such things as religion, ethnic background, and income level.

There are more uses for these groupings than just polling. For instance, a respected member of a particular group can write and send a campaign letter to other members of that group. Or the

members of a group can be sent a letter emphasizing issues that strongly concern that group. Or requests for contributions can be sent to the groups most likely to favor a particular candidate.

But how can we identify the members of a particular group? Sometimes the necessary information can be obtained from public records or from the records the campaign has been able to purchase from various organizations. For instance, the membership list of an environmental organization would contain the names of people known to be concerned about environmental issues. The subscriber list for a conservative newspaper would provide names of people with conservative views, and so on.

But sometimes the job is more difficult. For instance, how can we identify people with a particular ethnic background? Once, when every large city had its Italian neighborhood, its Jewish neighborhood, and so on, this was easy. Now, Italians, Jews, and other ethnics are likely to be found anywhere. How can they be singled out for special campaign mailings?

A computer program has been developed to do this job. The program works by analyzing people's names. That is, it looks for Italian names, Jewish names, and so on.

An early version of the program used a list of common names for each ethnic group. Each person's name was checked to see if it was on the list of Italian names, the list of Jewish names, and so on. Later versions of the program were more sophisticated. In addition to using tables of first and last names, they used tables of prefixes and suffixes likely to occur in names of different ethnic origins.

The author of the program claims it can identify members of seven different ethnic groups with 90 percent accuracy and 90 percent completeness. The program can approach 100 percent accuracy at some sacrifice in completeness. That is, almost all the people it identifies as belonging to a particular ethnic group actually will belong to it, but the program may overlook some members of the group. Or, the program can approach 100 percent completeness at some sacrifice in accuracy. That is, it can find almost everybody who belongs to a particular group but at the expense of including some people who do not actually belong.

Fund Raising　No political campaign is going to get very far without money. For one thing, all those polls we've been talking about cost plenty. And, of course, there are other reasons. For instance, advertising, particularly television advertising, is notoriously expensive. Nowadays, the money has to come from the people. Reforms in campaign spending laws have done away with the traditional "fat cats" who footed campaign bills in return for special favors after the candidate was in office.

Political fund raising is handled much like any other direct-mail campaign, such as selling magazine subscriptions. It starts with mailing lists, which now are commodities that are bought, sold, and rented, not only by political campaigns but by most business concerns as well. These lists originate with clubs, magazines, businesses, and other political campaigns that have sold their mailing lists to mailing-list companies. The mailing lists often come on magnetic tape, ready for use with a computer.

The value of a mailing list depends on how specific it is and, how likely it is to yield results. A general list would consist of people who (because of their memberships, political affiliations, or other reasons) might possibly be interested in contributing. A better list would consist of the names of people who had contributed to a candidate with a similar political background in the past. An even better list would consist of the names of people who had contributed to the present candidate in the past.

The first two kinds of lists can be purchased. The last kind has to be developed by the candidate himself. A good set of mailing lists is one of the most valuable assets a campaign organization can have.

Once the mailing lists have been obtained, they can be used in several ways. The cheapest way is simply to have the computer print out the mailing labels. These are stuck on envelopes carrying appeals and campaign literature. But it is often more effective to have the computer print the entire appeal. The computer can insert the name of the prospective contributor throughout the message, making it seem like a personal letter. Also, the content of the letter can be chosen differently for different groups of contributors.

(Having a computer insert the addressee's name at several points throughout a letter seems like a transparent trick to people familiar with computers. But many people who receive these letters feel that the use of their names proves that they received a personal appeal from the candidate.)

Canvassing   When election day finally arrives, every political party is interested in "getting out the vote." But the vote a party wants to get out is the vote for its candidate. It certainly doesn't want to spend time urging someone to vote who is likely to vote for the opposition. How can election workers be directed to the people who are most likely to vote the right way?

A computer can keep track of every registered voter in a city or state. The voters can be contacted, and those who express an interest in a particular party or candidate can be noted. Also, it can be noted which voters have received favors from the party, such as employment for relatives. On election day, the computer can use this information to print a list of people for each campaign worker to contact, urge to vote, and transport to the polls if necessary.

COUNTING
THE
BALLOTS

Tabulating the results of an election is a major data-processing task. Depending on whether it is a city, state, or national election, hundreds, thousands, even millions of votes have to be tallied.

Complicating this task is the fact that some of the issues to be voted on will be different in different precincts. Because of this, many different kinds of ballots have to be counted. And election officials are often under intense pressure from the press to do the job quickly—perhaps in time for a certain newspaper edition or television news program.

Computers can do this kind of job well, of course. But, as with any other large computer application, running a vote-counting operation smoothly is easier said than done. In the early 1970s, when computerized ballot counting was first introduced on a substantial scale, there were some spectacular election-night foul-ups. Computer problems sometimes delayed returns for hours. And these foul-ups usually were well-publicized by the press while it waited impatiently for the election results.

Pitfalls　In some cases, the problems have been with the machinery itself, such as the special card readers that read the votes from the ballots. A machine that handles papers or cards can jam, particularly if a mutilated card is fed into it. This is no problem if the operator knows how to unjam the machine or if a repairperson is on the scene. But it can be a major problem if poorly trained operators have no idea what is wrong or what to do about it.

In one case, for instance, the problem was traced to a machine that punched information from ballots onto paper tape. The operator had failed to insert a required "end of file" code after the data from each precinct. Before the computer would process the erroneous paper tapes, someone had to reprogram it so that it would not expect the missing "end of file" codes.

One solution to this kind of problem is to have a trial run before the election, using the same personnel and equipment that will be used on election night. During the trial run, special test data for which the results are known is processed.

But even this reasonable procedure can backfire. In one case, a reel of test data got mixed up with the tapes produced on election night. The test data was included in the reported election results!

Operator training is not the only reason for holding dry runs. After one city had turned down a request from election observers for a dry run, it was found on election night that the card readers would not read the ballots because their left edges were torn. Results were held up until the computer could be reprogrammed to read the ballots backwards.

Fraud　Some people may be actively working to make the count come out wrong—wrong in favor of their candidate. Some computing equipment vendors have nurtured the myth that, with computerized vote tabulation, fraud is technically impossible. But this is nonsense. A programmer with access to a vote-counting program would have little trouble modifying it to bias the results. A defense against this kind of tampering would be to keep a certified copy of the program under lock and key until election night. At that time, the certified program could be loaded into the computer under proper supervision.

But even that precaution could be futile. For at least one vote-counting program, it has been shown that the results could be biased by tampering with the computer's operating system. The observers, whose job it is to keep an election honest, probably don't even know that a computer *has* an operating system. How could they cope with fraud caused by tampering with something they don't even know exists? In the future, at least one election observer should be required to have a background in computer science.

Another myth is that computer professionals would never be guilty of fraud. Sadly, there is little support for this assumption. Computer operators and programmers have used their skills to embezzle money from their employers. And professionals in every field do break the law: remember, most of the defendants in the infamous Watergate scandal were lawyers.

Actually, most professionals are honest. But, inevitably, a few are subject to blackmail, receptive to bribery, or simply willing to do anything to see their candidate win. And people with dirty work to do seem to have an uncanny ability to locate the few people willing to cooperate.

Perhaps the best protection against fraud is to recount some or all of the ballots, either by hand or using a computer system with different hardware, software, and operating personnel. An independent machine count has the advantage that all the ballots can be recounted.

197

If hand recounting is to be used, it may be possible to recount only a sample of the ballots. Statisticians can tell how large a sample is required for reliable results. If the results of recounting the sample are far out of line with the original count, then the original count was in error, and all the ballots should be recounted.

To date, no case of computer-based election fraud has come to light. This means one of two things: either such fraud has not taken place, or it has taken place successfully.

ELECTRONIC VOTING

So far, we've assumed that people will continue to vote in the future as they do now—by marking ballots or manipulating levers in voting machines. But instead of going to the polls, people could vote electronically from their own homes. Such elections would be far less expensive for the government and more convenient for voters; thus, many more elections could be held, giving people a greater voice in how their government is run.

Televote A pioneer system of this kind, called Televote, has been tried out in the San Jose (California) Unified School District.

To get public opinion on a school issue, officials send a multiple-choice questionnaire to all authorized voters—the parents of schoolchildren and the children themselves, if they are over the age of twelve. After a voter makes his choices, he dials a special telephone number, a six-digit identification code, and then the numbers indicating his choices. The system punches this information on paper tape for later tabulation by a computer. (In an up-to-date system, a microcomputer could take the calls directly, eliminating the need for the paper tape.)

QUBE This prototype information utility, mentioned in chapter 8, is part of an advanced cable-TV system that provides viewers with everything from all-day nonviolent programs for preschool children to soft-core pornography. Educational films also are included, as are first-run movies, live sporting events, and specialized programs for doctors and lawyers.

But QUBE is not all one-way. By pressing buttons on a device attached to the television set, the viewers can express their opinions of politicians, amateur talent, or features in a local paper. Although the system is not used for official voting, it can make possible a true dialog between a political candidate and a large audience by letting the audience express its opinion on every issue the candidate raises. This kind of on-the-spot feedback could be worth considerably more to the candidate than a great many traditional polls.

Systems similar to QUBE also are being tried out in England and
Japan.

Possible Future Voting Systems   The future of electronic voting is much more likely to go the way of QUBE than of Televote.

For frequent widespread use (say, several times a month over a city, state, or the whole country), printed ballots would be cumbersome and expensive. For this reason, most proposals for electronic voting have the issues presented on television. With television, people for and against an issue could speak on the same program. The viewer would have the arguments for both sides fresh in mind when he voted.

If the voting could be done instantaneously, the results could be given to the participants while the program was still on the air. The result would be a kind of "national town meeting" where the voters would be able to express themselves on the issues their elected representatives are debating.

If instantaneous response was desired, collecting the results by telephone almost surely would not work. The lines would quickly jam as everyone tried to vote at once. People who could not get through the first few times would just give up trying.

But, by the time electronic voting becomes widespread, most homes probably will subscribe to an information utility like those described in chapter 8. Each person or family could enter a vote into a computer terminal connected to the home computer. A central computer then would poll all the home computers to collect the votes.

For those without home computers, a special-purpose "voting termi-nal" could be provided. The computers would communicate over the TV cable as described in chapter 8.

Possible Problems   One problem with electronic voting would be the positive identification of the voter. There must be some way to ascertain that each person votes only once and only on those issues appropriate for the precinct in which the person resides. The problem of positive identification of computer users, which we will examine again in a later chapter, has not been completely solved. But it probably will be solved for business and banking purposes long before electronic voting becomes widespread.

Although a person must be identified when he votes so that he cannot vote twice, his name must not be paired with his vote inside the computer. To do so would make the secret ballot a mockery. Not only must the system not keep track of how individuals vote, the people must be convinced that it is not doing so.

Needless to say, convenient provisions for voting must be made for those who own neither TV sets nor telephones, to say nothing of home computers.

Good or Bad?   The most exciting possibility of electronic voting is that it might raise voter participation to 90 percent or more, instead of the dismal 50 percent or less often typical of even presidential elections.

Also, many more specific issues could be referred directly to the public, or at least the public could make its opinions clear to its representatives. Our government might move in the direction of a pure democracy, like that of ancient Greece, where the citizens vote on every issue, instead of electing representatives to do their voting for them.

On the other hand, if the public is given greater input into the executive and legislative processes, will it necessarily make wise decisions? Or will it be governed by fashion, prejudice, fear, and narrow self-interest, instead of what is good for the country as a whole? Will bold new ideas ever be given a chance to prove themselves? Or will they be shouted down at birth by a populace fearful of change? Or might a government go in the opposite direction and become erratic and unstable because its position on fundamental issues varied from day to day, according to the whim and mood of the public?

Electronic voting offers the exciting possibility of giving ordinary citizens much greater participation in the affairs of government. On the other hand, any fundamental changes in a system of represent-ative government that has functioned (more or less) for over 200 years should be made with extreme caution and forethought.

FOR FURTHER READING

Acocella, Nicholas. "Polls, Pols, and Power: The Computer on the Hustings." *Creative Computing*, Sept.-Oct. 1976, pp. 54-57.

Burdick, Eugine. *The 480*. New York: Dell Publishing Co., 1964.

Farmer, James. "Computerized Voting: Many Happy Returns?" *Computer Decisions*, Nov. 1974, pp. 20-23.

Flato, Linda, and Wiener, Hesh. "Washington Slept Here." *Computer Decisions*, Nov. 1974, pp. 28-37.

Holmes, Edith. "Election Systems Win the Vote Count Race." *Computerworld*, Nov. 13, 1974, pp. 1-2.

"Living: Pushbutton Power." *Time*, Feb. 20, 1978, pp. 46-49.

de Solla Pool, Ithiel, *et al. Candidates, Issues, and Strategies*. Cambridge: MIT Press, 1964.

REVIEW QUESTIONS

1. What are some ways computers can play a role in the political process?

2. What is a *sample*?

3. Why were some of the early pollsters ludicrously wrong in their predictions?

4. What is a *random sample*? A *stratified sample*? What are the advantages and disadvantages of each?

5. Why do some politicians find election-night predictions by TV networks objectionable?

6. Give six kinds of polls used by campaign managers, and state the purpose of each one.

7. Compare what Simulmatics set out to do with what conventional pollsters achieve.

8. Describe the model of the electorate Simulmatics used.

9. What advice did Simulmatics give John Kennedy on handling the religious issue?

10. Describe how computers can be used to identify members of ethnic groups.

11. Describe how computers are used in political fund raising.

12. How can computers be used to make naive voters think they have received personal letters from the candidate?

13. How can computers help election workers get out the vote that is most likely to favor their candidate?

14. What are some factors that can complicate the ballot-counting process?

15. Has computerized voting always gone smoothly? What are some of the problems that have been encountered?

16. Why is it not necessarily reassuring to know that no cases of fraud in computerized elections have been verified?

17. Describe the Televote system.

18. How is QUBE used for electronic voting?

19. Describe how electronic voting might take place in the future.

20. List the possible benefits and dangers of electronic voting.

DISCUSSION QUESTIONS

1. Can political polls be too accurate? That is, can a too-detailed knowledge of what the public wants and expects force ambitious political leaders to conform to those wants and expectations instead of developing original solutions to outstanding problems?

2. Discuss the possibility that future political campaigns might become elaborate games, with all sides using computers and with the public as pawns. It has been cynically suggested that the responses of the public could be simulated by the computers, thereby eliminating the need for any real elections.

3. An electronic voting system requires identification of each voter (to make sure nobody votes twice), but it does not keep track of how each person votes. How can the voters be persuaded that the system is not keeping track of their votes?

4. It has been suggested that electronic voting will greatly increase the number of people who vote. Do you think this will be the case? And, if it is, do you think it will result in an increase or a decline in the quality of government?

5. Some students of government consider the increasing influence of special-interest groups a serious problem. How do you think electronic voting will affect the powers of special-interest groups?

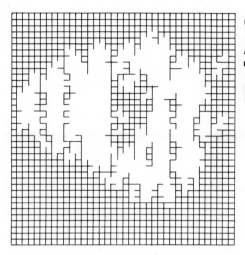

CHAPTER 14

COMPUTERS AND TRANS-PORTATION

Getting people from where they are to where they want to go is a major industry everywhere. More and more, this industry is relying on computers and electronics.

Computers may become even more important if energy shortages change traditional transportation patterns. The private automobile might have to be replaced with mass transit, for instance. If alternate energy sources are not developed, the energy crisis will only get worse, and considerable ingenuity will be needed to keep people moving.

Computers have applications in both private automobiles and public mass transportation. They can help with the exacting jobs of scheduling passengers, controlling traffic, and operating vehicles with maximum efficiency and safety.

In particular, computers can help resolve the conflict between energy conservation (which demands that vehicles operate with the highest possible efficiency) and pollution control (which often sacrifices efficiency for the sake of low exhaust emissions). With computer control, cars can be both clean and efficient.

**AUTOMOBILE
TRAFFIC
CONTROL**

Who hasn't been frustrated by having to wait at a red light when there was no car in sight along the road that had the green light? Or how about seeing a traffic light favor a main highway, which was hardly being used, while a long line of cars waited on a side road? Situations like these sometimes force the police to switch off the traffic lights and direct traffic by hand.

Computerized Traffic Control   A computer traffic-control system can eliminate many of these problems. The computer uses special sensors to measure the traffic flow on all the streets in the system. It then cycles the lights to favor the streets that are carrying the heaviest traffic *at that moment*. When traffic patterns change, the computer changes the operation of the traffic lights accordingly.

But this isn't all a computerized traffic control system can do. With the help of electrically operated traffic signs, the computer can declare some streets to be one-way when needed. Or it can direct traffic along alternate routes to avoid detours, accidents, or traffic jams.

With the aid of a speech synthesizer, the computer can automatically send traffic reports to radio and television stations for broadcast to the public. Or the computer can have its own radio channel, which drivers can pick up on their car radios. Or, again using a radio channel, the traffic-control computer can send information in digital form to a computer in each automobile, which would display the information for the driver.

Using Traffic Models   Scientists have used mathematical and computer models to investigate traffic flow, often with unexpected results. For instance, a line of heavy traffic can be sped up by *stopping it* occasionally. The occasional stops let gaps develop between groups of cars. These gaps prevent wave-like disturbances from rippling through the line of traffic. When such disturbances occur, all drivers are forced to slow down or stop to keep from hitting the car ahead. A computer program based on a model can take such unobvious steps as stopping traffic occasionally in order to speed up the overall flow.

Entering Freeways   In Tampa, Florida, a computer-controlled signal is being used to help motorists enter an expressway. It works like this. Sensors on the expressway transmit traffic information to a computer, which uses this information to locate gaps in the traffic flow. A series of computer-controlled green lights is placed along the guard rail of the entrance ramp. When the computer finds a gap, it turns on the lights in a precisely controlled sequence. The driver waiting to enter the expressway sees what appears to be a green bar moving along the guard rail. The bar starts slowly and gradually accelerates to highway speed. A motorist who drives to keep pace with the green bar will move precisely into the gap the computer has detected.

Observation shows that the system is used most by skilled drivers who no doubt could merge into traffic fairly quickly without it. The inexperienced and timid drivers who could make the best use of the system usually ignore it. Of course, if they doubt its reliability, their hesitation may be well-founded. But the more likely explanation is that they don't know what the device is for and have never bothered to find out. In that case, more publicity seems to be necessary. Getting people to change the habits of a lifetime is usually difficult.

COMPUTERS
IN CARS

For a long time, Detroit ignored automotive electronics with a "not invented here" attitude. But, in the face of demands for energy conservation, emissions control, and increased safety, Detroit finally seems willing to make some changes. Each year, more and more cars are using microprocessors for efficiency, safety, and driver convenience. By the late 1980s, probably all cars will do so.

System Monitoring   An automobile computer can monitor a car's systems and warn the driver of impending trouble. It might estimate how far the car could be driven before the breakdown actually occurred and inform the driver whether additional driving would do more damage. Recent-model Volkswagens have the sensors in place for such a diagnostic system. But the computer is at the Volkswagen dealer's, not in the car.

Information also can be provided just for the driver's convenience. As we saw in chapter 7, computers are available that will display such things as the amount of fuel remaining, the number of miles you can travel (at your current speed) before needing to fill up,

Data from the Indianapolis 500 racing car is monitored with the minicomputer and computer terminal shown in the background. This photo was taken in 1975; the monitoring system is still being used.

The computer and terminal are shown installed in the engine test area. This photo was taken in 1975.

the number of miles to your destination, and your estimated time of arrival.

It has been suggested that a receiver in the automobile could pick up the LORAN signals that ships use for radio navigation. The signals could be fed to the automobile computer, which would display the current position of the car on a map.

Another interesting possibility for the future is to let computers in automobiles communicate with a city's traffic-control computer. A driver in a strange town could get directions through town or to any particular destination. All drivers would rely on the traffic-control computer for the route with the fewest traffic problems. The automobile computer could monitor the transmissions of the traffic computer and warn the driver whe he was approaching a dangerous situation.

Improving Engine Performance As we also discussed in chapter 7, a computer can monitor the operation of the engine continuously and adjust it for maximum performance. The driver now has an advantage previously enjoyed only by the pilots of large airplanes—an "engineer" solely responsible for monitoring the operation of the engine.

Under the constant control of the computer, cars should be able to operate at air-fuel ratios of 18:1 or better, instead of the 15:1 or 16:1 used today. This situation should improve fuel economy and reduce emissions to the point where the catalytic converter, which is expensive, troublesome, and emits pollutants of its own, can be eliminated.

An Electronic Chauffeur The computer can even help you drive your car. It can maintain a constant speed so the driver can take his foot off the accelerator. With the help of a small radar (or some other distance-measuring device), the computer could "station keep" with the car ahead, following it at a constant distance or (even better) at a constant headway. (The headway is the time that elapses between two cars passing the same point.) Or the computer could maintain a constant speed except that it would slow down as necessary to keep from getting too close to the car ahead.

With the radar, the computer could detect an impending collision, warn the driver, and then inflate airbags. Since the computer could detect the collision several seconds before impact, the airbags would not have to be inflated with the explosive violence of existing ones.

What about that old science-fiction cliché, the "automatic driver," which would take over driving completely, like the automatic pilot of an airplane? Here's one way such a system could work. Cables buried beneath the road would carry electrical signals that the automobile computer could pick up and use to locate the center of its lane. The cables would also carry coded information about exits and intersections to help the computer with its navigation.

A traffic-control computer now really could control the traffic, not just the traffic lights. For instance, the traffic computer, communicating through the roadway cables, could instruct one car to slow down slightly and the one in front to speed up slightly, thereby creating a gap into which a car entering the highway could be inserted. As a car approached the entrance to a freeway, the traffic-control computer would already be working to make a place for it in the traffic flow.

A system like this would be expensive, of course. The control cables would have to be installed under miles of existing highways. And since uncontrolled cars could not be allowed on a computer-controlled highway, everyone who wanted to travel on the highway would have to buy control computers for their cars.

Another application for an onboard computer is as an intoxication tester. When the driver tried to start his car, the computer would display a series of digits. To demonstrate his sobriety, the driver would have to punch the displayed digits on a keyboard within a certain time limit. Otherwise, the car would not start.

The problem with this is that once a driver has been deterred from starting his own car a few times, he no doubt would change the car's wiring in order to disable the intoxication tester. But laws might be passed requiring people who have been convicted of drunken driving to have such a system and to have it inspected regularly to make sure it has not been tampered with.

SCHEDULING

One inconvenience of mass transportation is that you must travel when the bus, plane, or train is ready, not when you are. And it's even more inconvenient to arrive at the terminal and find that no

seats are left. Computerized scheduling and reservation systems can help alleviate these problems.

Airline Reservations   All major airlines now operate complex computerized reservtion systems. In order to make reservations for a long trip involving many flights over a period of days, weeks, or months, a passenger has only to call the nearest airline office. The computer system keeps track of who has reservations on what flights and will print out the tickets when the passengers call for them. Some systems allow credit-card-carrying passengers to get their tickets from a vending machine. If space on a certain flight is not available, the computer will put the person requesting space on a waiting list, and he will be called in the event of cancellations.

It's not uncommon for a long trip to involve flights on several airlines. The computer of the airline selling the tickets will contact the other airlines' computers and make the necessary reservations. The computers keep track of how much one airline owes another as a result of having sold tickets for the other airline's flights. Before computers, airlines found it next to impossible to keep track of who owed whom how much.

Car Pools   To conserve energy, authorities urge people to form car pools instead of each person driving his own car. In some places, computers have been used to make up car pools by matching up

people living in the same area who have a common destination. Even though this use of computers is a bit trivial, it does help to glamorize and publicize the car-pool plan. Obviously, there are more ways to use computers than for computing!

Computer-Scheduled Buses A computer can be used to provide a type of transportation that is about midway between a taxicab and a city bus. A person wishing to be picked up near his home phones the bus company. The computer works the person into the schedule of the nearest bus and tells him when he will be picked up. After the bus driver picks up each passenger, he is notified by radio where to go next. The bus route is not fixed but takes shape in the computer's memory as passengers call in.

In some places where this has been tried, there have been problems with people who request a pick-up but who don't show up at the appointed place and time. In some cases, this might be caused by thoughtless negligence. But it might also be that many people just don't understand the nature of the service being offered. As noted before, a tremendous amount of public education is needed to get people to use a new system properly.

In one city, a bus system of this type fell victim to legal suits by taxicab companies, which claimed that the service the buses provided was reserved by law for taxicabs.

THE
TROUBLES OF
BART

The first fully automated railroad is BART, the Bay Area Rapid Transit System, which operates in the San Francisco Bay area. Except in case of trouble, human operators don't actually drive the trains. The computer schedules the trains, oprates them, and monitors their speeds and locations. If the system breaks down, the operators can drive the trains at a maximum of twenty miles an hour (the normal maximum speed is eighty miles an hour) until repairs can be made.

For some time after BART went into operation, it was plagued with problems. The system tended to imagine "phantom trains" and bring everything to a grinding halt until it could be convinced that the tracks were in fact clear. Even worse, it sometimes ignored the presence of real trains. For months, a BART employee had to stand at each station and telephone the station behind when a train went by to indicate that the way was clear for the next train.

The programs that controlled the train's brakes would malfunction. Sometimes a train would go past a station without stopping. On one memorable occasion, the train went past the station, off the end of the tracks, and down an enbankment. Fortunately, it was only a small embankment, so the incident was an embarrassment instead of a disaster.

When the train did stop at the right place, there were problems
209 with the doors. Sometimes the doors would not open at the station.

Sometimes they opened when there was no station. And when they did open at the station, they frequently opened on the wrong side of the train.

Nor was it possible to shunt a malfunctioning train off to a siding. The computer knew how many trains it had, and it was not about to let anybody make off with one. If a train "disappeared," the computer became confused and brought the whole system to a halt.

Actually, it's doubtful that any of these problems can be blamed directly on the computer. Other components of the system were just as culpable. For instance, the rails were used to carry signals between the computer and the trains. But when the rails picked up a thin coating of rust, they did not make good electrical contact with the train, and this interfered with the signals.

Still, the computer's software seemed very inflexible. It did nothing to help handle the problems that occurred elsewhere.

Murphy's Law   Because of the troubles BART encountered, some people have suggested that mass transit systems should not rely so much on advanced technology. But perhaps a better suggestion is just to make sure that all the bugs are worked out of a new system before passengers start to use it.

All new systems have problems. And the time to solve them is *before* regular service begins. Furthermore, contracts for new systems should be written in such a way that the builders are committed to make any necessary changes found during the debugging phase. Also, builders who want this kind of contract should be responsible for building prototype systems to test the feasibility of their ideas.

Engineers summarize the problems encountered in a new technology in what they call *Murphy's law: Anything that can go wrong will go wrong.* Few major computer applications have been spared at least one reaffirmation of Murphy's law.

AIR-
TRAFFIC
CONTROL

The Problem   Air traffic control has long been a problem, especially near major airports where the traffic is dense. For a long time, the controllers complained that the manual air-traffic-control system was inadequate: the controllers were overworked, and safety was compromised as a consequence. A number of mid-air collisions have taken place, with tragic results. And many "near misses" occur that the public never hears about.

RDP   In response to these problems, the Federal Aviation Administration implemented a computer-based *Radar Data Processing* (RDP) traffic control system. The system uses high-precision radar to locate aircraft. The radar works best if the aircraft is equipped with a "transponder," a device that automatically transmits a return signal when it receives a signal from the radar. It's possible for airplanes not equipped with transponders not to show up on radar at all.

The data from the radars is processed by the computer system. The positions of the planes are displayed as spots of light, called "targets," on a CRT. The target corresponding to each aircraft is accompanied by a data block giving the plane's call sign, speed, altitude, and other information. Before RDP, controllers had to write this information on plastic cards and attach them to the radar screen.

Although RDP is now in widespread use, it occasionally has been severely criticized by controllers. The FAA denied the criticisms. The following are some of the alleged problems.

- Fast-climbing planes, such as business jets and military fighters, can outrun the system. When this happens, the altitude readout is cancelled.

- The data blocks for nearby aircraft can get swapped.

- Data blocks can drift away from the targets they are supposed to accompany.

- The data blocks may be incorrect.

- The location shown for a plane may be as much as twenty miles off.

- The controllers are not alerted if the system goes down.

If these problems do exist (or even existed when the system was first put into operation), then here is another example of the foolhardiness of rushing a system into service before it's fully debugged. A new airplane is tested most thoroughly before it is licensed for passenger service. Why not take the same care in testing the computer system that controls the airplane?

FOR FURTHER READING

"Computerized Cars." *Scientific American*, Aug. 1975, p. 48.

Hallen, Rod. "The Joy of Computerized Motoring." *Creative Computing*, April 1979, pp. 132-134.

Spencer, Donald D. *Computers in Society*. Rochelle Park, N. Y.: Hayden Book Co., 1974, pp. 131-147.

"Trouble in Mass Transit. Why Can't the People Who Put a Man on the Moon Get You Downtown?" *Consumer Reports*, March 1975, pp. 190-195.

Ward, Patrick. "Critic Says FAA Control System Has Bugs." *Computerworld*, May 7, 1975, pp. 1-2.

REVIEW QUESTIONS

1. Why may there be a future trend away from private automobiles and toward mass transit?

2. Describe how computerized traffic control would work.

3. Give an example of an unexpected result of using a mathematical model to investigate traffic flow.

4. How can a computer help a driver enter an expressway?

5. Give some possible explanations why the system referred to in question 4 is not as widely used as it could be.

6. What are some of the reasons Detroit is finally taking an interest in automotive electronics?

7. How would an automotive computer be able to warn a driver of an impending breakdown?

8. What are some of the ways an automotive computer could increase the driver's convenience?

9. How might automotive computers allow the expensive and troublesome catalytic converters to be eliminated?

10. Describe one way a system could be implemented to allow a computer to drive a car.

11. Give some ways computers simplify flight booking, both for the airlines and the passengers.

12. What is the main advantage of using computers to form car pools?

13. Describe how computer scheduling of buses works.

14. What are two problems encountered by computer-scheduled buses?

15. What is *BART*?

16. Describe some of the problems BART encountered when it first began operating.

17. Even if the computer system was not mainly responsible for BART's troubles, how could greater flexibility in its design help to alleviate problems that arose elsewhere?

18. Give Murphy's law and its application to computer systems.

19. Describe the FAA's Radar Data Processing system.

20. What are some of the criticisms that controllers have made against the RDP system?

DISCUSSION QUESTIONS **1.** Suppose that computer-controlled automobiles have been developed to the point where they could reduce deaths from highway accidents to almost zero. On the other hand, if computer-controlled cars were used, all highways would have to be modified at a cost of billions. And manually controlled cars could not be allowed on the same highways as computer-controlled ones. What should be considered before deciding whether or not to modify the country's highways for computer-controlled cars?

2. What might be done about the problem of people requesting a computer-scheduled bus but not showing up at the appointed place and time?

3. As mentioned in this chapter, taxicab drivers sometimes have been able to prevent the operation of innovative busing systems. Discuss the pros and cons of the taxi drivers' case. (The discussion should be on moral grounds, not on the legal technicalities of a particular city's ordinances.)

4. What steps could be taken to prevent the kinds of inconveniences suffered by the early users of the BART system?

5. When charges are made that a system is unsafe, what steps should be taken to make sure that people have enough information to decide whether or not they want to risk using the system in question?

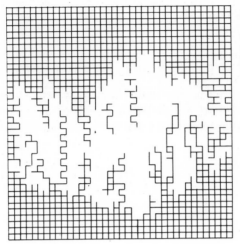

CHAPTER 15

COMPUTERS AND CRIME

No one who reads the newspapers can doubt the seriousness of crime in this country. Not a day goes by without numerous robberies, rapes, and murders being reported. In many cities, it's extremely dangerous to walk the streets at night.

Crime is a complex problem with many causes. Poverty, unemployment, conditions in the cities, and increasing disregard for authority all play their roles and no single remedy is going to solve the problem overnight.

But perhaps at least one of the causes can be dealt with—the inefficiency of the criminal justice system. For instance, the police usually are able to solve only a fraction of the crimes committed. And when offenders are apprehended, there is usually a long delay in trial and sentencing. During the delay, the offenders may be out on bail committing more crimes.

Much police work concerns informaton—information about stolen property, fugitives from justice, the methods of operation of known criminals. The computer can make an important contribution to processing this information effectively and efficiently.

Unfortunately, there is almost no other area in which computers inspire such fear. The reason is obvious: the police can initiate proceedings that can take a person's liberty away. And, sometimes with good reason, not everyone is convinced that those proceedings will be carried out fairly. Even worse, the police keep records that can haunt us the rest of our lives. Even those people who have the most to fear from crime may fear even more anything that increases the effectiveness of the police.

(The fact that large segments of the population do distrust the police is one more reason there will be no easy solutions to the problem of crime.)

In one way, the computer can be considered a mixed blessing for law enforcement. To be sure, it helps the police solve crimes and apprehend criminals. But it also opens up a whole new world of ways to commit crimes. As far back as 1974, authorities estimated that over $200 million were being lost each year through computer-related crime. That figure certainly has not diminished in the intervening years.

COMPUTERS
AND THE
POLICE

Patrol Car Dispatching When you call the police, the police dispatcher has to locate the car nearest you that is free to respond. This means the dispatcher has to keep track of the status and location of every police car—not an easy task for a large department.

Another problem, which arises when cars are assigned to regular patrols, is that the patrols may be *too* regular. If criminals find out that police cars will pass a particular location at regular intervals, they simply plan their crimes for times when no patrol is expected. Therefore, patrol cars should pass by any particular location *at random times*; the fact that a car just passed should be no guarantee

In the mid-1970s, two minicomputers were used to monitor doors, windows, and fire and smoke detectors in Sugar Creek, Texas. In the event of a fire or break-in, a computer turned on all the lights in the house and sounded an audible alarm. A message typed out in the computer control center informed a security officer of the nature and location of the problem.

that another one is not just around the corner. Yet simply ordering the officers to patrol at random would lead to chaos.

A computer dispatching system can solve both these problems. The computer has no trouble keeping track of the status and location of each car. With this information, it can determine instantly which car should respond to an incoming call. And with the aid of a pseudorandom number generator, the computer can assign routine patrols so that criminals can't predict just when a police car will pass through a particular area.

(Before computers, police sometimes used roulette wheels and similar devices to make random assignments.)

Computers also can relieve police officers from constantly having to report their status. The police car would contain a special automatic radio transmitter and receiver. The officer would set a dial on this unit indicating the current status of the car—patrolling, directing traffic, chasing a speeder, answering a call, out to lunch, and so on. When necessary, the computer at headquarters could poll the car for its status. The voice radio channels would not be clogged with cars constantly reporting what they were doing. A computer in the car automatically could determine the location of the car, perhaps using the LORAN method mentioned in the previous chapter. The location of the car also would be sent automatically to the headquarters computer.

Stolen Property Files   Often a police officer's hardest problem is recognizing stolen property as being stolen. A computerized file that lets the police quickly check descriptions and serial numbers of possible stolen items can help them recover stolen property as well as catch thieves and fences.

These files often are most useful and most needed for stolen cars. An officer can report the tag number of a suspicious vehicle or of one stopped for a routine traffic violation. The reply will come back while the suspected car is still in sight or in custody. Since stolen cars often are used as getway cars in other crimes, spotting one may prevent or solve some other crime.

Fugitives from Justice   The old "Wanted Dead or Alive" posters have given way to electronic systems that let officers identify a fugitive from justice in seconds.

One system of this kind is the FBI's National Crime Information Center (NCIC) in Washington, D. C. NCIC maintains computerized files on both fugitives and stolen property. State police information systems throughout the nation access NCIC directly. City and county systems work through the state systems.

NCIC can be accessed either through a terminal or a local computer. In either case, the information requested comes back in about ten seconds. When a local computer is used, it must be limited to law enforcement and justice work. This restriction helps prevent unauthorized access to NCIC files.

When a police officer stops a suspicious person or automobile, he radios the information from the car registration or the person's driver's license to the police dispatcher. The dispatcher checks the information out with NCIC. Within a minute or two, the officer will know if the person is wanted or if the car or its license plate has been reported stolen.

National Driver Register Service   A person whose driver's license has been revoked may attempt to obtain a new one in another state. To curtail this, the National Driver Register Service keeps information on persons whose licenses have been denied, revoked, or suspended. Before granting a license, a state can query this computerized system to see whether or not the applicant has had his license revoked in another state. All states use this service.

CRIMINAL JUSTICE RECORDS

Arrest Records   When a person is arrested in the United States, an arrest record is forwarded to the FBI, where it becomes a part of the person's FBI file. Even if the charges are later dropped or the person is acquitted, the arrest record still will be forwarded to employers who request an FBI check.

(A court ruling now requires that the disposition of the case be supplied with all records sent to employers. But law enforcement officials still can get arrest records where the disposition is unknown.)

People who favor the distribution of arrest records argue that just because an arrest did not lead to a conviction doesn't mean it was without foundation. Members of organized crime may go unconvicted because witnesses were intimidated or murdered. Sex criminals may escape justice because the victims don't wish to subject themselves to the ordeal of a trial. And the cases against many criminals have been dismissed because the police made some technical error during arrest or questioning.

The people who oppose the distribution of arrest records argue that people sometimes are arrested "on suspicion" or "for investigation," particularly if they have prior police records. People who participate in political demonstrations may be arrested, sometimes with justification, sometimes without. A person's chance of being arrested may be influenced by the person's race, sex, or social or economic status.

It has been estimated that one out of every two males will be arrested at some time in his life. For black males, the chances are even greater.

At least one court has maintained that using arrest records to deny employment constitutes racial discrimination. Residents of black ghettos are much more likely to be picked up "for questioning" or "on suspicion" than people who live in affluent, white suburbs.

It is a basic assumption of American justice that a person is innocent until proven guilty. It is difficult to see how the use of arrest records to deny employment and other benefits can be consistent with this assumption.

Conviction Records Conviction records are harder to argue against than arrest records. After all, a court has determined that a person did indeed commit a crime and has required the person to pay a penalty. Surely, the proponents of conviction records argue, employers have a right to keep convicted criminals out of their businesses.

And yet, when a person is convicted of a crime, society exacts a fixed penalty—so many years in jail or so many dollars for a fine. Conviction records can turn every sentence into a *life sentence* by denying the former convict employment in many areas for the rest of his life. Indeed, he may be excluded from the very job he was trained for while in prison. Unable to get work, he is all too likely to return to crime.

Some argue that a person's conviction record should be destroyed after a certain number of years. (Seven is a popular number.) But others argue that destroying the record after seven years is too late. After all, when a convict is first released from prison, he needs employment to further his rehabilitation.

So far, we haven't mentioned computers in this section. In fact, all the problems mentioned existed before anyone ever dreamed of using computers for arrest and conviction records. Now that computers are being used for some of these records, much controversy has surfaced. But the real problems lie not with the use of computers but with the records themselves.

This situation is typical when someone proposes storing certain types of records in a computer. People react to the proposal with alarm and concern, but usually this concern is misplaced. It should be focused not on whether the files should be stored in a computer but on whether they should exist at all. Any files that should not be allowed to exist inside a computer should not be allowed to exist outside one either.

USING COMPUTERS TO COMMIT CRIMES

A New Kind of Crime More and more, the operations of our businesses, governments, and financial institutions are controlled by information that exists only inside computer memories. Anyone clever enough to modify this information for his own purposes can reap substantial rewards. Even worse, a number of people who have done this and been caught at it have managed to get away without punishment.

These facts have not been lost on criminals or would-be criminals. A recent Stanford Research Institute study of computer abuse
was based on 160 case histories, which probably are just the proverbial tip of the iceberg. After all, we only know about the unsuc-
cessful crimes. How many successful ones have gone undetected is
anybody's guess.

Here are a few areas in which computer criminals hve found the
pickings all too easy.

Banking   All but the smallest banks now keep their accounts on
computer files. Someone who knows how to change the numbers in
the files can transfer funds at will. For instance, one programmer was
caught having the computer transfer funds from other people's
accounts to his wife's checking account. Often, traditionally trained
auditors don't know enough about the workings of computers to catch
what is taking place right under their noses.

Business   A company that uses computers extensively offers many
opportunities to both dishonest employees and clever outsiders. For
instance, a thief can have the computer ship the company's products
to addresses of his own choosing. Or he can have it issue checks to
him or his confederates for imaginary supplies or services. People
have been caught doing both.

Credit Cards   There is a trend toward using cards similar to credit
cards to gain access to funds through cash-dispensing terminals. Yet,
in the past, organized crime has used stolen or counterfeit credit
cards to finance its operations. Banks that offer after-hours or remote
banking through cash-dispensing terminals may find themselves
unwilingly subsidizing organized crime.

Theft of Information   Much personal information about individuals is
now stored in computer files. An unauthorized person with access to
this information could use it for blackmail. Also, confidential information about a company's products or operations can be stolen
and sold to unscrupulous competitors. (One attempt at the latter
came to light when the competitor turned out to be scrupulous and
turned in the people who were trying to sell him stolen information.)

Software Theft   The software for a computer system is often more
expensive than the hardware. Yet this expensive software is all too
easy to copy. Crooked computer experts have devised a variety of
tricks for getting these expensive programs printed out, punched on
cards, recorded on tape, or otherwise delivered into their hands. This
crime has even been perpetrated from remote terminals that access
the computer over the telephone.

Theft of Time-Sharing Services   When the public is given access to a
system, some members of the public often discover how to use the
system in unauthorized ways. For example, there are the "phone

freaks" who avoid long-distance telephone charges by sending over
their phones control signals that are identical to those used by the
telephone company.

Since time-sharing systems often are accessible to anyone who
dials the right telephone number, they are subject to the same kinds
of manipulation. Of course, most systems use account numbers and
passwords to restrict access to authorized users. But unauthorized
persons have proved to be adept at obtaining this information and
using it for their own benefit. For instance, when a police computer
system was demonstrated to a school class, a precocious student
noted the access codes being used; later, all the student's teachers
turned up on a list of wanted criminals.

Perfect Crimes It's easy for computer crimes to go undetected if no
one checks up on what the computer is doing. But even if the crime is
detected, the criminal may walk away not only unpunished but with
a glowing recommendation from his former employers.

Of course, we have no statistics on crimes that go undetected. But
it's unsettling to note how many of the crimes we do know about were
detected by accident, not by systematic audits or other security
procedures. The computer criminals who have been caught may have
been the victims of uncommonly bad luck.

For example, a certain keypunch operator complained of having
to stay overtime to punch extra cards. Investigation revealed that the
extra cards she was being asked to punch were for fraudulent
transactions. In another case, disgruntled employees of the *thief*
tipped off the company that was being robbed. An undercover
narcotics agent stumbled on still another case. An employee was
selling the company's merchandise on the side and using the computer to get it shipped to the buyers. While negotiating for LSD, the
narcotics agent was offered a good deal on a stereo!

Unlike other embezzlers, who must leave the country, commit
suicide, or go to jail, computer criminals sometimes brazen it out,
demanding not only that they not be prosecuted but that they be
given good recommendations and perhaps other benefits, such as
severance pay. All too often, their demands have been met.

Why? Because company executives are afraid of the bad publicity that would result if the public found out that their computer had
been misused. They cringe at the thought of a criminal boasting in
open court of how he juggled the most confidential records right
under the noses of the company's executives, accountants, and
security staff. And so another computer criminal departs with just
the recommendations he needs to continue his exploits elsewhere.

COMPUTER
SECURITY

Emphasis on Access and Throughput For the last decade or so,
computer programmers have concentrated on making it easy for

people to use computer systems. Unfortunately, in some situations, the systems are all to easy to use; they don't impose nearly enough restrictions to safeguard confidential information or to prevent unauthorized persons from changing the information in a file.

It's as if a bank concentrated all its efforts on handing out money as fast is it could and did very little to see that the persons who requested the money were entitled to it. Of course, a real bank works just the opposite way, checking very carefully before handing out any money. Computer systems that handle sensitive personal and financial data should be designed with the same philosophy in mind.

Positive Identification of Users A computer system needs a sure way of identifying the people who are authorized to use it. The identification procedure has to be quick, simple, and convenient. It should be so thorough that there is little chance of the computer being fooled by a clever imposter. At the same time, the computer must not reject legitimate users. Unfortunately, no identification system currently in use meets all these requirements.

At present, signatures are widely used to identify credit-card holders, but it takes an expert to detect a good forgery. Sometimes even a human expert is fooled, and there is no reason to believe that a computer could do any better.

A variation is to have the computer analyze a person's hand movements as he signs his name instead of analyzing the signature itself. Advocates of this method claim that different persons' hand movements are sufficiently distinct to identify them. And while a forger might learn to duplicate another person's signature, he probably would not move his hand exactly the way the person whose signature he was forging did.

Photographs are also sometimes used for identification. But, people find it inconvenient to stop by a bank or credit-card company and be photographed. Companies might lose business if they made the pictures an absolute requirement. Also, photographs are less useful these days, when people frequently change their appearance by changing the way they wear their hair. Finally, computer programs for analyzing photographs are still highly experimental.

Cash-dispensing systems often use two identification numbers: one is recorded on a magnetic stripe on the identification card, and the other is given to the card holder. When the user inserts his card into the cash-dispensing terminal, he keys in the identification number he has been given. The computer checks to see that the number recorded on the card and the one keyed in by the user both refer to the same person. Someone who stole the card would not know what number had to be keyed in in order to use it. This method currently is one most widely used for identifying computer users.

For a long time, fingerprints have provided a method of positive identification. But they suffer from two problems, one technical and one psychological. The technical problem is that there is no simple system for comparing fingerprints electronically. Also, most methods of taking fingerprints are messy. The psychological problem is that fingerprints are strongly associated in the public mind with police procedures. Because most people associate being fingerprinted with being arrested, they almost surely would resist being fingerprinted for routine identification.

Voiceprints may be more promising. With these, the user has only to speak a few words into a microphone for the computer to analyze his voice. There are no psychological problems here. And technically it's easier to take and analyze voiceprints than fingerprints. Also, for remote computer users, the identifying words could be transmitted over the telephone.

However, voiceprints still require more research. It has yet to be proved that the computer cannot be fooled by mimics. Also, technical difficulties arise when the voice is subjected to the noise and distortion of a telephone line.

Even lipprints have been suggested. But it's doubtful that kissing computers will ever catch on.

To date, the most reliable method of positive identification is the card with the magnetic stripe. If the technical problems can be worked out, however, voiceprints may prove to be even better.

Data Encryption Even sensitive data is transmitted to and from remote terminals, it must be *encrypted* (translated into a secret code) at one end and *decrypted* (translated back into plain text) at the other. Files also can be protected by encrypting the data before storing it and decrypting it after it has been retrieved.

Since it is impractical to keep secret the algorithms that are used to encrypt and decrypt data, these algorithms are designed so that their operation depends on a certain data item called the *key*. It is the key that is kept secret. Even if you know all the details of the encrypting and decrypting algorithms, you cannot decrypt any messages unless you know the key that was used when they were encrypted.

For instance, the National Bureau of Standards has adopted an algorithm for encrypting and decrypting the data processed by federal agecies. The details of the algorithm have been published in the *Federal Register*. Plans are underway to incorporate the algorithm in special purpose microprocessors, which anyone can purchase and install in his computer.

So the algorithm is available to anyone who bothers to look it up or buy one of the special purpose microprocessors. But the operation of the algorithm is governed by a sixty-four-bit key. Since there are about 10,000,000,000,000,000,000,000 possible 64-bit keys, no one is likely to discover the correct one by chance. And, without the correct key, knowing the algorithm is useless.

A recent important development involves what are called *public-key cryptosystems*.

In a public-key cryptosystem, each person using the system has two keys, a public key and a private key. Each person's public key is published in a directory for all to see; each person's private key is kept secret. Messages encrypted with a person's public key can be decrypted with that person's (but no one else's) private key. Messages encrypted with a person's private key can be decrypted with that person's (but no one else's) public key.

If I wanted to send you a secret message, I would look up your public key in the directory and use it to encrypt my message. When you received the message, you would decrypt it using your private key.

Now, suppose I wanted to send you a *signed* message—that is, one that you could verify came from me. I would encrypt the message, using my private key, and send it to you along with an unencrypted note telling you whom it came from. You would decrypt the message using my public key. The fact that my public key works to decrypt the message proves that the message was encrypted with my private key; obviously, the message had to come from me.

To send a *signed, secret* message, the two techniques just described would be used in combination. That is, I would first encrypt the message using my private key, then encrypt it again using your public key. The first encryptation signs the message; the second is for secrecy. You would decrypt the message twice. The first time you would use your private key, and, the second time, you would use my public key.

Protection through Software The software of a computer system, particularly the operating system, can be designed to prevent unauthorized access to the files stored on the system.

The protection scheme uses a special table called a *security matrix* (see figure 15-1). Each row of the security matrix corresponds to a data item stored in the system. Each entry in the table lies at the intersection of a particular row and a particular column. The entry tells what kind of access the person corresponding to the row in which the entry lies has to the data item corresponding to the column in which the entry lies.

Usually, there are several kinds of access that can be specified. For instance, a person may be able to read a data item but not change it. Or he may be able to both read and modify it. If the data is a program, a person may be able to have the computer execute the program without being able either to read or modify it. Thus, people can be allowed to use programs without being able to change them or find out how they work.

Needless to say, access to the security matrix itself must be restricted to one authorized person.

Also, the software has to be reliable. As we have already mentioned, even the software issued by reputable vendors may be full of bugs. One or more bugs may make it possible for a person to circumvent the security system. The security provisions or more than one computer system have been evaded by high school and college

students.

	Data-A	Data-B	Data-C
User-A	Read Modify Execute	Modify	Read
User-B	Read	Modify Execute	Modify
User-C	Read Modify	Read Execute	Read

Figure 15-1. The security matrix specifies the rights that each individual has to each data item. For instance, User-A can read, modify, or execute Data-A, but can only modify Data-B and can only read Data-C.

Restricting the Console Operator Most computer systems are extremely vulnerable to the console operator. That's because the operator can use the switches on the computer's control panel to insert programs of his own devising, to read in unauthorized programs, or to examine and modify confidential information, including the security matrix. In the face of these capabilities, any software security system is helpless. Computer systems for handling sensitive information must be designed so that the console operator, like other users, works through the software security system and cannot override it. One solution is to incorporate the security system in firmware instead of software, so that unauthorized changes to it cannot be made easily.

FOR FURTHER READING

Knight, Gerald. *Computer Crime.* New York: Walker and Co., 1973.

Meushaw, Robert V. "The Standard Data Encryption Algorithm." *Byte,* March 1979, pp. 66-74, and April 1979, pp. 110-126.

Neier, Aryeh. *Dossier: The Secret Files They Keep on You.* New York: Stein and Day, 1975.

Parker, Donn B. "Computer Security: Some Easy Things to Do." *Computer Decisions,* Jan. 1974, pp. 17-18.

Rivest, R. L.; Shamir, A.; and Aldeman, L. "A Method for Obtaining Digital Signatures and Public-Key Cryptosystems." *Communications of the ACM,* Feb. 1978, pp. 120-126.

REVIEW QUESTIONS

1. Give some reasons why there are strong feelings both for and against the use of computers in law enforcement.

2. How can computers aid patrol-car dispatching?

3. What is the advantage of having patrol cars pass through any given area at random times?

4. How can computers relieve officers of the necessity of frequently reporting the status and locations of their cars?

5. Give an example of how a stolen-property file might be used?

6. What is NCIC? How is it used?

7. What is the National Driver Register Service? How is is used?

8. Give the pros and cons of making arrest records available to (1) law enforcement officials and (2) employers.

9. Repeat the arguments of question 8 for conviction records.

10. Describe six kinds of computer crime.

11. Why are computer crimes often difficult to detect?

12. Why are those who commit computer crimes sometimes able to escape punishment even if the crime is discovered?

13. What change in philosophy is necessary to design secure computer systems?

14. Describe some proposals for positively identifying computer users.

15. What is a *key*? How is it used?

16. Describe the two keys that each person using a public-key cryptosystem would possess.

17. Describe how to use a public-key cryptosystem to send a secret but unsigned message.

18. Describe how you would send a signed, secret message using a public-key cryptosystem.

19. What is a *security matrix*?

20. Describe three kinds of access that a person may have to a data item or program stored in a computer system.

DISCUSSION QUESTIONS

1. Discuss the pros and cons of releasing arrest records to employers.

2. Discuss the pros and cons of destroying conviction records (or at least making them difficult to obtain) as soon as the convict is released from prison.

3. Why do you think some people who are highly trained in a valuable technical skill, such as computer programming, nevertheless turn to crime?

4. Public-key cryptosystems should make it possible for all communications and documents to be impervious to snooping and to carry (when desired) unforgeable signatures. Discuss the impact of these developments on society.

5. According to a news report, an inventor has developed a computerized device that can be worn like a wristwatch and can analyze a person's voice to indicate whether or not the person is lying. What would be the impact of such a device on society?

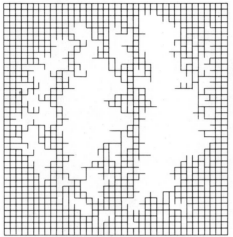

CHAPTER 16

AUTOMATION, ROBOTS, AND UNEMPLOY-MENT

When should a human being do a particular job and when should it be done by a machine? The idealistic answer is that if the job is interesting, challenging, and fulfilling, a person should do it. If it is tedious, boring, and repetitious, it is best turned over to a machine.

But practical difficulties arise at once. What about the people who make their livings doing those boring, tedious, and repetitious jobs? What about union leaders who owe their positions to *other people* going out and doing these jobs? Neither is likely to agree that the jobs that support them should be eliminated.

In fact, technology that changes patterns of employment is likely to be opposed by the people whose burdens supposedly are being lightened. This has been true from the machine-smashing Luddites of the nineteenth century through the union that strikes over automation today. The reason for the opposition, of course, is that the technology that improves working conditions in the long run causes people to lose their jobs in the short run.

Our society is based on a "work ethic," which demands that everyone "earn his bread by the sweat of his brow." The work ethic and the economic system based on it demand full employment or, at least, almost full employment coupled with some kind of welfare for those who cannot find jobs. As long as we remain committed to this

228

ethic and the economic system that goes with it, we will find ourselves deliberately rejecting automation and preserving much inhuman drudgery just to supply everybody with jobs. Indeed, this is exactly what happens when unions block or slow down automation for fear the members will lose their jobs.

But before we examine these social questions in more detail, let's look at some of the possibilities of automation and industrial robots.

AUTOMATION

Automation refers to machines carrying out some process under automatic control. Don't confuse automation with *mechanization*, where the machine is supervised by a human operator even though it may carry out many individual steps automatically. Automatic control is the essence of automation.

It was mechanization that produced the Industrial Revolution, which replaced most individual craftspeople with factories and machines. Automation promises (or threatens) a second industrial revolution in which human-supervised machines are replaced by machines that largely supervise themselves.

The first question is: Do we really need automation? Can automated machinery substantially improve our mass production techniques, which are envied and copied throughout the world?

Mass Production Most industries use the technique of mass production, which was made famous by Henry Ford (although he didn't originate the idea). The item being manufactured moves down a production line. At each station on the line, a worker performs some operation on the item—a part is installed, a weld is made, paint is applied, and so on. Each worker does the same small job on each item that passes his station.

Although mass production is highly efficient, it is hardly the answer to every production problem. For one thing, it requires many special machine tools, each designed to do just one job at one station on the production line. Each has to be foolproof, since it will be operated by a semiskilled or unskilled worker, not a skilled machinist. Many items must be sold to recover the costs of these special tools. So mass production means *mass* production; the technique is not economical for small runs.

Also, changing the design of the product being manufactured is expensive because special tools have to be changed. The retooling necessary to produce a new model car, for instance, greatly increases the cost of the car.

The products of mass production are uniform. The customer's options consist mainly of specifying whether or not certain parts are to be included. There is no possibility of ordering customized versions that the manufacturer did not anticipate originally. We cannot give a production line special instructions as we could an individual craftsperson.

A production-line worker has to do the same simple job over and over again. Often he is urged to do it at fairly high speed, to keep up with the conveyer that brings work pieces to his station. In short, people are asked to keep up with (and, to a certain extent, behave like) machines. When this is the case, jobs often become unfit for human beings.

General Purpose Machines   One alternative to mass production is to use general purpose machines operated by skilled machinists. General purpose machines are those usually found in any machine shop —lathes, drill presses, milling machines, shapers, and so on.

This approach is more expensive than mass production for two reasons. First, the skilled machinists command higher salaries than production-line workers. Second, the general purpose machines spend only a fraction of their time doing useful work. The rest of the time, the machinists are inserting and removing work pieces, changing tools (drill bits and the like), and making adjustments. Because of the higher labor cost and lower productivity of the machines, an individually machined part can cost a hundred times as much as a mass-produced one.

Computer Integrated Manufacturing Systems   Another alternative to mass production is automation. At the highest level, this would be a Computer Integrated Manufacturing System, or CIMS.

A CIMS would use computers to aid in the planning and design of a product, to control the manufacture of its parts, to supervise the movement of materials and parts through the plant, and to assemble the finished product. In short, CIMS would give us the fabled automatic factory. Completely automatic factories still lie in the future, although perhaps not the too-distant future. To date, none has been demonstrated.

Computer Managed Parts Manufacture   Although CIMS is still in the future, CMPM—Computer Managed Parts Manufacture—is feasible right now.

In CMPM, a computer oversees the operations of the machines and the conveyor that moves work from one machine to another. Any machine can select any one of about sixty tools from an adjoining carousel. The processes of inserting and removing work, changing tools, and making necessary adjustments to the machines are accomplished in seconds under the control of the computer. Although the machines are general purpose machines, they spend most of their time doing useful work, just like the machines on a production line.

At present, computer-controlled machine tools are much more expensive than conventional ones. How, then, can CMPM be economical?

One way is by eliminating skilled labor. But, even more important, the machines are kept constantly busy. The more expensive machines justify themselves by turning out more work. It has been estimated that CMPM might save as much as 80 percent of the cost of jobs that don't justify mass production. If this estimate turns out to be correct, then CMPM will be widely adopted in the future.

And the economics of CMPM might get even better in the years ahead. Machine tools are expensive because they themselves are not produced in large enough quantities to justify mass production. If CMPM were used to make cheaper computer-controlled machine tools and these tools were, in turn, used to make still cheaper computer-controlled machine tools, soon computer-controlled machine tools would be cheaper than conventional ones are now.

This kind of economy already can be seen in the computer industry. Older computers are now used to help design and manufacture new ones. This is at least partly responsible for the drastic price reductions of recent years. Certainly, microprocessors would not be so plentiful or so cheap if they had to be designed and manufactured without the aid of computers.

CMPM is flexible as well as economical. All the machines used are general purpose machines. Depending on what orders a machine receives from the computer, it might carry out completely different operations on successive work pieces that are brought to it.

This flexibility permits a factory to produce a number of different and unrelated products at the same time. The computer keeps track of which product each item moving through the factory is for. Since the computer gives each machine individual instructions for each item it works on, it doesn't matter that the items might be for different products. In the end, the computer sees that all the items for each product are brought together and assembled.

This is very much like time sharing, which allows many people to use a computer for different purposes at the same time. The time of a machine is shared among the many different jobs moving through the factory. The machine does a little bit of work on one job, a little bit on another, and so on as each item comes past. Because the machine is kept busy, it justifies its cost.

With such a system, even very small quantities of an item can be

Computers are used to help design and manufacture other computers. Here a plotter draws a pattern for an electronic-circuit board. Using photographic techniques, the circuit board can be manufactured directly from the drawing. Similar techniques are used to manufacture integrated circuits.

manufactured at reasonable cost. This can result in a greater variety of products at lower prices.

For instance, a manufacturer could have a large catalog of products, each of which could be available with many options. When a customer orders a product with a particular set of options, the instructions for turning it out are sent to the computer-controlled factory. At the same time the factory is manufacturing this product, it is turning out many other custom products for many other people. The efficiency of the factory approaches that of mass production, even though each customer has a wide range of choices concerning the details of the item manufactured for him.

In fact, even a single copy of an item could be turned out with production-line efficiency. In the future, you may be able to order almost any item for which you can provide instructions to the factory computer on how to manufacture the desired item. Software would be available for your home computer that would guide you through the task of preparing the necessary instructions.

Robots The greatest obstacle to full CIMS is the assembly operation, where individual parts are screwed, riveted, soldered, or welded together to form the final product. This kind of work calls for robots, machines with mechanical arms and hands that have the same capabilities (if not the same shape) as human appendages.

Industrial robots are already in use, although none of the current ones is sophisticated enough for tricky assembly operations. The simplest of these robots are "pick and place" machines capable of only very simple motions.

These machines are guided through preprogrammed movements by impulses of electricity or compressed air. The machine does not sense its surroundings and use feedback to guide its movements. Instead, mechanical stops determine the limits of each movement.

This kind of machine is usually programmed by means of a *plugboard*, which looks something like a telephone switchboard. The plugboard is divided into rows and columns. Each column represents a step in the robot's program. Each row represents a motion of a particular joint in a particular direction.

Plugs are inserted at the intersections of the rows and columns. When a plug is inserted at the intersection of a particular row and column, it specifies that the movement corresponding to that row will be carried out in the program step corresponding to the column. The program steps are carried out one after another. That is, the motion specified in the first column is carried out first, then the motion specified in the second column, and so on.

A slightly more advanced method of control uses a *potentiometer board* instead of a plugboard. A potentiometer is a control like the volume control on a TV set. It works by adjusting an electrical voltage or *potential*, hence the name *potentiometer*.

The potentiometer board is similar to the plugboard except that, **232** at the intersection of each row and column, there is a potentiometer instead of a receptacle for a plug. The settings of the potentiometers determine the positions of the robot's joints for each program step. Since the positions of the joints are determined, and not just which joints will move, the mechanical stops are no longer needed. The robot is programmed by adjusting the potentiometers.

We can make the robot still more versatile by replacing the plugboard or potentiometer board with an electronic memory. To store a program in the memory, a human tutor leads the robot through the desired motions using a hand-held box. The motions are stored automatically in memory. When the robot is ordered to play them back, it faithfully will duplicate the motions it learned from its human tutor.

How smoothly the robot moves depends on how much memory it has. If the memory holds only a few hundred steps, for instance, then each step must involve fairly large motions. Consequently, the robot moves rather jerkily. This is satisfactory for many jobs. But for others, such as wielding a paint sprayer, a smoother motion is essential. For these purposes, thousands of steps may be stored. Each individual step is so small that the robot appears to be moving continuously and smoothly.

Adding a computer to these simple electronic robots greatly increases their capabilities. For instance, we can simply order the robot to move its hand in, say, a straight line or a circle. The computer will work out the actual movements of the joints needed to carry out the motion. Without the computer, each separate position of the robot's joints necessary to move the robot's hand in the line or circle would have to have been stored in memory.

Even more important, the computer makes it possible for the robot to use feedback from its surroundings to adjust its movements. If the piece the robot is to pick up is not exactly where it should be, the robot can sense where it actually is and adjust the position of its hand as necessary. If the parts the robot is assembling don't go together easily, the robot can work them back and forth until they fit, just as a human assembler would do. In advanced (and still highly experimental) systems, the robot uses screwdrivers and other tools to assemble parts picked out of a bin.

What kinds of sensory feedback can a robot use? Our first thought is to give the robot a TV camera and let it use its "eyesight" to guide its work. Unfortunately, getting a computer to break a TV image down into the various objects it consists of is a difficult problem in pattern recognition. And methods for resolving this problem are still only experimental.

For the present, we need simpler methods than image analysis to provide sensory feedback for robots. One such method uses a laser beam. For objects close to the robot, the brightness of the beam reflected from the object is used to gauge its distance. For objects more than a meter away, a technique similar to radar can be used. A pulse of laser light is directed toward the object, and the time required for the reflected pulse to come back is measured. The distance to the object is proportional to this time. Sonar, which is used to focus some automatic cameras, also can be used.

These techniques allow a robot to locate objects, such as the parts it is to assemble. But they don't provide the fine positioning information needed to fit the parts together.

One approach to the fine positioning is to let the robot put the parts together by feel. That is, sensors on the robot's hand measure the amount of force that a part exerts back on the hand when the robot tries to move it in a certain direction. Suppose, for instance, the robot is trying to insert a rod in a hole that it just fits, but the rod is not precisely aligned with the hole. The robot can determine the nature and degree of the misalignment from the resistance it encounters as it tries to insert the rod. It uses this information to make the necessary adjustments in the position of the rod.

An even more advanced robot would be able to pick up randomly scattered parts and assemble them with screwdrivers, wrenches, soldering irons, and other tools. Such a robot would have to depend on vision. Also, it would have to be able to form and carry out fairly elaborate plans to deal with the problems (such as parts that don't fit precisely) that might arise.

We are now in the domain of *artificial intelligence*. Artificial-intelligence researchers are actively working on such problems as planning and robot vision. But the obstacles are formidable. Although these obstacles doubtless will be overcome in time, success does not seem to be just around the corner.

AUTOMATION AND SOCIETY

Employment   Back in the fifties, people were warned that the use of computers would lead to massive unemployment in the near future. It was feared that only the most highly skilled would be able to hold jobs.

Obviously, this dire prediction has not come true. Current employment levels are in the range of 90 percent to 95 percent, and employment as low as 90 percent is taken as a sign of serious recession. Of course, we cannot dismiss 5 percent to 10 percent unemployment as these figures represent millions of people out of work. But the situation the early students of automation feared, of perhaps 10 percent *employment*, obviously has not come about.

In fact, massive layoffs due to automation have been quite rare. More often, jobs have been lost to automation not because the people holding the jobs are fired but because people are not hired for new jobs at automated plants. Economic fluctuations have caused far more people to lose their jobs than has automation.

(There are exceptions to this in particular industries. For instance, modern word-processing and computerized-typesetting equipment has eliminated the need for many printing craftspeople, such as linotype operators. There have been some extremely bitter newspaper strikes when newspapers tried to dismiss unneeded personnel. In some cases, where the union "won" the strike, the newspaper was forced to cease publication because it could not afford to pay the extra personnel.)

What effects on employment can we trace to automation? There seem to be two.

(1) Worker productivity—the amount a single worker produces each hour—has increased, but not drastically.

(2) Some jobs have disappeared while other new ones have been created. The *nature* of the available jobs has changed more than their *number.*

In most cases, the jobs lost have been those calling for unskilled labor. The newly created ones demand much higher skills. Here is the real change automation has produced in the employment picture: people seeking jobs today need far greater skills than was once the case.

Most people manage to acquire sufficient skill to become usefully employed. Those who, for one reason or another, have not yet acquired the necessary skills, such as the young and the educationally disadvantaged, are the hardest hit by unemployment.

The solution, then, seems to be one of improved education for the more demanding jobs of today. But will the state of affairs just described continue indefinitely? If it does, then the appropriate social forces will have more to do with retraining people to keep up with changing job markets than with changing fundamental approaches to work and leisure.

It now seems that the populations of the developed countries will decline in the latter part of the century. With fewer people seeking jobs, the unemployment problem will be relieved. In fact, some industries may be forced to automate because they are unable to hire sufficient human workers.

But, in the long run, the problem will remain. When the technology for automating a process exists and has proved itself, then the process probably will be universally automated. The change may take place gradually, if for no other reason than the large investment in existing nonautomated factories. Opposition by labor unions can slow down automation but rarely can stop it. Conventional factories usually cannot compete with automated ones, so when one company in an industry automates, the others probably will have to follow suit.

The companies in question need not be in the same country. For instance, Japan is conducting extensive research in industrial robots and other advanced automation. An automated Japan could force the rest of the world to automate as well.

Yet, just because the change is taking place slowly, should we bury our heads in the sand and pretend it isn't taking place at all? Or is it time to start preparing for an age in which much of the world's work will be done by machines instead of people?

235

The Work Ethic   In the beginning, man was a hunter. For the hunter, this activity is interesting, challenging, and exciting. So much so, in fact, that many people still pursue it as a sport.

Agriculture, the history books tell us, was a tremendous technological step beyond hunting since a farmer can get a lot more food out of an acre of land than a hunter can. Yet, in one sense, agriculture was a step backwards. The hunter was replaced by the field hand. An interesting and challenging occupation was replaced with one that was pure drudgery.

In an agricultural society, it is imperative that every able person put in his time in the fields. A person who doesn't work is a social menace who cannot be tolerated. If too many emulate his ways, then the crops will fail for lack of attention, and everyone will go hungry.

And so the "work ethic" came into being; it is sometimes called the "Protestant work ethic" or the "Puritan work ethic," but it no doubt predated both Protestants and Puritans. It can be expressed in many ways: "One must earn his bread by the sweat of his brow"; "One must eat his bread with sweat on his face"; "There is no such thing as a free lunch"; and many more.

The trouble with these kinds of principles is that they do not remain simply handy rules of thumb for particular kinds of societies. Instead, they work their way into a society's mores and perhaps even into the orthodoxy of a religion. The principle in question becomes Right, Good, and Never to Be Questioned. Members of the society are trained from childhood to accept it on faith. Those who manage to throw off this early conditioning and re-examine a deep seated "ethic" are condemned by all right-thinking citizens in the harshest possible terms.

The work ethic may very well be an example of a principle that was once quite valid but that now or in the near future will have outlived its usefulness. Agricultural or early industrial societies *had* to insist that as many people as possible toil in the fields, the sweatshops, or the "dark, satanic mills." But advanced industrial processes often work best *without* people. Machines can do the jobs faster, better, and certainly cheaper. If automation is held back for the sake of supplying people with jobs, then the work ethic—and the economic system that enforces it—may not be in the best interests of society.

Times of Change   One problem is that no society will automate overnight. We have seen that automation is a gradual process. Therefore, we can expect substantial periods of time in which *some skills are needed and some are not.* Indeed, this situation already exists with respect to unskilled labor, which is largely unneeded.

The need for some people to work while others remain idle can cause social unrest. Those who work feel that those who don't are getting a free ride at everyone else's expense.

To put the matter another way, transitions are socially painful. There was little cause for dissatisfaction years ago, when our society had full employment. There will be little cause for dissatisfaction in future society where there is little employment, and wealth is distributed on some other basis than wages. But the transition may be a time of social unrest, particularly if people remain oblivious to the fact that a transition is in progress and insist on judging events on the basis of outmoded mores.

TOWARD
AN AUTOMATED
SOCIETY

Suppose we do opt for a society in which production is largely turned over to machines, and the wealth the machines generate is distributed to the people. Is there any practical political and economic way to bring such a society about?

Certainly it's not enough to outline some fanciful utopia and then sit back and wait for it to materialize. Nor is it productive to think in terms of revolutions or other violent unheavals, as the radicals of the sixties found out. No, if our utopian visions are to be taken seriously, then we must explain how to get from here to there. That is, what realistic political and economic steps can we take that:

(1) will appeal to the majority of the people,

(2) will not threaten too many vested interests, and

(3) will bring about the desired changes?

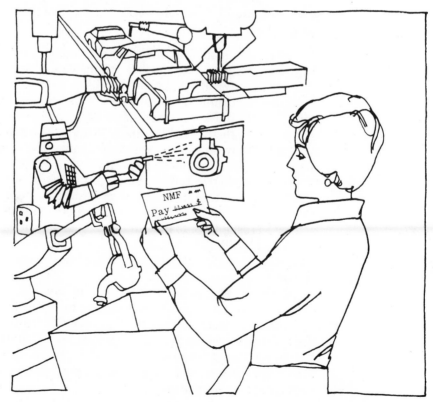

The National Mutual Fund Computer scientist James S. Albus has proposed a plan for distributing the wealth produced by automation. And his plan does specify how to get from our present state to the desired one without stepping on too many toes.

Any such plan is bound to be controversial, and the Albus plan is certainly that. Because it's presented here doesn't necessarily mean it's *the* answer. But whether or not it's the final solution, it's an interesting approach and one that makes a good starting point for discussions.

The Albus plan calls for the creation of an institution called the National Mutual Fund, or NMF. (A *mutual fund*, in stock-market jargon, is an organization that buys and sells stocks, distributing the profits from this activity to its own shareholders.)

The NMF would work like this.

- Every citizen automatically would be a shareholder in NMF.

- NMF would borrow its investment capital from the Federal Reserve Bank. No contributions by shareholders would be required.

- NMF would concentrate its investments in highly automated industries, thus providing an incentive for automation, which is one of the goals of the plan. Also, this feature might ease the fears of vested interests that traditional industries would be "taken over" by NMF.

- NMF would distribute its profits biweekly to all citizens over the age of eighteen. Each citizen would get the same amount. The payments would be a right of citizenship and would not be based on need.

NMF would stand in the same relation to a company as does any large stockholder (particularly the privately owned mutual funds that exist today). It would exert neither more nor less control than any other stockholder who owns the same amount of stock. NMF would participate in a company only through stock voluntarily offered for sale by the company. There would be no question of nationalization. In most cases, a company would be held partly by private interests and partly by NMF.

Because NMF would have great political and economic power, Albus proposes that its board of governors be publicly elected. This would assure that NMF would always be responsive to the public (or at least as responsive to the public as elected officials ever are).

Albus estimates that, twenty-five years after the plan was initiated, it could be paying six to twelve thousand dollars to each person.

What kind of world would NMF (or something like it) produce? Some people, no doubt, would choose to spend their lives in social activities, sports, hobbies, and other forms of recreation. And if that's their choice, who's to say it's the wrong one? Others probably would turn to art, music, literature, and crafts. They would hve the freedom to enrich their own lives, the lives of their friends and neighbors, and perhaps the entire world.

FOR FURTHER READING

Albus, James S. "The Economics of the Robot Revolution." *Analog Science Fiction/Science Fact*, April 1975, pp. 70-81. For reader comment, see the issue of Aug. 1975, pp. 171-176.

———— "Automation and the Sleeping Nation." *Computer Decisions*, Aug. 1975, pp. 28-34.

———— and Evans, John M. "Robot Systems." *Scientific American*, Feb. 1976, pp. 76-86B.

Cook, Nathan H. "Computer-Managed Parts Manufacture." *Scientific American*, Feb. 1975, pp. 22-29.

Gotlieb, C. C. and Borodin, A. *Social Issues in Computing*. New York: Academic Press, 1973, pp. 164-193.

Mosher, Ralph S. "Industrial Manipulators." *Scientific American*, Oct. 1964, pp. 88-96.

Nevins, James L. and Whitney, Daniel F. "Computer-Controlled Assembly." *Scientific American*, Feb. 1978, pp. 62-74.

Pylyshyn, Zenon W. *Perspectives on the Computer Revolution*. Englewood Cliffs, N. J.: Prentice-Hall, 1970, pp. 402-455, 480-496.

REVIEW QUESTIONS

1. What are some of the advantages of automation? What, in our present society, are some of its disadvantages?

2. Distinguish between automation and mechanization.

3. Contrast the first Industrial Revolution with the one that automation is causing.

4. Why is mass production more economical than using a skilled machinist and general purpose tools?

5. What are some of the disadvantages of mass production?

6. Why may some production-line work be unfit for human beings?

7. What is CIMS?

8. Describe CMPM in some detail.

9. What is the greatest obstacle to full CIMS?

10. How is it possible for computer-controlled tools to be more economical than conventional tools, even though the computer-controlled tools cost more?

11. Compare an automatic factory with a time-shared computer system.

12. Describe several ways of controlling industrial robots and the advantages and disadvantages of each.

13. Describe some ways industrial robots can sense their environments.

14. Have the predictions of the early fifties concerning the impact of automation on employment come to pass?

15. Name one industry that has been seriously affected by automation. Why has this industry been affected more than many others? (*Hint*: What does it deal in?)

16. Give two effects of automation on the job market.

17. How did the transition from hunting to agriculture affect the nature of work?

18. Describe the work ethic.

19. Why is the transition to an automated society likely to produce social unrest? What evidence of this can you see today?

20. Describe the Albus plan.

1. Discuss the morality of eliminating dreary, dangerous, and dehumanizing jobs on which large numbers of people depend for their livelihood.

2. Discuss the value of the work ethic in a society where most of the work could (if the people desire it) be done by machines.

3. Discuss why you do or do not think that the National Mutual Fund would work in practice.

4. Try to think of some alternatives to the National Mutual Fund that would accomplish the same objective—provide a fair means of distributing the wealth created by robots.

5. Suppose that the technical and social problems are all solved and most of the work of the world is turned over to machines. Describe how people might live in such a world. How would they spend their time? What kind of art and music would they have? Which activities would they consider serious and which frivolous? What would they talk about? Do you think the world you have described would be more or less interesting to live in than the existing one?

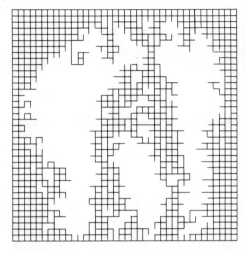

CHAPTER 17

COMPUTERS IN BUSINESS AND FINANCE

The first computers were used for scientific and engineering calculations. To keep these expensive machines busy when the scientists and engineers were not using them, managers put them to work keeping records and doing other administrative tasks. Now, far more computers are used for business data processing than for scientific calculations.

We should not be surprised that computers are widely used in business, since so much business is devoted to information processing. A corporation, for instance, has two components—production and management. The production component works directly with the products and services the company provides. But the management component works with information—reports, memos, orders, invoices, accounts, paychecks, and guidelines.

Financial institutions are even more devoted to information processing. After all, money itself is just a means of conveying financial information. About the only task a bank engages in that is not information processing is the storage of valuable items in its vaults—and this is a very small part of its activities.

BUSINESS DATA PROCESSING

Every transaction a company engages in requires some paperwork. Every order received, every invoice sent, every payment received, every payment made—each of these carries its burden of paperwork. In all but the very smallest companies, at least some of this paperwork is done by computers. And the microprocessor revolution is bringing the advantages of computers to even the smallest companies.

For example, whenever a customer places an order, a packing slip must be printed to get the order shipped, an invoice must be sent to the customer, and the amount owed must be entered in the customer's account. When the payment is finally received (perhaps after repeated requests and threats), it must be credited to the proper account.

Permanent files, such as customer accounts, are stored on magnetic tape or disks. Traditionally, such transactions as orders and payments are punched on cards. Periodically, the transaction cards are read into the computer by a program that updates the permanent files and produces any needed printout, such as invoices and packing slips.

Nowadays, more and more systems are being designed so that employees can update files directly from remote terminals. This eliminates the card-punching step. Also, the terminals make it easier to modify the files when necessary to correct errors.

MANAGEMENT INFORMATION SYSTEMS

The Need for Input A manager's job is primarily one of information processing. Therefore, the manager is helpless without good input—accurate, up-to-date information about the organization and its environment.

More and more small computers are being put to use by business and professional persons.

Ideally, the manager should be provided only with the information relevant to his responsibilities; otherwise, he has the added burden of separating the relevant information from the irrelevant. The level of detail also must be appropriate: too little detail and the manager lacks essential information; two much and he cannot see the forest for the trees.

The system that is responsible for getting the right information to the right people at the right time is called the *Management Information System* (MIS). In the past, this was a manual system and often a rather informal one. Crucial information might be imparted over lunch or on the golf course, for instance. But, nowadays, management information systems usually employ computers.

A management information system can produce four kinds of output—scheduled listings, demand reports, exception reports, and predictive reports.

Scheduled Listings are the most traditional and commonly used computer outputs. Each month, when the payroll or the customer accounts or the inventory records or some other file is processed, reports are generated and sent to whomever might be able to use them. Scheduled listings are thus a byproduct of business data processing.

Unfortunately, a manager who is responsible for a number of activities is apt to find himself deluged with computer printout once a month. Most of the information is not needed at the moment. And the manager has trouble finding the information he does need, since it is buried in mountains of useless information. (Replacing the printouts with microfilm makes the problem less visible but no less serious.)

A *demand report* is produced only at the request of the person who is going to receive it and contains only the information that was specifically requested. Usually a demand report meets the manager's needs far better than any scheduled listing.

In fact, a demand report does not have to be a printed report at

Business and professional persons can obtain graphical presentations of statistical information from a desk top computer (as shown here) or from a terminal connected to a remote computer.

all. The manager can use a CRT terminal in his office to request the information he needs. The items requested—perhaps only a few numbers—would appear at once on the screen. The computer also could display data as charts, graphs, and pictures instead of numbers. The manager would request printed output only if he wanted to study the data at length or take it home or to a meeting. Studying lengthy reports would be replaced by asking the computer questions.

An *exception report* alerts the manager to some abnormal condition. Exception reports might list people who failed to pay their bills, overdrew their checking accounts, or exceeded their lines of credit.

Unfortunately, exception reports sometimes become so large that managers find it difficult to decide which exceptions are due to minor oversights and which represent more serious problems, such as the activities of a thief. The art of deciding what to call an exception needs refinement. As always, a computer system errs just as much by producing too much output as by producing too little.

Predictive reports are produced with the aid of mathematical or computer models, such as those discussed in chapter 9. These reports attempt to forecast the future behavior of the company and the economy based on their past performance. If a manager is considering a decision, he may want to try it out on the model to see what the predicted consequences will be.

DATABASE MANAGEMENT

Frequently, all the information about a business is collected into one set of files for the benefit of the management information system and business data processing. The collection of files is called a *database*.

Many different computer programs have to manipulate the information in database. We would like to make these programs as independent of the details of how the data is organized as we possibly can. Otherwise, if we have to make some small change in the organization of the data—in order, say, to accommodate a change in the way the company does business—we will have to modify all the programs that use the data.

The solution is to use a *database management system* (DBMS). This is a set of programs that serves the same function for the database that the operating system serves for the computer system as a whole. The database management system is in charge of the database. Other programs obtain data by making requests of the database management system. The requests are based on a simple, logical picture of how the data is organized. The programs state their requests in terms of the logical picture. The database management system worries about the messier physical details of exactly where each item is stored in auxiliary memory.

Relational Databases There are several methods for organizing databases. The easiest kind of database to understand is the *relational database*. Since conceptual simplicity is a strong advantage in database management, relational databases are being used more and more.

We think of the data in a relational database as being stored in a series of tables called *relations*. (How it is actually stored in auxiliary memory is up to the database management system. The whole point of database management is that we don't have to worry about how the data is actually stored.) We retrieve information from the relational database by (in effect) cutting up the tables and pasting the rows and columns back together in different ways.

To make this clear, let's look at a simple example. The following relation shows the employees of a company, the salary of each employee, and the division in which each employee works.

EMPLOYEE

NAME	SALARY	DIVISION
JONES	13,500	AEROSPACE
SMITH	15,000	AUTOMOTIVE
ROBERTS	20,000	AEROSPACE
YOUNG	10,000	AEROSPACE
CLARK	40,000	AUTOMOTIVE

Each row of the relation contains information about one *entity*— that is, one of the individuals about whom we are storing information. The column headings NAME, SALARY, and DIVISION are the *attributes* of the entities. Finally, the entries in each row of the relation give the *values* of the attributes for a particular entity.

To extract information from the relations, we use a set of operations known as the *relational algebra*. Two of the operations in the relational algebra are RESTRICTION and PROJECTION. RESTRICTION selects particular rows from a relation. PROJECTION selects particular columns.

For instance, suppose we need the names of all the workers in the AEROSPACE division. We start by giving the database management system the following command:

A = RESTRICTION of EMPLOYEE on DIVISION = 'AEROSPACE'

Here, A is the name of a new relation that is obtained from EMPLOYEE by retaining only those rows of EMPLOYEE for which the value of DIVISION is AEROSPACE. The new relation is as follows:

A

NAME	SALARY	DIVISION
JONES	13,500	AEROSPACE
ROBERTS	20,000	AEROSPACE
YOUNG	10,000	AEROSPACE

245

Sales and economic information can be displayed as easy-to-interpret graphs using a desk top computer.

We are not, however, interested in all the information in relation A. The salaries of the employees were not requested in the original question. And we know the division for each employee since we asked for the names of the employees in the AEROSPACE division. In short, all the information we need is in the NAME column. We extract the NAME column using the PROJECTION operator:

B = PROJECTION of A on NAME

Again, B is a new relation. But it has only one column, the NAME column:

B

NAME
JONES
ROBERTS
YOUNG

The three values in the relation B answer our original question, "Which employees work for the aerospace division?"

A third important operation of the relational algebra is JOIN. JOIN is used to coordinate the data found in two different relations. For instance, suppose we have the following relation, giving the location and the manager of each division:

ORGANIZATION

DIVISION	LOCATION	MANAGER
AEROSPACE	LOS ANGELES	JACKSON
AUTOMOTIVE	DETROIT	THOMAS

Now, suppose we want to know which employees work in Detroit. Neither table by itself can provide this information. EMPLOYEE tells which division each employee works in, and ORGANIZATION gives the location of each division. We must use both

relations together to answer our question.

To do this, we JOIN EMPLOYEE and ORGANIZATION on DIVISION. That is, if a row in EMPLOYEE and a row in ORGANIZA-TION both have the same value for DIVISION, the two rows are joined together. We build a new relation C consisting of all the joined-together rows. The following command requests the database management system to construct the relation C:

C = JOIN of EMPLOYEE and ORGANIZATION on DIVISION

The relation C is as follows:

C	NAME	SALARY	DIVISION	LOCATION	MANAGER
	JONES	13,500	AEROSPACE	LOS ANGELES	JACKSON
	SMITH	15,000	AUTOMOTIVE	DETROIT	THOMAS
	ROBERTS	20,000	AEROSPACE	LOS ANGELES	JACKSON
	YOUNG	10,000	AEROSPACE	LOS ANGELES	JACKSON
	CLARK	40,000	AUTOMOTIVE	DETROIT	THOMAS

Now that we have the locations and the names in the same relation, the next step is to restrict ourselves to those rows of A for which LOCATION has the value Detroit:

D = RESTRICTION of C on LOCATION = 'DETROIT'

This gives us the following relation:

D	NAME	SALARY	DIVISION	LOCATION	MANAGER
	SMITH	15,000	AUTOMOTIVE	DETROIT	THOMAS
	CLARK	40,000	AUTOMOTIVE	DETROIT	THOMAS

To extract the names we are interested in and discard everything else, we use a PROJECTION on NAME:

E = PROJECTION of D on NAME

The relation E contains the information we want:

E	NAME
	SMITH
	CLARK

Interfaces A database can be used two ways. One way is to write programs that manipulate the data by means of commands given to the database management system. When the programs are executed, the appropriate data will be stored in the database or retrieved from it. Using information stored in the database, we might, for instance, use this method to write a program to print employees' paychecks.

The other approach is to have a user interface that accepts requests from a terminal and passes them on to the database management system. Data received back from the database management system is returned to the user at the terminal. This technique makes possible the kind of ask-the-computer-a-question information retrieval that already has been mentioned.

For the first approach, the language in which the program is written must contain commands for manipulating the database. These commands constitute the interface between the programming language and the database management system.

Unfortunately, most programming languages were designed before database management became popular. Therefore, these languages have no built-in commands for manipulating databases.

Almost all languages, however, have provisions for calling *subroutines*—programs that are intended to be invoked by other programs. It is possible to write a set of subroutines that (with the help of the database management system) will manipulate the database. These subroutines can be invoked from almost any programming language. For instance, there might be one subroutine for RESTRICTION, another for PROJECTION, and another for JOIN.

For communicating with the user through a terminal, even such operations as RESTRICTION, PROJECTION, and JOIN are usually not suitable. Since the person at the terminal is a businessperson, not a programmer, he will find it tedious to have to remember the particular relations stored in the database or the particular sequences of RESTRICTIONs, PROJECTIONs, and JOINs needed to fetch a particular result. Instead, the user should be able to ask questions in English, or something reasonably close to it, and let the interface translate the English questions into commands for the database management system.

These considerations have led to the development of *natural-language interfaces*. A natural-language interface accepts questions in ordinary English, translates them into the necessary commands for the database management system, and passes the results back to the user. For instance, the question

What are the salaries of the employees of the aerospace division?

would be translated by the natural-language interface into the following commands for the database management system:

E = RESTRICTION of EMPLOYEE on DIVISION = 'AEROSPACE'

248 F = PROJECTION of E on SALARY

A relatively
inexpensive
computer system
designed for use in
professions and
small businesses.

The interface would return the relation F to the user:

F	SALARY
	13,500
	20,000
	10,000

Programs processing natural languages still fall far short of perfection. Therefore, we must not expect a natural-language interface to understand unrestricted English that can include such things as allusions, subtle references, elliptical language, and so on.

Fortunately, the questions that can be asked about the data in a database—if they are asked in a straightforward way—usually follow one of a reasonable number of patterns. These patterns can be stored in the computer's memory along with the commands for the database management system necessary to handle each pattern. Every question can be analyzed into some combination of these basic patterns.

Still, the possibility exists that the computer might misunderstand a question—that is, translate it into the wrong combination of patterns. Therefore, after a question has been analyzed, the natural language interface may translate the analyzed question back into English. The user then can judge whether this paraprase is equivalent to the original question.

Occasionally, the system may encounter a query that it cannot analyze. In that case, the questioner will have to fall back on commands such as RESTRICTION, PROJECTION, and JOIN. If the user is not a programmer, he probably will have to call on one to translate his question manually.

**POINT-OF-SALE
EQUIPMENT**

The traditional cash register is being replaced by a variety of electronic terminals that serve many functions besides totaling up orders. These terminals are known as *point-of-sale equipment*, and this application of computers is called *POS*, for *point of sale*.

Price Marking It is an expensive and time-consuming job to mark the price on every item in a supermarket. With POS, this chore can be avoided. Whether it *should* be avoided has become the subject of a controversy that has slowed down the acceptance of POS considerably.

Each item carries a unique ten-digit identification number coded as a series of black and white bars. The scheme for coding numbers using bars is formally known as the Universal Product Code and informally as the "bar code." Bar codes now appear on almost every supermarket item. Manufacturers print the codes on the labels. Each digit of the identification number is represented by the ratio of the widths of a black bar and an adjacent white bar. Since only the ratios of the widths of the bars are important, the codes can be printed as large or as small as desired.

The coded numbers are fed into the POS terminal through either a hand-held scanning wand or a scanner built into the counter. The exact angle at which the scanner or the wand passes over the code is unimportant, again because only the relative widths of the bars count. The terminal transmits the identification number to a computer, which looks up the product identification number in a disk file and sends back to the terminal the price of the item and its description. Both the description and the price are displayed to the customer and printed on the sales slip. In addition, the computer updates the store's records to reflect the sale of that particular item.

The Controversy Controversy has arisen over whether POS systems are more convenient or less convenient for consumers than the

A small computer being used at the sales counter in an automobile parts store.

traditional practice of marking the price on each item.

The stores point out that the prices are still placed on the shelves below the items being sold. And the sales tickets contain not only the prices but the descriptions of the items as well. Also, some stores make a scanner available to the customers so that they can check the prices of items after they have removed the items from the shelves.

In spite of this, however, many consumers' groups oppose eliminating individual price marking. Without the price stamped on each item, they argue, the consumer's ability to compare the prices of different brands of the same item and the same brand in different stores is impaired. They also voice suspicions that the price stored in the computer for an item might be higher than the price displayed below the item on the shelf.

Opposition comes from another quarter as well. Eliminating individual price marking would save the store money mainly by making possible about a 25 percent reduction in store personnel. This fact has not been lost on store employees and their unions, who regard it with considerably less enthusiasm than the store managers do. In a number of localities, consumer groups and store employees' unions have teamed up to oppose the elimination of individual price marking. In a few states, they actually have gotten laws passed requiring that all items be individually marked.

This opposition has greatly deterred the move to POS systems. Even though all supermarket items now carry the bar codes, the scanners to read these codes are not nearly so much in evidence.

Data Capture   Another feature of POS terminals ultimately may be more important than the elimination of price marking. This is the ability of the terminals to collect data for keeping track of a store's inventory and keeping up with the buying habits of the public.

It is often difficult for a store manager to decide just what items to stock and how many of each. The public taste changes rapidly. A certain item may be very much in demand today but find few takers several weeks later. The retailer has to follow these changes as best he can. He needs to know which items are currently being bought so he can reorder them while the demand lasts. He needs to know which items are not moving so he can sell them at reduced prices and replace them with more profitable items. And he needs to know how many of each item is being purchased each month so he knows how many to reorder.

POS terminals can help collect this kind of information. For each item sold, the POS terminal sends the identification number of the item to the computer. In addition to providing the terminal with the price and description of the item, the computer can update an inventory file to reflect the fact that the store now has one less of the item sold. Thus, the POS terminals provide important input for the store's management information system.

By letting the manager keep better track of the store's inventory, POS terminals also help combat "shrinkage," or the theft of merchandise by store employees.

ELECTRONIC FUNDS TRANSFER (EFT)

Too Much Paper Every year, billions of canceled checks and credit card slips pass from one bank to another. Transporting all that paper is cumbersome and expensive. In spite of partial automation (using those oddly shaped magnetic characters printed on checks), processing one check still calls for about ten manual operations and costs from fifteen to twenty cents. Bankers would like to stop moving all that paper around and substitute electronic messages instead.

Electronic Checks However, a bank that accepts a check does not have to send the check itself to the bank on which it is drawn. An electronic message can be sent instead. The bank on which the check was drawn would return a message indicating whether or not the check is good. If it is, then the computers at both banks would adjust their records to reflect the transfer of funds. This isn't too different from the way things are done now, except that electronic messages would change hands instead of paper checks.

Of course, this means that you would not get back your canceled checks. This could be a problem because many people use canceled checks for record keeping and as proof of payment. One solution would be to replace canceled checks with printed confirmation slips generated at your local bank and useful for record keeping.

252

Another problem is privacy. The bank's computers would have a record of everyone to whom you sent a check. (For instance, the name of the person to whom you sent a check would have to appear on the printed confirmation if the confirmation was to serve the same purposes as a canceled check.) Conceivably, this information could be misused—to say, identify people contributing to an unpopular political movement. The same problem arises with most other applications of EFT as well.

Teller Terminals Computer technology is often used to allow a teller to display the status of a customer's account instantly on a CRT terminal. This is particularly convenient for check cashing, since many banks will not cash personal checks without first verifying that the money is actually in the account. Having to wait while the teller phones to check the account is annoying; the customer often feels that he is suspected of attempting to pass bad checks.

With the terminal, the teller immediately can inform any customer of the exact balance in his account. Previously, customers needing this information had to go to the bookkeeping office and perhaps even pay a fee to have their records checked.

The computer system that supports these terminals can generate useful management information. For instance, it could record the number of transactions taking place during each hour of the day at a particular teller station or branch office. Managers could use this information to plan banking hours and staff assignments in order to operate as efficiently as possible while still giving depositors satisfactory service.

Customer Terminals Some banks have started to install remote banking terminals in supermarkets, shopping malls, and other convenient public places. Sometimes the terminal is located right outside the bank, so customers can use it when the bank is closed.

In some cases, the terminal is manned by a bank or store employee who handles the actual cash. But more and more terminals are unmanned; an automatic cash dispenser passes out the money.

The customer inserts a card similar to a credit card—often called a money card in bank advertising—and enters an identifying number on a calculator-like keyboard. A magnetic stripe on the card carries

A remote banking terminal. The customer's "money card" is inserted in the slot at bottom right. Instructions to the customer appear on the screen at top right.

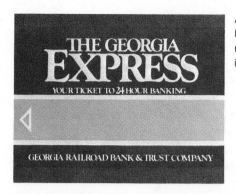

A "money card" for use with a remote banking terminal. The card contains a magnetic stripe on which identifying information is recorded.

an additional identification code. If the identifying number and the identifying information on the magnetic stripe both refer to the same person, then the card is accepted, and the customer can enter the details of the desired transaction. The requested money comes out of a slot.

Small banks have expressed considerable opposition to EFT in general and remote banking terminals in particular. They fear that a large bank, by installing remote terminals over a wide area, could take business away from smaller banks that cannot afford EFT equipment. Most of today's opposition to EFT comes from these smaller banks.

Automatic Payments and Deposits Another service possible with EFT is to allow people to pay recurrent bills automatically. A utility, say, would transmit your bill for electricity, gas, water, or telephone directly to the bank, which automatically would deduct the payment from your account. You would not have to make out a check each month, spend money on postage to mail it, and perhaps have it get lost in the mail after all.

For instance, a California water company has initiated such a system with two key features. First, the customer still gets a monthly statement showing the amount of the bill and the date on which the payment was deducted from his account. Second, the customer has the right to withdraw the payment within fifteen days in the event of a dispute over the bill.

In the same way, wage and salary checks could be deposited with the bank, protecting the wage earner against loss and robbery. Already, people who receive social security checks can arrange to have them automatically deposited.

A Nationwide EFT Network These developments seem to point toward a nationwide electronic funds transfer network. With such a system, cash would be used only for transactions between individuals or with very small businesses. All other transactions would be handled by checks or credit cards. Point-of-sale terminals could, through a connection to the bank's computer, transfer cash the instant a purchase was made.

254 Also, customers could transact certain business from their homes, using Touch-Tone phones to communicate with the bank's computer. The user would punch the numbered buttons to enter identification numbers, requests for information, and instructions. With a speech synthesizer, the computer would provide information, repeat back instructions to guard against error, and confirm that instructions had been carried out.

Aside from the matter of competition among banks, the dangers of a nationwide EFT system seem to be threefold.

1. *Privacy.* Every financial transaction we make would be recorded on the system. There is the danger that someone—an oppressive government, perhaps—could obtain this information and use it against us.

2. *Crime.* People might find ways of making unauthorized funds transfers for their own advantages. Bank employees already have been caught programming the bank's computer to transfer other people's money to their own accounts. The proliferation of home computers and, as a result, of computer-wise people may aggravate the problem.

3. *Failure.* Complex systems can fail dramatically, as did the power system that caused a blackout of most of the eastern United States. A similar failure in an EFT system would result in a "credit blackout," in which the economy of an entire region of the country would be thrown into chaos. The failure could be caused by sabotage as well as accident. Saboteurs might be able to "get into" an insufficiently protected system with their home computers and disrupt its operation.

EFT Legislation   In 1978, Congress passed the Financial Institutions Regulatory Act. Two parts of this, the Fair Funds Transfer Act and the Right to Financial Privacy Act, regulate EFT systems.

The Fair Funds Transfer Act defines EFT as "any transfer of funds which is initiated through an electronic terminal, telephone instrument, or computer magnetic tape." The act requires financial institutions to

- notify customers of the terms and conditions of EFT services;

- give written documentation of all EFT transactions at the time they take place; and

- provide periodic statements at least every three months.

The act limits the liability of a consumer for an EFT transaction to $500. The burden of proof is on the financial institution to show that the consumer authorized a disputed EFT transaction.

The Right to Financial Privacy Act details the procedures the government must follow in obtaining financial records. The individual must be notified that his financial records have been requested.
255   He also must be advised of his rights to attempt to keep the records

from the agency requesting them. Records requested by one agency cannot be provided to any other agency or department of the government.

AUTOMATING THE STOCK EXCHANGE

The Stock Market   Suppose you place an order for a stock with your hometown stockbroker. He will forward your order by telephone or Teletype to his firm's main office in New York. From there it will be sent to the floor of the appropriate stock exchange. A clerk will transcribe the order on a piece of paper and pass it to the firm's broker on the trading floor. The broker makes his way to the "trading post" at which the stock is traded. There is negotiates either with another broker or with the "specialist" who mans the trading post. Through these negotiations, the broker tries to get the stock at the best possible price.

The specialist at each trading post is charged with maintaining an orderly market in each stock traded at that post, buying and selling from his own account, if necessary, to accomplish this. Also, the specialist is responsible for handling "limit orders," those to be executed only when (or if) the stock reaches a certain price.

Brokerage firms use computers extensively to keep track of their customers' accounts. But the actual trading on the floor of the exchange is still manual. However, this may well change in the not-too-distant future. A prototype trading facility called SIMFAC— Simulated Trading Facility—has been built for the American Stock Exchange.

SIMFAC   The simulated trading facility uses four kinds of terminals —booth terminals, broker terminals, specialist terminals, and terminals for exchange personnel to use for the surveilance of trading in particular stocks. The terminals are of the CRT type, although booth terminals have provisions for producing printed copy as well.

An order is received on the booth clerk's terminal directly from the brokerage firm's computer. If the order does not require active negotiation (as many orders do not), the clerk need only press a button to have the order transferred to the specialist's "book file" for execution. If, because of the size of the order or the market conditions for the stock, the skills of a broker are needed, then the clerk will have the order printed out and pass it on to the floor broker.

The broker terminals are arranged around the rims of the trading posts. From any of these, the broker can get information about a stock or execute a trade, either with another broker or with the specialist. To avoid misunderstandings, the information entered by both parties to a trade is compared while the parties are still at their terminals.

The exchange personnel use the surveilance terminals to keep track of trading in certain stocks. One purpose of this might be to decide when to stop trading on a certain stock in order to preserve an orderly market.

Each terminal incorporates a badge reader. The terminal's screen remains blank and its keyboard inoperative until a valid plastic badge is inserted. This badge grants the user access to certain files and the ability to order certain transactions. Thus, a broker can use any broker terminal, a clerk any clerk terminal, and so on. Identification resides in the badge and not in the terminal used.

Computers and Speculators Computers can be used not only by brokers but by their customers as well. The customers use computers to help them *play* the stock market. A computer can examine a mass of stock-market data, looking for patterns that would point to situations ripe for speculation. Computers have been programmed to make buy-and-sell decisions for particular stocks. In short, the computers play the market while their owners look on.

At one time, it was feared that the use of computers by large institutions would squeeze out the small investor. But now, with home computers, the small investor can get in on the fun. It seems likely that people who invest or speculate in the stock market will be among the prime users of personal computers.

But it may not matter very much whether or not computers are used to play the stock market. Mathematical economists strongly question the validity of the methods that Wall Streeters use to

attempt to predict market bahavior. Programming these methods in computers will not make them any more effective. Computerized trading may turn out to involve just as much guesswork as the manual kind.

FOR FURTHER READING

Computer Decisions, April 1974. This issue contains four articles on POS.

"EFT Bill, Consumer Privacy Act Passed." *Communications of the ACM*, Dec. 1978, p. 1093.

Flato, Linda. "Checking on EFTS." *Computer Decisions*, May 1975, pp. 22-26.

Kling, Rob. "Value Conflicts and Social Choice in Electronic Funds Transfer System Developments." *Communications on the ACM*, Aug. 1978, pp. 642-657.

"Smith, Adam." *The Money Game*. New York: Dell Publishing Co., 1969, pp. 127-154.

Zussman, Ronald, *et al.* "Towards an Automated Stock Exchange." *Computer Decisions*, Jan. 1974, pp. 24-27.

REVIEW QUESTIONS

1. Describe the data processing a company must do to handle a customer's order.

2. Describe four kinds of reports produced by management information systems. Which is the most common but least useful?

3. What is a *database*?

4. Compare a database management system to the operating system of a computer.

5. What is the logical organization of a relational database?

6. What is the *relational algebra*?

7. Give examples of how the operations of the relational algebra can be used to extract information from a database.

8. What is a *natural-language interface* for a database management system?

9. What is the Universal Product Code? How is it used?

10. What are the advantages to the retailer of eliminating individual price marking? What are the advantages to the consumer? The disadvantages?

11. What purposes could POS terminals serve besides eliminating individual price marking?

12. Why would bankers like to replace paper checks and credit card slips with electronically transmitted messages?

13. Why is the installation of remote banking terminals controversial?

14. Describe how the automatic payment of bills would work. What are some of the advantages of this to the consumer and the company? What are some of the possible disadvantages?

15. What would be some of the consequences of a nationwide EFT network?

16. Give three possible dangers of a nationwide EFT system.

17. What rights do users of EFT systems have under the Fair Funds Transfer Act and the Right to Financial Privacy Act?

18. Describe the automated stock exchange now under study.

19. How can computers be used to play the stock market?

20. What may be the impact of personal computing on the use of computers to play the stock market?

**DISCUSSION
QUESTIONS**

1. The price-marking controversy has been based on people's *opinions* of how the elimination of individual price marking would affect consumer convenience. Can you think of a way this could be tested objectively? Do you think the parties to the controversy would be willing to accept the results of an objective test?

2. Discuss the cashless society that EFT may bring about. How would transactions between individuals take place? How would vending machines work? How could children be provided with money? Should children be provided with "money cards" that give them access to all the money in their fathers' or mothers' or even their own bank accounts?

3. Give a dramatic description of a "credit blackout."

4. According to a news report, a man received a "money card" from a bank at which he no longer had an account and was able to withdraw $1000 before being stopped. What does this incident say about the abilities of banks to implement sophisticated EFT systems?

5. If present trends continue, trading on the stock exchange floors will be done with the aid of computers, and most investors and speculators will use computers to help them make their decisions. Characterize the stock market as a computer game played for high stakes.

CHAPTER **18**

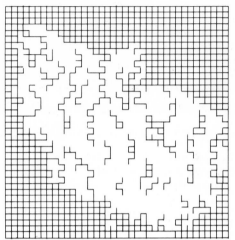

COMPUTERS AND PEOPLE

The only purpose for building computer systems is to help people. And most computer systems do help *some* people—those who ordered them designed and built, for instance. Unfortunately, not every system helps every person who comes into contact with it. Some systems can affect some people quite adversely—say, by invading their privacy.

If computer systems are to serve all the people and not just the selected few, then steps must be taken to assure that the systems will interact with everyone who comes into contact with them in convenient, helpful, and nonharmful ways.

PRIVACY

Computers can maintain files on individuals and make the contents of those files instantly available to anyone with access to the system. Furthermore, the contents of those files can be transmitted electronically from one computer to another. Information that originally was collected by different agencies for diverse and individually justifiable purposes can be merged to yield a computerized dossier on an individual. The citizen needs protection against the misuses of computerized files that seriously can compromise his right of

privacy.

These high school students just finished a ten hour marathon volleyball game to raise money for a computer. It was not too long ago that students were demonstrating against computers instead of trying to raise money to buy one.

A number of individuals and groups have suggested guidelines for information systems that will assure the privacy of the persons on whom the information is being kept. Most of these guidelines cover essentially the same ground, and most are incorporated in the Privacy Act of 1974. Unfortunately, this act applies only to files maintained by government agencies. Files maintained by private organizations, such as businesses, are excluded.

Here is a typical set of guidelines.

▪ *An individual can inspect his own file.* Every person has the right to inspect the information kept on him by any organization, institution, or government agency.

▪ *An individual can correct errors in his file.* There must be a procedure whereby an individual can challenge the correctness of information kept on him and force the information to be changed if he can prove it is not correct. It should not be necessary for him to engage in a prohibitively expensive court battle to do this.

▪ *Information should be routinely evaluated for accuracy.* Although an individual has the right to examine his own file, it should not be his responsibility to catch errors. The institution that maintains the file should have routine procedures for keeping files accurate and up-to-date.

▪ *An individual can add information he feels should be included.* An individual may feel that, although the information in his file is accurate, it does not tell the whole story and so gives a misleading impression. In that case, the individual should have the right to include his side of the story in the file.

▪ *Operators of a system should notify individuals about the kind of information stored and the uses to which it will be put.* Any right to have access to a file or to make corrections is meaningless if the individual doesn't know what files are being kept on him and how they are being used.

UNIVERSAL IDENTIFIERS

Identifiers In most files, each record contains a unique *key* or *identifier*, a data item that uniquely identifies the person to whom the record refers.

The most obvious identifier is a person's name. Unfortunately, different people do have the same name. Since a person's name does not always uniquely identify a single person, names are not satisfactory identifiers.

It's possible to construct an identifier that has a high probability of being correct. This is done by combining the person's name with other information—the person's address and date of birth, for instance. However, parts of the identifier, such as the address, would quickly become outdated in many cases. Other parts, such as the date of birth, are confidential and should not be available to everyone who happens to see the identifier.

What we are left with, then, are the various account numbers, social security numbers, customer numbers, employee numbers, and so on that we constantly must keep track of.

The Universal Identifier Instead of making each person keep track of dozens of account numbers, why not assign to each person a unique identifier? This "computer name" for the person would be used by every information system with which that person comes into contact.

Even though such a universal identifier would simplify our lives by giving us only one identifying number to remember, opposition to assigning universal identifiers is strong. The fear is that the existence of a universal identifier would make it easier to match up the records corresponding to the same person in different files. In short, it would improve the efficiency with which information about a person would be exchanged among different computer systems. But people who fear computers are reluctant to agree to anything that would make computer systems more efficient.

In fact, however, the absence of universal identifiers does not prevent separate files from being merged or information from being exchanged among different computer systems. The constructed identifiers mentioned earlier could be used for these purposes. The only difference is that the constructed identifiers occasionally may cause errors when files are merged, whereas the universal identifiers would not. People might do well to encourage the passage of laws that forbid the mergings and exchanges they consider improper, instead of relying on the inefficiency of computer systems to protect them.

The Social Security Number As a Universal Identifier The social security number is used as an identifier not only by the Social Security Administration but by the Internal Revenue Service and many state agencies as well. For years, the social security number has been on its way to becoming a universal identifier.

The Privacy Act of 1974, however, placed limitations on the use of the social security number. Individuals were given the right to refuse to supply their social security numbers for purposes not authorized by law.

But, since then, additional legislation has been passed that allows some exceptions, particularly for state government systems that already were organized around social security numbers when the Privacy Act was passed. As a result, the use of social security numbers by state and federal governments is still widespread. As far as the government is concerned, the social security number is still about to become a universal identifier.

THE INTERACTIONS OF COMPUTER SYSTEMS AND THEIR USERS

A computer system should be considerate of the human feelings, limitations, and idiosyncracies of the people who use it. After using the system, people should not feel that they have been "folded, spindled, or mutilated."

Understandable Output The output of a computer system should be understandable to the people who use it. This should be true regardless of who the people are. Output for programmers and computer operators should be as understandable as that supplied to the general public.

In the mid-1970's this talking computer system was being used by over 5,000 blind people in the Boston area. With the aid of the system a blind person could type letter-perfect correspondence, proofread manuscripts, do bookkeeping problems, and write computer programs. The computer responded to the typist in words and sentences, telling him precisely what he had typed or giving him the results of commands or computations carried out by the computer.

Many systems violate this principle by printing obscure codes that can only be interpreted by consulting a manual provided by the manufacturer. (Sometimes even consulting the manual is not very enlightening, since the explanation found there may be obscure.) Again, there's plenty of room for improvement. The "job control languages" used to specify how jobs are to be handled by a computer system are major offenders.

To be sure, many manual systems fail to produce understandable output. Government documents, for instance, are often unreadable—including that most widely circulated of all government documents, the instructions for preparing income tax forms. But perhaps computers can do better.

Courtesy We might do well to program our computers with the elementary courtesies, such as saying "please" when making a request and "thank you" when a request is carried out. Admittedly, these words are as empty for the computer as they often are for the human beings who mouth them. But if they make the user feel a little less manipulated, they are worthwhile.

Quick Response and Reaction A system should acknowledge its input as quickly as possible. If a person has made a request, then the system should act on it promptly. When immediate action is impossible, the person should be informed of what steps are being taken to satisfy the request. If possible, a time estimate of when the request can be fulfilled should be given.

One reason for using computers, of course, is to improve the response times for systems. Manual systems are most likely to respond slowly.

Provisions for Corrections We've already mentioned the importance of people being able to correct errors in files that are kept on them.

But all information systems should have provisions for corrections. System designers must realize that, despite everybody's best efforts, incorrect information *will* get into the system and will have to be found out and corrected. Many of the horror stories told about computers and erroneous bills arise from the lack of provisions for corrections. The employee who promises to "take care of" the erroneous bill may, in fact, be powerless to do so.

Different Classes of Individuals   The system must "realize" that it deals with different classes of individuals with different backgrounds and needs. Sometimes this requirement conflicts with privacy: a system may need certain personal information about someone in order to deal with that person as an individual.

This can be a touchy subject. In other circumstances, treating different classes of individuals in different ways is known as *discrimination*. To prevent discrimination, there is a movement towards eliminating references to race and sex from certain documents. But such elimination also could prevent a system from providing assistance tailored to the special problems of a particular race or sex.

User Choices   The user should have as much freedom of choice as possible in the ways he deals with the system. For instance, a person may be allowed to provide requested information in any order he wishes, instead of having to fill out a rigid form.

Provisions for Override   The designers of a complex system like to believe that they have thought of every possible situation that can occur. But, of course, they have not. "Improbable events permit themselves the luxury of occurring," as Charlie Chan once put it. Eventually, the system will have to be modified to handle the unforeseen cases routinely. But, in the meantime, there must be some way of overriding the system occasionally, so people in special situations will not be inconvenienced.

SYSTEM RELIABILITY

Some innovative systems (such as BART, which we looked at in chapter 14), have proved to be notoriously unreliable during their first few years of operation. And some computer applications, such as computer translations of natural languages, have yet to live up to the enthusiastic claims once made for them. In some situations, the public needs to be protected from systems that are not reliable or do not live up to the claims made by their designers.

Research Objectives and Engineering Realities   Anyone who goes into a new project is enthusiastic about the anticipated positive results. This reaction is both human and undesirable. Spare us the person who isn't optimistic and enthusiastic about what he's doing. Still, this enthusiasm can be detrimental when the public is led to confuse the hoped-for results of a research project with what already has been proved and is ready for use.

Classification of Systems   One approach to preventing this confusion would be to place proposed systems in three categories.

1. *Under Investigation.*   Researchers currently are studying ways to implement the proposed system. They may well expect their research to be highly successful and to yield important benefits. But these successes have yet to be achieved.

2. *Implemented but Unproved.*   The proposed system has been constructed, and preliminary tests indicate that it operates as desired. However, it has not been extensively tested in the field, so it probably suffers from the numerous bugs that extensive field testing invariably uncovers. People who use the system at this point do so at their own risk.

3. *Proved.*   The system has been tested in actual use over an extended period of time. All the bugs apparently have been eliminated. Implementing another copy of the system should be a routine job for competent engineers in the appropriate specialties.

OWNERSHIP OF INFORMATION

Protection of Computer Software   The software for a computer system may be as valuable as the hardware or more so. The software of a large system represents years of labor by many people. Yet software vendors are finding it increasingly difficult to protect their products from appropriation by unauthorized persons.

At present, software protection often relies on complex licensing agreements, which can be annoying to both the vendor and the buyer. The vendor must take it upon himself to detect violations of the licensing agreement and bring suit. The buyer must agree to tedious restrictions and security precautions. Often, important documentation is kept secret, an annoyance to all who must work with the system.

The problem is even more serious with personal computing. Businesses accept software costs as business expenses. But it's hard to convince hobbyists who are merely "having fun" that it is wrong to get a copy of a program from a friend instead of buying it from its author or publisher. There has been considerable copying of software in the personal computing field, and this probably has held back the development of more advanced software for personal computers.

Software vendors have attempted to obtain patent protection for their products but with little success. Patent applications have been rejected on the grounds that to patent a program is to patent ideas, which the patent law specifically forbids. In one case, which reached the Supreme Court, the court rules that no patent should be granted. However, that case concerned an algorithm stated in abstract form rather than a program stated in the language of a particular computer. Also, the court did not rule out patenting a program that was part of a machine, such as a piece of firmware.

The question of patent protection for software is still muddled. But the weight of the latest court decisions seems to be against it.

Copyright is another avenue of protection. Most software is routinely copyrighted. Copyright protects the form in which information is expressed but not the ideas the information carries. On the other hand, copyright does protect a book from being translated into a foreign language and a play from being performed, even though these acts radically change the form of the information.

It's still not clear just how the copyright laws will be interpreted for computer programs, since not enough cases have gone to court. But some interesting possibilities have been suggested. For instance, when a program is loaded into a computer memory from cards, disk, or tape, it is being copied—illegal without the copyright holder's permission. And when a computer executes the instructions of a program, is this not the same as when actors perform a play or musicians perform a composition from a written score?

The present copyright law serves to protect information in conventional forms—books, photographs, recordings, and so on. But information stored in computer systems presents some new problems. For one thing, it's easy to copy: often, a command to the computer's operating system is all that is needed to get a copy produced. Second, the copy is identical in every respect to the original; it may be hard to distinguish between the copy and the original, or between an authorized copy and an unauthorized one.

These problems have to be overcome. All the systems described in this book require extensive effort on the part of human beings to develop programs and other information. People will not be motivated to create this information if their creations cannot be protected so that they can profit from them.

Commercial Use of Personal Information   The law provides businesses with some protection when their information is misused. When industrial spying occurs or when one business hires key personnel away from another for the purpose of picking their brains, damage suits are often successful.

But what about the misuse of personal information? In some cases, such as when someone's photograph is used for advertising purposes without the person's consent, a suit usually will be successful. But what about when a business profits from selling mailing lists? Do individuals have any right to say whether or not their names should be on the lists? And should they not have a right to some of the

profit made through the use of their names?

More and more, information is becoming a commodity to be bought and sold. We need to develop a legal concept of ownership of information, similar to the concept of ownership we now have for real property.

Such a concept is a long way from development. At this point, we can only suggest possibilities. Perhaps a person should own all the information about him and his activities, except where the ownership would conflict with some need of society, such as freedom of the press. Beyond that, an individual should be able to control whether personal information is used to make a profit; when it is so used, the individual should be able to demand a share of the profit.

FOR FURTHER READING

ACM Committee on Computers and Public Policy. "A Problem-List of Issues Concerning Computers and Public Policy." *Communications of the ACM*, Sept. 1974, pp. 495-503.

IBM advertisement. "Four Principles of Privacy." *Newsweek*, July 8, 1974, p. 48.

Mooers, Calvin N. "Computer Software and Copyright." *Computing Surveys*. March 1975, pp. 45-72.

Neier, Aryeh. *Dossier: The Secret Files They Keep on You.* New York: Stein and Day, 1975.

Secretary's Advisory Committee on Automated Personal Data Systems. *Records, Computers, and the Rights of Citizens.* Cambridge: Massachusetts Institute of Technology, 1973.

Sterling, Theodor D., "Guidelines for Humanized Computerized Information Systems: A Report from Stanley House." *Communications of the ACM*, Nov. 1974, pp. 609-613.

REVIEW QUESTIONS

1. Give the five guidelines for access to files that were mentioned in this chapter.

2. What is an *identifier?*

3. People sometimes complain that they are being turned into numbers because computer systems use numbers in place of their names. Why are names not good identifiers? What would be the effect if the turned-into-numbers people were heeded, and names were used as identifiers?

4. What is a *universal identifier?*

5. Why do some people object to the assignment of universal identifiers?

6. How could separate files be merged and information exchanged among computer systems without the aid of universal identifiers?

7. Describe how a computer system must behave in order to have each of the following properties:

- understandable output

- courtesy

- quick response

- provisions for corrections

- recognition of different classes of individuals

- allowance for user choices

- provisions for override

8. Why is the public sometimes misled about the actual workability of proposed systems?

9. Describe three categories in which systems could be placed to indicate their states of development.

10. Give three approaches to the protection of software.

11. Why is software for personal computers particularly hard to protect?

12. What is the main objection to patent protection for software?

13. What are some suggestions that have been made for applying the copyright law to loading and executing computer programs?

14. What would be the likely effects on the development of computer systems if it proved impossible to protect programs and other information against unauthorized use?

15. What are some questions that can be raised about the use of personal information for commercial purposes?

**DISCUSSION
QUESTIONS**

1. Discuss the privacy guidelines given in this chapter. Do you think any of them are unnecessary? Do you think any additional guidelines are necessary?

2. Discuss the attitudes of people toward universal identifiers. Ask some of your friends for their feelings on the matter and discuss their responses. Are these attitudes based more on logic or emotion?

3. Can you think of some steps, other than those described in this chapter, than can be taken to make interactions between human beings and computer systems go more smoothly?

4. From your own experience, describe a computer application or other technological innovation that did not work as planned when it first was put into service.

5. Discuss the pros and cons of giving individuals much more control over the commercial use of information about them than they now have.

CHAPTER 19

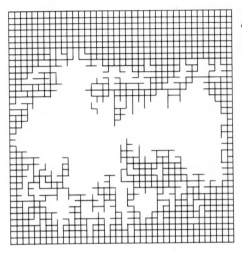

ARTIFICIAL INTELLIGENCE

Intelligent computers and robots are stock characters in science-fiction stories and films, and often they turn out to be the most memorable ones. Who can forget HAL of *2001: A Space Odyssey*, the drones of *Silent Running*, Robby of *Forbidden Planet*, or the half-comic, half-serious 'droids, C3PO and R2-D2, of *Star Wars*?

Are science-fiction stories about intelligent machines and robots predicting the future accurately? Or are they wide of the mark, like the 1930s science-fiction stories that predicted everyone would have his own private helicopter by 1950? (By 2050, people will be lucky if they still have their own private automobiles!)

In short, will we ever be able to program a computer to exhibit intelligent behavior? Without a working crystal ball, we can't give an absolute answer one way or the other. Only time will reveal the levels of performance that computers eventually will reach. But we can look at some of the possibilities and see why the question of machine intelligence is an open one in spite of the unsupported, dogmatic assertions we sometimes hear.

IMITATIONS OF MAN

Are human beings the only thinking creatures on earth? Or is it possible that other things, living or nonliving, possess or could possess the power of reason?

Philosophers have long enjoyed debating this point. In the seventeenth and eighteenth centuries, for instance, a heated dispute raged over whether or not animals could think. And, even today, studies are being done on the intelligence of dolphins and the ability of chimpanzees to use language.

Machines were brought into the debate when elaborate clockwork automata became popular. These ingenious machines could mimic human behavior to a surprising degree. People were startled to see a robot boy seated at a desk write a page-long letter complete with signature at the end, pausing from time to time to dip a quill pen in an inkwell. Musical automata were particularly fashionable; robots that played pianos, organs, violins—even whole robot orchestras—were not uncommon.

Sometimes the fascination and curiosity turned to fear, hatred, and suspicion. Pierre Droz, one of the most prolific creators of clockwork automata, was jailed by the Holy Inquisition when he displayed his work in Spain. The dreaded Inquisition was dedicated to stamping out witchcraft and heresy.

The last word in automata of this type exists today in (of all places) Disneyland. In the Audio Animatronics exhibit, robot historical figures (Abraham Lincoln is one) act out scenes from the lives of their human counterparts. This kind of mimicry no longer seems to bother people as it once did. We are now sophisticated enough to realize that recorded voices and preprogrammed movements do not endow a robot with humanity.

WHAT IS THINKING

"Can a computer think?" we ask. Before we can even start to get an answer, we need to know what is meant by the word *think*. Unfortunately, it is difficult for people to agree on a definition. In fact, many arguments over the possibilities of thinking machines break down precisely because the participants aren't talking about the same thing when they use the word *think*. To begin our discussion, therefore, let's look at four proposed definitions of *thinking*.

Thinking Is a Uniquely Human Activity   Those who advance this definition are unwilling to admit that a computer can think unless it can duplicate all the intellectual, emotional, and sense-related activities of human beings. For them, thinking is the same as being human. To be sure, they seldom state their definition quite so baldly. But this is the definition that seems to lie behind statements that computers cannot think because they cannot do some uniquely human thing, such as feel hatred, fall in love, or enjoy friendship.

Thinking Is the Ability to Solve "Deep" or Difficult Problems   If a
machine could play a masterly game of chess or reason out solutions

to deep problems in science, mathematics, and the humanities, many people would grant it the ability to think. We also might require that it communicate in some natural language, such as English, so that it could discuss these problems with human beings in their own language.

The point is that, by this definition, we judge the intelligence of a computer only by its ability to reason and to communicate the results of its reasoning. We don't require it to have human emotions or behave like human beings in ways that don't involve reasoning.

The Turing Test   Alan Turing, the pioneer British computer scientist, proposed that the question, "Can a machine think?," be replaced by another question that can be stated without ambiguity. To state this new question, Turing started out by describing something called the *imitation game*, which is somewhat similar to the television panel show *To Tell the Truth*.

The imitation game has three players—a computer, a human being, and a (human) interrogator; the latter is separated from the computer and the human. The interrogator communicates with the other two players through intermediaries, by Teletype, or by some other means that will conceal whether a particular message originated with the human or the computer.

The object of the game is for the interrogator to determine which of the other two players is the computer. He knows the players only as X and Y. At the end of the game, he will announce that either X or Y is the computer.

The object of the computer is to try to imitate a human as closely as possible. The real human plays a somewhat neutral role, simply answering the interrogator's questions as truthfully and accurately as possible. But the computer labors under no such restrictions. For instance, it might pretend to be unable to do mathematics to throw the interrogator off. If asked about its physical appearance, it would just lie. But if asked to analyze a love poem, it would be put to the test.

Now, suppose the game is played many times. Will the interrogator usually be able to identify which player is the computer? Or will he make the wrong choice as often as not? This last question is the one that, according to Turing, should replace the question, "Can a machine think?"

Turing's definition of thinking (or substitute for it) is behavioral: whether or not a machine can think hinges on how it behaves and not on its physical appearance or what its innermost thoughts and feelings (if any) might be.

Since Turing compares a computer to a human being, his concept of thinking is close to the one that maintains thinking is a human activity. A human can think; therefore, if a machine can think, it must be able to imitate a human. To be sure, Turing limits the imitation to matters of the mind and does not require the machine to resemble a human physically. On the other hand, an interrogator could ask a

player to comment on a poem, a novel, or a work of art. A highly intelligent but emotionless computer might find this hard to do.

ELIZA When playing the imitation game, we must beware of cheap imitations. There exists a program, called ELIZA, that can carry on superficial conversations. This is done entirely with conversational tricks, such as taking the other person's statements and turning them into questions.

For instance, if a person talking to ELIZA said (typed, actually)

YOU ARE NOTHING BUT A DUMB COMPUTER.

ELIZA might reply,

WHAT MAKES YOU SAY I AM NOTHING BUT A DUMB COM-PUTER?

This sounds as if the computer understood the original statement and is asking why it was made. Actually, the computer understood nothing. In the computer's memory are stored a number of sentence patterns, such as

YOU ARE _____ .

and

273 WHAT MAKES YOU SAY I AM _____ ?

The program recognizes that YOU ARE NOTHING BUT A DUMB COMPUTER is an example of the first pattern, with NOTHING BUT A DUMB COMPUTER in place of the blank. By consulting a table stored in memory, the computer finds that a possible reply to a sentence having the first pattern is one having the second pattern and with the same phrase substituted for the blank. The dumb computer made no attempt to understand the phrase that characterizes it so well.

A well-written program of this kind can be surprisingly glib, using all the conversational tricks that people fall back on when they have nothing really intelligent to say. For instance, the program occasionally repeats a person's last statement almost exactly ("I went to Paris last summer." "You went to Paris last summer?"), a surprisingly effective conversational gambit. And when ELIZA really gets stuck, it tries to change the subject.

People who have carried on conversations with ELIZA-like programs have been deceived into thinking they were talking to human beings. It has been said that this is an example of a computer passing the Turing test. But, actually, the people who were duped allowed themselves to be taken in by ELIZA's inane conversational tricks. Any attempt to get the program to discuss a serious subject—art, music, sports, human affairs—quickly would have revealed the deception. The interrogator in the imitation game must be careful not to be fooled by a clever word manipulator like ELIZA.

Degrees of Thinking   All the definitions of thinking we have discussed so far assume that thinking is an all-or-nothing proposition: either a computer can think, or it cannot. Computer scientist Paul Armer has suggested another approach, which is based on two premises. One, thinking involves a number of features we can examine separately. And, two, we can measure the degree to which each feature is present.

For instance, one feature of thinking is the speed with which it is done. We all admire fast thinkers. Of course, computers can process information much faster than humans can. On the speed scale, then, we might give computers a high rating and human beings a much lower one.

But speed, obviously is not everything. Another feature of thinking is the complexity and sophistication of the information processing that occurs. Setting up a scale to measure this would not be easy, but, for the sake of argument, assume that it can be done. Then, on the "sophistication scale," humans would have a high rating, and present-day computers would have a much lower one.

By Armer's definition, then, humans, computers, and animals all can be said to think in some sense. But the thought processes of each are quite different, and each has its own strengths and weaknesses. The merit of a particular combination of strengths and weaknesses depends on the job to be done. If complex arithmetic must be done very fast, then we need a computer. For sophisticated problem solving, a human would be the right choice. For quick reactions to subtle sense impressions, we might turn to an animal.

From this point of view, there is no vast gap between being able to think and not being able to think. To be sure, humans currently rate far higher than computers on many of the features of thinking. But we should not be surprised if future research vastly improves the ability of programs to handle certain features. At first, this will be done on a feature-by-feature basis, so we will see here a program that can handle natural languages and there a program that can play chess. But if enough programs that rate highly in enough different features of thinking are developed, eventually someone may be able to put them together and give us our imitation-game challenger after all.

SOME METHODS OF ARTIFICIAL INTELLIGENCE

Artificial intelligence is the field of research that seeks to program computers for more intelligent behavior. More specifically, it seeks to improve the computer's abilities in those areas of intelligent behavior where humans currently rate high and computers currently rate low.

It was Lady Lovelace who first stated the problem that faces a

worker in artificial intelligence. "The Analytical Engine," she wrote, "has no pretensions to originate anything. It can do *whatever we know how to order it to perform.*" The modern way of saying the same thing is, "A computer can only do what it is told to." How can anything that can only follow orders be considered intelligent?

The answer lies in making the instructions we give to the computer sufficiently general. We will not be content to instruct the computer merely in how to do this or that job—how to make up a payroll, for instance, or how to track a spacecraft. Instead, our aim is nothing less than instructing the computer how to think. Once this is done, the computer, executing the "thinking" program, can figure out how to make up payrolls and track spacecraft as well as how to do many other tasks.

Of course, it is much easier to *talk* about programming a computer to think than it is to *do* it. We don't really know how to tackle the general problem at all. But we have seen that thinking can be broken down into a number of separate features, and progress has been made in programming computers to exhibit some of these features.

Problems and Search   Surely, one of the most important features of thinking is the ability to solve problems. The key to general purpose problem solving is *search.* When a human being encounters a problem he has no idea how to solve, he falls back on trial and error. He tries one thing and then another until he finds something that takes him a step closer to his goal. Once that step is taken, the problem solver may have to resort to trial and error again to find the next step toward the solution.

The search continues this way until the problem is solved or until the search comes to a dead end. If the latter occurs, the problem solver has to backtrack to a previous step and strike out in another direction from there.

The investigations of a detective, as chronicled by so many mystery writers, are a good example of this kind of problem solving.

Heuristics   A blind search, however, is unlikely to get us anywhere. No problem solver ever will have time to follow up every possible line of investigation that conceivably could lead to a solution. The arguments we used in chapter 6 to show that the number of paths through a large flowchart is astronomical can be used to show that the number of paths facing a problem solver is just as large.

No, the search somehow has to be guided. At each step, the problem solver must be restricted to those alternatives that are most likely to lead to a solution. But how can we tell whether or not an alternative is promising before investigating it in detail?

The trick is to use rules of thumb that are technically known as *heuristics.* (*Heuristic* comes from a Greek word meaning "serving to discover.") A heuristic suggests a certain course of action to be taken in certain situations. But there is no guarantee that the suggestion is the *right* course or the *only* course to follow. The suggested action is

simply one that has worked well in similar situations in the past and, therefore, is worth trying now. Most proverbs—for example, "A stitch in time saves nine"— are heuristics. So are most household hints—"To remove a stuck jar lid, place the lid under hot water."

The advice given to beginners in a profession usually consists of heuristics. Beginning writers, for instance, are urged to use short sentences, avoid the passive voice, and prefer words of Anglo-Saxon derivation to those derived from Latin. Each of these rules is worth knowing, yet good reasons exist for violating every one of them.

The rules of harmony composers use provide another example. Traditional composers follow these rules for the most part. But even (perhaps especially) the most famous composers violate the rules from time to time. In fact, one well-known textbook on harmony states that following the rules without exception would lead to very dull music.

A heuristic, then, recommends some action we should *think about* taking in a particular situation. Whether we should actually take that action depends on the details of the particular situation we are facing. Heuristics never guarantee success. The most promising approach to a problem may turn out to be a dead end. Worse yet, the heuristic might lead the problem solver to reject as unpromising the only path that leads to a solution.

The advantage of heuristics is that they reduce the number of alternative paths that have to be explored. If we consider all the heuristics that apply to a particular situation, then the number of actions they recommend is much smaller than the total number of actions possible. The number of things we have to try to each step of solving our problem is vastly reduced. And, although there is no guarantee that any of these things will take us closer to solving our problem, it's a good bet that one of them will.

Pattern Recognition Usually, the conditions under which a particular heuristic can be used are rather specialized. A rule of thumb for starting a flooded car, say, helps you only when you are faced with starting a flooded car; it will do nothing for you if you are trying to remove a stuck jar top. And none of the heuristics for removing stuck jar tops will do anything to help you start a flooded car.

Often, the difference between an apprentice and a master at a craft is that the apprentice knows only the heuristics that almost always work, while the master also knows many that apply only to very special situations. Yet these special situations occur often enough to give the master a considerable advantage over the apprentice.

To decide which heuristics to apply, the problem solver looks for *patterns* in the problem situation. A chess player, for instance, is guided by the patterns formed by the men on the board. A detective will notice that a crime follows a certain pattern and plan his investigation accordingly.

Thus, a problem-solving program needs a capacity for *pattern recognition*. This is the ability to extract examples of patterns from complex information and use these to select the applicable

277

heuristics. We can think of the heuristics a problem solver has at his command as being filed according to the patterns that suggest their use.

Planning   Another way to eliminate unpromising alternatives is to work out a plan or a strategy in advance. One then follows up only those alternatives that are consistent with the plan.

The plan could be a previously memorized one. Police and fire departments, for instance, plan how they will handle certain situations. The members of these departments are required to learn these plans. When faced when one of these situations, the police officer or firefighter does *not* try everything that can be thought of but carries out the steps called for by the previously memorized plan.

On the other hand, we can make up a plan as we go along, basing it on information extracted from the problem situation. For instance, a poker player bases his strategy on the hand he has been dealt and the hands he *thinks* the other players have. His information about the other players' hands varies as the game proceeds, and new information may require a change in plans.

Just as with heuristics, a plan not only does not guarantee success, it may cause you to miss the correct solution altogether. So a problem solver must be prepared to abandon a plan that is not working and switch to an alternate one. On the other hand, if the problem solver switches too often, the number of alternatives to explore will become unmanageble.

Current problem-solving programs are not nearly as good at planning as they should be. A common criticism of chess-playing programs, for instance, is that while they sometimes make very good moves, they seem to have no overall plan for achieving victory. Even the good moves are motivated by immediate tactical skirmishes, not by some overall strategy.

Representation of Knowledge   Each of us has in his head a kind of model of the real world. The model allows us to imagine situations before they arise and plan our actions in advance. It allows us to work out in our heads how to accomplish a task before we ever take any physical action.

If a computer is to think about the real world, then, it has to have some way to represent knowledge about the real world in its memory. Although we have seen how we can model real-world systems inside computers, the models invariably were constructed by people, not by the computer itself. As yet, no one has thought of a way to put everything a person knows about the real world in a computer's memory in such a way that the computer can use the knowledge effectively. The problem of representation of knowledge is an important area of research in artificial intelligence.

Communication in a Natural Language   Many people, including all the advocates of the Turing test, would insist that a computer be able to communicate in a human language, such as English, before they would accept the machine as intelligent.

The ability to communicate in English varies from one program to another. Many programs can understand some English words, phrases, or sentences. When the discourse is limited to a particular subject, some programs do surprisingly well. But no program has yet demonstrated the ability to understand and use unrestricted English.

One of the earliest attempts to apply artificial intelligence to a practical problem was the attempt in the late 1950s and early 1960s to program computers to translate Russian into English. At that time, there was a fear that we were falling behind the Russians because most of our scientists and engineers could not read Russian technical journals.

These attempts failed. Using fairly simple techniques, such as looking up Russian words in a dictionary and using simple grammar and context rules when more than one translation was possible, about 80 percent of the Russian text could be translated. But the remaining 20 percent proved remarkably difficult. Since 80 percent translations were not good enough, the funds eventually were withdrawn from the translation projects, and they all disappeared.

Present workers in artificial intelligence believe that a computer must somehow extract the meanings of sentences before it can translate them into another language. No mere juggling of words will do the job.

THEY SAID
IT COULDN'T
BE DONE

Some scientific ideas draw more than their share of laughter and ridicule. In recent history, air travel was one of these, and space travel was another. And, today, people who raise the possibility of intelligent machines seem to be laughed at more than those who propose equally far-out ideas.

The famous science and science-fiction writer Arthur C. Clarke, in his book *Profiles of the Future*, analyzes why those who "said it couldn't be done" are so often wrong. Clarke points out two roadblocks to successful prophecy—*failure of nerve* and *failure of imagination.*

Failure of nerve occurs when someone has all the facts at hand but cannot bring himself to draw the proper conclusion from them. Failure of the imagination occurs when someone finds it impossible to visualize where current trends are leading.

People outside the computing field who vehemently deny the possibility of intelligent machines often seem to suffer from failure of nerve. To have machines as intelligent as human beings, or even more so, is just too frightening and unpleasant for them to think about. Therefore, they deny the possibility in the strongest possible terms.

People in the computing field, on the other hand, seem more

subject to failure of imagination. And no wonder. If you spend your days struggling to program simple applications for a machine that shows not the slightest hint of intelligence, you may find it hard to believe that anyone could ever program the machine for intelligent behavior. After all, one has enough trouble getting it to do those simple applications correctly.

Vitalism. According to vitalism, living things obey different natural laws than do nonliving things. Life possesses some "vital force" that can never be duplicated in the laboratory. Although this idea goes back to the eighteenth century, its influence can be seen in many recent discussions of artificial intelligence.

For instance, it was once widely believed that the chemicals found in living organisms could not be synthesized from nonliving substances in the laboratory. Thus, the world of chemistry was profoundly shocked in 1828 when the German chemist Friedrich Whöler synthesized a component of urine.

Vitalism suffered this kind of defeat again and again. Over the years, it became clear that the chemical reactions taking place in living things obeyed the same laws as those taking place in the laboratory. The circulation of the blood was explained in terms of hydraulics, the motion of the body in terms of mechanics, the activities of the nerves in terms of electricity and chemistry. Nobody found a trace of any "vital force."

But one last outpost of vitalism remains—the human brain. So far, biologists have not been able to explain in detail how the brain thinks, and artificial intelligence researchers have not been able to duplicate its functions in the laboratory. Until this is done, those who wish to can still cling to the hope that the human body is governed by something more than the mere principles of physics and chemistry. Vitalism dies hard, and some of the diehards are the most vehement critics of artificial intelligence.

Now let's look at four objections that are frequently raised against the possibility of artificial intelligence.

In the Image of Man? We touched on this objection before when we talked about the definition of thinking. Some people say a machine can never think because it cannot, they assert, fall in love, experience anger, appreciate a joke, enjoy strawberries and cream, and so on and on.

But does something have to be human to be intelligent? Does something have to be like us in every respect before we will admit it can think? Consider this: Some radio astronomers are trying to contact beings on the planets of distant stars. Suppose we someday do contact creatures from outer space. They surely will differ from us in almost every respect. Will we grant them the ability to think? Strawberries and cream would most likely poison them.

Able to Leap Tall Buildings in a Single Bound? People have said, with
apparent seriousness, that they will believe a computer can think

when it has written a symphony as magnificent as one of Beethoven's or a play as eloquent as one of Shakespeare's or when it has defeated the current world champion at chess.

What makes this idea laughable is that the overwhelming majority of human beings can't do these things either. If these are the criteria for intelligence, then almost all of us are very unintelligent indeed.

In fact, someone once went even further and said that a convincing thinking machine would have to be able to prove Fermat's Last Theorem in mathematics. Now, Fermat's Last Theorem is the most famous unsolved problem of mathematics; after years and years of struggle, mathematicians have been unable to prove Fermat's elusive theorem. By this criterion, then, *nobody* can think, nor has anybody been able to think during the last several hundred years that mathematicians have struggled with Fermat's Last Theorem.

I Know Just What You're Going to Say How can a computer ever do anything original when its behavior can be completely predicted from its program?

In principle, it's true that one could look at a computer program and predict everything the computer would ever do. But, in practice, this is ridiculous except for the simplest programs. In chapter 6, we saw that there is an astronomical number of paths through the flowchart of a complicated program. No human being could ever work out the consequences of following each of those paths. Indeed, program performance is so difficult to analyse that we find it extremely hard to determine whether or not a program has an error in it.

Furthermore, a program, like a human being, can learn from experience. What the program will do in the future depends on the experiences it has had in the past. We may know every detail of a program; but, without a history of the computer's day-by-day experiences, we will not even be able, in principle, to predict the future behavior of the program.

On the practical side, programs that play chess and checkers often are able to beat their own programmers. If a programmer could predict every move his program was going to make, would he ever lose a game to his own creation?

Limitations of Current Machines In the fifties, it was said that a computer with as many tubes as the human brain had cells would "not fit into the Empire State Building, would require the entire output of Niagara Falls to power it, and would need the Niagara River to cool it."

Here is a clear failure of the imagination. No part of this statement is true today. The bulky, hot, power-wasting vacuum tubes have given way to the tiny, cool, efficient transistors, tens of thousands of which can be packed onto a single integrated-circuit chip.

Besides, it is still uncertain that an intelligent machine would require as many transistors as the human brain has cells. The computer has access to auxiliary memory devices, such as magnetic tape and disk, while the human brain does not. Also, the computer operates much faster than the human brain, and this could make up for a shortage of cells. Even at the hardware level, a computer might work in quite a different way than the human brain yet still be able to think.

Intelligent computers may well require hardware advances over current machines. In view of the progress that electronics has made in recent years, dare we say that those advances will not be made?

So What Should We Expect?   At first sight, it may seem that most of this chapter has been devoted to arguing *for* the possibility of intelligent machines. But this isn't so. The arguments have been *against* some of the poorly thought-out objections that other people have raised against the possibility of thinking computers. But even if we agreed that all these objections were invalid, the technical challenge of building and programming an intelligent computer still could prove to be beyond our abilities.

What are the arguments *for* the possibility of thinking computers? The best ones seem to come from current research on artificial intelligence and from the history of technology.

Artificial intelligence researchers have made some progress in understanding and duplicating most of the features of intelligence. The progress has not been spectacular; it has not been rapid; and, in every area, far more remains to be done than has already been accomplished. Yet these successes, small as they are, encourage us to believe that achieving artificial intelligence is not totally beyond our ability. A start has been made. The work that has been done has borne (very modest) fruit. It's not unreasonable to expect that more work will yield more impressive results.

What the history of technology teaches us is that, once the first steps have been taken toward a technical goal, it is usually just a matter of time and research until the goal is reached. The first steps may be short and halting: the radio, the telephone, and the airplane were all useless toys in their earliest incarnations. But once the pioneers took the first steps, it was just a matter of time until those inventions were perfected for everyday use.

FOR FURTHER READING

Asimov, Isaac. *The New Intelligent Man's Guide to Science.* New York: Basic Books, 1965, p. 798.

Clarke, Arthur C. *Profiles of the Future.* New York: Harper & Row, 1963.

Feigenbaum, Edward A., and Feldman, Julian, eds. *Computers and Thought.* New York: McGraw-Hill Book Co., 1963.

Minsky, Marvin L. "Artificial Intelligence." *Computers and Computation.* San Francisco: W. H. Freeman, 1971, pp. 123-131.

Phlyshyn, Zenon W., ed. *Perspective on the Computer Revolution.* Englewood Cliffs, N. J.: Prentice-Hall, 1970, pp. 208-217, 224-245, 334-348.

Rorvik, David. *As Man Becomes Machine.* Garden City, N. Y.: Doubleday, 1971.

Sagen, Carl. *The Dragons of Eden.* New York: Random House, 1977.

Taube, Mortimer. *Computers and Common Sense.* New York: McGraw-Hill Book Co., 1963.

Weizenbaum, Joseph. *Computer Power and Human Reason.* San Francisco: W. H. Freeman, 1976.

Winston, Patrick Henry. *Artificial Intelligence.* Reading, Mass.: Addison-Wesley, 1977.

As we mentioned in the introduction to this chapter, robots and intelligent computers have often been the subjects of science fiction. The following are representative of the ways science-fiction writers have handled these subjects:

Asimov, Isaac. *I, Robot.* Garden City, N. Y.: Doubleday, 1963.

Clarke, Arthur C. *2001: A Space Odyssey.* New York: New American Library, 1968.

Gerrold, David. *When Harlie Was One.* Garden City, N. Y.: Nelson Doubleday, 1972.

Lucas, George. *Star Wars.* New York: Ballantine Books, 1976.

Heinlein, Robert A. *The Moon Is a Harsh Mistress.* New York: G. P. Putnam's Sons, 1968.

Jones, D. F. *Colossus.* New York: G. P. Putnam's Sons, 1966.

Mowshowitz, Abbe. *Inside Information: Computers in Fiction.* Reading, Mass.: Addison-Wesley, 1977.

Pohl, Fredrik. *Gateway.* New York: St. Martin's Press, 1977.

REVIEW QUESTIONS

1. Describe some ways you have seen robots and intelligent computers portrayed in science-fiction films or stories.

2. What was the subject of one of the earliest debates over whether something other than human beings could think?

3. What development brought machines into the debate over what could think?

4. What is the modern version of clockwork automata?

5. Give four approaches to defining the word *think* for computers.

6. Describe one kind of cheap imitation we may encounter in playing the imitation game.

7. What is the relation of search to problem solving?

8. What is the disadvantage of blind search?

9. What is a *heuristic*?

10. Give some examples of proverbs and household hints that are heuristics.

11. What is *pattern recognition*? Why is it important for heuristic search?

12. What is the role of planning in problem solving?

13. What is one of the most frequent criticisms of chess-playing computer programs?

14. What do we mean by the *representation of knowledge*?

15. Describe the attempts at computer translation of Russian in the 1950s.

16. Describe what is meant by *failure of nerve* and *failure of imagination*. Give examples of each from the history of familiar inventions.

17. What is *vitalism*?

18. In what sense can we say that the human brain is the last outpost of vitalism?

19. Give the four arguments against the possibility of intelligent machines that were discussed in this chapter. Evaluate the validity of each argument.

20. Give the arguments for the possibility of intelligent machines presented in this chapter. Again, evaluate the validity of the arguments.

DISCUSSION QUESTIONS

1. Discuss the various definitions of thinking presented in this chapter. Which one do you think is most suitable for asking the question: Can a machine think?

2. Read and discuss the article, "Turing Point," by Thomas A. Easton, in *Analog Science Fiction / Science Fact*, May 1975, pp. 93-104.

3. Read Isaac Asimov's *I, Robot*. and discuss whether or not future robots should be equipped with Asimov's Three Laws of Robotics. Can you think of any *disadvantages* of equipping every robot with the Three Laws?

4. Describe life in a future society in which highly intelligent machines are facts of life. What tasks might people purposely reserve for themselves even though machines could carry them out faster and more accurately?

5. Read the chapter, "The Obsolescence of Man," in Arthur C. Clarke's *Profiles of the Future*. Discuss Clarke's ideas about the inevitability of intelligent machines eventually replacing human beings as the dominant life form on this planet.

PART
THREE

BASIC

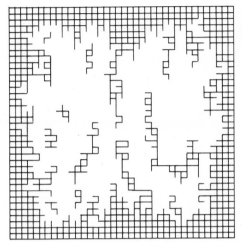

CHAPTER 20

GETTING STARTED

The previous chapters of this book have dealt with computers, programs, and programming. But reading about programming is not enough. To find out why programming can be so much fun, so challenging, and sometimes so tricky, you have to try it yourself.

In this part of the book, we will get a chance to try out programming for ourselves. We will learn to write programs in a programming language called BASIC. As the name indicates, BASIC is a simple programming language especially intended for beginning programmers. BASIC is easy to learn and easy to implement on small computers. For these reasons, it is the most widely used programming language in education and personal computing, and it is widely used on the computers found in small businesses.

USING THE COMPUTER

When the time comes for you to write a program in BASIC, you probably will use either a small, self-contained computer or a terminal connected to a larger computer. Either way, you will have a keyboard for typing information to be sent to the computer and either a printer or a display screen on which the computer can send information to you.

It would be pointless for us to present the fine details of any one computer system here, because these details vary so much from one system to another; the details of your system no doubt would be different. Therefore, you will have to rely on your instructor to explain how to enter BASIC programs into your computer and get them executed.

To give you an idea of what to expect, here is a list of the things that most BASIC systems will let you do. If you aren't sure how to do any of these things on your system, check with your instructor before you use the computer.

▪ You can type in your BASIC program line by line, just as if you were typing it out with a typewriter.

When you write and execute your basic programs, you will probably use either a computer terminal similar to the one shown on the left or a desk top computer similar to those shown below.

■ If you hit the wrong key, you can hit a special *delete* key that causes the computer to erase the error. You then hit the correct key and continue typing. By hitting the *delete* key more than once, you can erase as many erroneous characters as necessary.

■ You can enter the lines of your program in any order. As we will see in a moment, each line has a *line number*. The line numbers determine the order in which the lines are stored inside the computer. This order is the same regardless of what order the lines were typed in. This means you can add new lines at any time and have the computer put them in the proper places in the program by giving them appropriate line numbers. For instance, if you wanted to add a line between line 20 and line 30 of your program, giving the new line a line number of 25 would do the trick.

■ You can retype a line at any time. The newly entered line replaces the old line having the same line number.

■ You can delete any line.

■ You can have the computer *list* your program. This means that the computer prints out or displays a copy of the program as it is stored in memory.

■ You can have the computer *run* or execute your program. This means that the computer will follow the instructions in the program. The reason you write a program, of course, is to get the computer to follow the instructions in it.

■ At any time, you can force the computer to stop executing your program and stand by for further commands. This is important since it is easy to accidentally write a program that will not stop of its own accord.

■ If your program contains grammatical errors in the BASIC language or if it requests impossible operations (such as dividing by zero), the computer will print an *error message* for each problem it finds. Just because the computer does not print any error messages, however, does not that mean that your program is correct. A program can be grammatically correct and not request any impossible operations; yet it still may not give the computer the correct instructions for accomplishing the task the program was intended to accomplish.

Generally, a programmer enters a program, gets it listed to check for typing errors, executes the program, makes changes in it, gets another listing, executes the program again, and so on. The programmer continues to revise the program and test it by executing it until he is satisfied with the results the program produces.

BASIC PROGRAMS

Lines and Line Numbers   A BASIC program is made up of a number of lines, each of which contains instructions for the computer. Unless the computer is specifically directed to do otherwise, it executes the lines (follows the instructions on each line) in the order in which the lines occur in the program.

Each line starts with a line number. The lines are stored inside the computer in order of increasing line numbers, regardless of the order in which the lines were typed. The first line in a BASIC program has the smallest line number; the second line has the next smallest line number; and so on. The last line always has the largest line number.

BASIC programmers usually choose line numbers in multiples of ten—10, 20, 30, 40, and so on. The reason for this is to leave room between the lines of the program if it becomes necessary to add new lines. For instance, if you find that your program will work better with additional lines between line 40 and line 50, then you can use the line numbers 41, 42, 43, 44, 45, 46, 47, 48, and 49 for the new lines. But if you found you needed another line between lines 60 and 61, you would be out of luck, since fractional line numbers are not allowed.

What follows the line number and contains the instructions for the computer is called a *statement*. The word *instruction* or *command* would be more descriptive, but *statement* is traditional.

Each statement starts with a *keyword* that indicates what the computer is supposed to do when it executes that statement. The keyword is used to name the statement. Thus, the statement that begins with the keyword READ is called the READ statement; the statement that begins with the keyword PRINT is called the PRINT statement; and so on.

The END Statement   The END statement consists of the keyword END and nothing else. Because its purpose is to tell the computer where the end of the program is, the END statement must always be the last one in the program.

Programmers frequently forget to put in the END statement after they have typed in all the other statements of the program. Here is a trick for avoiding that. Since you can enter the lines of a program in any order, get in the habit of starting off by entering the END statement first. Give it a large line number, say 999 or 9999. As long as none of the other lines in the program have line numbers this large, the END statement will be the last statement in the program.

Here is a BASIC program illustrating line numbers and the END statement. At this point, don't worry about the meanings of any of the statements except the END statement:

```
10 PRINT "GOOD MORNING"
20 PRINT "HOW ARE YOU?"
30 PRINT "IS THERE SOMETHING I CAN DO FOR YOU?"
999 END
```

**THE
PRINT
STATEMENT**

A computer is of little use if it cannot print or display the results it reaches. Therefore, one of the first statements we learn in any computer language is the one that directs the computer to print or display information for the user. In BASIC, the statement that does this is the PRINT statement.

(In the reminder of the book, we will use the words PRINT, *print*, and *printout* as if the output were to be printed on paper. But if you are using a CRT display instead of a printer, the output will be displayed on the screen instead of actually being printed.)

Printing Strings   In BASIC, a series of letters, digits, and punctuation marks is called a *character string*, or simply a *string*. Strings are one of the types of data that can be stored in the computer's memory and manipulated by BASIC programs.

A string is always enclosed in quotation marks. The quotation marks themselves are not part of the string; they just show where it begins and ends. The following are examples of strings:

```
"HELLO"
"I AM YOUR FRIENDLY COMPUTER"
"COMPUTER PROGRAMMING IS FUN"
"DON'T YOU AGREE?"
```

A PRINT statement consists of the word PRINT followed by the items to be printed. For example, the following BASIC program uses PRINT statements to print the four strings just given:

```
10  PRINT "HELLO"
20  PRINT "I AM YOUR FRIENDLY COMPUTER"
30  PRINT "COMPUTER PROGRAMMING IS FUN"
40  PRINT "DON'T YOU AGREE?"
999 END
```

When the computer executes this program, it will print the following:

```
HELLO
I AM YOUR FRIENDLY COMPUTER
COMPUTER PROGRAMMING IS FUN
DON'T YOU AGREE?
```

Notice two things here. First, the computer executes the statements in the order in which they appear in the program; PRINT "HELLO" is executed first, PRINT "I AM YOUR FRIENDLY COMPUTER" is executed next, and so on. Second, the quotation marks are not printed, since they are not part of the strings but merely enclose them.

(When strings appear in running text, as they do in the preceding paragraph, the quote marks are slightly different from the ones used in displayed items, such as programs. This difference is not significant and should be ignored.)

Quotation marks can only be used to enclose strings. They are not allowed as parts of the strings themselves. If we allowed quotation marks to be parts of strings, the computer would not be able to tell the quotation marks that were part of a string from those that enclosed the string. If you need to quote something inside a string, use single quotes (apostrophes):

```
"'HOLD IT RIGHT THERE,' SAID THE POLICEMAN."
```

Printing Numbers   Numbers constitute another type of data that can be stored in the computer's memory and manipulated by BASIC programs. Numbers in BASIC programs can be written the way we usually write them, except that commas in the numbers are not allowed. The following are all acceptable numbers in BASIC:

```
25      1000      -50      9.75
```

The following are not acceptable:

```
1,000      2,500      1,000,000      -5,200
```

A PRINT statement will print numbers as well as strings. For instance, the program

```
 10 PRINT 25
 20 PRINT 100
 30 PRINT -50
 40 PRINT 9.75
999 END
```

causes the computer to print the following:

```
25
100
-50
9.75
```

Floating-Point Notation   When the computer has to print a very small number or a very large one, it uses a special notation to keep the printed number from taking up too much space. This notation is variously called floating-point notation, scientific notation, and exponential notation. You may already be familiar with floating-point notation, since many pocket calculators use a form of it for displaying very small and very large numbers.

To illustrate, suppose the computer executes the following program:

```
10 PRINT .000125
20 PRINT 12345000
999 END
```

The computer would print something like this (some details of the printout may be slightly different for your computer):

```
1.25000E-04
1.23450E+07
```

Let's see how to interpret numbers printed in this form. The number to the right of the letter E is called the *exponent*; it tells us how many places to the right or left the decimal point should be moved. If the exponent has a + sign, the decimal point is to be moved to the right. If the exponent has a − sign, the decimal point is to be moved to the left.

Let's take 1.25000E-04 as an example. To interpret this, we must start with 1.25000 and move the decimal point four places to the left. While we are moving the decimal point, we add any zeros that become necessary:

```
  1.25000
   .125000      (one place to the left)
   .0125000     (two places to the left)
   .00125000    (three places to the left)
   .000125000   (four places to the left)
```

Finally, the three zeros on the *right* serve no purpose and can be dropped. When we drop them, we are left with .000125.

Now, let's try to interpret 1.23450E+07. We must start with 1.23450 and move the decimal point seven places to the right:

```
1.23450
12.3450      (one place to the right)
123.450      (two places to the right)
1234.50      (three places to the right)
12345.0      (four places to the right)
123450.      (five places to the right)
1234500.     (six places to the right)
12345000.    (seven places to the right)
```

Again, we add extra zeros when they are needed.

To give a few more examples, here are some numbers in both conventional and floating-point notation:

Conventional Notation	Floating-Point Notation
500	5.00000E+02
−.0025	2.50000E-03
125749	1.25749E+05
.000001	1.00000E-06

When you write numbers in a BASIC program, you may use floating-point notation if you wish. If you do, you don't have to write any unneeded zeros, and you can omit plus signs. For example, consider this program:

```
 10  PRINT .000125
 20  PRINT 1.25E-4
 30  PRINT 12345000
 40  PRINT 1.2345E7
999  END
```

When the computer executes this program, it prints the following:

```
1.25000E-04
1.25000E-04
1.23450E+07
1.23450E+07
```

Notice that the computer prints each number the same way, regardless of whether it is written in conventional or floating-point notation in the program.

We must always be careful to distinguish between numbers and strings. Numbers are never enclosed in quotation marks; strings always are. Therefore, .000125 is a number, but ".000125" is a string.

Computer scientists say that numbers and strings belong to different *data types*. This means they are stored inside the computer differently, and the operations that can be carried out on them are different. The computer treats numbers and strings differently when they appear in PRINT statements. A string is always printed out, character by character, exactly as it appears in the program. A number, however, may be printed in exponential notation to save space. The following program illustrates this:

```
 10  PRINT ".000125"
 20  PRINT .000125
 30  PRINT "12345000"
 40  PRINT 12345000
999  END
```

When the computer executes this program, it prints the following:

```
.000125
1.25000E-04
12345000
1.23450E+07
```

Spacing Printed Items   A PRINT statement may contain more than one string or number to be printed. The punctuation marks used to separate the strings or numbers in the PRINT statement determine **296** how much space will be left between the printed items.

For instance, if the items are separated by *semicolons*, they will be printed close together. The program

```
10 PRINT 10; 20; 30; 40; 50
20 PRINT "AL"; "TO"; "GET"; "HER"
999 END
```

produces the printout

```
10 20 30 40 50
ALTOGETHER
```

We notice a difference between printing numbers and printing strings. When numbers are separated by semicolons, the numbers are printed close together, but they are not run together. There is at least one space between each pair of numbers. When strings are separated by semicolons, however, the individual strings are run together in the printout, with no space between them.

Exactly how much space is left between numbers will vary from one BASIC system to another. With this, as with some other details, you will have to experiment to see exactly what your system does.

You can mix numbers and strings in the same PRINT statement. Most systems will put spaces around the numbers. For instance,

```
10 PRINT 5; "PLUS"; 3; "EQUALS"; 8
999 END
```

causes the computer to print

```
5 PLUS 3 EQUALS 8
```

Again, exactly how much space is left between the items will vary from one version of BASIC to another.

If we ever need more space than the computer provides we can always include additional spaces inside quotation marks. The following program illustrates the use of spaces inside quotation marks:

```
10 PRINT "AL"; "TO"; "GET"; "HER"
20 PRINT "AL "; "TO "; "GET "; "HER"
999 END
```

The printout from this program is

```
ALTOGETHER
AL TO GET HER
```

Blank spaces can be used anywhere in a string. BASIC treats blank spaces just like any other characters.

If the items in the PRINT statement are separated by *commas* instead of semicolons, then the printed items are arranged in columns instead of being printed next to one another. The usual number of columns is five, although this number can vary, depending on the kind of display device your computer uses.

The following program illustrates the use of commas:

```
10 PRINT 1, 2, 3, 4, 5
20 PRINT "A", "B", "C", "D", "E"
30 PRINT "AL", "TO", "GET", "HER"
999 END
```

Notice that the commas go *outside* the quotation marks, not inside them as they would if we were writing English. The program produces the following printout:

1	2	3	4	5
A	B	C	D	E
AL	TO	GET	HER	

This feature of BASIC is useful for making up tables or reports in which the data is to be printed in columns. For instance, the following program prints a table giving the hourly wages of five workers:

```
10 PRINT "EMPLOYEE", "HOURLY"
20 PRINT "NAME", "RATE"
30 PRINT "--------", "------"
40 PRINT "ANDERSON", 10.25
50 PRINT "BAKER", 15.75
60 PRINT "CARSON", 25.38
70 PRINT "DAVIS", 40.25
80 PRINT "ERICSON", 12.63
999 END
```

The printout looks like this:

```
EMPLOYEE   HOURLY
NAME       RATE
--------   ------
ANDERSON   10.25
BAKER      15.75
CARSON     25.38
DAVIS      40.25
ERICSON    12.63
```

Skipping Lines   To cause the computer to skip a line in the printout, we use a statement consisting of the word PRINT with nothing following it. The following program illustrates how to make the computer skip a line:

```
10 PRINT "EMPLOYEE", "HOURLY"
20 PRINT "NAME", "RATE"
30 PRINT
```

```
40 PRINT "ANDERSON", 10.25
50 PRINT "BAKER", 15.75
60 PRINT "CARSON", 25.38
70 PRINT "DAVIS", 40.25
80 PRINT "ERICSON", 12.63
999 END
```

Line 30 causes the computer to skip a line between the column headings and the columns:

```
EMPLOYEE    HOURLY
NAME        RATE
                        (This line skipped)

ANDERSON    10.25
BAKER       15.75
CARSON      25.38
DAVIS       40.25
ERICSON     12.63
```

Keeping the Computer on the Same Line   Normally, when the computer finishes executing a PRINT statement, it sends a code that causes the printer or display device to go to a new line. When the next PRINT statement is executed, the data it prints is printed on the new line.

Sometimes, however, we want to keep the computer from going to a new line after each PRINT statement. That way, we can use more than one PRINT statement to print on a particular line.

We can suppress the transition to a new line by ending a PRINT statement with either a comma or a semicolon. After the PRINT statement has been executed, the computer stays on the same line, and the only spacing done is that called for by the final comma or semicolon.

An example program will make this clearer:

```
10 PRINT "AL";
20 PRINT "TO";
30 PRINT "GET";
40 PRINT "HER"
50 PRINT 1, 2,
60 PRINT 3, 4,
70 PRINT 5
999 END
```

This program prints the following:

```
ALTOGETHER
1           2           3           4           5
```

The semicolons at the ends of lines 10, 20, and 30 caused "TO",
"GET", and "HER" to be printed on the same line as "AL". The

spacing is the same as if the four strings had all been in the same PRINT statement, separated by semicolons.

The commas at the ends of lines 40 and 50 caused 1, 2, 3, 4, and 5 all to be printed on the same line. The spacing is the same as if all five numbers had appeared in the same PRINT statement, separated by commas.

We can mix commas and semicolons in a single PRINT statement. This includes commas and semicolons used at the ends of lines. For instance, consider the following program:

```
10 PRINT 1, 2; 3, 4
20 PRINT 1; 2;
30 PRINT 3, 4,
40 PRINT 5; 6
999 END
```

The printout from this program is

```
1             2 3           4
1 2 3         4             5 6
```

As you can see, a semicolon always produces close spacing, and a comma always produces spacing to the next column. This is true regardless of whether the semicolon or comma occurs within a PRINT statement or at the end of one.

ARITHMETIC IN BASIC

The following five signs are used to indicate arithmetic operations in BASIC:

```
+    addition
-    subtraction
*    multiplication
/    division
^    exponentiation
```

The + and − signs are familiar from everyday arithmetic and should cause no problems.

Most computer printers and display devices don't have the × and ÷ signs for multiplication and division. Therefore, * and / are used instead. In BASIC, then, 3 × 5 is written 3*5 and 12 ÷ 4 is written 12/4.

The exponentiation operation and the sign ^ may not ring any bells at all. Even if you have encountered the concept of exponentiation in a math course, the name "exponentiation" and the sign ^ were probably not used.

Actually, exponentiation is nothing more than a method for
indicating repeated multiplications, such as the following:

$5 \times 5 \times 5 \times 5 = 625$
$2 \times 2 \times 2 = 8$
$10 \times 10 = 100$

As we mentioned in chapter 4, mathematicians use a shorthand notation for such repeated products. They write 5^4 for $5 \times 5 \times 5 \times 5$, 2^3 for $2 \times 2 \times 2$, and 10^2 for 10×10. Therefore,

$5^4 = 625$
$2^3 = 8$
$10^2 = 100$

The small raised number is called the *exponent*, and the operation of repeated multiplication is called *exponentiation*.

(We have already mentioned that, in floating-point notation, the number to the right of the letter E is called the exponent. That's because 1.2345E7, for instance, could just as well be written 1.2345×10^7. Only the first form is allowed in BASIC. But scientists and engineers often use the second form.)

How can we indicate exponentiation in a programming language? Computer terminals have no provisions for printing numbers above or below the line or for printing some numbers smaller than others. However, the Teletype machines used with the early BASIC systems had an upward-pointing arrow. It struck the designers of BASIC that this upward-pointing arrow could suggest the raised exponents of mathematics. Therefore, in these early versions of BASIC (and in many BASIC textbooks), 5^4 is written 5↑4, 2^3 is written 2↑3, and 10^2 is written 10↑2.

Unfortunately, the upward arrow is one character for which the Teletype does not conform to the standard ASCII character set used by most BASIC systems. The character code that corresponds to ↑ on the Teletype corresponds to ˆ in the standard character set. That is, if we disconnect the Teletype from the computer and connect, in its place, a terminal that uses the standard character set, then everywhere the Teletype would have printed ↑, the terminal will print ˆ.

Teletypes are being used less and less with computers that run BASIC, and terminals that use the standard character set are being used more and more. As a result, ˆ has replaced ↑ as the sign for exponentiation in BASIC. We can think of ˆ as an arrow that has lost its shaft due to conditions beyond our control.

In any event, the only thing you have to remember is that the exponentiation sign indicates repeated multiplication, as the following examples illustrate:

$10\char94 3 = 1000$ $12\char94 2 = 144$
$\ \ 2\char94 4 = 16$ $\ \ 3\char94 3 = 27$

The signs for the operations of arithmetic are called *arithmetic operators* in BASIC. Thus, +, −, *, /, and ˆ are the arithmetic operators in BASIC.

When we write an arithmetic operator between two numbers, the result is called an *expression*. The following are examples of expressions:

```
3+5     8*4     9^2
7-2     12/3
```

When the computer encounters an expression in a BASIC program, it carries out the indicated arithmetic operation and obtains the result. What it does with the result depends on how the expression is used in the program.

If the expression is used in a PRINT statement, then the computer prints the result it calculates. For example, the program

```
 10 PRINT 3+4, 7-2, 8*4, 12/3, 9^2
999 END
```

causes the computer to print

```
7           5           32          4           81
```

Expressions in PRINT statements can be mixed with other items to be printed, as the following program shows:

```
 10 PRINT "THE SUM OF"; 5; "AND"; 3; "IS"; 5+3
 20 PRINT "THE PRODUCT OF"; 5; "AND"; 3; "IS"; 5*3
999 END
```

The printout is

```
THE SUM OF 5 AND 3 IS 8
THE PRODUCT OF 5 AND 3 IS 15
```

THE REM STATEMENT

The keyword REM stands for *remark*. The REM statement allows the programmer to insert remarks into the program. The remarks are intended for a person reading the program, not for the computer. The computer ignores REM statements when it executes the program.

For example, the program at the end of the last section can be provided with REM statements:

```
  5 REM THIS PROGRAM ILLUSTRATES THE PRINTING
  6 REM OF STRINGS, NUMBERS, AND THE VALUES OF
  7 REM ARITHMETIC EXPRESSIONS
 10 PRINT "THE SUM OF"; 5; "AND"; 3; "IS"; 5+3
 20 PRINT "THE PRODUCT OF"; 5; "AND"; 3; "IS"; 5*3
999 END
```

Since the computer ignores the REM statements, this version of the program produces exactly the same printout as the previous version.

The purpose of remarks is to explain to a person reading a program what the program does and how it works. Text intended to explain the workings of a program is known as *documentation*. There are two ways to document a program. One is to use remarks in the program itself. The other is to accompany the program with a separate text that explains its operation.

In this book, we usually will use the second method of documentation: all programs will be discussed in detail in the surrounding text. Therefore, our programs will not have nearly as many REM statements as would be necessary if we were relying on the REM statements alone for documentation.

What we refer to as remarks in BASIC are usually known as *comments* in other programming languages.

EXERCISES **1.** Write a program that will cause the computer to print the following price list:

```
ITEM         ITEM
NUMBER       PRICE
------       -----
11325        24.95
24321        16.95
32431        10.28
49872        29.35
67250        19.95
```

2. A computer can be programmed to print out pictures and designs. Examples of this kind of computer art (?) adorn the walls of computer rooms everywhere. Subjects range from cartoon characters to *Playboy* centerfolds. For example, the following program prints out a childish drawing of a tree:

```
10 PRINT "       *"
20 PRINT "      ***"
30 PRINT "     *****"
40 PRINT "    *******"
50 PRINT "   *********"
60 PRINT "  ***********"
70 PRINT "      ***"
80 PRINT "****************"
999 END
```

Enter this program into your computer and execute it to see that it performs as advertised. Then write a program to produce some picture or design of your own. The picture need not be any more complicated than the one in the example. On the other hand, the artistically inclined can have fun with this assignment by doing
303 something much more elaborate.

3. Give the printout produced by the following program:

```
 10 PRINT 1; 2; 3;
 20 PRINT 4, 5;
 30 PRINT 6, 7; 8,
 40 PRINT 9
999 END
```

4. Give the printout produced by the following program

```
 10 PRINT 8+4, 8-4, 8*4, 8/4, 8^4
999 END
```

5. Write a program to work out each of the following arithmetic problems, and print the results. Each result should be printed on a separate line.

(a) $128 + 375$

(b) $1923 - 754$

(c) 35×78

(d) $1813 \div 37$

(e) 2^{10}

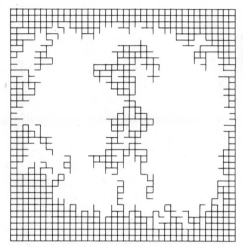

CHAPTER 21

USING THE COMPUTER'S MEMORY

When the computer executes a statement such as

10 PRINT 27+35

it carries out the calculation and prints the result. It does not, however, save the result to be used again later in the program.

If the result of a calculation will be needed again later, then we need some way to save the result until then. Saving results for later use is the function of the computer's memory. In this chapter, we will see how to use the computer's memory for this purpose.

VARIABLES

Named Memory Locations   We can think of the computer's memory as a large array of boxes, like post-office boxes or pigeonholes. Each box contains either a number or a string. And each box has an address by which the computer can refer to it.

Usually a program will use only a few of these boxes, and these few will be the only ones in which we are interested. We can display these boxes and ignore the rest. For example, suppose a program has stored the numbers 25 and 3.14 and the string "JOHN SMITH" in memory. Then, the part of memory we're interested in looks like this:

| 25 |

| 3.14 |

| "JOHN SMITH" |

If we are going to use the information stored in memory, we must have some way of referring to particular memory locations. The computer does this using binary-coded addresses. But we aren't particularly keen about having to refer to location 1101010111011010 or location 1010000011010001.

Therefore, higher-level languages such as BASIC allow us to use *names* for memory locations. These names are much easier to write and remember than binary codes. The computer keeps track of the correspondence between the names and the actual memory locations.

BASIC uses two kinds of memory locations—*numeric locations*, which hold numbers, and *string locations*, which hold strings. The two different kinds of locations are given different kinds of names so the computer can tell easily whether a particular name refers to a numeric location or a string location.

The name of a numeric location can consist of a single letter of the alphabet. The following are examples of names of numeric locations:

A   C   D   H   L   X   Y   Z

The name of a numeric location also can consist of a single letter followed by single digit. For example, the following are all valid names for numeric locations:

B2   D0   G1   K3   M9   Y5   Z7

The digits come in handy when we have more than one quantity whose name begins with a particular letter. For instance, suppose a program has to store three values in memory that are best described by the words *price, payment,* and *percent*. Then we could use P1 to stand for *price*, P2 to stand for *payment*, and P3 to stand for *percent*.

The name of a string location consists of a letter of the alphabet followed by a dollar sign. The dollar sign stands for *string*. The following are all names of string locations:

A$ C$ D$ L$ U$ X$ Y$ Z$

To illustrate named memory locations, suppose that 25 has been **306** stored in the location named A, 3.14 has been stored in the location named P, and "JOHN SMITH" has been stored in the location named N$. Then we can picture the computer's memory like this:

A | 25
P | 3.14
N$ | "JOHN SMITH"

When we need to use these locations, we refer to them by name. Thus, whenever A occurs in the program, the computer refers to the location containing 25; whenever P occurs, the computer refers to the location containing 3.14; whenever N$ occurs, the computer refers to the location containing "JOHN SMITH."

We can request the computer to change the contents of the locations. For instance, suppose we told the computer to store 150 in location A and 6.28 in location P. After the computer had carried out our orders, its memory will look like this:

A | 150
P | 6.28
N$ | "JOHN SMITH"

Notice that the contents of N$ were not changed, since we did not request the computer to store anything in that location. The contents of a location always remain the same until we explicitly request the computer to store a new value in that location.

Variables and Values   Although it's perfectly all right to speak of memory locations, names, and the contents of locations, just as we've been doing, programmers often use a different terminology with which we should be familiar.

A named memory location is often called a *variable*. The term comes from the fact that the contents of a location vary as the program stores different values in the location.

The name of a memory location is also the name of the variable. We always refer to variables by name. Thus, we speak of the variables A, P, and N$ just as we speak of our friends Jack, Bill, and Mary.

The number or string stored in a memory loction is called the *value* of the variable. Thus, in the last example, the value of A was 150, the value of P was 6.28, and the value of N$ was "JOHN SMITH."

Because the contents of a memory location can change, the value of a variable can change as well. Suppose, for instance, the value of A is 25. If we order the computer to store 150 in location A, then the new value of A will be 150. Whenever a new value is stored in a memory location, the value of the corresponding variable is changed accordingly.

Instead of drawing a picture of the memory locations with their names and contents, as we've been doing, we can list all the variables and their values, like this:

Variable	Value
A	150
P	6.28
N$	"JOHN SMITH"

This kind of list of variables and their values is called a *symbol table*. Some computer systems will print the symbol table at the programmer's request. Being able to examine the values of all the variables at any time during the execution of a program helps the programmer locate errors in the program.

THE LET STATEMENT

Now we'll look at some BASIC statements that refer to and change the contents of memory locations. The most frequently used of these is the LET statement.

Consider the following statements:

```
10 LET X = 5
20 LET Q$ = "GOOD MORNING"
```

Each of these statements causes the value on the right-hand side of the equal sign to be stored in the memory location whose name appears on the left-hand side of the equal sign. In the example, then, line 10 causes 5 to be stored in location X, and line 20 causes "GOOD MORNING" to be stored in location Q$. After the two statements have been executed, the values of X and Q$ are as follows:

Variable	Value
X	5
Q$	"GOOD MORNING"

We also can describe the effects of these statements using variable-value terminology. The LET statement is often called the *assignment* statement, because the effect of a LET statement is to *assign* a new value to a variable. Thus, line 10 assigns the value 5 to the variable X, and line 20 assigns the value "GOOD MORNING" to the variable Q$. After a value has been assigned to a variable, the variable retains that value until a new value is assigned to it. Figure 21-1 illustrates the process of assigning values to variables.

Using Variables on the Right-Hand Side of the Equal Sign Instead of using a value such as 5 or "GOOD MORNING" on the right-hand side

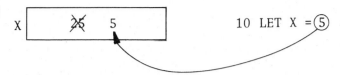

Figure 21-1. The assignment statement LET X = 5 stores the value 5 in the memory location named X. The 5 replaces the previous contents of location X.

of the equal sign, we can use a variable instead. The value of the variable on the right-hand side of the equal sign is assigned to the variable on the left-hand side. Or, in terms of memory locations, the contents of the memory location named on the right-hand side of the equal sign are copied into the memory location named on the left-hand side of the equal sign.

For example, suppose that the variables A, B, C$, and D$ have the following values:

Variable	Value
A	5
B	10
C$	"JACK"
D$	"JANE"

Now suppose the computer executes the following statements:

```
10 LET A = B
20 LET C$ = D$
```

Line 10 assigns the value of B to A. Line 20 assigns the value of D$ to C$. The variables now have the following values:

Variable	Value
A	10
B	10
C$	"JANE"
D$	"JANE"

Notice that the values of B and D$ remain the same. Only the values of A and C$, the variables that appeared on the left-hand sides of equal signs, were changed.

Figure 21-2 illustrates the assignment statement with a variable on the right-hand side of the equal sign.

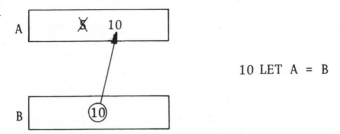

10 LET A = B

Figure 21-2. The assignment statement LET A = B stores the contents of memory location B in memory location A. The previous contents of location A are replaced by the contents of location B. The contents of location B are not changed.

Using Expressions on the Right-Hand Side of the Equal Sign Observe the following examples:

10 LET A = 3+5
20 LET B = 10-4
30 LET C = 8*5
40 LET D = 24/8
50 LET E = 3^4

We've already seen that, when the computer encounters an expression in a program, it works out the value of the expression by carrying out the indicated arithmetic operation. What the computer does with the calculated value depends on how the expression is used in the program.

When the expression is used on the right-hand side of the equal sign in an assignment statement, the computer assigns the value of the expression to the variable on the left-hand side of the equal sign. So, after all five statements in the example have been executed, the values of the variables are as follows:

Variable	Value
A	8
B	6
C	40
D	3
E	81

Figure 21-3 illustrates assignment statements containing expressions.

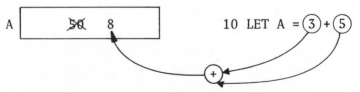

10 LET A = ③ + ⑤

Figure 21-3. The assignment statement LET A = 3+5 adds the values 3 and 5 and stores their sum in memory location A. The sum replaces the previous contents of location A.

BASIC allows us to use variables as well as values in expressions. When the computer encounters a variable in an expression, it gets the value of the variable from memory and substitutes the value for the variable in the expression.

For example, suppose that the variables P and Q have the following values:

Variable	Value
P	12
Q	15

Now, suppose the computer encounters the expression

P+Q

It first substitutes 12 for P and 15 for Q, getting the expression

12+15

The computer then adds 12 and 15, getting 27, the value of the expression.

Variables and numbers can be mixed in expressions. For instance, when the computer encounters the expression

5*P

it first substitutes 12 for P to get

5*12

It then multiples 5 by 12, getting 60, the value of the expression.

The following program illustrates expressions containing variables:

```
10 LET P = 12
20 LET Q = 15
30 PRINT P+Q, 5*P
999 END
```

This program prints the following:

27   60

THE INPUT, READ, AND DATA STATEMENTS

We have seen how to do arithmetic using variables, expressions, and assignment statements. We also have seen how to print out the results of our calculations using PRINT statements. Now we need some way of getting the data we are to process into the computer in the first place. BASIC provides two slightly different ways of doing this.

The INPUT Statement   The INPUT statement accepts data typed at the terminal by the user. The simplest INPUT statement has the following form:

10 INPUT X

Any other variable could have been used in place of X.

When the computer executes this statement, it prints a question mark on the terminal:

?

The question mark is the user's cue to enter the data the program needs. Whatever value the user types in will be assigned to X. If the user types in 25, the line on the terminal now looks like this:

? 25

The computer accepts this value and assigns it to the variable X. We can display the effect of the INPUT statement by displaying the value of the variable X:

Variable	Value
X	25

The INPUT statement is another statement that can store values in memory locations and so change the values of variables.

More than one variable can appear in an INPUT statement. The different variables are separated by commas:

10 INPUT X, Y, Z

Now when the computer types the question mark, it expects the user to respond with three values, separated by commas. The first value will be assigned to X, the second to Y, and the third to Z.

For instance, suppose the exchange with the user goes like this:

? 49, 10, 30

After the input statement has been executed, the variables X, Y, and Z will have the following values:

Variable	Value
X	49
Y	10
Z	30

312

The question mark the computer types gives the user no clue as to what type of data or how much data is being requested. To let the user know what data is to be entered, a PRINT statement providing this information must be executed before the INPUT statement. The PRINT statement *prompts* the user to type in the necessary data.

For instance, suppose the data a certain program needs is the length, width, and height of a room. To get the user to enter this data, we could use the following statements:

```
10 PRINT "ENTER LENGTH, WIDTH, AND HEIGHT"
20 INPUT L, W, H
```

The dialog with the user might go like this:

```
ENTER LENGTH, WIDTH, AND HEIGHT
? 15, 10, 7
```

The computer typed the first line and the question mark. The user typed the rest. After the exchange, the variables L, W, and H have the following values:

Variable	Value
L	15
W	10
H	7

We can shorten the exchange slightly by using a semicolon at the end of the PRINT statement. This causes the question mark to be typed on the same line as the prompt. Since the question mark implies that data is being requested, the word ENTER is no longer needed:

```
10 PRINT "LENGTH, WIDTH, HEIGHT";
20 INPUT L, W, H
```

Now the exchange with the user goes like this:

```
LENGTH, WIDTH, HEIGHT? 15, 10, 7
```

The computer typed everything through the question mark. The user typed the rest.

Now let's write a complete program using the INPUT statement. The program is one that an electronic cash register could use to calculate the sales tax on a purchase. The program inputs the amount of the purchase and the tax rate. It prints the sales tax and the amount that must be paid.

The sales-tax rate will be entered as a decimal. That is, a 3 percent sales-tax rate will be entered as .03, a 4 percent sales tax rate as .04, and so on.

We will use the following variables to store the values with which the program works:

Variable Name   *Description of Value*

P	amount of purchase
R	sales-tax rate
T	sales tax on purchase
A	amount to be paid

Here is the program:

```
10  REM SALES TAX
20  PRINT "AMOUNT OF PURCHASE";
30  INPUT P
40  PRINT "SALES-TAX RATE (AS DECIMAL)";
50  INPUT R
60  LET T = R*P
70  LET A = P+T
80  PRINT "SALES TAX IS"; T
90  PRINT "AMOUNT TO BE PAID IS"; A
999 END
```

Line 10 provides a short descriptive title for the program. Lines 20 through 50 get the data the program needs for its calculations. The amount of the purchase is assigned to P, and the sales-tax rate is assigned to R.

Lines 60 and 70 do the calculations. Line 60 calculates the sales tax by multiplying the sales-tax rate by the amount of the purchase. Line 70 calculates the amount to be paid by adding together the amount of the purchase and the sales tax.

Lines 80 and 90 print out the results of the calculation.

When the program is executed, the dialog with the user will go like this:

```
AMOUNT OF PURCHASE? 200.50
SALES-TAX RATE (AS DECIMAL)? .04
SALES TAX IS 8.02
AMOUNT TO BE PAID IS 208.52
```

The only things typed by the user are 200.50 and .04. The computer typed everything else.

The READ and DATA Statements   The INPUT statement allows the user to engage in a dialog with the program as it executes. This kind of dialog is essential for game-playing programs, computer-assisted instruction, and many other programs in which there is a give and take of information between the user and the computer.

On the other hand, if we know in advance all the information the program will need, we may as well provide it all at once, instead of piece by piece. The READ and DATA statements allow us to do this.

Like the INPUT statement, the READ statement obtains values and assigns them to variables. But, instead of requesting the values from the user, the READ statement obtains the values from another statement, the DATA statement.

For example, look at the following statements:

```
10 READ P, R
20 DATA 200.50, .04
```

When the READ statement is executed, the computer turns to the DATA statement for the needed values. The first value in the DATA statement is 200.50; this value is assigned to P. The second value in the DATA statement is .04; this value is assigned to R.

The DATA statement does not have to come immediately after the READ statement. It can come anywhere in the program. In fact, programmers often place the DATA statements near the end of the program. That way, the DATA statements are easy to locate when we want to change them in order to run the program with a different set of data.

The following version of the sales-tax program illustrates the use of the READ and DATA statements:

```
10 REM SALES TAX (USING READ AND DATA STATEMENTS)
20 READ P, R
30 LET T = R*P
40 LET A = P+T
50 PRINT "SALES TAX IS"; T
60 PRINT "AMOUNT TO BE PAID IS"; A
800 DATA 200.50, .04
999 END
```

When this program is executed, no data is requested from the user, since all the needed data is included in the DATA statement. The program prints

```
SALES TAX IS 8.02
AMOUNT TO BE PAID IS 208.52
```

If we want to use the same program with different data, we have to change line 800. (Most BASIC systems provide simple methods for changing a line in a program.) For instance, if we change line 800 to

```
800 DATA 500, .03
```

and execute the program again, the printout is

```
SALES TAX IS 15
AMOUNT TO BE PAID IS 515
```

If the data will not fit in a single DATA statement, we can spread it over as many as necessary. The computer considers all the data in all the data statements to be made up of one long list of data items.

For example, consider the following statements:

```
10 READ A, B
20 READ C, D
30 READ E, F
40 DATA 10, 15, 30
50 DATA 64, 85, 87
```

The computer makes up one long list containing all the data items in all the DATA statements. The data list for the program containing the statements just given is

```
10, 15, 30, 64, 85, 87
```

The computer keeps its place in the data list much as you might use your finger to keep your place in a list you are reading. We'll use an arrow to represent the computer's "finger." Then, before the first READ statement is executed, the data list and arrow look like this:

```
↓
10, 15, 30, 64, 85, 87
```

Now, suppose that line 10 is executed. The computer reads the values 10 and 15 and assigns them to A and B. The arrow is moved to reflect the fact that the first two data values have been read:

```
         ↓
10, 15, 30, 64, 85, 87
```

Line 20 is executed next. The variables C and D are assigned the values 30 and 64. The computer moves the arrow to reflect the fact that two more values have been used:

```
             ↓
10, 15, 30, 64, 85, 87
```

Now line 30 is executed, and you won't be surprised to find out that E and F are assigned the values 85 and 87. The arrow is moved again:

```
                 ↓
10, 15, 30, 64, 85, 87
```

All the values have been read. The variables have the following values:

Variable	Value	Variable	Value
A	10	D	64
B	15	E	85
C	30	F	87

Since the arrow has run off the end of the data list, there is no more data to be read. If another READ statement is now executed, the computer will print an error message saying that the program tried to read nonexistent data.

Occasionally, we may want a program to process the same data more than once. For this purpose, BASIC has a statement that allows us to reset the arrow back to the beginning of the data list so the same data can be read once again. The statement that does this is the RESTORE statement:

```
60  RESTORE
```

After a RESTORE statement, the data list and arrow look like this:

```
↓
10, 15, 30, 64, 85, 87
```

Now additional READ statements can be executed. The first of these will begin by reading the value 10.

EXPRESSIONS HAVING MORE THAN ONE OPERATOR

So far, we have used expressions that have only one operator in each expression. Such expressions are easy to use, and, by using enough of them, we can carry out any arithmetical calculation, no matter how complex. Nevertheless, they have certain disadvantages, which are best illustrated with an example.

Suppose we have five variables—A, B, C, D, and E—and we wish to do the following:

(1) Multiply the values of A and B.

(2) Multiply the values of C and D.

(3) Add the two products and assign the sum to E.

Using the one-operator expressions we have encountered so far, we can do the job with three statements:

```
10  LET  S = A*B
20  LET  T = C*D
30  LET  E = S+T
```

Two additional variables, S and T, are needed to store the two products until they can be added. The need for extra variables is a disadvantage of this method: if a complicated program already uses many variables, introducing additional ones can only complicate matters further.

Fortunately, BASIC allows us to do the same calculation using only a single statement:

```
10 LET E = A*B + C*D
```

This method is simpler than the three-statement method in two ways. First, only one statement is required instead of three. Second, we don't have to introduce any additional variables. BASIC automatically stores the products in memory and automatically retrieves them when it is ready to add them together.

In fact, the only slight drawback is that we have to learn a few rules about how BASIC evaluates expressions having more than one operator. Fortunately, these rules are extremely simple.

The question that arises for expressions containing more than one operator (and, therefore, calls for more rules) is this: In what order will the computer carry out the operations designated in the expression? For example, how do we know that for A*B + C*D the computer first will work out A*B and C*D and then add the two products? In writing the expression, I have used spaces to make the two products stand out, but the computer pays no attention to spaces. The expression also could have been written as A*B+C*D, and the computer would have evaluated it the same way.

As far as we can tell just by looking at A*B+C*D, the computer might just as well do the addition first and then the multiplications. This certainly would give a different result than if the multiplications were done first and then the addition. To illustrate, suppose the values of A, B, C, and D are 10, 20, 30, and 40. The following shows the two different ways of evaluating 10*20+30*40:

Multiplications Done First	*Addition Done First*
10*20+30*40	10*20+30*40
200+1200	10*50*40
1400	20000

As you see, the two different methods of evaluation give quite different answers. Since we will be in some trouble if we can't tell whether an expression will work out to 1400 or 20000, we have to learn a few rules.

Using Operator Priorities   The order in which arithmetic operations are to be performed is decided by assigning priorities to the arithmetic operators, as follows:

```
^          high priority
* and /    medium priority
+ and -    low priority
```

The operator priorities are used in conjunction with the following two rules for evaluating arithmetic expressions.

• Rule 1. The arithmetic operators in an expression are applied in order of their priorities—high priority operators first, low priority operators last. (We say that an operator is "applied" when the corresponding operation is carried out.) Thus, the exponentiations in an expression are carried out first, then the multiplications and divisions, and, finally, the additions and subtractions.

▪ Rule 2. Operators having the same priority are applied in left-to-right order as they occur in the expression.

Now let's look at some examples:

Example 1:

```
2*4+2*4^3
2*4+2*64      High priority operators first
  8+128       Medium priority operators next
  136         Low priority operators last
```

Example 2:

```
12/4-2^2/4
12/4-4/4      High priority operators first
  3-1         Medium priority operators next
  2           Low priority operators last
```

If there are no high priority operators in an expression, then, of course, we would apply the medium priority operators first. And if there were no high or medium priority operators, then we obviously would start with the low priority operators.

Example 3:

```
10*20+30*40
  200+1200    Medium priority operators first
  1400        Low priority operators last
```

The next example illustrates Rule 2: Operators having the same priority are applied in left-to-right order as they occur in the expression:

Example 4:

```
4*3/6*2
12/6*2        Leftmost operator first
  2*2         Now the next operator to the right
  4           Rightmost operator last
```

Example 4 sometimes causes people trouble, particularly those who have studied algebra. They confuse 4*3/6*2 with the built-up fraction

319

$$\frac{4*3}{6*2} \;=\; \frac{12}{12} \;=\; 1$$

But in BASIC, the numerator and denominator are *not* evaluated separately. Instead, the operators are applied as they are encountered in reading the expression from left to right. Here's another example of the same kind of expression:

Example 5:

```
24/8*2      Operators have the same priority
   3*2      so apply the operators
   6        working from left to right
```

Now let's write a BASIC program to illustrate the use of expressions containing more than one operator. Suppose we have some boxes that are to be used for shipping. We know the dimensions of the boxes—their lengths, widths, and heights. We are interested in two things. One is the volume of each box—how much it will hold. The other is the "length-plus-girth" of the box—the length of the box added to the distance around it. We want to know this curious combination of dimensions because it appears in shipping regulations. Some carriers will not take a shipment for which the length-plus-girth exceeds a certain amount.

Suppose we use the variables L, W, and H to store the length, width, and height of the box. We can write expressions using these variables for both the volume of the box and its length-plus-girth.

The volume of a box is simply the product of its three dimensions. We calculate it with the following expression:

```
L*W*H
```

In going around a box, we traverse its width twice and its height twice. The girth of a box, then, is given by

```
2*W + 2*H
```

To get length-plus-girth, all we have to do is add the length to the girth:

```
L + 2*W + 2*H
```

Now we're ready to write our program. We use the variables V and G to store volume and length-plus-girth:

```
10 REM BOX
20 PRINT "LENGTH, WIDTH, HEIGHT";
30 INPUT L, W, H
```

```
40 LET V = L*W*H
50 LET G = L + 2*W + 2*H
60 PRINT "VOLUME IS"; V
70 PRINT "LENGTH-PLUS-GIRTH IS"; G
999 END
```

Line 50 of this program can be simplified to eliminate one arithmetic operation. In order to do the simplification, we must see how to use parentheses in expressions.

Using Parentheses   There is one problem with the operator-priority method for evaluating expressions. Sometimes we don't want the operators to be applied in the order dictated by their priorities.

For example, suppose we want to evaluate the built-up fraction

$$\frac{8*3}{3*2} = 4$$

We have seen that the expression

8*3/3*2

will *not* do the job. In fact, this expression works out to be 16, not 4.

What we want to do is to force the 3 and the 2 to be multiplied together first and the result divided into the product of 8 and 3. We can make this happen by enclosing 3*2 in *parentheses*. The rule for using parentheses is very simple.

▪ Rule 3. Any part of an expression that is enclosed in parentheses is evaluated before any part of the expression that is not enclosed in parentheses.

The following examples illustrate this rule:

Example 6:

```
8*3/(3*2)
8*3/6          Parentheses first
24/6           then left-to-right order
4
```

Example 7:

```
2*(20+30)
2*50           Parentheses first
100            then multiplication
```

In example 7, notice that the addition inside the parentheses was done before the multiplication outside the parentheses in spite of the fact that addition has a lower priority than multiplication. The parentheses override the usual priorities.

Now let's go back to our example program and the expression for girth, which we wrote as follows:

2*W + 2*H

Instead of multiplying the width by 2 and the height by 2 and adding the two results, we could just as well add the width and height first and then multiply the sum by 2. Doing it that way gives us the following expression for girth:

2*(W+H)

Therefore, we can replace line 50 in the example program by

50 LET G = L + 2*(W+H)

Notice that this version of line 50 contains one less operator than the old version, so the computer has one less operation to carry out. Using parentheses not only made the expression simpler, it saved the computer work.

EXERCISES **1.** Suppose that the variables A, B, C, and D have the following values:

Variable	Value
A	10
B	20
C	30
D	40

Give the values of the variables after the execution of each of the following statements:

```
10 LET A = B+C
20 LET D = D/B
30 LET C = A-D
40 LET B = B^2
50 LET D = B
```

Note that before the execution of each statement but the first, the variables will have the values they had after the execution of the previous statement.

2. Evaluate each of the following expressions:

(a) 2*9-5*3   (b) 3*3^2*3
(c) 10/2*5   (d) 12/2-3

3. Evaluate each of the following expressions:

(a) 3*(5+4)   (b) 10/(2*5)
(c) 2*(9-5)*3   (d) (10+5)/(3+2)

4. A store gives a percentage discount on certain items. That is, it may give 5 percent off on one kind of item, 10 percent off on another kind of item, and so on. Write a program that prints the amount of the discount and the discounted price for an item. The program accepts as data the regular price of the item and the discount rate. The discount rate is expressed as a decimal—.05 for a 5 percent discount, .1 for a 10 percent discount, and so on.

5. The diameter of a circular pool and the depth to which it is filled are both given. Both of these dimensions are in meters. Write a program to calculate the number of liters of water needed to fill the pool to the specified depth.

We can use a formula from geometry to calculate the volume of water needed:

$$\text{volume} = \frac{3.14 \times \text{depth} \times \text{diameter}^2}{4}$$

This formula gives the volume of water in cubic meters. Each cubic meter contains 1000 liters, so

number-of-liters = 1000 × volume.

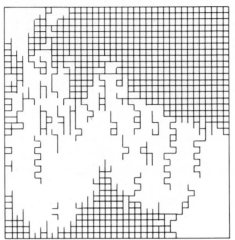

CHAPTER 22

REPETITION

The programs in the previous chapter may have struck you as being rather trivial. After all, who needs a computer to work out the volume and length-plus-girth for a single box? It would be easier to do the job with a pocket calculator than it would be to write a program and then execute that program on a computer.

But suppose you're a box manufacturer who has to do these calculations for hundreds of different styles of boxes. Now using the computer makes more sense. If you're going to use a program hundreds of times, then the effort invested in writing it will be amply repaid.

Therefore, almost all practical computer programs involve repe-*tition* in some way. That is, at least some of the program statements are written only once but used many times. Of course, the repetition could occur because the program as a whole is written only once but executed many times. But the more usual case is that, during a single execution of the entire program, some of the statements will be executed more than once.

THE FOR AND NEXT STATEMENTS

BASIC has two statements that are especially designed for controlling repetition—the FOR statement and the NEXT statement. We can best illustrate their operation with an example:

```
10 FOR I = 1 TO 5
20    PRINT I
30 NEXT I
```

The execution of the statement PRINT I is controlled by the FOR and NEXT statements. We emphasize this fact by indenting PRINT I with respect to the FOR and NEXT statements. The indentation is not required and, in fact, is ignored by the computer. The only purpose of the indentation is to make it easy to see at a glance that the execution of line 20 is controlled by lines 10 and 30.

Line 20 is executed five times, and the value of I is different for each execution. The first time line 20 is executed, the value of I is 1. The second time, the value of I is 2. The third time, the value of I is 3. The fourth time, the value of I is 4. The fifth and last time, the value of I is 5. The effect is the same as if the following five statements had been executed:

```
20 PRINT 1
21 PRINT 2
22 PRINT 3
23 PRINT 4
24 PRINT 5
```

When the statements are executed, the computer prints the following:

```
1
2
3
4
5
```

The FOR and NEXT statements are useful for printing tables, such as those found in mathematical handbooks. For example, let's write a program to print a short table giving the squares of numbers. (The square of a number is equal to the number multiplied by itself.)

```
10 REM SQUARES
20 PRINT "NUMBER", "SQUARE"
30 PRINT
40 FOR N = 1 TO 6
50    LET S = N^2
```

```
60      PRINT N, S
70 NEXT N
999 END
```

Lines 50 and 60 are executed with the value of N equal in turn to 1, 2, 3, 4, 5, and 6. For each value of N, line 50 calculates its square, and line 60 prints both the number and its square. The printout looks like this:

NUMBER	SQUARE
1	1
2	4
3	9
4	16
5	25
6	36

We also can use a table to summarize the results of processing data read from DATA statements. For example, suppose we need to calculate the volumes of five boxes whose dimensions are given as data. The following program will do the job:

```
10 REM VOLUMES
20 PRINT "LENGTH", "WIDTH", "HEIGHT", "VOLUME"
30 PRINT
40 FOR I = 1 TO 5
50     READ L, W, H
60     LET V = L*W*H
70     PRINT L, W, H, V
80 NEXT I
800 DATA 10, 7, 3, 12, 8, 4, 10, 8, 5, 15, 7, 5
810 DATA 9, 6, 4
999 END
```

The first time the READ statement is executed, it assigns the values 10, 7, and 3 to L, W, and H. The second time the READ statement is executed, it assigns the values 12, 8, and 4 to L, W, and H. And so on. To make out the DATA statement, we list the length, width, and height for the first box, then the length, width, and height for the second box, and so on.

The program produces the following printout:

LENGTH	WIDTH	HEIGHT	VOLUME
10	7	3	210
12	8	4	384
10	8	5	400
15	7	5	525
9	6	4	216

This program works fine if we always want to calculate the volumes of exactly five boxes. But suppose we want to calculate the volume of four boxes one time, six boxes another time, ten boxes another time, and so on. In other words, we may want the program to process the data for a different number of boxes each time it is executed. To make this possible, the number of boxes must be included in the data instead of being written into the program.

We can do this by letting the first number in the DATA statement be the number of boxes for which the calculation is to be done. The remaining entries in the DATA statement give the dimensions of the boxes as they did before.

We want to modify the program so that it will do the calculation for exactly the number of boxes specified in the DATA statement. Before processing any other data, the program reads the first data item (the number of boxes) and assigns it to the variable N. The rest of the program is the same as before, except that the value of N is used in place of 5 in the FOR statement.

```
10  REM VOLUMES (MODIFIED)
20  PRINT "LENGTH"; "WIDTH", "HEIGHT", "VOLUME"
30  PRINT
35  READ N
40  FOR I = 1 TO N
50      READ L, W, H
60      LET V = L*W*H
70      PRINT L, W, H, V
80  NEXT I
800 DATA 5, 10, 7, 3, 12, 8, 4, 10, 8, 5, 15, 7, 5
810 DATA 9, 6, 4
999 END
```

With the DATA statements shown, the new version of the program produces the same printout as the old one. But suppose we modify the DATA statements as follows:

```
800 DATA 3, 10, 7, 3, 12, 8, 4, 10, 8, 5
810 (deleted)
```

Now the program produces the following printout:

LENGTH	WIDTH	HEIGHT	VOLUME
10	7	3	210
12	8	4	384
10	8	5	400

The first item in the DATA statement was 3. This value was read, assigned to N, and used in the FOR statement to specify exactly three repetitions. Therefore, the statements for reading the data, calculating the volume, and printing the table entries were executed three times.

Computing Totals   When we print a table like the one for LENGTH, WIDTH, HEIGHT, and VOLUME, we frequently want the total of one or more columns. Even if the total is not otherwise significant, it is sometimes used for error checking. If a set of data items has to be processed a number of times, we can calculate the total of the items each time they are processed. If one of the totals turns out to be different from the others, we can be sure that an error has been made.

Let's start with a simple program to add up an arbitrary number of values:

```
 10 REM TOTAL
 20 READ N
 30 LET T = 0
 40 FOR I = 1 TO N
 50    READ V
 60    PRINT V
 70    LET T = T+V
 80 NEXT I
 90 PRINT "---"
100 PRINT T
800 DATA 5, 120, 247, 105, 275, 183
999 END
```

As before, the first entry in the DATA statement tells how many items are to be processed. The value 5 is read, assigned to N, and used in the FOR statement to control the repetition.

The variable T is used to hold the running total. We can think of it as playing the same role as does the display on an adding machine. Every time we add a new value, the display shows the new total.

Before we add any values on an adding machine, we clear the display by pressing the *clear* key. In BASIC, the statement

```
30 LET T = 0
```

is equivalent to pressing the *clear* key on the adding machine. It sets the starting value of T to 0.

The three repeated statements

```
50 READ V
60 PRINT V
70 LET T = T+V
```

do the equivalent of punching a new value into the adding machine. Line 40 reads a value; line 50 prints the value just read; and line 60 adds the value just read to the running total.

When the program is executed, it produces the following print-out:

```
120
247
105
275
183
---
930
```

Now let's modify our VOLUMES program again to calculate the total volume of all the boxes and print this total at the foot of the VOLUME column:

```
10 REM VOLUMES AND TOTAL VOLUME
20 PRINT "LENGTH", "WIDTH", "HEIGHT", "VOLUME"
30 PRINT
35 READ N
37 LET T = 0
40 FOR I = 1 TO N
50    READ L, W, H
60    LET V = L*W*H
70    PRINT L, W, H, V
75    LET T = T+V
80 NEXT I
90 PRINT , , , "---"
100 PRINT , , , T
800 DATA 3, 10, 7, 3, 12, 8, 4, 10, 8, 5
999 END
```

In lines 90 and 100, the three commas cause the computer to skip three columns. Whenever the computer encounters a comma, it skips immediately to the beginning of the next column. There need not be any data items between the commas.

When the program is executed, it produces the following print-out:

LENGTH	WIDTH	HEIGHT	VOLUME
10	7	3	210
12	8	4	384
10	8	5	400

			994

The variable whose name appears in the FOR and NEXT statements is called the *controlled variable*. In the preceding programs, the controlled variable has always been stepped by 1. That is, it has taken on the values 1, 2, 3, ... on successive repetitions.

We can cause the controlled variable to be stepped by any amount we wish if we add a STEP phrase to the FOR statement. If we write STEP 5, for instance, then the controlled variable will be stepped in increments of 5. If we write STEP 2, then the controlled variable will be stepped in increments of 2.

For instance, suppose we want to find the sum of all the even numbers from 2 through 100. To step through the even numbers, we "count by twos." That is, we start with 2 and step by 2 each time:

```
10 REM SUM OF EVEN NUMBERS
20 LET T = 0
30 FOR N = 2 TO 100 STEP 2
40     LET T = T+N
50 NEXT N
60 PRINT T
999 END
```

If, instead, we wanted to add up all the odd numbers from 1 through 99, then we would replace line 30 by

```
30 FOR N = 1 TO 99 STEP 2
```

By making the step negative, we can count down as well as up:

```
10 REM COUNTDOWN
20 FOR J = 10 TO 1 STEP -1
30     PRINT J
40 NEXT J
50 PRINT "LIFTOFF"
999 END
```

What will this program print when it is executed?

REPETITION USING THE GO TO AND IF STATEMENTS

The FOR and NEXT statements control repetition by counting the number of times the repeated statements are executed. But this is by no means the only way to control repetition. Often we want the repetition to continue while a certain condition is true or until a certain condition becomes true. These conditions may have nothing to do with counting.

Some programming languages provide statements to control repetition by these other means, much as the FOR and NEXT statements in BASIC control repetition by counting. The statements that do this are similar to the WHILE and REPEAT-UNTIL constructions described in chapter 6. BASIC, however, does not provide these statements. If we want to control repetition in BASIC by some means other than counting, we must build our own repetition constructions out of more general purpose statements.

The statements in BASIC that are used for this purpose are the GO TO statement and the IF statement.

The GO TO Statement The GO TO Statement directs the computer to jump to a specified line of the BASIC program and continue execution from there. For example,

```
10 GO TO 50
```

instructs the computer to jump to line 50. Therefore, line 50 is executed immediately after line 10.

We can program a repetition using the GO TO statement alone. For example, let's modify the program VOLUMES to use the GO TO statement:

```
10 REM VOLUMES (WITH GO TO STATEMENT)
20 PRINT "LENGTH", "WIDTH", "HEIGHT", "VOLUME"
30 PRINT
40    READ L, W, H
50    LET V = L*W*H
60    PRINT L, W, H, V
70 GO TO 40
800 DATA 10, 7, 3, 12, 8, 4, 10, 8, 5, 15, 7, 5
810 DATA 9, 6, 4
999 END
```

Let's work through this program. When the computer gets to line 40 for the first time, it reads the first three data items and assigns them to L, W, and H. Line 50 calculates the volume, and line 60 prints a line of output.

The GO TO statement in line 70 sends the computer back to line 40. Therefore, the computer reads another three values, computes another volume, prints another line of output, and now it is back at line 70 again. Line 70 sends the computer back to line 40 to start processing another set of values, and so on.

Notice that, as in previous versions of the program, the controlled statements are indented with respect to the statements that control their execution. The controlled statements are lines 40, 50, and 60. There is only one controlling statement, the GO TO statement in line 70.

But all is not well with this program: we neglected to provide any means for stopping the repetition. Theoretically, the repetition will go on forever. Practically, it will go on until the data is exhausted. Then it will be stopped automatically, and an error message will be printed.

The program produces the following printout:

LENGTH	WIDTH	HEIGHT	VOLUME
10	7	3	210
12	8	4	384

```
10              8              5              400
15              7              5              525
9               6              4              216
OUT OF DATA IN LINE 40
```

The last line of the printout is an error message. (Your computer may print error messages in a slightly different form.) The error message indicates that the computer failed in an attempt to execute line 40 because there was no more data to be read.

A program whose execution ends with the computer printing an error message is considered to be an example of shoddy workmanship. Anyone besides the programmer who uses the program is going to be confused. Did the program work as it was intended to? Or did it fail to work properly because the user entered some data incorrectly?

Also, we could not use this approach to repetition for the version of the program that calculates the total volume. The statements that print the separating line and the total at the foot of the VOLUME column have to be executed after the repetition is terminated. But in the program just given, no statements can be executed after the repetition terminates, since the repetition is terminated only when the computer terminates the execution of the entire program.

So, at this point, we know how to produce a repetition, but we don't yet have any way of stopping one gracefully. That's why we need the IF statement.

The IF Statement   Like the GO TO statement, the IF statement causes the computer to jump to a specified line. But the jump is *conditional;* that is, it takes place only if a certain condition is true. If the condition is not true, then the IF statement has no effect, and the computer continues executing the program at the statement following the IF statement.

For example, suppose the computer executes the following IF statement:

```
10 IF X = Y THEN 50
```

When the computer executes line 10, it compares the current value of X with the current value of Y. If the two values are equal, then the computer jumps to line 50 and continues executing the program from there. If the two values are not equal, then the computer goes on to the line following line 10—line 20, if the usual numbering scheme is being used.

In the example, $X = Y$ is a *condition*, and the equal sign is a *relation*. (Don't confuse the use of $=$ in the IF statement with its use in the LET statement. The two uses have nothing to do with one another.) Six relations can be used to form conditions in BASIC. All six are shown in the following table:

X = Y	The value of X equals the value of Y.
X < Y	The value of X is less than the value of Y.
X > Y	The value of X is greater than the value of Y.
X <= Y	The value of X is less than or equal to the value of Y.
X >= Y	The value of X is greater than or equal to the value of Y.
X <> Y	The value of X is not equal to the value of Y.

Each condition stands for a statement about the possible values of X and Y, where X and Y can be constants, variables, or expressions. If the statement is true, the computer jumps to the specified line. If the statement is false, the computer goes on to the next line in the program.

The following are some examples of conditions:

```
2 > 5      (false)
2 <> 5     (true)
3 < 2      (false)
9 > 9      (false)
9 >= 9     (true)
```

The same relations also can be used to compare strings. For strings, < means "precedes in alphabetical order" and > means "follows in alphabetical order."

Repetition with GO TO and IF Now let's rewrite the program VOLUMES using both the IF and the GO TO statements. This time, the program will not terminate with an error message. And this version of the program will print the total volume, which the version using only the GO TO statement could not.

We need to provide some way for the program to recognize that it has processed all the data before it actually tries to read a nonexistent data item. We do this by using a *sentinel*, which is a special dummy data value whose only purpose is to signal the program that there is no more data to follow. Since we will be reading data items in groups of three, we will use three dummy data items, all 0, as our sentinel. This sentinel cannot be confused with a legitimate data item, since it isn't possible for any of the dimensions of a box to be zero.

Here, then, is yet another version of VOLUMES:

```
10 REM VOLUMES (WITH IF AND GO TO STATEMENTS)
20 PRINT "LENGTH", "WIDTH", "HEIGHT", "VOLUME"
30 PRINT
40 LET T = 0
50 READ L, W, H
60 IF L = 0 THEN 120
```

```
70      LET V = L*W*H
80      PRINT L, W, H, V
90      LET T = T+V
100     READ L, W, H
110 GO TO 60
120 PRINT , , , "---"
130 PRINT , , , T
800 DATA 10, 7, 3, 12, 8, 4, 10, 8, 5, 0, 0, 0
999 END
```

Line 50 reads the first three data items and assigns them to L, W, and H. Line 50 is used only to read the first three data items. All the remaining data is read by line 100.

When the computer reaches line 60, it checks to see if the sentinel has been read by testing to see if the value of L is 0. If the value of L is 0, then the sentinel has been read, all the data has been processed, and the computer jumps to line 120 to print the total. If the value of L is not 0, then the data just read is not the sentinel, and so that data is processed.

Lines 70, 80, and 90 process the data just read. Line 100 reads a new set of three data items. Line 110 sends the computer back to line 60 to check whether the data just read by line 100 is the sentinel. If it is, then, as before, the computer will jump to line 120 to print the total. Otherwise, the data read by line 100 will be processed.

Obviously, lines 60-110 will continue to be executed repeatedly until eventually the sentinel is read by line 100. Then, when line 60 is next executed, the value of L is found to be 0, so the computer jumps to line 120, terminating the repetition.

As you read the program, it might occur to you that line 100 could be omitted, provided line 110 was changed to GO TO 50. This change would work, but it would make the structure of the program harder to see, since one of the statements controlling the repetition (line 60) would occur in the midst of the controlled statements (lines 50, 70, 80, 90, and 100). The modern trend in programming is to try to make the structure of a program as clear as possible, even if this occasionally means writing a statement we once would have avoided writing.

Flowcharts Flowcharts can help us see the structure of programs that use IF and GO TO statements. Figure 22-1 is a flowchart of the program VOLUMES.

As we saw in chapter 6, the oval-shaped symbols in the flowchart indicate the points at which the computer is to start and stop carrying out the instructions.

The parallelograms (rectangles with slanting sides) indicate the input and output operations, those specified with the READ, INPUT, and PRINT statements in BASIC. Note that lines 20 and 30 in the program, which print the column headings and the space separating the headings from the data, are merely summarized with the phrase "Print column headings" in the flowchart.

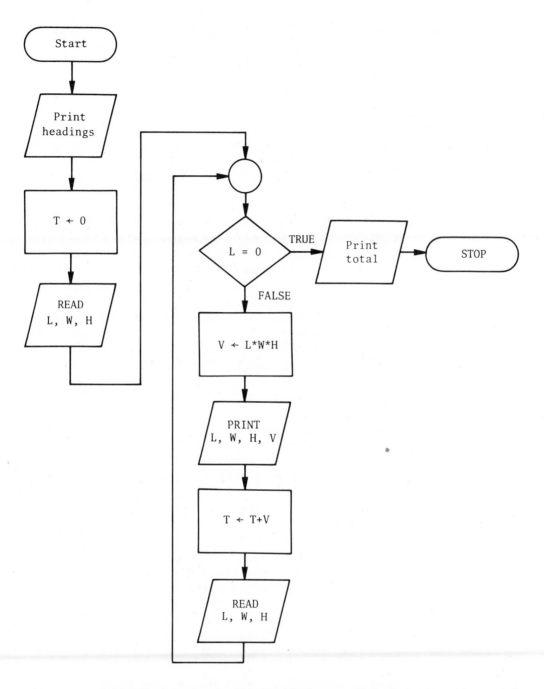

Figure 22-1. The flowchart of the VOLUMES program. Notice the loop around the repeated statements. Also note that the check for whether or not the repetition should terminate is made at the start of the loop, before the repeated statements have been executed.

The rectangles contain the assignment statements, which carry out the calculations. Note that, in the flowchart, we write the assignment statements in a slightly abbreviated form. The word LET is omitted, and the equal sign is replaced with a left-pointing arrow.

The arrow signifies that the value of the expression on the right-hand side of the arrow is to be stored in the memory location named on the left-hand side. The following compares the way in which assignment statements are written in BASIC and in the flowchart:

BASIC	Flowchart
40 LET T = 0	T ← 0
70 LET V = L*W*H	V ← L*W*H
90 LET T = T+V	T ← T+V

The diamond-shaped symbol corresponds to the IF statement in BASIC. The condition inside the diamond is the same as the one in the IF statement. If the condition is true, the computer follows the path marked TRUE. Otherwise, it takes the path marked FALSE.

A collector circle marks a point at which separate paths through the flowchart come together to form a single path.

The GO TO statement is represented by one of the connecting lines in the flowchart. Can you tell which of the connecting lines corresponds to the GO TO statement?

Notice that the repetition forms a loop in the flowchart. As we mentioned in chapter 6, a repetition is often referred to as a *loop* for this reason.

Prechecked and Postchecked Loops   The repetition in the VOL-UMES program is sometimes called a *prechecked loop*. By *prechecked* we mean that the IF statement that checks whether or not the repetition is to continue is executed *before* any of the repeated statements. With a prechecked loop, it is possible for the repeated statements not to be executed at all. This would happen in the VOLUMES program if the first entry in the DATA statement were 0.

Sometimes, however, it does not make sense to test whether or not the repetition should continue until the repeated statements have been executed at least once. In that case, we need a *postchecked loop*, one in which the IF statement is executed after the repeated statements.

For instance, consider the following problem. A college offers a scholarship to the first student who applies whose high-school average is greater than 95. Our data consists of the names of the applicants and their averages, listed in the order in which the persons applied. We want the program to read the names and averages from this list until it finds an average greater than 95, and then to print out the name of the person who gets the scholarship.

Obviously, we want to read names and averages from the DATA statement until we find an average greater than 95. Since we cannot test an average until we have read it, we cannot tell whether or not the repetition needs to continue until after the repeated statement—the one that reads the names and averages—has been executed at least once.

The following BASIC program determines who will receive the scholarship:

```
10  REM  SCHOLARSHIP
20      READ N$, A
30  IF  A <= 95  THEN  20
40  PRINT N$
800 DATA "BARRY", 80, "CHARLIE", 95, "DORIS", 93
810 DATA "JOHN", 98, "ZACK", 99, "NONE", 100
999 END
```

Notice that the repeated statement, line 20, is always executed at least once. It is then executed repeatedly as long as the average read remains less than or equal to ninety-five.

Figure 22-2 is a flowchart of the SCHOLARSHIP program. Note the position of the decision diamond at the "bottom" instead of at the "top" of the loop.

What is the purpose of the data items "NONE" and 100 in line 810?

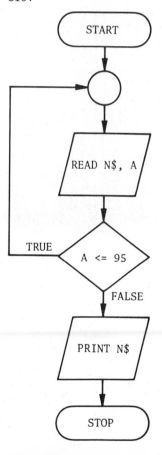

Figure 22-2. The flowchart of the SCHOLARSHIP program. The loop here is called a "postchecked loop," since the check for whether or not the repetition should terminate is made after the repeated statement has been executed.

1. Write a program to print a line of ten asterisks, like this:

****

The program should use only one PRINT statement:

30 PRINT "*";

(The line number may be different in your program, of course.) *Hint:* When this statement is executed repeatedly, the semicolons cause the asterisks to be printed on the same line.

2. Write a program to print the following pattern:

```
*
**
***
****
*****
******
*******
********
*********
**********
```

The program should have the following structure:

```
10 FOR N = 1 TO 10
        (Statements to print N asterisks on a line)
50     PRINT
60 NEXT N
999 END
```

Line 50 causes the computer to go to a new line in the printout after it has finished printing each line of asterisks.

3. Write a program to print the following pattern:

```
*
***
*****
*******
********
```

4. Write a program to print the following pattern:

```
*
***
*****
*******
********
*******
*****
***
*
```

5. Write a program to print the following pattern:

```
X000000000
XXX0000000
XXXXX00000
XXXXXXX000
XXXXXXXXX0
XXXXXXX000
XXXXX00000
XXX0000000
X000000000
```

6. Write a program to read a list of numbers and compute their average. The first entry in the DATA statement gives the number of values to be averaged. The remaining entries are the numbers whose average is to be found. For instance,

```
800 DATA 5, 1, 2, 3, 4, 5
```

tells the program that there are five numbers to be averaged and that those numbers are 1, 2, 3, 4, and 5. With this DATA statement, the program should print 3 as the average.

7. This is the same as problem 6 except that a sentinel will be used to tell the program when there are no more numbers to be averaged. The values being averaged can be positive or zero but not negative. Therefore, we can use -1 as the sentinel. Thus, the DATA statement.

```
800 DATA 0, 1, 2, 3, 4, 5, 6, -1
```

tells the program to find the average of 0, 1, 2, 3, 4, 5, and 6. The program should find the average of these numbers to be 3.

CHAPTER 23

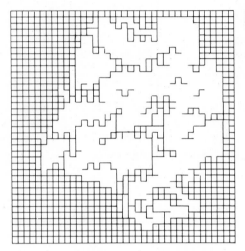

SELECTION

Selection refers to selecting particular statements for execution depending on the conditions that are true when the program is executed. As usual, the conditions are stated in terms of relations among the values of constants, variables, and expressions. Selection greatly increases a program's flexibility by allowing it to respond in different ways to different kinds of input.

In BASIC, the raw materials for selection are the same as those for repetition—the IF and GO TO statements.

ONE-WAY SELECTION

In one-way selection, a particular set of statements is either to be executed or not executed. If the statements are not to be executed, then the computer simply skips over them and continues on with the rest of the program.

For instance, suppose we want to print the names and grades of the students who passed a certain course. Let the values of N$ and G be the name and grade, respectively, of one student. If the student passed—if the value of G is greater than or equal to 60—then the student's name and grade are to be printed. But if the student failed —the value of G is less than 60—we want to skip the statement that prints the name and grade.

The following BASIC program reads a list of names and grades and prints the names and grades of the students with passing grades. The data for each student consists of a name followed by a grade, such as "BILL", 85. The sentinel is "/*", 0. (The string "/*" is frequently used as a sentinel in data processing.)

```
10  REM PASSING GRADES
20  PRINT "NAME", "GRADE"
30  PRINT
40  READ N$, G
50  IF N$ = "/*" THEN 100
60      IF G < 60 THEN 80
70          PRINT N$, G
80      READ N$, G
90  GO TO 50
100 PRINT "END OF PASSING GRADE LIST"
800 DATA "BILL", 85, "CHARLIE", 45, "DORIS", 60
810 DATA "FRED", 59, "MARY", 90, "SUE", 40, "/*", 0
999 END
```

Lines 60 and 70 make up the one-way selection. If the value of G is greater than or equal to 60, then line 70 is executed, and the values of N$ and G are printed. If the value of G is less than 60, line 70 is skipped, and the values of N$ and G are not printed.

Note that we continue the practice of indenting controlled statements with respect to controlling ones. Thus, the PRINT statement in line 70 is indented with respect to the IF statement in line 60, which controls whether or not the PRINT statement is executed.

Figure 23-1 is a flowchart of the PASSING GRADES program. Find the part of the flowchart corresponding to lines 60 and 70.

The program produces the following printout:

```
NAME        GRADE

BILL        85
DORIS       60
MARY        90
END OF PASSING GRADE LIST
```

TWO-WAY SELECTION

One-way selection gives us the option of having a set of statements either executed or not executed, depending on whether or not a

certain condition is true. Sometimes, however, we would like to have

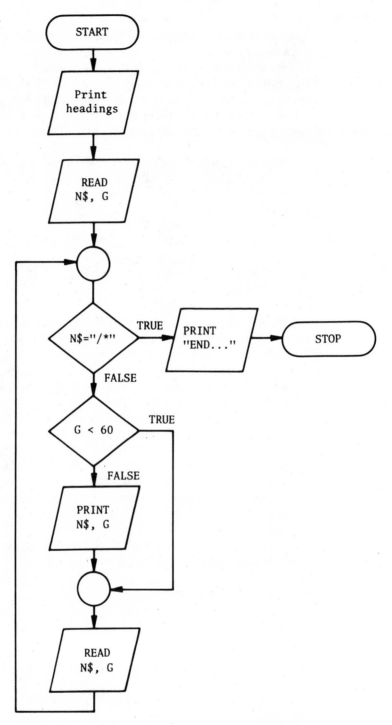

Figure 23-1. One-way selection. If G < 60 the statement PRINT N$, G is skipped over.
Otherwise is executed.

one set of statements executed if a condition is true and another set executed if it is false. This is known as *two-way selection*. We select one out of two possible sets of statements, depending on whether a condition is true or false.

Let's see how to use two-way selection to compute an employee's weekly wages. In the simplest case, the calculation is

wages = pay-rate × hours-worked

That is, if I make $20 an hour and work 35 hours one week, my wages for that week are

20 × 35 = 700

In BASIC, if we let the values of W, R, and H be wages, pay-rate, and hours-worked, then the calculation is done like this:

80 LET W = R*H

But this is not the whole story. Most workers who are paid by the hour are entitled to extra pay for overtime. The usual rule is "time-and-a-half for overtime" where overtime is anything in excess of 40 hours a week.

Therefore, if someone has worked more than 40 hours, we must pay for the first 40 hours at the normal rate R and for the remaining hours at the overtime rate 1.5*R. In BASIC, we can express this calculation as follows:

100 LET W = 40*R + 1.5*R*(H−40)

The first term 40*R pays for the first 40 hours at the normal rate. The second term 1.5*R*(H-40) pays for the remaining H-40 hours at the overtime rate of 1.5*R.

So we have two statements for calculating wages—one for people who have not worked more than 40 hours and another one for those who have. We can use two-way selection to make sure that the correct statement is executed depending on how many hours the person worked. In BASIC, the two-way selection looks like this:

```
 70 IF H > 40 THEN 100
 80     LET W = R*H
 90 GO TO 110
100     LET W = 40*R + 1.5*R*(H−40)
110 ...
```

We start by checking whether or not the value of H is greater than 40. If it is, we jump to line 100, which does the overtime calculation. If the value of H is not greater than 40, we go on to line 80, which does the calculation for those who did not work any overtime.

343

Notice line 90 carefully, because beginners have a tendency to leave it out. When we have finished calculating the wages for someone who did not work any overtime, we must jump over the calculation for persons who did work overtime. Otherwise, both calculations will be done, which is incorrect. Therefore, after the computer has executed line 80, line 90 causes it to jump to line 110, the next line following the entire two-way selection.

Now let's incorporate these statements into a program for printing a weekly wage report:

```
10  REM WAGE REPORT
20  PRINT "NAME", "RATE", "HOURS", "WAGES", "TOTAL WAGES"
30  PRINT
40  LET T = 0
50  READ N$, R, H
60  IF N$ = "/*" THEN 150
70      IF H > 40 THEN 100
80          LET W = R*H
90      GO TO 110
100         LET W = 40*R + 1.5*R*(H-40)
110     PRINT N$, R, H, W
120     LET T = T+W
130     READ N$, R, H
140 GO TO 60
150 PRINT , , , , T
800 DATA "BILL", 3.58, 44, "CHARLIE", 3.25, 35
810 DATA "DORIS", 2.75, 46, "FRED", 5.31, 38
820 DATA "MARY", 6.83, 48, "/*", 0, 0
999 END
```

Figure 23-2 is a flowchart of this program. Notice that there is a statement to be executed in each of the paths leading from the decision diamond to the collector circle. In one-way selection, statements to be executed appear in only one of these paths, and the other path goes straight from the decision diamond to the collector circle.

The program produces the following printout:

NAME	RATE	HOURS	WAGES	TOTAL WAGES
BILL	3.58	44	164.68	
CHARLIE	3.25	35	113.75	
DORIS	2.75	46	134.75	
FRED	5.31	38	201.78	
MARY	6.83	48	355.16	
				970.12

Using a separate column for the total is another way to arrange a report, one that frequently is used in business and accounting.

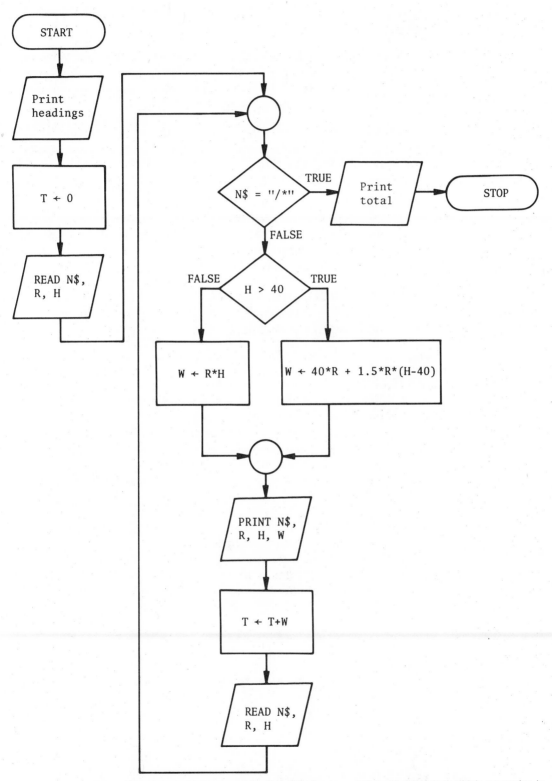

Figure 23-2. Two-way selection. Whether or not H > 40 determines which expression is
345 used to calculate the value of W.

**MULTIWAY
SELECTION**

We have had one-way selection and two-way selection. Why stop there? Why not allow the computer to select from among an arbitrary number of alternatives? Selection from among more than two alternatives is known as *multiway selection*.

The ON-GO TO Statement   BASIC has a special statement, the ON-GO-TO statement, that is designed specifically to help us program multiway selection. The following example illustrates the ON-GO TO statement:

```
100 ON N GO TO 110, 140, 170
```

If the value of N is 1, the computer jumps to line 110; if the value of N is 2, the computer jumps to line 140; if the value of N is 3, the computer jumps to line 170. It is an error if the value of N is not 1, 2, or 3.

The ON-GO TO statement can be written to refer to any number of lines. The only limit is how many line numbers will fit onto a single line in the BASIC program. For instance, the statement

```
100 ON S GO TO 50, 80, 100, 200, 350, 400
```

will send the computer to line 50, 80, 100, 200, 350, or 400, depending on whether the value of S is 1, 2, 3, 4, 5, or 6. For this statement, it is an error if the value of S is not in the range 1-6.

Let's look at an example that uses the ON-GO TO statement. Suppose we have data consisting of sales reports from three sales territories. Each report consists of a territory number and an amount sold. We want to print a sales summary in which all the amounts for territory 1 are printed in the first column; all the amounts for territory 2 are printed in the second column; and all the amounts for territory 3 are printed in the third column. We also want to compute totals for each of the three territories.

Let's use N for the territory number, A for the amount sold, and T1, T2, and T3 for the totals for the three territories. The following statements will print the value of A in the proper column and add its value to the proper total. The proper column and the proper total are determined by the territory number:

```
100 ON N GO TO 110, 140, 170
110     PRINT A
120     LET T1 = T1+A
130 GO TO 190
140     PRINT , A
150     LET T2 = T2+A
160 GO TO 190
170     PRINT , , A
180     LET T3 = T3+A
190 ...
```

Notice carefully the GO TO 190s, which are necessary to cause the computer to jump to the next statement following the entire selection construction after either of the first two alternative sets of statements have been executed. As with two-way selection, these important GO TOs are sometimes inadvertently omitted.

Here is the complete program for the sales summary:

```
10 REM SALES SUMMARY
20 PRINT , "TERRITORIES"
30 PRINT "FIRST", "SECOND", "THIRD"
40 PRINT
50 LET T1 = 0
60 LET T2 = 0
70 LET T3 = 0
80 READ N, A
90 IF N = 0 THEN 210
100     ON N GO TO 110, 140, 170
110        PRINT A
120           LET T1 = T1+A
130     GO TO 190
140        PRINT , A
150           LET T2 = T2+A
160     GO TO 190
170        PRINT , , A
180           LET T3 = T3+A
190     READ N, A
200 GO TO 90
210 PRINT "---", "---", "---"
220 PRINT T1, T2, T3
800 DATA 1, 125, 2, 200, 2, 250, 3, 100, 1, 200, 3, 225
810 DATA 2, 150, 1, 300, 3, 200, 2, 100, 1, 150, 3, 105
820 DATA 0, 0
999 END
```

The program produces the following printout:

TERRITORIES

FIRST	SECOND	THIRD
125		
	200	
	250	
		100
200		
		225
	150	
300		
		200
	100	

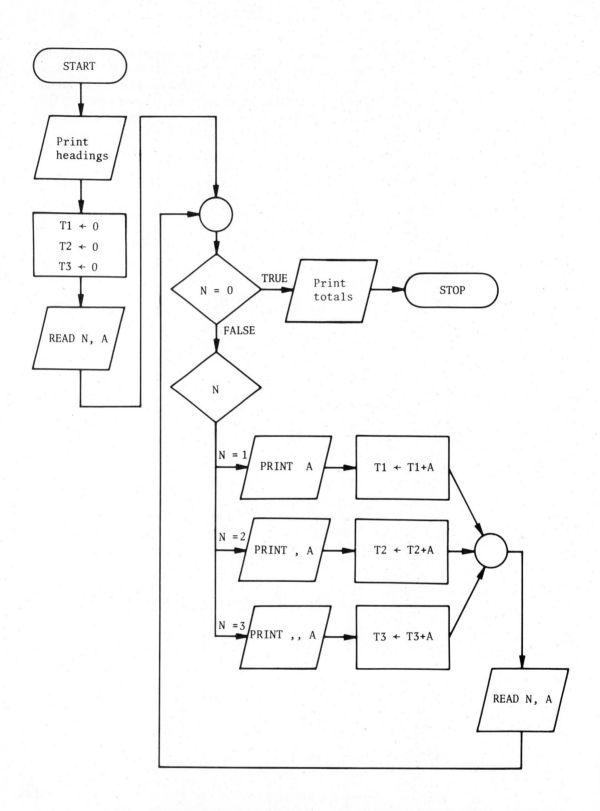

Figure 23-3. Multiway selection. The value of N determines in which column the value of A will be printed and to which total the value of A will be added.

150

                                       105

---   ---   ---

775   700   630

Figure 23-3 is a flowchart of the preceding program. Multiway selection is the only case in which more than two lines join at a collector circle.

EXERCISES   **1.** Suppose that a weather station records the temperature every hour. Write a program to read the temperatures recorded on a particular day, and print out the high and the low for that day. *Hint:* As the program reads the temperatures, let the values of H and L be the highest and lowest temperatures that have been read so far. If the temperature just read is greater than the value of H, then it replaces the value of H. If the temperature just read is less than the value of L, then it replaces the value of L. After all the temperatures have been read, the values of H and L will be the high and low for the day. Start the program by setting the values of both H and L to the first temperature read.

2. Modify PASSING GRADES so that it prints the names and number grades of all the students. But the program should now print a third column that contains either PASS or FAIL for each student, depending on whether that student got a passing or a failing grade.

3. Rewrite the program PASSING GRADES again, as follows. The printout should have two columns, one headed PASS and the other headed FAIL. The name of each person who passed is printed in the PASS column. The name of each person who failed is printed in the FAIL column. Only one name is printed on each line.

4. Modify the program WAGES to handle workers who are paid in three different ways.
Case 1. These workers are paid a fixed amount each week, regardless of how many hours they work. A typical DATA statement entry for a worker of this type is

"CHARLIE", 1, 250

meaning that this is a worker of type 1, and he earned $250 this week. *Case 2.* These workers do not get overtime; they are paid at the regular rate regardless of how many hours they work. A typical DATA statement entry for a worker of this type is

"FRED", 2, 6.70, 50

meaning that this is a worker of type 2, and he gets $6.70 per hour for
50 hours of work.

Case 3. These workers get time-and-a-half for overtime, just as in the example in this chapter. A typical DATA statement entry for a worker of this type is

"DORIS", 3, 7.50, 45

meaning that this is a worker of type 3, and she gets $7.50 an hour (plus overtime) for 45 hours of work.

The printout should show the type of each worker. Payrate and hours worked should be shown for workers of types 2 and 3 but not for those of type 1.

5. A company is looking for people with the following qualifications:

Degree	Specialty	Years Experience
BS	ENGINEER	at least 5
PHD	PROGRAMMER	at least 2
MS	MANAGER	at least 1
BS	PROGRAMMER	at least 6
MS	ENGINEER	at least 3

Write a program to read the name, degree, specialty, and years of experience for each person applying for a job. The program will print this data for each person who qualifies for a job (and will print nothing for those who don't qualify). The DATA statement entry for each applicant gives the person's name, degree, specialty, and years of experience, in that order. For example:

"SMITH", "BS", "MANAGER", 3

Hint: Draw a flowchart of the program before attempting to write it in BASIC.

350

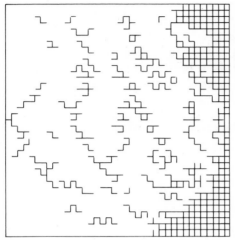

CHAPTER 24

FUNCTIONS AND SUBROUTINES

A program carries out calculations for the user. A function or subroutine carries out calculations *for a program.* Functions and subroutines differ from one another in the way they are invoked by the program that uses them, the way they receive their data, and the way they return their results.

Functions and subroutines are two of the programmer's most important tools. Suppose, for instance, a certain calculation has to be done at several points in a program. Instead of writing the statements to do the calculation several times, we write them once in a function or subroutine. Then, at every point in the program where the calcultion has to be done, we write a single statement that invokes the function or subroutine.

BUILT-IN FUNCTIONS

Built-in functions are part of the BASIC language. You don't have to write them yourself. They are written into the BASIC language processor and are available to any programmer who needs them.

To illustrate how functions are used in BASIC, let's start with the simplest built-in function, *the absolute value function,* ABS. ABS is

THE MIND TOOL used to remove the minus sign from a negative number but leave a positive number unchanged. Thus, ABS converts −5 to 5 but leaves 7 unchanged.

The value a function operates on is called its *argument*. The argument is written in parentheses after the name of the function. Thus, in

ABS(-4)

the argument is −4. That is, ABS is applied to −4, and the result is 4.

Now ABS (−4) is an *expression*. That is, it has the value 4 just as 3+5 has the value 8 and 3*5 has the value 15. We can use an expression involving functions anywhere we can use any other expression. For instance, consider the following statements:

```
10 LET A = ABS(-7)
20 LET B = ABS(10)
30 PRINT A, B
40 PRINT ABS(-7), ABS(10)
```

When these statements are executed, the computer prints

```
7           10
7           10
```

The argument of a function can be variable or an expression, as well as a constant. If the argument is an expression, the expression is evaluated before applying the function:

```
10 LET A = 10
20 LET B = 25
30 LET C = A-B
40 PRINT A, B, C, ABS(C), ABS(A-B)
```

These statements produce the printout:

```
10          25          -15         15          15
```

BASIC has a number of built-in functions, not all of which will be of interest to every user. For reference, all of them appear in the following list, but only a few of them will be used later in the book. The functions are organized according to who might find them useful. In each case, X stands for the argument, and the passage to the right of a function defines its value.

The following functions will be useful to all programmers:

ABS(X)   The absolute value of X. That is, the value of X with its sign changed to +, regardless of whether the sign was + or - originally.

INT(X)   The largest integer (whole number) not greater than X, thus INT(3.14) = 3. But notice that INT(-3.14) = -4; -4 is less than -3.14, which is less than -3, so the largest integer less than -3.14 is -4.

SGN(X)   -1 if X is negative; 0 if X is 0; 1 if X is positive. Thus SGN(-5) = -1; SGN(0) = 0; SGN(3) = 1.

SQR(X)   The square root of X--that is, the value that, when multiplied by itself, gives X. Thus SQR(25) = 5 and SQR(6.25) = 2.5.

The following functions mainly will be of interest to those who have studied trigonometry. All the angles are in radians:

SIN(X)   The sine of X
COS(X)   The cosine of X
TAN(X)   The tangent of X
ATN(X)   The arctangent of X

Although you may occasionally run across the following two functions in elementary mathematics, they mainly will be of interest to those who have studied more advanced subjects, such as calculus and differential equations:

EXP(X) e^X
LOG(X)   The natural logarithm of X

The functions we will use most are INT, ABS, and SGN. For instance, let's see how we can use these to round numbers to the nearest integer.

Rounding   Suppose we need to round values to the nearest integer, so that 25.4 becomes 25, 25.5 becomes 26, and 25.6 becomes 26.

Let's see how to do this arithmetically. The first step, called *half adjusting*, consists of adding .5 to the number to be rounded:

25.4	25.5	25.6
+ .5	+ .5	+ .5
25.9	26.0	26.1

The next step is to discard everything to the right of the decimal point. *For positive numbers only*, the INT function does this job:

INT(25.9) = 25   INT(26.0) = 26   INT(26.1) = 26

In general, if N is a positive number, then the expression

353   INT(N+.5)

gives the value of N rounded to the nearest integer. The following program demonstrates this:

```
10 REM ROUND
20 FOR J = 1 TO 5
30    READ N
40    PRINT N, INT(N+.5)
50 NEXT J
800 DATA 25.45, 50.63, 18.95, 10.49, .51
999 END
```

The printout is

24.45	25
50.63	51
18.95	19
10.49	10
0.51	1

The method we've been discussing doesn't work for all negative numbers. For instance, $INT(-25.5 +.5) = INT(-25.0) = -25$, so -25.5 is rounded to -25 instead of -26, as we would expect.

The easiest way to handle negative numbers is, first, to use the ABS function to change the negative numbers to positive ones. The positive numbers are rounded as before, after which the SGN function is used to give them back their correct signs.

For instance, suppose we want to round -25.4, -25.5, and -25.6. First, we apply the ABS function to each:

$$ABS(-25.4) = 25.4 \quad ABS(-25.5) = 25.5 \quad ABS(-25.6) = 25.6$$

Since the negative numbers have been changed to positive ones, we can round as before:

$$
\begin{array}{ccc}
25.4 & 25.5 & 25.6 \\
+\ \ .5 & +\ \ .5 & +\ \ .5 \\
\hline
25.9 & 26.0 & 26.1
\end{array}
$$

$$INT(25.9) = 25 \quad INT(26.0) = 26 \quad INT(26.1) = 26$$

Now the rounded values have to given back their negative signs:

```
SGN(-25.4)*25 = -1*25 = -25
SGN(-25.5)*26 = -1*26 = -26
SGN(-25.6)*26 = -1*26 = -26
```

We see, then, that any negative number can be rounded to the nearest integer by using the expression

354 $SGN(N)*INT(ABS(N)+.5)$

The same expression also works for positive numbers. Why?

Making Change A traditional program for illustrating the capabilities of the INT function is a program for making change. A practical application for such a program would be in a microprocessor-controlled vending machine.

Let the value of C be the amount of change that is to be returned to the customer. We want to know how many twenties, tens, fives, dollars, half dollars, quarters, dimes, nickels, and pennies to give back.

To begin with instead of working with both dollars and cents, it is easier to work with just cents alone. Therefore, we will convert the amount to be returned entirely into cents. That is, $23.75 will be converted to 2375 cents, $61.98 will be converted to 6198 cents, and so on.

At first, it would seem that all we have to do is multiply the value of C by 100:

```
10 LET C = 100*C
```

However, a problem arises because numbers usually are stored inside the computer in binary notation, and many common decimal fractions, such as .10, can only be represented approximately in binary notation. Thus, $35.10, say, might be stored inside the computer as the binary equivalent of 35.0999. If we multiply this by 100, we get 3509.99, which is not the result we want. If, however, we round 3509.99 to the nearest integer, we get 3510, which is the result desired.

Therefore, we will convert the value of C to cents as follows:

```
10 LET C = INT(100*C + .5)
```

The multiplication by 100 converts the value of C to cents. Rounding to the nearest integer defends against the incompatibility between binary and decimal notation.

Let's start our change making with the twenty-dollar bills. How many twenties should the customer get? Since a twenty-dollar bill is worth 2000 cents, we divide the value of C by 2000. Since we can only hand out a whole number of twenty-dollar bills, we are only interested in the integer part of the quotient.

For instance, suppose the change is $50 or 5000 cents. Dividing 5000 by 2000 gives 2.5. Taking the integer part of 2.5, we find that INT(2.5) = 2. Therefore, we should hand the customer two twenties.

The part of our program that computes the number of twenties to be handed back looks like this:

```
20 LET N = INT(C/2000)
30 PRINT "TWENTIES", N
```

Now we need to know how much change we still have to deal with after we have given back two twenties. To get this, we subtract the amount handed back from the value of C:

```
40 LET C = C - 2000*N
```

Now we are ready to hand out the tens:

```
50 LET N = INT(C/1000)
60 PRINT "TENS", N
70 LET C = C - 1000*N
```

Proceeding in this way, we have no trouble with fives, ones, halves, quarters, dimes, nickels, and pennies. One of your exercises will be to write the complete change-making program.

RND AND TAB

RND and TAB are both referred to as functions in BASIC, although neither is quite what a mathematician would call a function. But whatever you call them, they are both quite useful.

RND The RND function generates *pseudorandom numbers.* These are numbers that seem to have been chosen at random, such as by spinning a roulette wheel, but actually have been calculated by a program. (In the case of RND, the program is part of the BASIC language processor.) We often drop the prefix "pseudo" and just refer to "random" numbers.

In the standard version of BASIC, the RND function doesn't require an argument, but this isn't true of all versions of BASIC. If the RND function requires an argument in the version of BASIC you are using, then your instructor will describe the necessary argument.

The random numbers produced by RND are greater than or equal to 0 and less than 1. Each time RND is used in an expression, its value is a new random number.

For instance, the statement

```
10 PRINT RND, RND, RND, RND, RND
```

produces something like

```
0.173425    0.519035    0.971423    0.312991    0.761852
```

Of course, the actual values produced will vary from one computer to another and will even be different each time the statement is executed. As another example, the program

```
10 FOR I = 1 TO 100
20     PRINT RND,
30 NEXT I
999 END
```

prints 100 random numbers, which will (very likely) all be different.

Often, we need random numbers that are integers lying in some particular range. For instance, to simulate the rolling of dice, we need integers in the range 1-6; to simulate a roulette wheel, we need integers in the range 1-36; for a guessing game in which the computer "thinks of" a number from 1 to 100, we need random integers in the range 1-100.

Let's focus our attention on the last case, random integers in the range 1-100. We can construct an expression for supplying these integers as follows:

Expression	Range of Values	
RND	0-.999999	
100*RND	0-99.9999	
INT(100*RND)	0-99	(integers)
INT(100*RND)+1	1-100	(integers)

The same idea works to produce random integers with other ranges:

Expression	Range of Values	
INT(100*RND)+1	1-100	(integers)
INT(36*RND)+1	1-36	(integers)
INT(6*RND)+1	1-6	(integers)

Normally, we get the same sequence of random numbers each time we execute a program that uses the RND function. This is helpful for debugging programs, since we can see how the changes we make in a program affect its output. (If a different sequence of random numbers was used each time the program was executed, we could not untangle the differences in the output produced by using a different sequences of random numbers and the differences resulting from our changes to the program.)

On the other hand, always using the same sequence of random numbers would be fatal to a game-playing program, since the computer would always play the same way. If we include the statement RANDOMIZE at the beginning of the program, however, the computer will generate a different set of random numbers each time the program is executed. Usually, we leave RANDOMIZE out when we are debugging the program; we put it in when the program is ready for use.

The following guessing-game program illustrates the use of RND and RANDOMIZE:

```
10 REM GUESSING GAME
20 RANDOMIZE
30 PRINT "I AM THINKING OF A NUMBER FROM 1 TO 100"
40 PRINT "TRY TO GUESS THE NUMBER I AM THINKING OF"
50 LET N = INT(100*RND)+1
60 PRINT "YOUR GUESS";
```

```
 70 INPUT G
 80 IF G = N THEN 160
 90    IF G > N THEN 120
100       PRINT "YOUR GUESS IS TO SMALL. TRY AGAIN"
110       GO TO 130
120       PRINT "YOUR GUESS IS TOO LARGE. TRY AGAIN"
130    PRINT "YOUR GUESS";
140       INPUT G
150 GO TO 80
160 PRINT "YOU ARE CORRECT. CONGRATULATIONS!"
999 END
```

If line 20 were omitted, why would people quickly tire of playing this game?

TAB The TAB function provides the programmer with greater control over how the printout is positioned on the page. TAB can only be used in PRINT statements; it cannot be used in expressions or assignment statements.

Let's suppose that the positions on a line in which a character can be printed are numbered, starting with 1 for the leftmost position. Thus TAB(10) in a PRINT statement causes the computer to space over to position 10 on the line; TAB(25) causes it to space over to position 25; and so on.

Consider the following statement:

```
10 PRINT TAB(5); "SEE"; TAB(19); "SPOT"; TAB(28); "RUN"
```

The computer produces the following printout (the "scale" above the printout lets you see the position in which each character is printed):

```
          1    1    2    2    3
1...5....0....5....0....5....0....
    SEE            SPOT    RUN
```

As you see, "SEE" is printed starting at position 5; "SPOT" is printed starting at position 19; and "RUN" is printed starting at position 28.

The TAB function can be used to provide columns of different widths than those produced by the comma. We also can use the TAB function for printing graphs and patterns. For instance, the program

```
10 FOR N = 1 TO 5
20    PRINT TAB(6-N)
30    FOR I = 1 TO N
40       PRINT "*";
50    NEXT I
60    PRINT
70 NEXT N
999 END
```

prints

```
    *
   **
  ***
 ****
*****
```

USER-DEFINED FUNCTIONS

You aren't limited to those functions whose definitions are built into BASIC. You also can define your own functions. Although the facilities for defining functions in BASIC are limited compared to those offered by some programming languages, BASIC functions still can be quite useful.

To begin with, we have to give a name to the function we are defining. The names of user-defined functions in BASIC consist of three letters each. Of the three letters, the first two must be FN. Therefore, the possible names for user-defined functions in BASIC are FNA, FNB, FNC, and so on.

We define a function using a DEF statement, which can be placed anywhere in the program but which usually is placed near the beginning. To see how the DEF statement works, let's define a rounding function, FNR, which will round any positive or negative number to the nearest integer. We define FNR as follows:

```
10 DEF FNR(X) = SGN(X)*INT(ABS(X)+.5)
```

X is the function *parameter*. Whenever the function is used, the argument that is supplied is substituted for X in the expression on the right-hand side of the equal sign. The value of the function is the value of the expression on the right-hand side of the equal sign with the argument substituted for X.

For instance, suppose we have the expression

```
FNR(-73.6)
```

The argument is −73.6. This is substituted for X in the expression on the right-hand side of the equal sign in the function definition:

```
SGN(-73.6)*INT(ABS(-73.6)+.5)
```

This expression is evaluated to get the value of the function:

```
SGN(-73.6)*INT(73.6+)+.5)
        -1*INT(73.6+.5)
        -1*INT(74.1)
        -1*74
        -74
```

359

Therefore, the statement

10 PRINT FNR(-73.6)

causes the computer to print

-74

The parameter X in the function definition has nothing to do with any variable X that might be used elsewhere in the program. Therefore, it's possible to use the same name as a parameter in one or more function definitions and as a variable name as well. The various uses will not intefere with one another.

A function that is useful for game-playing programs yields random integers in the range 1-N, where N is the argument of the function:

20 DEF FNI(N) = INT(N*RND)+1

Thus, the value of FNI(6) is a random integer in the range 1-6; the value of FNI(100) is a random integer in the range 1-100; and so on.

SUBROUTINES

A subroutine is a part of a BASIC program that can be invoked from elsewhere in the program. The subroutine must contain at least one RETURN statement. When the computer executes the RETURN statement, it leaves the subroutine and continues execution at the statement following the one that originally invoked the subroutine.

A subroutine is invoked using a GOSUB statement. For example, the statement

100 GOSUB 500
110 ...

causes the computer to jump to line 500, the first line of the subroutine. Before jumping, however, the computer saves the line number of the line immediately following the GOSUB statement— line 110, in this case. When the RETURN statement in the subroutine is executed, the computer comes back to line 110 and continues execution from there.

GOSUB differs from GO TO in that GOSUB makes provisions for returning to the statement immediately following the GOSUB statement. GO TO is a one-way ticket to another part of the program; GOSUB provides for a round trip.

It is convenient to think of a GOSUB statement as a command to the computer to do whatever calculation is done by the subroutine. In effect, subroutines allow us to define new commands that the computer will obey.

For example, consider the program WAGES, which calculates the wages an employee earns. Let's rewrite that program so that it uses a subroutine starting at line 500 to do the actual wage calculation. Having decided to do this, we can use GOSUB 500 as if it were the command "calculate the wages W for an employee who worked H hours at R dollars per hour."

The part of the program that reads the data and prints the results is as follows:

```
10  REM WAGES (USING SUBROUTINE)
20  PRINT "NAME", "RATE", "HOURS", "WAGES"
30  PRINT
40  READ N$, R, H
50  IF N$ = "/*" THEN 100
60      GOSUB 500
70      PRINT N$, R, H, W
80      READ N$, R, H
90  GO TO 50
100 STOP
```

Notice two things.

First, when we write this part of the program, we can assume that GOSUB 500 will get the wages calculated. At this point, we don't have to worry about any of the details of how the calculation is done. Therefore, we have separated the problem of reading and printing the data from the problem of calculating the wages. We can concentrate our attention on one problem at a time.

Second, this part of the program ends with a STOP statement. The STOP statement, which has the same effect as the END statement, can be used anywhere in a program, not just at the end. We need the STOP statement because the subroutine is going to follow the main program. It would be an error if, when the computer finished executing the main program, it kept on going and executed the subroutine as well. The subroutine is only to be executed when it is invoked by a GOSUB statement in the main program. Therefore, the STOP statement terminates execution of the program before the computer gets to the statements of the subroutine.

Now, of course, we have to write the subroutine. But as we write it, we only have to concentrate on one thing—calculating wages. We don't have to worry about reading the data or printing the results.

The subroutine goes like this:

```
500 IF H > 40 THEN 530
510     LET W = R*H
520 GO TO 140
530     LET W = 40*R + 1.5*R*(H-40)
540 RETURN
```

Regardless of which statement is executed to calculate the value of **361** W, the computer will end up at line 540, the RETURN statement. This statement causes the computer to go back to the main program and pick up execution with line 70, the statement following the GOSUB statement.

The complete program looks like this:

```
10 REM WAGES (USING SUBROUTINE)
20 PRINT "NAME", "RATE", "HOURS", "WAGES"
30 PRINT
40 READ N$, R, H
50 IF N$ = "/*" THEN 100
60    GOSUB 500
70    PRINT N$, R, H, W
80    READ N$, R, H
90 GO TO 50
100 STOP
500 IF H > 40 THEN 530
510    LET W = R*H
520 GO TO 540
530    LET W = 40*R + 1.5*R*(H-40)
540 RETURN
800 DATA "BILL", 3.58, 44, "CHARLIE", 3.25, 35
810 DATA "DORIS", 2.75, 46, "FRED", 5.31, 38
820 DATA "MARY", 6.83, 48, "/*", 0, 0
999 END
```

EXERCISES

1. Write the complete change-making program. The program should interact with the user as follows:

```
AMOUNT OF CHANGE? 33.47
   TWENTIES   1
   TENS       1
   FIVES      0
   ONES       3
   HALVES     0
   QUARTERS   1
   DIMES      2
   NICKELS    0
   PENNIES    2
```

2. People like to imagine patterns in random data, whether they are the positions of the stars in the sky or the fluctuations of the stock market. It's interesting to print random star patterns and see what constellations you can find. Write a program to print such a pattern. For each print position in the pattern, the program computes

INT(2*RND)

If the value of this expression is 1, print an asterisk. If the value of the expression is 0, leave a space. Note that, when BASIC fills up one line

with characters, it automatically goes to the next line, so you don't
have to worry about arranging your pattern into lines.

3. Write a program to print the following pattern:

```
    *
   ***
  *****
 *******
*********
 *******
  *****
   ***
    *
```

The only PRINT statements in the program should be PRINT "*"; and
PRINT. PRINT "*"; should appear twice at the most.

4. Define a function FNC that will round off amounts of money to
the nearest cent. For instance,

FNC(21.4762) = 21.48   FNC(35.163) = 35.16

Hint: The argument should be multiplied by 100, rounded to the
nearest integer, and the result divided by 100. To test your function
definition, use it to write a program that reads in values and prints
them out rounded to two decimal places.

5. Write a subroutine to be used by a program that plays craps.
Every time the subroutine is invoked, it simulates the rolling of a pair
of dice. The subroutine prints the numbers rolled and assigns their
sum to the variable D. For instance, the subroutine might print

YOU ROLLED A 5 AND A 3

and set the value of D to 8.

6. Use the subroutine of problem 5 to write a complete craps-
playing program. After the dice have been rolled the first time, there
are three cases, depending on the value of D, the sum of the two
numbers rolled.
   Case 1.   D = 7 or 11. The player wins.
   Case 2.   D = 2, 3, or 12. The player loses.
   Case 3.   D = 4, 5, 6, 8, 9, or 10. The value of D for the first roll
becomes the player's "point." The dice are rolled repeatedly until
the player "makes his point" (by rolling the same number he did on
his first roll) or "craps out" (by rolling a 7). The player wins if he
makes his point and loses if he craps out.

CHAPTER 25

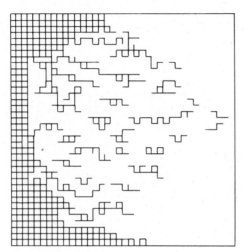

ARRAYS

There are two basic ways a computer can process data. One way is to calculate the results from the data given, as we do when we work out an arithmetic problem. The other way is to use the data to look up the results, as we do when we use a person's name to look up a telephone number.

For instance, suppose a program needs baseball statistics, say, or the populations of major cities. There is no computation that will yield the winner of the World Series for a particular year or the number of people who have decided to live in a particular city.

When we solve mathematical problems, the results usually can be obtained by computation. But the further away we get from mathematics and the closer we get to the subjects of everyday experience, the more we have to use lists and tables to hold arbitrary data.

In programming languages, lists and tables are known as *arrays*.

ONE-DIMENSIONAL ARRAYS

So far, we have used names, such as A, M, and Z, to refer to single memory locations. Now we want to see how to use a name to refer to a number of memory locations.

For instance, suppose we use L to refer to five memory locations containing the values 25, 48, 15, 96, and 72. We can think of L as being laid out in memory like this:

L
25
48
15
96
72

The individual memory locations making up L are called its *elements*. We refer to individual elements by placing the number of the element after L in parentheses. Thus L(1) refers to the first element of L, the one containing the value 25. L(2) refers to the second element of L, the one containing the value 48. L(3) refers to the third element of L, and so on.

Thinking in terms of values instead of memory locations, the value of L is a *list* of numbers. We refer to the individual entries on the list by referring to the elements of L. Thus, the value of L(1) is 25; the value of L(2) is 48; and so on.

The number in parentheses that specifies the element to which we are referring is called a *subscript*. The word *subscript* means *written below* and comes from mathematics. Mathematicians write subscripts as small numbers below the printed line. Thus, a mathematician would write the elements of L as L_1, L_2, L_3, L_4, and L_5. Most computer printers can't print small numbers below the line, so the subscripts must be placed in parentheses after the array name. This is just as well, since the computer-science notation for array elements is easier to read than the mathematical one.

We refer to L as an *array variable* or just as an *array*. L(1), L(2), and so on are called *subscripted variables*.

We can use subscripted variables anywhere we can use ordinary variables. We can use them in PRINT statements, for instance:

```
10 PRINT L(1), L(2), L(3), L(4), L(5)
```

This statement produces the printout

```
25          48          15          96          72
```

We can also use subscripted variables in expressions and assignment statements. For instance, after the assignment statement

```
10 LET L(5) = L(1) + L(2)*L(3) + L(4)
```

has been executed, L looks like this:

L
25
48
15
96
841

365

Finally, we can use subscripted variables in READ and INPUT statements. After the following are executed

```
10 READ L(1), L(2), L(3), L(4), L(5)
20 DATA 7, 3, 9, 8, 4
```

L looks like this:

L
7
3
9
8
4

As long as we just use constants, such as 1, 2, 3, 4, and 5, for subscripts, we gain nothing from using arrays. We could just as well have used separate variables, such as V, W, X, Y, and Z, in place of L(1), L(2), L(3), L(4), and L(5). Arrays come into their own when we use variables or expressions as subscripts.

For example, let's write the statements to add up the values of the elements of the array L:

```
10 LET T = 0
20 FOR I = 1 TO 5
30    LET T = T+L(I)
40 NEXT I
50 PRINT T
```

As usual, the value of T is the running total. We start off with the value of T equal to 0 and then add the value of each element of L to it. Adding the values of the elements of L to the value of T is done by the statement

```
30   LET T = T+L(I)
```

Here is the crucial point. Line 30 is only written once, yet it is used five times, once for each element of L. The first time the statement is executed, the value of I is 1, so the value of the first element of L is added to T, just as if we had written

```
30 LET T = T+L(1)
```

The second time line 30 is executed, the value of I is 2, and the effect is the same as if we had written

```
30 LET T = T+L(2)
```

And so on for I equal to 3, 4, and 5. *By using a variable or an expression as a subscript, we can cause a repeated statement to refer*
366 *to a different array element each time it is executed.*

The DIM Statement   Before we use an array in BASIC, we must tell the computer how many elements the array will have, so the computer will know how much memory to set aside for the array. We do this with a DIM statement. DIM stands for *dimension*, which in this context simply means *size*.

In the DIM statement, we list all the arrays that will be used in a program. Following the name of each array, we give the number of elements in the array. The number of elements is enclosed in parentheses. For instance,

10 DIM L(5), A(10), B(50)

specifies that the program will use three arrays—L, A, and B. L has 5 elements, A has 10 elements, and B has 50 elements.

The DIM statement for an array must come before the point in the program where the array is first used. Usually, it is best to put all DIM statements near the beginning of the program.

Some versions of BASIC allow the DIM statement to be omitted under certain conditions. Since the conditions vary from one version of BASIC to another, the safest course is always to include the DIM statement.

The Change-Maker Revisited   The change-making program described in the previous chapter offers a good opportunity to use arrays. Without arrays, the program is rather clumsy, because we have to use a separate set of statements for each denomination of bill or coin that we use in making change. With arrays, we can write these statements once and repeat them for each denomination.

We will use two arrays. One will give the value (in cents) of each bill or coin. The other will give the English name of each bill or coin in plural form. The two arrays, V and N$, are specified as follows:

20 DIM V(9), N$(9)

(*Note:* Because some versions of BASIC don't allow arrays of strings, this program can't be used with all versions of BASIC.)

The contents of the two arrays are as follows:

V		N$	
	2000		"TWENTIES"
	1000		"TENS"
	500		"FIVES"
	100		"ONES"
	50		"HALVES"
	25		"QUARTERS"
	10		"DIMES"
	5		"NICKELS"
	1		"PENNIES"

Notice that we have made a two-column table by using a
separate one-dimensional array for each column. This technique is

used frequently. The arrays are referred to as "parallel arrays," since we can think of the two arrays as lined up side by side, as in the preceding illustration. For any value of I from 1 through 9, V(I) refers to an element of V, and N$(I) refers to the corresponding element of N$. In particular, V(I) gives the number of cents a particular bill or coin is worth, and N$(I) gives the English name for bills or coins of that kind.

Our first job is to give the arrays the contents that were just shown. We can do this with READ and DATA statements:

```
30  FOR I = 1 TO 9
40      READ V(I)
50  NEXT I
60  DATA 2000, 1000, 500, 100, 50, 25, 10, 5, 1
70  FOR I = 1 TO 9
80      READ N$(I)
90  NEXT I
100 DATA "TWENTIES", "TENS", "FIVES", "ONES", "HALVES"
110 DATA "QUARTERS", "DIMES", "NICKELS", "PENNIES"
```

(Remember, we can place DATA statements anywhere we wish in a program. When the DATA statements are used to supply constants— as opposed to the data being processed—it is often clearer to place the DATA statements immediately after the statements that read the constants.)

With the help of these arrays, we can write a single repetition to handle the entire change-making process. If C is the amount of change yet to be returned and K is the number of coins or bills of a particular kind to be handed out, then the following statements do the job:

```
160 FOR I = 1 TO 9
170     LET K = INT(C/V(I))
180     PRINT N$(I), K
190     LET C = C - K*V(I)
200 NEXT I
```

If you compare this simple repetition with the long list of statements required for the change-making program in the previous chapter, you can't help but appreciate how arrays let us use the same statements repeatedly, with the statements referring to different data each time they are used.

Now let's write a complete version of the change-making program using one-dimensional arrays:

```
10  REM CHANGE (USING ARRAYS)
20  DIM V(9), N$(9)
30  FOR I = 1 TO 9
40      READ V(I)
50  NEXT I
```

```
 60 DATA 2000, 1000, 500, 100, 50, 25, 10, 5, 1
 70 FOR I = 1 TO 9
 80    READ N$(I)
 90 NEXT I
100 DATA "TWENTIES", "TENS", "FIVES", "ONES", "HALVES"
110 DATA "QUARTERS", "DIMES", "NICKELS", "PENNIES"
120 PRINT "AMOUNT OF CHANGE";
130 INPUT C
140 IF C = 0 THEN 999
150    LET C = INT(100*C + .5)
160    FOR I = 1 TO 9
170       LET K = INT(C/V(I))
180       PRINT N$(I), K
190       LET C = C - K*V(I)
200    NEXT I
210    PRINT
220    PRINT "AMOUNT OF CHANGE";
230    INPUT C
240 GO TO 140
999 END
```

Table Look-up   In the change-making example, we used all the information in the table made up of the two arrays. Therefore, we simply started at the beginning of the arrays and worked through them, element by element.

Frequently, however, we have to search for the information we need, just as when we look up words in a dictionary or numbers in a telephone directory.

For an example of a problem of this kind, suppose a certain manufacturer gives quantity discounts on certain items. The following table gives the cost per item for different quantities purchased:

Quantity Purchased	Cost Per Item
1-99	25.00
100-299	23.50
300-599	20.75
600-999	18.45
1000 or over	16.30

Let's think for a moment about how we want to store this table inside the computer. As we saw for the change-making program, it's convenient to store a two-column table by using a separate one-dimensional array for each column. There is no problem in storing the cost-per-item column as a one-dimensional array, since each entry of the column consists of a single number. But each entry of the quantity-purchased column represents a *range* of values and consists of two numbers, one for the lower limit of the range and one for the

369

upper limit. We can only store one number in each element of a one-dimensional array, however.

But do we really need to store both the lower limit and the upper limit of each range? No, we don't. If we know only the upper limits, it is clear what the lower limits must be.

The lower limit of the first range must be 1, if we assume that table is to cover all possible quantities and if we assume that single orders are allowed. And the lower limit of every other range is simply one more than the upper limit of the preceding range. That is, 100 = 99+1, 300 = 299+1, 600 = 599+1, and 1000 = 999+1. Since the lower limits can be worked out from the upper limits, only the upper limits have to be stored. We will store the quantity-purchased column, then, as a one-dimensional array, each of whose elements contains the upper limit of one of the ranges.

But now a new problem arises. The last range, the one listed as "1000 and over" in the table, has no upper limit. What will we store in the last element of the array representing the quantity-purchased column?

We can solve the problem this way. Suppose that the program has inputted the number of items that the customer purchased and is preparing to look up this number in the quantity-purchased column. Before doing so, the program stores the number of items purchased, the number it is about to look up, in the last element of the quantity-purchased array. If the customer purchased 1500 items, for instance, then 1500 would be stored as the last element of the quantity-purchased array. When this is done, the last range becomes 1000-1500. When the program proceeds to look up 1500, it finds that 1500 lies in the last range. The cost per item for 1500 items, then, is 16.30.

By storing the number of items purchased as the last entry in the quantity purchased array, we make sure that, no matter how large the number of items purchased is, that number always will lie in the last range, if it did not lie in any of the preceding ones. And that, in fact, is exactly what the phrase "1000 and over" implies.

We can look at this another way. By storing the value we are looking up in the last element of the quantity-purchased array, we make sure that the last range will contain that value, even if no other range does. The value we are looking up, then, acts as a sentinel that makes sure the search will stop with the last range in the table and will not try to "run off the end of the table." Hereafter, we will refer to the last entry in the quantity-purchased array as the *sentinel value*.

Let's use Q for the quantity-purchased array and C for the cost-per-item array. The two arrays look like this:

Q
| 99 |
| 299 |
| 599 |
| 999 |
| *sentinel* |

C
| 25.00 |
| 23.50 |
| 20.75 |
| 18.45 |
| 16.30 |

Q consists of the upper limits of the ranges and the sentinel. C consists of the costs per item.

In three steps, our program will find the cost per item corresponding to a certain number of items purchased. First, the number of items purchased is stored in the sentinel position. Then, the program starts at the beginning of Q and scans down the array until it finds a value greater than or equal to the number of items purchased. Finally, the price per item is the entry in the C array corresponding to the value found.

Suppose, for example, that 700 items were purchased. Then 700 is stored in the last element of Q. Scanning Q from top to bottom, the first value we find that is greater than or equal to 700 is 999. Therefore, the cost per item for a purchase of 700 items is 18.45.

On the other hand, suppose that 2000 items were purchased. Then 2000 is stored in the last element of Q. Scanning Q from top to bottom, the first value we find that is greater than or equal to 2000 is 2000. Therefore, the cost per item for a purchase of 2000 items is 16.30.

Now let's see how to program this. Let the value of N be the number of items purchased. The first step is to store this value in the last element of Q:

```
140 LET Q(5) = N
```

Next, we scan Q from top to bottom—that is, from Q(1) to Q(5)—looking for the first element whose value is greater than or equal to the value of N:

```
150 LET I = 1
160 IF Q(I) >= N THEN 190
170     LET I = I+1
180 GO TO 160
```

The program looks at each element of Q until it finds one whose value is greater than or equal to the value of N. When this element is found, the computer jumps to line 190. The value of I is the subscript of the element found. The cost per item is the value of the corresponding element of C, C(I). The total cost of the items is the number of items purchased times the cost per item, or

```
N*C(I)
```

The following is the complete cost-finding program:

```
10 REM COSTS
20 DIM Q(5), C(5)
30 FOR I = 1 TO 4
40     READ Q(I)
50 NEXT I
60 DATA 99, 299, 599, 999
70 FOR I = 1 TO 5
```

```
 80     READ C(I)
 90 NEXT I
100 DATA 25.00, 23.50, 20.75, 18.45, 16.30
110 PRINT "NUMBER OF ITEMS PURCHASED";
120 INPUT N
130 IF N = 0 THEN 999
140     LET Q(5) = N
150     LET I = 1
160     IF Q(I) >= N THEN 190
170         LET I = I+1
180     GO TO 160
190     PRINT "THE COST OF THE PURCHASE IS"; N*C(I)
200     PRINT
210     PRINT "NUMBER OF ITEMS PURCHASED";
220     INPUT N
230 GO TO 130
999 END
```

TWO-DIMENSIONAL ARRAYS

The arrays we have used so far are said to be *one-dimensional*, since they only extend in one direction—the vertical direction in our illustrations. Two-dimensional arrays extend in two directions. If we think of a one-dimensional array as a list, then a two-dimensional array is a table with both rows and columns.

A two-dimensional array is specified as follows:

```
10 DIM T(5, 4)
```

This informs the computer that T is a two-dimensional array with five rows and four columns. The number of rows is always given first, followed by the number of columns. The number of elements in the array is the number of rows multiplied by the number of columns. T, then, has twenty elements.

We can visualize T as being laid out in memory as follows:

Columns

		1	2	3	4
T	1	25	38	72	91
	2	43	69	21	54
Rows	3	71	38	63	49
	4	87	51	29	18
	5	10	77	94	61

To refer to a particular element of T, we need two subscripts, one to give the row in which the element is located and the other to give the column in which the element is located. Thus, T(3, 2) refers to the element in the third row and second column; T(5, 1) refers to the element in the fifth row and first column. For the values of T shown in the illustration, the value of T(3, 2) is 38 and the value of T(5, 1) is 10.

A Political Poll   For an example illustrating the use of two-dimensional arrays, let's consider the following problem. Three candidates, Jack, Bob, and Carol, are running for a political office. A poll is taken in which Democrats, Republicans, and Independents are asked which candidate they prefer. We would like to display all combinations of party affiliation and candidate preferences—how many Democrats are for Jack; how many Democrats are for Bob; how many Democrats are for Carol; how many Republicans are for Jack; and so on.

We can display this information conveniently by using a table whose rows correspond to Democrats, Republicans, and Independents and whose columns correspond to Jack, Bob, and Carol. Each entry in the table tells how many people with a certain political affiliation favor a certain candidate.

Suppose, for instance, the results of the poll were as follows:

	Jack	Bob	Carol
Democrats	100	10	50
Republicans	25	150	75
Independents	45	60	150

According to this data, of all the Democrats questioned, 100 preferred Jack, 10 preferred Bob, and 50 preferred Carol. Of all the Republicans questioned, 25 preferred Jack, 150 preferred Bob, and so on.

Our first job is to collect the data in this table. The data the poll takers return consists of the political affiliation and the preferred candidate for each person questioned. We need to read this data and total up the number of persons of each political affiliation who prefer a particular candidate.

Let's use an array D to accumulate this data. The array D is dimensioned as follows:

```
10 DIM D(3, 3)
```

Each of the three rows of D corresponds to a political affiliation; each of the three columns corresponds to a candidate.

Before starting to accumulate any data, we have to clear all the entries of D to 0. The following statements will do this:

```
10 FOR I = 1 TO 3
20    FOR J = 1 TO 3
30        LET D(I, J) = 0
40    NEXT J
50 NEXT I
```

This kind of construction, with one FOR-NEXT repetition nested inside the other, is extremely common in processing two-dimensional arrays. Therefore, we will look at it closely to make sure we understand how it works.

Let's start with the innermost FOR and NEXT:

```
20     FOR J = 1 TO 3
30        LET D(I, J) = 0
40     NEXT J
```

This sets the values of the elements in one row of D to 0. Which row? That is determined by the value of I. If the value of I is 1, then lines 20-40 are equivalent to

LET D(1, 1) = 0   LET D(1, 2) = 0   LET D(1, 3) = 0

If the value of I is 2, then lines 20-40 are equivalent to

LET D(2, 1) = 0   LET D(2, 2) = 0   LET D(2, 3) = 0

If the value of I is 3, then lines 20-40 are equivalent to

LET D(3, 1) = 0   LET D(3, 2) = 0   LET D(3, 3) = 0

We see, then, if the value of I is 1, the elements of the first row are set to 0; if the value of I is 2, the elements of the second row are set to 0; if the value of I is 3, the elements of the third row are set to 0. A more concise way of describing this is to say that the elements of the Ith row are set to 0.

Obviously, then, if we want to set the values of the elements in all three rows of I to 0, we should execute lines 20-40 first with I = 1, then with I = 2, and finally with I = 3. This is exactly what the outer FOR-NEXT repetition causes to be done. The effect of the two nested repetitions, then, is to set all the elements of D to 0.

We usually use two nested FOR-NEXT repetitions when we want to carry out some operation on all the elements of a two-dimensional array.

Now, suppose that each person questioned stated a political affiliation and a preferred candidate. This information is coded as two numbers. The first number gives the political affiliation of the person questioned, and the second number indicates which candidate that person prefers. The codes are as follows:

Political Affiliation		Candidate Preferred	
Democrat	1	Jack	1
Republican	2	Bob	2
Independent	3	Carol	3

The code numbers have been chosen to correspond to the rows and
columns of D used for each affiliation and candidate. Thus, row 1 of

D corresponds to Democrats; row 2 to Republicans, and so on.

The data the poll takers collect might look something like this:

```
800 DATA 1, 3, 2, 1, 3, 3, 1, 1, 1, 1, 2, 3, 0, 0
```

Each pair of numbers represents one person's response. Thus, 1, 3 means that the person questioned was a Democrat who preferred Carol; 2, 1 means that the person questioned was a Republican who preferred Jack. The last two values, 0, 0, constitute the end-of-data sentinel.

Of course, this is just a tiny set of data for illustration. The results of an actual poll would contain hundreds or thousands of responses.

Now, suppose that the values of the elements of D have been set to 0 as previously described. The following program segment counts the number of people of each affiliation who prefer each candidate:

```
10 READ I, J
20 IF I = 0 THEN 60
30     LET D(I, J) = D(I, J)+1
40     READ I, J
50 GO TO 20
60 ...
```

The values read for I and J determine a particular element of D, namely D(I, J). The value of this element is increased by one to count one more person with the corresponding political affiliation and preferring the corresponding candidate. Preference data is read and counted until the end-of-data sentinel is encountered.

Once the raw data has been collected, we can do a number of things with it. For one thing, we might be interested in simply printing out the data for our inspection. To print a two-dimensional array, we use the same kind of repetition-within-a-repetition that we used to set the elements of D to 0:

```
10 FOR I = 1 TO 3
20     FOR J = 1 TO 3
30         PRINT D(I, J),
40     NEXT J
50     PRINT
60 NEXT I
```

Lines 20-50 print one row of D. The value of I determines which row is printed. The comma at the end of line 30 causes all the elements of the row to be printed on a single line. After each row has been printed, line 50 causes the computer to go to a new line for the next row. Lines 10 and 60 cause lines 20-50 to be repeated for I = 1, 2, and 3, thus printing out all three rows of D. The printout looks like

this:

100	10	50
25	150	75
45	60	150

Can you think of a way to get the rows and columns labeled with the names of the political parties and candidates?

Usually, we are less interested in the *number* of people who gave a particular response than we are in the *percentage* of all those questioned who gave that response.

To calculate the percentages, we first must know the total number of people questioned. We can get this by adding up the values of all the elements of D. Again, we use nested FOR-NEXT constructions:

```
10 LET T = 0
20 FOR I = 1 TO 3
30    FOR J = 1 TO 3
40       LET T = T+D(I, J)
50    NEXT J
60 NEXT I
```

We calculate the percentage of people giving a particular response by dividing the number of people giving that response by the total number of people questioned and multiplying the result by 100. That is,

```
100*D(I, J)/T
```

gives the percentage of people questioned whose affiliation and preference correspond to the values of I and J. Let us use an array P with three rows and three columns to record the percentages:

```
10 FOR I = 1 TO 3
20    FOR J = 1 TO 3
30       LET P(I, J) = 100*D(I, J)/T
40    NEXT J
50 NEXT I
```

Another thing we probably are interested in is the percentage of people questioned who preferred each particular candidate. We can get this result by summing up the *columns* of P to get a total percentage for each candidate.

Let's use a three-element, one-dimensional array C to hold the percentages for the candidates. The value of C(1) will be the percentage of people who preferred Jack; the value of C(2) will be the percentage who preferred Bob; the value of C(3) will be the percentage who preferred Carol. We add up the columns of P as follows:

10 FOR J = 1 TO 3

```
20      LET C(J) = 0
30      FOR I = 1 TO 3
40          LET C(J) = C(J)+P(I, J)
50      NEXT I
60 NEXT J
```

This example differs slightly from our previous ones in that the inner FOR-NEXT sums one *column* (instead of one row) of P. Which column is summed depends on the value of J. The outer FOR-NEXT steps J from 1 to 3, thus causing a sum to be computed for each column.

We also might want to know the percentage of people questioned who were of each affiliation. For instance, if our sample is to give reliable results, then these percentages should be the same for the sample as for the population as a whole.

Let's use a three-element, one-dimensional array A to hold the percentages for the political affiliations. We calculate the value of each element of A by summing the corresponding row in P:

```
10 FOR I = 1 TO 3
20     LET A(I) = 0
30     FOR J = 1 TO 3
40         LET A(I) = A(I)+D(I, J)
50     NEXT J
60 NEXT I
```

This example works more like our earlier ones, with the inner FOR-NEXT summing the elements of a particular row and the outer FOR-NEXT stepping through the three rows.

Of course, all the arrays we have introduced so far would have to be included in DIM statements. The following is a DIM statement for these arrays:

```
10 DIM D(3, 3), P(3, 3), C(3), A(3)
```

EXERCISES   **1.** Write a program that will read in five numbers and print them out in reverse order. That is, if the DATA statement is

```
800 DATA 1, 3, 5, 7, 9
```

the program will print

```
9   7   5   3   1
```

2. Write a program that reads and stores a price list. One column of the price list contains the order numbers of the items; the other column contains their prices. When you enter the order number of an item, the program either will print the price of the item or inform you that the order number you entered is not in the table.

377

You can use the table-look-up program in this chapter as a guide to writing this program. However, here we are looking for a particular value instead of trying to find the range in which a particular value lies. This means that when you compare the order number entered with the order numbers in the table, you will use = instead of $>$=.

3. Write a program to read in nine numbers and print them as a three-by-three array. The first three numbers read will be in the first column of the array; the second three numbers in the second column; and the last three numbers in the third column. For instance, if the DATA statement is

800 DATA 1, 3, 5, 7, 9, 11, 13, 15, 17

the program will print

1	7	13
3	9	15
5	11	17

4. A *magic square* is a square array of numbers such as

8	1	6
3	5	7
4	9	2

Note that all the rows, columns, and diagonals have the same sum. (In the example, for instance, $8 + 1 + 6 = 15$, $3 + 5 + 7 = 15$, $4 + 9 + 2 = 15$, $8 + 3 + 4 = 15$, $1 + 5 + p = 15$, $6 + 7 + 2 = 15$, $8 + 5 + 2 = 15$, and $4 + 5 + 6 = 15$.) The number of rows or columns is the *order* of the square; the example is a magic square of order 3. Write a program that will read in a square of any order and print out whether or not the square is "magic." For the example, the DATA statement for the given square would be

800 DATA 3, 8, 1, 6, 3, 5, 7, 4, 9, 2

5. Write a complete program to process the results of a political poll. The various counts and percentages discussed in the chapter should be calculated and printed out in easy-to-read form. As a class project, you might take a poll on some issues that are of concern on your campus and use the computer to process the results. Your student newspaper might be interested in publishing a summary showing how different groups on campus feel about the issues in question.

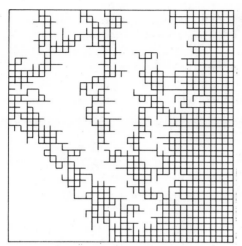 **STRINGS**

We have been using strings all along, but, so far, we haven't done too much with them. Mainly, we have read them in and printed them out unchanged. Now we want to look at some of the kinds of processing that computers can carry out on strings.

One reason we haven't explored string processing in depth is that the facilities for handling strings vary greatly from one version of BASIC to another. We have already tripped over this problem once with the change-making program using arrays; there, we pointed out that some versions of BASIC don't allow arrays of strings.

The version of BASIC you are using, then, may not have all the string-handling features described in this chapter, and those it does have may differ in detail from those described here. Differences such as these are extremely confusing to beginners still struggling with the elements of a language. But you're an old hand at BASIC by now, so you should be able to cope with a few differences between what is discussed in the text and what is available on your computer system.

Besides, you might as well get used to coping with such differences. It is a rare implementation of a programming language that does not have at least one feature that is different from every other **379** implementation of the same language.

STRING OPERATIONS AND FUNCTIONS

Concatenation   To *concatenate* two strings is to join them together. *Join* would have been a much better word than *concatenate*, but we seem to be stuck with *concatenate*.

In BASIC, the + sign is used for the concatenation operator. Thus, + has different meanings when applied to numbers and to strings. When applied to numbers, it means addition. When applied to strings, it means concatenation. The use of the same sign to represent different operations on different kinds of data is a common feature of many programming languages.

The following shows the values of some string expressions formed with the concatenation operator:

```
"STRAIGHT"+"FORWARD" = "STRAIGHTFORWARD"
"UN"+"LIKELY" = "UNLIKELY"
"AL"+"TO"+"GET"+"HER" = "ALTOGETHER"
```

The concatenation operator never introduces blanks. If blanks are needed, they must be included explicitly in the expression:

```
"GOOD"+"MORNING" = "GOODMORNING"
"GOOD"+" "+"MORNING" = "GOOD MORNING"
```

Like the arithmetic operators, the concatenation operator can be used with variables and in expressions. For instance, suppose that A$, B$, C$, and D$ have the following values:

Variable	Value
A$	"CON"
B$	"CAT"
C$	"EN"
D$	"ATE"

The statement

```
10  E$ = A$+B$+C$+D$
```

assigns the value "CONCATENATE" to E$.

LEFT$, RIGHT$, and MID$ In many versions of BASIC the only string operator is +. All other string manipulations are done with built-in functions.

The functions LEFT$, RIGHT$, and MID$ are all used to extract substrings from a string.

A substring is simply a part of a string. For instance, some of the substrings of "CONCANTENATE" are

"CON"   "CAT"   "TEN"   "NATE"   "ATE"

Notice that the substring "ATE" occurs in two different positions in the string "CONCATENATE".

For the purpose of identifying substrings, the characters of a string are assumed to be numbered, starting with 1 for the leftmost character. For example, the following shows the numbering of the characters in the string "ALL RIGHT":

```
"ALL  RIGHT"
 123456789
```

Notice that the blank space is counted, too.

An invocation of the function MID$ has the following form:

```
MID$(A$, I, J)
```

Here, A$ is the string from which the substring is to be extracted; I is the position of the first character of the substring; and J is the number of characters in the substring. The following examples should make clear how MID$ is used:

```
MID$("ALL RIGHT", 1, 3) = "ALL"
MID$("ALL RIGHT", 5, 5) = "RIGHT"
MID$("ALL RIGHT", 1, 2) = "AL"
MID$("ALL RIGHT", 5, 3) = "RIG"
MID$("ALL RIGHT", 4, 1) = " "
MID$("CONCATENATE", 4, 3) = "CAT"
```

When the substring to be extracted occurs as the first part or the last part of the string, the functions LEFT$ and RIGHT$ are slightly easier to use than MID$. LEFT$(A$, 5), for instance, returns the first five characters of A$. RIGHT$(A$, 5) returns the last five characters of A$. The following examples illustrate LEFT$ and RIGHT$:

```
LEFT$("ALL RIGHT", 2) = "AL"
LEFT$("ALL RIGHT", 3) = "ALL"
RIGHT$("ALL RIGHT", 5), = "RIGHT"
RIGHT$("THAT'S ALL RIGHT", 5) = "RIGHT"
RIGHT$("CONCATENATE", 3) = "ATE"
```

LEN   The LEN function gives the length of a string—the number of characters in it:

```
LEN("TOGETHER") = 8
LEN("CONCATENATE") = 11
LEN("ALL RIGHT") = 9
```

381   Note that the blank in "ALL RIGHT" is counted.

Can a string have a length less than 1? Yes, BASIC allows the *null* string, which contains no characters and has a length of zero. The null string is represented as

""

that is, two sets of quotation marks with nothing whatever in between. Therefore,

LEN ("") = 0

Concatenating the null string with another string does not change the other string:

"COMPUTER"+"" = "COMPUTER"
""+"COMPUTER" = "COMPUTER"

Sometimes we give a string variable a starting value equal to the null string and then concatenate various strings with it, just as we might give a numerical variable the value zero and then add various values to it. For instance, after the following statements have been executed, the value of A$ is "ALL RIGHT".

```
10 LET A$ = ""
20 FOR I = 1 TO 9
30     READ C$
40     LET A$ = A$+C$
50 NEXT I
60 DATA "A", "L", "L", " ", "R", "I", "G", "H", "T"
```

INSTR   Frequently, we need to determine the position of a substring inside the string that contains it. For instance, if we are interested in breaking a string down into words or sentences, we might want to know the positions of the blanks or periods.

Some versions of BASIC provide a function for finding the position of a substring. The function goes under different names in the different versions of BASIC that provide it. INSTR is the name we will use here.

An invocation of the INSTR function has the following form:

INSTR(K, A$, B$)

A$ is the string that is being searched for the substring B$. K is the position in A$ where the search is to begin. The value returned by INSTR is the position of B$ in A$:

INSTR(1, "FORGET", "GET") = 4
INSTR(1, "CONCATENATE", "TEN") = 6
382   INSTR(1, "ALL RIGHT", " ") = 4

If the substring is not found in the string being searched, INSTR returns the value zero:

```
INSTR(1, "FORGET", "GOT") = 0
INSTR(1, "CONCATENATE", "CATER") = 0
INSTR(1, "ALL RIGHT", "LLL") = 0
```

If the substring occurs more than once in the string being searched, INSTR returns the position of the leftmost occurrence that it finds:

```
INSTR(1, "CONCATENATE", "ATE") = 5 (not 9)
```

On the other hand,

```
INSTR(6, "CONCATENATE", "ATE") = 9
```

Since the search for "ATE" started in position 6, the first occurrence is missed, and the position of the second occurrence is returned.

If the first argument of INSTR is omitted, it is assumed to be 1. Thus

```
INSTR("CONCATENATE", "ATE") = 5
INSTR("FORGET", "GET") = 4
INSTR("WAKIKI", "KI") = 3
```

If your version of BASIC does not have any function that will do the job of INSTR, you can write a subroutine to do it. The subroutine will be equivalent to

```
10 LET K = INSTR(K, A$, B$)
```

That is, before the subroutine is invoked, the value of K is set to the position at which the search is to start. The value of A$ is set to the string to be searched, and the value of B$ is set to the string to be searched for. After the subroutine returns, the value of K is the position of the first occurrence of the substring (or 0 is the substring not found in the string being searched).

As shown in figure 26-1, the subroutine compares B$ with successive substrings of A$ having the same length as B$:

```
500 IF K+LEN(B$) > LEN(A$)+1 THEN 540
510 IF MID$(A$, K, LEN(B$)) = B$ THEN 570
520     LET K = K+1
530 GO TO 500
540 REM CASE WHERE SUBSTRING NOT FOUND
550     LET K = 0
560     RETURN
570 REM CASE WHERE SUBSTRING FOUND
580     RETURN
```

A$ = "CONCATENATE"

B$ = "TEN"

CONCATENATE
TEN   *Does not match*

CONCATENATE
TEN   *Does not match*

CONCATENATE
TEN   *Does not match*

CONCATENATE
TEN   *Does not match*

CONCATENATE
TEN   *Does not match*

CONCATENATE
TEN   *Matches*

Figure 26-1. The subroutine compares B$ with successive substrings of A$ having the same length as B$.

Line 500 determines when the entire string has been searched. (How does it do this?) Line 510 compares B$ with the substring of A$ that starts at position K and has the length LEN(B$). If the two are equal, then the sought-after substring has been found, and the subroutine returns. Otherwise, the value of K is increased by 1, and, if the entire string has not yet been searched, the comparison is repeated.

The following version of the subroutine is equivalent to the previous one but is more efficient because it doesn't require LEN(A$) and LEN(B$) to be evaluated repeatedly:

```
500 LET L = LEN(B$)
510 LET M = LEN(A$)-L+1
520 IF K > M THEN 560
530 IF MID$(A$, K, L) = B$ THEN 590
540    LET K = K+1
550 GO TO 520
560 REM CASE WHERE SUBSTRING NOT FOUND
570    LET K = 0
580    RETURN
590 REM CASE WHERE SUBSTRING FOUND
600    RETURN
```

As is often the case, the more efficient subroutine is not as easy to read as the less efficient one. It is left as an exercise to explain in detail how these subroutines work.

AN APPLICATION TO WORD PROCESSING

A word-processing program consists of two parts: (1) a *text editor*, which allows the text to be entered, revised, and corrected; and (2) a *formatter*, which does such jobs as printing running heads and page numbers, centering titles, making all lines the same length, and leaving space for illustrations.

Some text editors have a CHANGE command that is used to make changes in a line of text. For instance, if the line being edited is

THE QUICK BROWN FOX JUMPS OVER THE LAZY DOG.

then the command

CHANGE "BROWN", "RED"

would replace BROWN by RED giving:

THE QUICK RED FOX JUMPS OVER THE LAZY DOG.

When a word to be changed occurs more than once in a line, you must include enough characters on one side of the word or the other to identify a single occurrence. For instance,

CHANGE "THE L", "A L"

gives us

THE QUICK RED FOX JUMPS OVER A LAZY DOG.

The inclusion of " L" assures that the second THE is changed and not the first.

Let's see how to implement the CHANGE command using the BASIC operators and functions we have studied. Let the value of L$ be the line of text to be edited. Along with the CHANGE command, the user enters two strings—a "pattern string," P$, which is to be located in the line of text, and a "replacement string," R$, which is to replace the pattern. For instance, in our first example, where the line being edited was

THE QUICK BROWN FOX JUMPS OVER THE LAZY DOG.

and the command was

CHANGE "BROWN", "RED"

we have that

L$ = "THE QUICK BROWN FOX JUMPS OVER THE LAZY DOG."
P$ = "BROWN"
R$ = "RED"

We will need to work with the lengths of the string being edited and the pattern string:

10 LET L = LEN(L$)
20 LET P = LEN(P$)

For the example, the values of L and P are

L = 44
P = 5

The next step is to locate the pattern in the line to be edited:

30 LET I = INSTR(L$, P$)

The value of I is the position of the leftmost occurrence of the pattern in the line to be edited. Using this value, we can break the line into three parts:

LEFT$(L$, I-1)	The part of L$ preceding the leftmost occurrence of the pattern
P$	The pattern
RIGHT$(L$, L-P-I+1)	The part of L$ following the leftmost occurrence of the pattern

386 The expression L−P−I+1 is the number of characters to the right of the first occurrence of the pattern. We start with the length L of the line being edited and subtract two things: (1) the number of characters in the pattern, P, and (2) the number of characters to the left of the first occurrence of the pattern, I−1. The result is

L-P-(I-1)

and a rule of algebra allows us to change this to L−P−I+1.

For instance, in the example just given, we have

```
I = 11
LEFT$(L$, 11-1) = LEFT$(L$, 10) = "THE QUICK "
RIGHT$(L$, 44-5-11+1) = RIGHT$(L$, 29)
                      = "FOX JUMPS OVER THE LAZY DOG."
```

The parts of the string to the left and right of the part that matched the pattern, LEFT$(L$, I−1) and RIGHT$(L$, L−P−I+1), are not to be changed. On the other hand, P$ is to be replaced by R$. Therefore, the changed value of L$ is computed using

```
80 LET L$ = LEFT$(L$, I-1)+R$+RIGHT$(L$, L-P-I+1)
```

We still have to consider a few special cases. First, the value of I may be 0 because the pattern is not a substring of the line being edited. When this happens, the user probably made a typing error in entering the pattern, so it's best to do nothing at all.

Special cases also arise if the pattern occurs at the very beginning or end of the line being edited. If the pattern occurs at the beginning of the line, then the value of I is 1, and the second argument of LEFT$(L$, I−1) is 0. When the pattern occurs at the end of the line, then the second argument of RIGHT$(L$, L−P−I+1) is 0.

Since at least some systems may not handle these zero arguments correctly, we will separate out these special cases. When the pattern occurs at the beginning of the line, the edited value of L$ is given by

```
110 LET L$ = R$+RIGHT$(L$, L-P)
```

When the pattern occurs at the end of the line, the edited value of L$ is given by

```
140 LET L$ = LEFT$(L$, I-1)+R$
```

By putting all these results together, we get the statements that implement the CHANGE command:

```
10 LET L = LEN(L$)
20 LET P = LEN(P$)
30 LET I = INSTR(L$, P$)
40 IF I = 0 THEN 150
```

```
 50 IF I = 1 THEN 100
 60 IF I-1+P = L THEN 130
 70 REM NO SPECIAL CASE
 80    LET L$ = LEFT$(L$, I-1)+R$+RIGHT$(L$, L-P-I+1)
 90 GO TO 150
100 REM PATTERN AT BEGINNING
110    LET L$ = R$+RIGHT$(L$, L-P)
120 GO TO 150
130 REM PATTERN AT END
140    LET L$ = LEFT$(L$, I-1)+R$
150 ...
```

1. Some versions of BASIC have MID$ but not LEFT$ or RIGHT$. Give expressions involving MID$ and LEN that are equivalent to LEFT$ and RIGHT$.

2. Some versions of BASIC have, in place of MID$, a function SEG$ defined as follows: SEG$(A$, I, J) returns the substring of A$ whose first character is in position I, and whose last character is in position J. For instance,

SEG$("CONCATENATE", 6, 8) = "TEN"

Write an expression using SEG$ that is equivalent to MID$. Write an expression using MID$ that is equivalent to SEG$.

3. Explain in detail the operation of the first version of the subroutine for INSTR.

4. Explain why the more efficient version of the subroutine for INSTR is equivalent to, or does the same job as, the less efficient version. Why is the second version more efficient?

5. Explain the operation of lines 110 and 140 in the implementation of the CHANGE command.

INDEX

393

†